CW00543252

Customer Engagement Marketing

Robert W. Palmatier • V. Kumar
Colleen M. Harmeling
Editors

Customer
Engagement
Marketing

Editors
Robert W. Palmatier
Foster School of Business
University of Washington
Seattle, Washington, USA

V. Kumar
Georgia State University
Atlanta, Georgia, USA

Colleen M. Harmeling
Florida State University
Tallahassee, Florida, USA

ISBN 978-3-319-61984-2   ISBN 978-3-319-61985-9   (eBook)
DOI 10.1007/978-3-319-61985-9

Library of Congress Control Number: 2017951630

This Palgrave Macmillan imprint is published by Springer Nature
The registered company is Springer International Publishing AG
The registered company address is: Gewerbestrasse 11, 6330 Cham, Switzerland

The authors thank Bharath Rajan, Ericka Yates, and Gayatri Shukla for their valuable feedback on earlier drafts and Renu for copyediting this manuscript.

Preface and Acknowledgments

en•gage /in gāj/ *verb*
   to occupy, attract, or involve (someone's interest or attention)
There is no better word to describe today's modern culture than "engaged."
In a typical day, it is hard to imagine a single moment where we are not
occupied or do not have something commanding our attention. We are
accustomed to instantaneous access to information, opinions, entertain-
ment, and even products, grand-scale (or even mundane) conversations
conducted in virtual public arenas, chronicled thoughts, feelings and experiences, and connections across space and even time.

   Yet, nothing is more telling of these dramatic cultural shifts than a comparison of life today to life just over a decade ago. Fifteen years ago, events
worthy of public recognition and widespread coverage were monumental
achievements or devastating crises. Personal experiences were reserved for
home videos only to be re-experienced by the original participants.
Acquiring a new skill required investment in a class, guidance from a
mentor, or effortful search often involving travel to an information source
(e.g., library). People sought advice from a small group of trusted peers,
typically friends, and family. Word of mouth was considered an inefficient
grassroots effort valuable only to small companies. Our personal networks
were comprised of connections to friends, family, and colleagues formed
through face-to-face interactions and known primarily only to the members
within it. As consumers, we had little power.

Today, the recognition and coverage we once only ascribed to culturally relevant, "newsworthy" events, we now apply to "postworthy" events such as "What I ate Tuesday night" or "My reaction to the latest episode of the current Netflix series." We capture, caption, edit, chronicle, and publicize mundane, personal experiences for an awaiting audience of loyal followers who will comment and redistribute to others who are often strangers. A voice command to a smartphone, typically less than five feet from where we are, gives us instantaneous access to information. YouTube videos and blogs with instructional guides ranging from "how to drive a car" to "how to build a super computer" have replaced traditional information outlets. Star ratings and reviews hold more influential positions than recommendations from sisters and friends. Our social networks are publically displayed and celebrated based on who we know and how many connections we have. And as evidenced by David Carroll and United Airlines, a single consumer has the power to use this social network to command losses of more than $180 million to a firm.

Nowhere, however, is this shift more relevant or evident than in the changing perspectives and practices in marketing, where "customer engagement" has been sneaking in to where we once said "relationship marketing" or "customer relationship management." Importantly, these cultural shifts were matched by an unprecedented visibility of customer thoughts, connections, and even moment by moment behaviors and reactions that provide the infrastructure for converting this movement into strategic insights. Where we once were limited by individual descriptors and transactional information, we now have a more holistic view of customers that has undoubtedly altered our understanding of key marketing concepts such as customer value, salespeople lifetime value, product innovation, customer support, marketing communication, and other fundamental marketing functions. In response, Social Media Managers and Directors of Customer Engagement are typical installations on firm organizational charts. While some have criticized that this "movement" is nothing more than a passing fad, this "passing fad" has only gained momentum fueled through these enduring cultural shifts.

This book is a response to the engagement movement and the new lens it provides for interpreting important marketing concepts. Throughout these 14 chapters, we explore how this new perspective alters the fundamental aspects of marketing where customers are no longer mere consumers of value but contributors to key marketing functions, products are no longer "offerings" from the firm but "co-creations" between the firm and the customer, and salespeople are more appropriately knowledge brokers. If you are a marketing researcher or just interested in marketing strategy, we hope this new perspective provides inspiration for new avenues of research and thought.

The book also provides a practical guide to marketing managers that outlines ways to embrace this new role of the customer. It describes new techniques for assessing customer value that recognize customer-owned resources such as access to customer social networks or customer knowledge. It discusses how to effectively motivate customers to contribute these resources through the use of incentive programs and how to empower them through engagement tools and platforms that amplify the impact of customer contributions on other current and potential customers. It acknowledges the data aspect of engagement and how to use this increased visibility of the customer to inform strategic decision-making. Finally, it provides a note of caution that discusses the potential dark side of customer engagement and how to proactively and reactively manage customer inter-actions. If you are a marketing manager, we hope that in the pages that follow you find guidance to enhance your current marketing strategies.

We would like to thank both Jazmine Robles and Marcus Ballenger, our editorial team at Palgrave Macmillan Publisher, for their invaluable support and guidance that made this a smooth and enjoyable process. We would also like to thank all of our contributing authors for making this book possible.

Robert W. Palmatier
Professor of Marketing
University of Washington

V. Kumar
Regents' Professor of Marketing
Georgia State University

Colleen M. Harmeling
Assistant Professor of Marketing
Florida State University

CONTENTS

List of Figures

LIST OF TABLES

CHAPTER 1

Customer Engagement Marketing

Anita Pansari and V. Kumar

CUSTOMER ENGAGEMENT: INTRODUCTION AND ORGANIZING FRAMEWORK

Managing customers has forever been the primary focus of firms. What has changed is how customers are managed. With the advent of customer and marketing databases, the strategies to manage customers have evolved from transaction to relationship marketing and now to customer engagement. This evolution is evident in the metrics used in the different phases of marketing. Till the early 1990s, managers analyzed customers' transaction data to develop metrics such as past customer value, share-of-wallet, and recency, frequency, and monetary value of purchases. Managers used only these measures to design strategies to increase customer value and firm profits. However, in the late 1990s and early 2000s, firms realized that customers need more than transacting with the firm which led to managers shifting their focus from transaction marketing to relationship marketing. Firms then aimed at improving customer trust, commitment, and loyalty through better products, services, and loyalty programs. In this

A. Pansari (✉)
Michigan State University, East Lansing, MI, USA

V. Kumar
Georgia State University, Atlanta, GA, USA

era, firms focused on retaining profitable customers by applying the metric of customer lifetime value (Kumar 2008).

Over the years, with the use of social media platforms for marketing activities, marketers realized that it is not enough to only understand how long the customer will stay with the firm but also to understand if there are other ways beyond purchases that customers can contribute to the firm. This led to the rise of the term Customer Engagement in marketing.

Consistent with the developments in the marketplace, this book of Customer Engagement Marketing covers a broad range of strategic issues regarding the antecedents and consequences of customer engagement. It also focuses on understanding customer engagement in different contexts and extending the concept of Customer Engagement. The book comprises 14 chapters which are organized into three parts (see Fig. 1.1) consisting of the antecedents, consequences, and the different contexts of customer engagement.

However, before we dive into the chapters, it is crucial to understand the basic foundation of customer engagement by focusing on the following questions:

a) What is customer engagement?
b) What is the theory driving customer engagement?

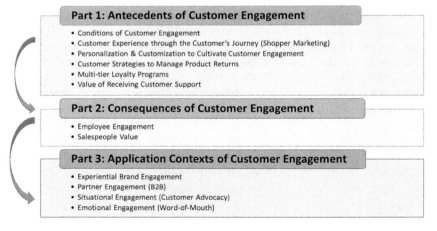

Part 1: Antecedents of Customer Engagement

- Conditions of Customer Engagement
- Customer Experience through the Customer's Journey (Shopper Marketing)
- Personalization & Customization to Cultivate Customer Engagement
- Customer Strategies to Manage Product Returns
- Multi-tier Loyalty Programs
- Value of Receiving Customer Support

Part 2: Consequences of Customer Engagement

- Employee Engagement
- Salespeople Value

Part 3: Application Contexts of Customer Engagement

- Experiential Brand Engagement
- Partner Engagement (B2B)
- Situational Engagement (Customer Advocacy)
- Emotional Engagement (Word-of-Mouth)

Fig. 1.1 Organization of the book

c) How is it different from other customer relationship management constructs?
d) Are there any benefits of engaging customers?
e) Are there situations/contexts where customer engagement would be enhanced?

UNDERSTANDING CUSTOMER ENGAGEMENT

Engagement has been discussed over the past century with various interpretations in numerous contexts. In the context of social welfare, engagement is discussed as civic engagement, social engagement, community engagement, etc. In the business world, it is discussed in a contractual relationship context, and in management, as an organizational activity with the internal stakeholders. In the marketing domain, engagement is associated with the level of an active relationship that a customer shares with a firm and is termed as customer engagement (CE).

Customer engagement has been discussed extensively in the past decade in both marketing academia and the business world. It was the eighth most frequently used buzz word in business in 2014. In the business world, it has been considered a strategy, investment, listening to the customer's voice, emotional connection, and interaction with the organization beyond what is necessary.[1] Gallup studies indicate that:

- In the consumer electronics industry, fully engaged shoppers make 44% more visits per year and spend $84 more than a disengaged customer.
- Fully engaged shoppers make 44% more visits per year to their preferred retailer than actively disengaged shoppers.
- In casual and fast food restaurants, fully engaged customers make 56% and 28% more visits per month respectively, as compared to disengaged customers.
- In the hospitality sector, fully engaged hotel guests spend 46% more per year.
- In the insurance sector, fully engaged policy owners purchase 22% more types of insurance products.
- In the retail banking industry, customers who are fully engaged bring 37% more annual revenue to their primary bank.[2]

The above statistics highlight the importance of customer engagement. Customer engagement has been a topic of discussion in marketing academia from 2010 (Vivek et al. 2012; Kumar et al. 2010; Van Doorn et al.

2010; Kumar and Pansari 2016). There have been various discussions, definitions, and arguments about customer engagement. We present a snapshot of those conceptualizations in Table 1.1. The latest definition provided by Pansari and Kumar (2017) provides a holistic view of customer engagement.

Pansari and Kumar (2017) define CE as "the mechanics of a customer's value addition to the firm, either through direct or/and indirect contribution." The direct contribution consists of customer purchases, and the indirect contributions consist of incentivized referrals that the customer provides, the social media conversations that customers have about the brand, and the customer feedback/suggestions given to the firm. Based on the customer engagement theory proposed by Pansari and Kumar (2017), when a customer is satisfied with his/her relationship with the firm and has an emotional attachment to the firm, then it can be said that the customer is engaged with the firm.

Although there are multiple definitions of engagement, confusion prevails on other CRM constructs and CE. For instance, customer experience, customer involvement, customer satisfaction, customer commitment, and so on are frequently misinterpreted as customer engagement. To clarify, customer experience is the customer's cognitive, affective, emotional, social, and physical responses to the entity, product, and service (Verhoef et al. 2009). This indicates that customer experience is the customer's response to the firm's actions, whereas customer engagement is the contribution the customer makes to the firm's revenue, directly or indirectly. Similarly, customer involvement is the importance that the consumer places on the product/service depending on his/her need. Customer involvement occurs before the customer makes a purchase and customer engagement occurs after the customer has made an initial purchase and has had an experience with the firm. Several other CRM constructs are often misinterpreted as CE. These constructs, while related to CE, are quite distinct from CE. Table 1.2 provides an effective summary of how these are distinct from, yet related, to customer engagement.

THEORY OF CUSTOMER ENGAGEMENT

Understanding the theory of customer engagement is a good way to enhance our understanding of the differences between customer engagement and other customer relationship constructs. The theory of engagement evolves from the relationship marketing theory in which the

Table 1.1 Select literature review on the conceptualization of customer engagement

Study	Type of firm	Type of variables	Conceptual/Empirical	Definition
Bowden (2009)	B2C	Attitude and behavior-based	Conceptual	A psychological process that models underlying mechanisms by which customer loyalty is formed for new customers as well as the mechanisms by which loyalty may be maintained for repeat-purchase customers of a service brand
Van Doorn et al (2010)	B2C	Behavior-based	Conceptual	Customers' behavioral manifestation toward a brand or firm, beyond purchase, resulting from motivational drivers such as word-of-mouth activity, recommendations, helping other customers, blogging, writing reviews
Brodie et al. (2011)	B2C	Attitude-based	Conceptual	A psychological state that occurs by virtue of interactive, co-creative customer experiences with a focal agent/object (e.g., a brand) in focal service relationships
Vivek et al. (2012)	B2C	Attitude and behavior-based	Conceptual	The intensity of an individual's participation and connection with the organization's offerings and activities initiated by either the customer or organization
Hollebeek (2011)	B2C	Attitude and behavior-based	Conceptual	The level of customers' motivational, brand-related, and context-dependent state of mind characterized by specific levels of cognitive, emotional, and behavioral activity in brand interactions

(continued)

Table 1.1 (continued)

Study	Type of firm	Type of variables	Conceptual/ Empirical	Definition
Kumar et al. (2010)	B2B and B2C	Attitude and behavior-based	Conceptual	(1) Customer purchasing behavior, whether it be repeat purchases or additional purchases through upselling and cross-selling [CLV]; (2) Customer referral behavior as it relates to the acquisition of new customers through a firm-initiated and incentivized formal referral programs [CRV]; (3) Customer influencer behavior through customers' influence on other acquired customers as well as on prospects [CIV]; (4) Customer knowledge behavior via feedback provided to the firm for ideas for innovations and improvements and contributing to knowledge development [CKV])
Kumar and Pansari (2016)	B2B and B2C	Behavior-based	Empirical	Same as Kumar et al. (2010)
Pansari and Kumar (2017)	B2B and B2C	Attitude and behavior-based	Conceptual	The mechanics of a customer's value addition to the firm, either through direct or/and indirect contribution

Adapted from Pansari and Kumar (2017, pp. 294–311)

Table 1.2 Constructs related to customer engagement

Related constructs	Definition	Measurement (One possible approach)	Relationship to customer engagement (CE)
Customer involvement	A person's perceived relevance of the object based on inherent needs, values, and interests (Zaichowsky 1985, p. 342)	Zaichowsky (1985) provides a 20-item scale. Some of the items of the scale reflect the importance, relevance, value, excitement, appeal, want, and benefits of the product. These items are measured as a seven-point semantic differential scale. The reliability of this scale exceeds 0.90	Involvement is the action of the customer to seek information that may be used to manage any potential risk in the decision-making process (Delgado-Ballester and Munuera-Aleman 2001). This would occur before the customer makes a purchase; hence, it would precede CE as CE includes customer purchases
Customer experience	It is holistic in nature and involves the customer's cognitive, affective, emotional, social, and physical responses to the entity, product, and service (adapted from Verhoef et al. 2009)	Gentile et al. (2007) identify six factors for CE—sensorial, emotional, cognitive, pragmatic, lifestyle, and relational—and measured these with a four-point scale	Customer experience is a cognitive measure which is an outcome of the firm's actions and does not include the actions of the customer toward the firm. CE is a measure of the customers' actions toward the firm
Customer satisfaction	It is a judgment that a product or service feature, or the product or service itself, provides (or is providing) a pleasurable level of consumption-related fulfillment, including levels of under- or over fulfillment (Oliver 1997, p. 13)	Bruner et al. (2001) suggest a generalized set of 12-item scales measuring various aspects of the purchase and use of the product and service with a high average reliability of over 0.90	If a customer is satisfied with a product or service, then he/she may buy the product/service again. Purchase (component of CE) is a consequence of satisfaction

(continued)

Table 1.2 (continued)

Related constructs	Definition	Measurement (One possible approach)	Relationship to customer engagement (CE)
Customer loyalty	It is a favorable attitude toward a brand resulting in the consistent purchase of the brand over time (Assael 1992)	Mittal (1994) provides a three-item scale measuring consumers' preference to a few brands and limiting their purchases to the same. It is measured using a five-point Likert scale, and scale reliability is 0.76	Loyalty measures only repeat purchase transactions of the customer and focuses only on the revenue of the firm. CE goes beyond purchases and includes referrals, influence, and feedback
Customer trust	Willingness to rely on an exchange partner in whom one has confidence (Moorman et al. 1993, p. 82)	Garbarino and Johnson (1999) develop a scale for consumer trust which measures confidence in quality and reliability, perceptions of risk and variability. They use a five-point Likert scale to measure the items	Trust is the breadth of the attitude toward the brand which is embedded in CE
Customer commitment	An enduring desire to maintain a valued relationship (Moorman et al. 1992, p. 316)	Garbarino and Johnson (1999) develop a scale for commitment which captures the identification with the company, psychological attachment, concern with long-term welfare, and loyalty. They use a five-point Likert scale to measure the items	Commitment is the depth of the attitude toward a brand which is embedded in the CE framework
Customer brand value	The differential effect of a customer's brand knowledge, brand attitude, brand purchase intention, and brand behavior on his or her response to the marketing of a brand (Kumar et al. 2015)	Kumar (2013) provides a scale that reflects brand awareness, image, trust, affect, loyalty, advocacy, purchase intention, and premium price. Each are measured on a 1–10 scale with scale reliability exceeding 0.80 (Kumar et al. 2015)	Customer brand value offers a quantitative view of the customer perceptions of the brand. It interacts with the components of CE

Adapted from Pansari and Kumar (2017, pp. 294–311)

foundation is based on commitment and trust (Morgan and Hunt 1994). Previously, the primary purpose of relationship marketing was to establish long-term relationships with the firm, thereby promoting efficiency, productivity, effectiveness, and cooperation. A firm's initial relationship with the customer was restricted to purchases, ensuring long-term loyalty, and continued patronage. However, this has evolved with the developments in the marketplace based on the ever-evolving needs and interests of the consumers. For instance, the current need of consumers is to always be connected with the firm through various social media platforms, interacting with other users of the product, and relying on customers' evaluations of the firm. Many consumers even provide free review videos and feedback to the firm as their contribution to the firm. All of this indicates that customers have evolved from merely conducting transactions with the firm to developing a bond with the firm and its other customers. This relationship between the customer and the firm evolves only if the customer is satisfied with his/her existing relationship with the firm and is also emotionally connected with the firm. In other words, for customer engagement to exist, the customer should have a satisfied and emotionally connected relationship with the firm. However, this relationship evolves over time and varies from customer to customer based on the experience with the firm. This experience is positive only if the initial purchase made by the customer meets the expectations of the customer as shown in Fig. 1.2.

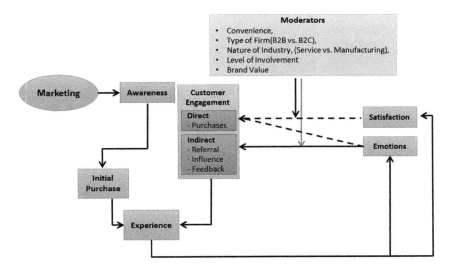

Fig. 1.2   Conceptual framework of customer engagement

Figure 1.2 shows the conceptual framework and the theory behind customer engagement. As products and services are introduced, firms invest in marketing activities to create awareness. This awareness helps customers identify if the firm's product and services fulfill a need. This awareness also sets an expectation in the mind of the customer. After identifying the need and expectations from the firm, the customer makes his/her initial purchase which creates an experience for the customer. This experience is positive if the firm meets or exceeds the expectations of the customer. Once the customer has a positive experience with the products and services of the firm, he/she would be satisfied with the firm which would induce repeat purchase. The positive experience that the customer has with the firm leads to positive emotions as discussed by Pansari and Kumar (2017).

The theory of CE states that if a customer is satisfied with the firm and has an emotional attachment with the firm, then he/she would be engaged with the firm in the form of purchases (direct contribution), referrals, influence, and feedback (indirect contribution). Specifically, satisfaction results in direct contribution, and emotional attachment results in indirect contribution. However, this relationship between satisfaction and direct contribution and emotion and indirect contribution is moderated by many factors—type of industry (service vs. product), type of firm (B2B vs. B2C), level of involvement, brand value, and convenience level.

For example, the nature of the industry (service vs. product) influences direct contribution (purchase). However, the impact of satisfaction on purchase is higher in the service industry because there is an immediate opportunity to recover from the service failure when the customer's expectations are unmet. On the other hand, with a product, the chance of recovery is lower as the customer must wait until the next production cycle to repurchase—that is if they provided feedback to improve the product and if the feedback can be implemented. Moreover, the impact of satisfaction on purchase is enhanced if the firm is B2B. This is owing to the heightened focus on the product/service's functionality and the approval from multiple decision-making units in a B2B firm. Additionally, the higher the involvement in purchasing a product, the higher the customer's expectations and investment meaning the product is purchased less frequently than low-involvement products. Therefore, the impact of satisfaction on direct contribution is higher for low-involvement products because they are repurchased more frequently. Furthermore, the influence of satisfaction on direct contribution is greater for brands with low brand value as the level of expectations and chances of disconfirmation are low (high-brand-value products carry high expectations and disconfirmation) which leads to repurchase behavior as the level of satisfaction will be higher. Lastly, the impact of satisfaction on direct contribution is greater depending on the level of convenience provided by a firm. It is boosted if the availability and ease of use is high because it ensures possible product repurchase.

On the other hand, the relationship between emotions and indirect contribution is enhanced in a service industry (vs. product) since customers share their service experiences more often than their experiences with using a product, which in turn can lead to referrals and feedback for the firm. In a B2C firm (vs. a B2B firm), the impact of emotions on indirect contribution is enhanced due to the actions of consumers being based on emotions. Where there is emotional attachment, the consumers are more likely to recommend and participate in social media discussions regarding the product/service. In the case of high-involvement products (vs. low-involvement), the impact of emotions on indirect contribution is higher because consumers have invested time into researching the product and are willing to provide valuable feedback and recommend. In addition, for high-brand-value products, the impact of emotions on indirect contribution is higher due to the increased consumer expectations and attachment to the brand. On the flip side, this also leads to a greater negative effect in the event of disappointment. Lastly, the higher the level of convenience that the firm provides to its customers, the greater the impact of emotions on indirect contribution. This is due to the increased opportunity for customers to interact with the firm and provide referrals and feedback, as well as promote the firm on social media platforms.

MEASURING CUSTOMER ENGAGEMENT

For firms to accrue the benefit of CE, they should be aware of the toolkit to measure CE. All the components of CE can be measured with transaction data (Kumar 2013), except customer knowledge value, as it comprises the feedback and suggestions that the customers provide. The firm may only use the feedback that is specific to enhancing their product/service, and thus may not consider all of the customer's suggestions. Tracking these suggestions and providing a monetary value is a challenge, which has not yet been fully explored in the literature (Kumar and Bhagwat 2010).

In spite of this, there is a robust Customer Engagement measure available where CE is measured as a second-order construct, with the components of CE (purchases, referrals, influence, and feedback) being the first-order constructs. Kumar and Pansari (2016) developed the CE scale, which comprises of 16 items. The scale is representative of all the dimensions of CE, as it is comprised of four items for each of the dimensions of customer engagement. The scale has been validated with multiple samples, and the overall scale reliability is 0.95.

IMPLEMENTING CUSTOMER ENGAGEMENT

The CE scale was used to measure CE in two time periods across 120 companies by Kumar and Pansari (2016) in 2013 and 2014. This sample of companies for the B2B sector comprised of multinational companies belonging to industries, such as lightweight metals, technology, engineering, manufacturing parts, and service companies including technology consulting services, computer hardware and software services, data/call centers, marketing research and analytics firms, advertising agencies, and media services. Some of the B2C companies included mail-ordering retail companies, and manufacturers of consumer products, electronics, and furniture, and mass media companies providing cable television, internet services, and telephone services, retail outlets, airlines, and rental businesses.

Based on the CE measures derived from the firms, Kumar and Pansari (2016) categorized the firm into four categories. A score of 16–31 on customer engagement indicates the lowest levels of engagement and is classified as "disengaged"; a score of 32–47 indicates low levels of engagement and is classified as "somewhat engaged"; scores of 48–63 on CE indicate that the customer is "moderately engaged" with the firm; and a score of 64–80 on CE indicates that the customer is fully engaged with the firm and are termed as "super engaged." After the first period, the firms were categorized into these four categories and relevant strategies to improve their level of CE were suggested. These strategies to improve CE were based on the level of satisfaction and emotional attachment of the customer to the firm. In order to maximize both the direct and indirect contribution, companies must figure out how to manage both satisfaction and emotion in a positive way since satisfaction positively influences direct contribution, and emotions influence the indirect contributions of customers. The set of strategies, also referred to as the Customer Engagement Matrix, to manage satisfaction and emotion are based on the intensity of positive emotions (low or high) and the level of satisfaction (low or high).

For example, when customers display a lower state of emotions and satisfaction and continue to transact with the company, it could be that the customer is transacting with the company because of a necessity. Such customers are termed as "fill in need" customers (Pansari and Kumar 2017). For these customers, the firm will have to work hard and capture them beyond the "fill in need." The firm must engage the customers by providing better service, understanding the customer's needs and preferences, and the reasons why the firm is not the customer's first preference. Firms can use appropriate strategies like discounts, promotions, and offer an improved quality of service to encourage the customers to transact more and form a strong relationship.

There could be some customers who have high positive emotions toward the firm but low levels of satisfaction. This could be because of low share-of-wallet, elevated expectations of quality, or disappointment with the quality. These customers are termed as "altruistic-focused" (Pansari and Kumar 2017), since they have high emotions toward the brand, despite being dissatisfied. For such emotionally attached customers, firms can use their attachment to their advantage to get more opportunities to meet the customer's expectations. Companies can take advantage of the emotional attachment and better understand the needs of the customer and work toward reducing the customer's dissatisfaction. Firms can segment these customers based on their level of emotions and use multi-level strategies to provide a better experience and improve the level of satisfaction.

Sometimes a customer may be satisfied with the firm but may not be emotionally connected with the firm. Such customers are aptly titled "value-based" (Pansari and Kumar 2017). As the name suggests, these customers focus on deriving maximum value from the firm. They would switch to any firm which provides higher value as they are not emotionally attached. Some managers may become complacent as this group of customers seem low maintenance as they already provide revenues to the firm. However, this would be short sightedness as it would be easy for the competition to lure such customers, and complacency from managers may hinder the objective of maintaining a long-term relationship with the customer. To maintain a long-term relationship with the customer, the firm has to have a deeper emotional connection with customers by duly recognizing them, providing personalized products, hosting events for them, providing better touchpoint experiences, being personal with them, and so on. All of these strategies may help the customers build an emotional attachment with the firm.

If the firm ensures that all its customers are satisfied with the relationship and are emotionally connected, then they can extract maximum value by using the appropriate strategies to enhance customer engagement. For instance, managers can use the "Wheel of Fortune" strategies by Kumar (2008) to increase the purchases of a satisfied customer. Each of the Wheel of Fortune strategies have been validated in the marketplace, with various firms generating an ROI of over eight to ten times after implementing these strategies. Some of the Wheel of Fortune strategies focus on resource allocation, pitching the right product to the right customer at the right time, and so on. In case of the indirect contribution (customer referrals, influence, and feedback), firms can provide incentives to their emotionally attached customers for providing referrals and use a social media metric like Customer Influence Value (Kumar et al. 2013) to offer financial incentives to its customers. Firms should also ensure that their infrastructure is seamless for customers to interact with them across various social media platforms like Facebook, Instagram, and so on. Firms should encourage customers to provide feedback by ensuring an infrastructure conducive to input by providing avenues such as feedback boxes, a page for feedback on the website, and so on. As an example of this approach, Dell Inc. has created the idea-sharing platform Idea Storm[3] to encourage their customers to provide feedback and to collect new product/service ideas from the customer base.

Firms can use various strategies to improve their CE which will then improve firm performance. This was validated by Kumar and Pansari (2016) when they measured CE in the second year for the same 120 companies. Their model-free evidence indicates that in the B2B manufacturing sector, on average, the CE per firm improved from a score of 36 to a score of 48. They also show an average increase of 8.2% in firm revenues. However, this revenue increase cannot be attributed to customer engagement alone. In their study, Kumar and Pansari (2016) measure the combined effect of customer engagement and employee engagement (EE). However, when isolating the effect of CE and EE, the influence of CE on increasing firm performance was twice that of EE. In the B2B services sector, which was dominated by information technology and consulting firms, on average, the customer engagement scores declined from a score of 50 to 43, along with firm revenues, which declined by 5.2%. This decline was seen across the industry and was due to macro-environmental factors, rather than firm-specific factors.

In the case of B2C firms in the manufacturing sector, they observe the CE scores improving from 55 to 62 and the average profits improving by 3.4%. In the services sector for B2C firms, they note that the CE scores improved from 35 to 41, and the average profits improved by 5.6%. This implementation indicates that the customer engagement scale can be effectively used across industries.

Further, it is also true that customer engagement positively affects firm performance across industries. Despite a clear definition, theory, process, and benefits of engagement, there still remain a few questions which remain unanswered:

a) How do product returns and customer loyalty affect customer engagement?
b) How does personalization and customization of a firm's offerings impact customer engagement?
c) What are the various factors which can help build customer engagement?
d) Does the impact of customer engagement go beyond firm performance?
e) Can the concept of customer engagement be extended and applied to the other stakeholders of the firm?

To answer these questions, the editors of this book solicited contributions from a pool of experts in the field to provide a better and in-depth understanding of customer engagement. The book is comprised of 14 chapters which are synthesized into a framework (see Fig. 1.3) which highlights the antecedents, moderators, and consequences of customer engagement.

This book provides strategies and an in-depth understanding of customer engagement. Overall, this book of Customer Engagement Marketing serves as an authoritative guide on customer engagement for professionals, researchers, and students.

ORGANIZATION OF THE BOOK

This book is divided into three parts. Each part contains several chapters which deal with a specific theme related to customer engagement and answer a set of questions. Part 1 focuses on the antecedents of CE, Part 2

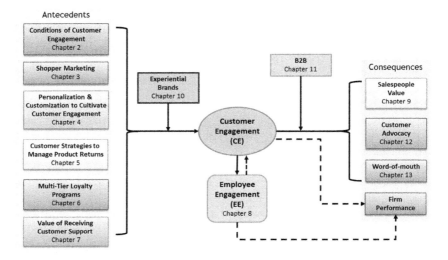

Fig. 1.3 Conceptual framework based on chapters in this book

examines the consequences of CE, and Part 3 discusses the various application contexts in which CE can be applied and extended, as shown in Fig. 1.1.

Part 1: Antecedents of Customer Engagement

The first part of the book discusses in depth the antecedents of customer engagement. Chapter 2 is aptly titled "If You Build Right, They Will Engage: A study of Antecedent Conditions of Customer Engagement" by Vivek, Beatty, and Hazod. In this chapter, the author(s) identify two major sources of customer engagement, one originating from the firm and the other originating from the customer. They note that the customer engagement programs facilitated by the originating firm that are authentic, relevant to the consumer, and promote a true dialog between the firm and consumers would be successful. Further, they state that if the consumers are experience seeking, feel psychologically safe with the program, perceive the program to be meaningful, and feel psychologically available, then they are more likely to engage with the firm. The authors conduct two studies to capture practitioner and customers' perspectives. Their findings indicate that successful CE relies on the presence of multiple factors (Chap. 2, titled "Conditions of Customer Engagement") by the originating firm and internal tendencies of the individual consumer.

For CE to be successful, it is very important for the firms to understand the different stages of customer relationships and the impact of each of them on CE. In the next chapter (Chap. 3, titled "Measuring and Managing Customer Engagement Value through the Customer Journey"), Venkatesan, Petersen, and Gussoni take the readers through a map-based view of customer engagement. In this chapter, the authors develop a framework for building the customer journey map based on customer engagement. They discuss the components of CE (CLV, CRV, CIV, and CKV) in the customer journey (pre-purchase, purchase, and post-purchase). The authors discuss the different customer relationship management streams like customer engagement, customer experience, and customer journey. In their framework, they recognize different stages of customer relationships (acquisition, growth, retention, and win back), and different stages of customer journey (pre-purchase, purchase and post-purchase). They discuss the various links in customer relationships which need to be further explored. For example, the link between customer retention, word-of-mouth, and influence is less clear, as are the best mechanisms for firms to use to engage with customers during their experiences. Their framework also highlights how customer experience would vary at each step of the CE process. For example, the pre-purchase phase of experience for acquiring high-lifetime-value customers would vary from that of the experience for acquiring high-influencer-value customers. The authors conclude by stating that firms will engage customers successfully when they can customize experiences that will appeal to a variety of preferences. Therefore, firms should develop customized strategies for enhancing customer engagement. This is discussed in depth in Chap. 4, which is aptly titled "Customer Engagement through Personalization and Customization" by Bleier, De Keyser, and Verleye.

The authors state that when a firm personalizes, it takes the lead and tailors marketing activities to individual customers; and when it customizes, the customers take on an active role to partially adapt the marketing mix as per their preferences. In this chapter, the authors discuss the different stages of a customer's life cycle (acquisition, retention, and attrition) with specific engagement goals at each stage and the customization and personalization strategies which the firms could use to tailor their marketing mix. Their findings indicate that the three main levels (mass, segment, and individual) of personalization are not mutually exclusive and can be combined. To modify strategies across the customer life cycle, relationship, and customer characteristics, certain tactics across the life cycle are discussed. Specifically, relationship characteristics include customer familiarity with the company and company familiarity with the customer. Customer characteristics include "customer role readiness" and "customer trait reactance." The authors suggest that for a successful strategy to achieve customer engagement, it is important that the level of autonomy for customization strategies and the level of granularity for personalization strategies both be aligned with customer characteristics, the level of familiarity, and the level of trust in the customer–firm relationship. Sometimes, regardless of personalization and customization, the customer may not be content with the final product and may return the product. However, product returns may not necessarily create a negative impact as they offer the firm one more opportunity to interact with the customer and fulfill his/her need.

In Chap. 5 titled "Managing Product Returns Within the Customer Value Framework," Minnema et al. discuss product returns in the context of the customer value framework as well as the antecedents and consequences of product returns. The antecedents of customer product return decisions include the impact of product return policies, pre-purchase information effects, customer characteristics, and product characteristics. The consequences of product returns on the transactional and non-transactional aspect of customer behaviors include the impact on future purchase and return behavior and customer engagement behaviors. The authors conclude that product returns, in fact, have positive consequences on future purchase behavior and help foster loyalty and engagement toward the retailer.

Loyalty can help stimulate engagement if firms follow the personalized-level loyalty strategies as discussed by Bijmolt et al. in Chap. 6, which is aptly titled "Multi-Tier Loyalty Programs to Stimulate Customer Engagement." In this chapter, the authors define and discuss the advantages and disadvantages of a Multi-Tier Loyalty Program (MTLP). They define MTLPs as "hierarchical structures that enable firms to prioritize customers based on past purchase behavior and target them accordingly." They state that MTLPs help firms promote engagement among the most profitable customers by managing and fostering behavioral and attitudinal loyalty. An MTLP is a long-term investment which rewards customers based on their past, current, or future value to a firm. It has a predefined structure, rules, and procedures which help identify and target customers according to tiers. The authors also provide strategies (rewards, symbolic benefits, customer-company identification, and consumer learning) through which firms can leverage MTLPs to stimulate customer engagement. They conclude by discussing the disadvantages of MTLPs, some of which are (1) the challenge of meeting customers' expectations and sense of entitlement; (2) the resulting customer heterogeneity with customers not reacting satisfactorily to the differences in how they are treated; (3) the complicated dynamics whereby customers are promoted or demoted to new tiers; and (4) the ambiguities regarding how best to design the tier structure. MTLPs can be a tremendous asset to firms but only if marketing practitioners are aware of the potential drawbacks.

Chapter 7 titled "Happy Users, Grumpy Bosses: Current Community Engagement Literature and the Impact of Support Engagement in a B2B Setting on User and Upper Management Satisfaction" by Beckers et al. discusses the importance of support services for online communities in the B2B context. In this chapter, the authors discuss the growing online communities and managerial interest in facilitating web-based support services in the B2B setting. They examine how the value placed by users and upper management on receiving online customer support for community engagement varies. Moving from a traditional service support model, or a one-to-one support model, to an online support model, or a one-to-many web-based support model, allows customers to be passively or actively involved in support solutions. There are positives and negatives for both the customer and service provider in each model. The authors note that it is important for higher-level managers to ensure that the interests of the customer, organization, and individual are aligned. They hypothesize several theories about the effects of service request activity on satisfaction, knowledge consultation, and community support, testing each hypothesis through data collected from employees at various corporate levels. In the B2B context, it is not only the customer who plays an important role in the smooth functioning of the firm but also the partners of the firm. Hence, it is important to assess the engagement level of the partners as well.

Part 2: Consequences of Customer Engagement

In Part 2 of the book, the various consequences of customer engagement are discussed. Customer engagement has an impact on firm performance which has been widely discussed in the literature and the practitioners' world. The impact of customer engagement on firm performance has been empirically validated by Kumar and Pansari (2016). In their study, they use a sample size of 120 companies across the B2B and B2C and manufacturing and services sectors, over a two-year period. Their results indicate that on average, after implementing the recommended customer engagement strategies, the average firm performance in terms of revenues increased. However, the impact of customer engagement goes beyond firm performance; it also impacts the employees of the firm and is manifested through employee engagement and improved salesperson value, as discussed in Chaps. 8 and 9. In Chap. 8 titled "Customer Engagement and Employee Engagement: A Research Review and Agenda," Mittal, Han, and Westbrook discuss "a review of extant research on the association between customer engagement and employee engagement, and the relationship of these two constructs with firm performance." Customer engagement impacts employee engagement, and employee engagement impacts firm performance directly and indirectly. The authors stress the importance of clearly defining customer engagement and employee engagement, especially because employee engagement is often conflated with related constructs. Drawing from a recent definition developed by Kumar and Pansari (2016), the authors discuss engagement as primarily behavioral, "with an explicit acknowledgment that the behaviors are causally driven by customer and employee attitudes toward a firm."

Earlier research was rooted in the service-profit chain (SPC) paradigm, in which employee efforts drive customer satisfaction, which in turn, drives the financial outcomes of the firm. The authors modify this approach with the help of stakeholder theory and the generalized exchange theory (GET). Empirically, the vast literature suggests a positive association between customer engagement and employee engagement, though it is clear that the relationship is moderated by a variety of circumstances. These moderators are explored in a section devoted to the context sensitivity of customer engagement and employee engagement. The authors analyze both the positive and negative outcomes of customer engagement and employee engagement.

Positive customer engagement drives customer loyalty, donations to charitable organizations associated with the firm, and so on, and negative customer engagement can result in dysfunctional customers who exhibit harmful behaviors. Finally, the authors highlight the methodological issues in examining customer engagement and employee engagement (i.e., the surfeit of single-firm studies, various measurement issues, etc.), and outline a few significant research gaps to be addressed in future studies.

In Chap. 9 titled "The Disruptive Impact of Customer Engagement on the Business-to-Consumer Sales Force," Hochstein and Bolander identify the challenges which in-store salespeople experience with customers who have a high degree of firm and product engagement. The authors note that there is a conflict between the firm and the customers. The firms want to place a great deal of value on maintaining a salesforce of value-adding knowledge brokers, but high-engagement customers simply want order takers or automated purchasing, not specialized "knowledge brokers." The authors held a focus group with executives in the retail jewelry industry to dive deep into this conflict. The findings of the focus group indicate that customers see salespeople as an obstruction or as irrelevant given previously acquired information. When customers' minds are already made up when they enter the store, it is difficult for salespeople to create value for them. The authors invoke regulatory focus theory, that is prevention vs. promotion focus. They note that highly engaged customers are more likely to be prevention focused and view salespeople as obstructions. Customers often overestimate their own knowledge, presumably leaving an opening for salespeople to assist in the creation of scarce knowledge. The authors propose that salespeople identify the determinant attributes that the customers used to make their decisions, and impart relevant information within this context. This requires a change in how salespeople typically conduct needs analysis from a general to a more swift and concise approach that seeks to understand exactly which attributes are most important to the customer. The authors conclude by laying out steps for future research in this area.

Part 3: Application Context of Customer Engagement

Customer engagement can also be extended to various contexts like experiential brands, B2B, brand engagement, and emotional attachment. The next section discusses the various contexts in which customer engagement can be applied. In Chap. 10 titled "Creating Stronger Brands through Consumer Experience and Engagement," Calder et al. address the conceptual distinction between materialistic/transactional brands. They discuss experiential brands as brands which engage with customers via personal, memorable experiences that transcend basic product attributes and ideally align with the customer's larger personal goals. Citing relevant literature in this stream, the authors define an "experientially engaging brand" as "one in which consumers make specific cognitive, emotional and behavioral investments for the purpose of gaining a valued experience from interacting with the brand."

Given this overview of the extant literature, the authors tackle the question of whether experientially engaging brands perform better than transactional/materialistic ones. Though brands can function both materialistically and experientially, studies have relied on consumer perception to arrive at the conclusion: "...the consumption of experiences tends to generate greater happiness than the consumption of more transactional offerings." Citing the limitations of this line of research and the aforementioned conceptual fuzziness of these two types of branding, the authors propose a research approach that emphasizes a consumer's ability to classify a purchase as either materialistic or experiential depending on his/her focus.

The authors propose a model of self-control to advance contemporary understanding of why experientially engaging brands generally perform better than materialistic ones. Three hypotheses are generated that together focus on the capacity of experiential brands for alignment with consumers' higher-order goals. By the same token, a materialistic brand can fulfill a lower-order goal at the expense of higher-order goals—the materialistic engagement can be successful and yet still create a negative impression on the consumer. The authors conclude the chapter by discussing engagement within a social media context, and how this line of inquiry can be developed in the future.

In Chap. 11 titled "From Customer to Partner Engagement: A Conceptualization and Typology of Engagement in B2B," Reinartz and Berkman analyze specific properties of business markets like the derived character of demand or formalization, the rationality of exchange, and so on, and discuss their impact on the phenomenon of customer engagement. They argue that the concept of customer engagement should be extended to partner engagement to reflect the complexity and network character of value chains in the business markets. They also develop a typology of partner engagement behaviors in business markets and deliberate upon the differences in the levels of organizational engagement and individual engagement, the underlying relational factors, as well as special cases. They conclude by drawing specific implications for B2B managers and provide avenues for future research in the domain of partner engagement.

The last two chapters (Chaps. 12 and 13) discuss situational engagement and emotional engagement. In Chap. 12 titled "Engaging with Brands: The Influence of Dispositional and Situational Brand Engagement on Customer Advocacy," Liu et al. discuss situational engagement and its relationship with brand engagement. They examine the influence of dispositional brand engagement on customer advocacy, as mediated through situational engagement with a specific brand. They also provide empirical validity for their framework. Their results show that brand engagement has a stronger influence on situational brand engagement than does brand schematicity. They also note that affective and behavioral engagement with a specific brand had an equal and positive impact on consumers' advocacy for the brand. They conclude by providing theoretical and managerial implications for their study.

In Chap. 13 titled "The Emotional Engagement Paradox," Aksoy et al. examine how customers' word-of-mouth (WOM) behaviors differ depending on the level of emotional engagement, or level of emotional arousal, toward brands across different industry categories. Their study links the emotional engagement level data to WOM behavior across different channels for 3022 US consumers. They draw distinctions in WOM behaviors between brands with different levels of emotional engagement using a simple exploratory means analysis on a limited sample of 696 respondents. Their findings provide insights signifying that positive/negative emotional engagement is associated with positive/negative WOM behaviors. Their study also shows that the highest levels of positive/negative online WOM and the most family and friend recommendations occur for customers having both positive and negative emotional engagement, which is also associated with the highest levels of self-brand connection. The authors conclude by providing implications for researchers and managers, and identifying a need for future research to determine whether the share of engagement reflects a managerially relevant outcome.

CONCLUSION

Collectively, the different chapters of this book provide a holistic picture of customer engagement marketing in various contexts. It provides an in-depth understanding of and clarity on customer engagement as it discusses the scope and definition of the construct, its antecedents, consequences, and the various contexts to which customer engagement can be applied. Although there has been some discussion on customer engagement, the conceptual framework of customer engagement (Pansari and Kumar 2017) is empirically validated only partially. It would therefore be interesting to understand and empirically validate the impact of marketing activities on customer engagement. This can be done by understanding the various marketing activities of the firm like advertising (online/offline) and promotions (free samples, coupons). Researchers could focus on empirically testing the complete process of the customer journey from the pre-purchase, purchase, and post-purchase stage as discussed in Chap. 3. They could then empirically test if customer engagement is part of the journey or if it is an outcome of the holistic customer journey.

This book has demonstrated various antecedents and outcomes of customer engagement. It would be thought-provoking to explore the antecedents and consequences of CE using other firm-controlled activities like innovation. For example, it would be especially interesting to explore whether product creativity affects customer engagement. Does this relationship vary based on the levels of creativity? Do engaged customers respond differently to new products of the same firm? It would be exciting to study these in the context of the fast-changing technology space where there is a creative product introduced almost every week.

Customer engagement has greatly benefited companies in the United States as demonstrated by Kumar and Pansari (2016). Would it help companies across the world? Can the existing customer engagement framework be applied to all the firms across the world, or should it be modified? The answers to these questions would help multinational firms launch new products and engage with customers as well as provide researchers with useful insights. The primary difference in the context of engaging customers between the United States and other nations would be influenced by the cultural and economic factors. The cultural factors of a country determine the tastes and preferences of consumers, and the economic behavior affects their ability to buy. It would be fascinating to observe the differences (if any) in the CE framework due to cultural dimensions. The integration of the CE framework with the cultural dimensions and the economic factors leads to some more intriguing questions like: Would the cultural dimensions affect all the components of CE, or only some? Would the economic conditions of a country affect only purchases or would it also affect the indirect CE dimensions? How would different industries across the world react to the CE framework?

Customers have always been important stakeholders to the firm. However, the other stakeholders like employees (as discussed in Chap. 8), suppliers, other partners (as discussed in Chap. 11), investors, society, and so on also play an important role in ensuring sustainable firm performance. Therefore, it would be beneficial to extend the concept of engagement to all the stakeholders of the firm and evaluate their impact on firm performance. Some questions that would then arise are—are all stakeholders equally important? How much should a firm spend on engaging all stakeholders? How much does each stakeholder contribute to firm performance?

If the firms want to ensure that their customers are always engaged, then the firm has to ensure that engagement is an integral part of their organizational culture. Researchers could focus on developing the next strategic orientation for engagement similar to market orientation and interaction orientation. In the 1990s, Narver and Slater (1990) and Kohli and Jaworski (1990) focused on the concept of market orientation, which recommends that firms should not only focus on their customers but also on their competitors and on the process. Additionally, interaction orientation proposed by Ramani and Kumar (2008) reflects the firm's ability to interact with customers and take advantage of the information obtained from them through successive interactions to achieve profitable customer relationships. Similarly, researchers could develop an Engagement Orientation approach focusing on effectively engaging all stakeholders and understanding the process of engaging all stakeholders and the benefits of the same.

This book is a great starting point for anyone who would like to discover the foundation of customer engagement and also understand its antecedents and consequences. There is also tremendous scope for researchers to explore customer engagement in depth and contribute to this growing body of knowledge.

NOTES

1. http://dalecarnegiewayohio.com/2013/10/18/is-the-business-buzzword-engagement/.
2. http://www.gallup.com/businessjournal/172637/why-customer-engagement-matters.aspx.
3. http://www.pcmag.com/article2/0,2817,2096798,00.asp.

REFERENCES

Assacl, H. (1992). *Consumer Behavior and Marketing Action* (4th ed.). Boston: Kent.

Bowden, J. L. H. (2009). The Process of Customer Engagement: A Conceptual Framework. *Journal of Marketing Theory and Practice, 17*(1), 63–74.

Brodie, R. J., Hollebeek, L. D., Juric, B., & Ilic, A. (2011). Customer Engagement: Conceptual Domain, Fundamental Propositions, and Implications for Research. *Journal of Service Research, 14*(3), 252–271.

Bruner, G. C., II, Gordon, C., James, K. E., & Hensel, P. J. (2001). *Marketing Scales Handbook* (Vol. III). Chicago: American Marketing Association.

Delgado-Ballester, E., & Luis Munuera-Alemán, J. (2001). Brand Trust in the Context of Consumer Loyalty. *European Journal of Marketing, 35*(11/12), 1238–1258.

Garbarino, E., & Johnson, M. S. (1999). The Different Roles of Satisfaction, Trust, and Commitment in Customer Relationships. *The Journal of Marketing, 63*(2), 70–87.

Gentile, C., Spiller, N., & Noci, G. (2007). How to Sustain the Customer Experience: An Overview of Experience Components that Co-create Value with the Customer. *European Management Journal, 25*(5), 395–410.

Hollebeek, L. (2011). Exploring Customer Brand Engagement: Definition and Themes. *Journal of Strategic Marketing, 19*(7), 555–573.

Kohli, A. K., & Jaworski, B. J. (1990). Market Orientation: The Construct, Research Propositions, and Managerial Implications. *Journal of Marketing, 45*, 1–18.

Kumar, V. (2008). *Managing Customers for Profit: Strategies to Increase Profits and Build Loyalty.* Upper Saddle River: Prentice Hall Professional.

Kumar, V. (2013). *Profitable Customer Engagement: Concept, Metrics and Strategies.* Los Angeles: SAGE Publications India.

Kumar, V., & Bhagwat, Y. (2010). Listen to the customer. *Marketing Research, 22*(2), 14–19.

Kumar, V., & Pansari, A. (2016). Competitive Advantage through Engagement. *Journal of Marketing Research, 53*(4), 497–514.

Kumar, V., Aksoy, L., Donkers, B., Venkatesan, R., Wiesel, T., & Tillmanns, S. (2010). Undervalued or Overvalued Customers: Capturing Total Customer Engagement Value. *Journal of Service Research, 13*(3), 297–310.

Kumar, V., Bhaskaran, V., Mirchandani, R., & Shah, M. (2013). Practice Prize Winner – Creating a Measurable Social Media Marketing Strategy: Increasing the Value and ROI of Intangibles and Tangibles for Hokey Pokey. *Marketing Science, 32*(2), 194–212.

Kumar, V., Luo, A., & Rao V. (2015). *Linking Customer Brand Value to Customer Lifetime Value* (Working Paper).

Mittal, B. (1994). A Study of the Concept of Affective Choice Mode for Consumer Decisions. *Advances in Consumer Research, 21*(1), 256–263.

Moorman, C., Zaltman, G., & Deshpande, R. (1992). Relationships Between Providers and Users of Market Research: The Dynamics of Trust Within and Between Organizations. *Journal of Marketing Research, 29*(3), 314.

Moorman, C., Deshpande, R., & Zaltman, G. (1993). Factors Affecting Trust in Market Research Relationships. *Journal of Marketing, 57*(1), 81–101.

Morgan, R. M., & Hunt, S. D. (1994). The Commitment-Trust Theory of Relationship Marketing. *Journal of Marketing, 58*(3), 20–38.

Narver, J. C., & Slater, S. F. (1990). The Effect of a Market Orientation on Business Profitability. *Journal of Marketing, 54*, 20–35.

Oliver, C. (1997). Sustainable Competitive Advantage: Combining Institutional and Resource-Based Views. *Strategic Management Journal, 18*(9), 697–713.

Pansari, A., & Kumar, V. (2017). Customer Engagement: The Construct, Antecedents, and Consequences. *Journal of the Academy of Marketing Science, 45*(3), 22–30.

Ramani, G., & Kumar, V. (2008). Interaction Orientation and Firm Performance. *Journal of Marketing, 72*(1), 27–45.

Van Doorn, J., Lemon, K. N., Mittal, V., Nass, S., Pick, D., Pirner, P., & Verhoef, P. C. (2010). Customer Engagement Behavior: Theoretical Foundations and Research Directions. *Journal of Service Research, 13*(3), 253–266.

Verhoef, P. C., Lemon, K. N., Parasuraman, A., Roggeveen, A., Tsiros, M., & Schlesinger, L. A. (2009). Customer Experience Creation: Determinants, Dynamics and Management Strategies. *Journal of retailing, 85*(1), 31–41.

Vivek, S. D., Beatty, S. E., & Morgan, R. M. (2012). Customer Engagement: Exploring Customer Relationships Beyond Purchase. *Journal of Marketing Theory and Practice, 20*(2), 122–146.

Zaichkowsky, J. L. (1985). Measuring the Involvement Construct. *Journal of Consumer Research, 12*(3), 341–352.

PART I

Antecedents of Engagement

If You Build It Right, They Will Engage: A Study of Antecedent Conditions of Customer Engagement

Shiri D. Vivek, Sharon E. Beatty, and Melanie Hazod

Noting that CE, a tier-one research priority of Marketing Science Institute (2014–16), is clearly a source of competitive advantage, and that a customer's emotional connection with a company is key to achieving this advantage (Kumar and Pansari 2016), researchers have explored its nature, dimensions, and fundamental propositions (Brodie et al. 2011; Vivek et al. 2012), proposed frameworks (Hollebeek et al. 2016; Pansari and Kumar 2016), and suggested its applicability in different platforms and fields of business (Kumar and Pansari 2016).

In the presence of right elements, hedonic and utilitarian brands are potentially capable of connecting with and engaging the customer (Hollebeek et al. 2016). In recent years, academicians have addressed the nature of CE as well as developed several measures to estimate it (Vivek et al. 2014), but, as indicated in Table 2.1, most academic work has concentrated on conceptually pinpointing the right mix of elements that make for effective engagement (Brodie et al. 2011). CE is "the intensity of an individual's participation in and connection with an organization's offerings or activities, which either

S.D. Vivek (✉) • M. Hazod
Eastern Michigan University, Ypsilanti, MI, USA

S.E. Beatty
University of Alabama, Tuscaloosa, AL, USA

© The Author(s) 2018
R.W. Palmatier et al. (eds.), *Customer Engagement Marketing*,
DOI 10.1007/978-3-319-61985-9_2

Table 2.1   Relevant CE antecedent literature

Authors	Methodology	Antecedents
Brodie et al. (2011)	Conceptual	Involvement, participation, flow, satisfaction, commitment, trust
Higgins and Scholer (2009)	Conceptual	Hedonic properties, need satisfaction, opposing interfering forces, overcoming personal resistance, regulatory fit, likelihood, use of proper means, customer role readiness
Hollebeek (2011)	Empirical exploration	CE investments: immersion, ardor, verve
Vivek et al. (2012)	Empirical exploration	Involvement, customer participation, social connection
Pansari and Kumar (2016)	Conceptual	Customer satisfaction, customer emotions with business characteristics moderating
Kumar and Pansari (2016)	Empirical	Employee engagement
Hollebeek et al. (2016)	Conceptual	Customer resource integration, customer knowledge-sharing and learning
Vivek et al. (2014)	Empirical	From the organization: dialogue, facilitative role, authenticity, relevance. From the individual: experience-seeking, meaningfulness, psychological safety, psychological availability
Prahalad and Ramaswamy (2004)	Conceptual on co-creation	Dialogue, access, risk-benefits, and transparency
Marbach et al. (2016)	Conceptual	Customer personality traits: introversion, disagreeableness, openness to experience, conscientiousness, neuroticism, altruism and need for activity, learning and arousal

the customer or the organization initiates" (Vivek et al. 2012, p. 133). Thus, offerings, programs, or activities initiated by the organization with a goal of connecting with or engaging their customers or potential customers may be referred to as customer engagement (CE) strategies, which is the focus of this paper.

While recent research overly focuses on online presence and social media in engaging customers, research seems to ignore that brands have successfully engaged customers in pre-social media days. Such engagement was evident in brand communities, such as the 90-year-old Macy's Thanksgiving Day Parade, Harley Davidson's enduring connections with its customers through rallies, as well as Subaru's enthusiast festivals. At the same time, recent studies discuss the failed online attempts by well-known brands, such as the Pepperidge Farms Goldfish crackers and the Porsche Cayenne (Fournier and Lee 2009). Thus, customer engagement strategies operate well beyond the online environment and should be considered broadly. Further, the recipe for developing effective engagement programs is not yet clear and needs further academic exploration.

Prahalad and Ramaswamy (2004) proposed the DART (dialogue, access, risk-benefit, and transparency) approach to target CE and co-creation. More recently, Kumar and Pansari (2016) posited that satisfaction and emotional connectedness lead to CE, though the influence may differ based on the customer's convenience desire and involvement levels, as well as by the industry and value of the brand. However, managers still seek answers to their many CE questions, such as what makes CE programs successful? What elements make up an effective engagement strategy? Do some customers have a higher propensity to engage than others? If so, what individual factors influence this inclination? We contribute to the understanding of the engagement ecosystem with our research program involving a series of qualitative interviews and in keeping with social exchange theory (Homans 1958) and the more recently proposed theory of engagement (Kumar and Pansari 2016). Our research involved reaching out to engaged customers plus executives involved with the design and implementation of CE programs. Thus, we identify four strategic elements of the CE ecosystem that make for a highly engaging marketing program, irrespective of the platform, online or otherwise. We also study CE efforts of the Bavaria region of Deutsche Bahn (DB), the German railway company, as a case study. We then discuss four factors that influence the level of engagement of an individual customer.

Data Collection and Analysis

We used qualitative research based in grounded theory (Corbin and Strauss 1990) and constant comparison (Glaser and Strauss 1999) to explore the antecedents of customer engagement. This method was appropriate given the exploratory nature of this research. Two studies were conducted to capture both the practitioner and customer perspective.

The first study identified the range of foci with which customers engage. Drawing from the previous research findings (Higgins and Scholer 2009; Vivek et al. 2012), we view engagement as a connection with not only with a brand but also with any of its marketing elements, such as outreach events, product co-creation, self-service, advertising, and social media activities.

The researchers asked participants to provide three examples of marketing programs they enjoyed engaging in. In addition, they were asked to elaborate on how and why they felt engaged with these programs. We gathered 178 incidences of engagement from 62 participants (28 females), across a series of focus groups, including varied ages and occupations to capture a whole range of CE foci.

The second study involved exploring engagement strategies from an organizational perspective. In-depth interviews were conducted with 18 (6 women) executives managing customer experience and engagement programs in a range of industries, involving both online and offline contexts (such as marketing consulting, cosmetics, logistics, hospitality, and retail). The participants represented different hierarchical levels (supervisors, managers, senior managers, and vice presidents) and ranged in age (29 to 67 years), experience (from 6 to 27 years), and region.

The researchers entered into a discussion with the executives that flowed as a conversation after the initial question, "Tell us about your marketing program and why you think it is able to engage (not engage) customers?" Probes and follow-up questions were used to fill in the gaps in the engagement stories discussed by the executives. The average length of interviews was 43 minutes. All interviews were recorded and transcribed.

The researchers used several methods to arrive at key findings, including text analysis, coding of transcripts, keyword search, and comparison of themes. The analysis increased our understanding of the key elements of engagement strategy, and individual's preconditions for engaging. We discuss those findings here.

FINDINGS

In analyzing data from the studies, we discovered two basic sets of elements that were quite different: first, the elements of an organization's engagement strategy and second, differences between customers based on their preconditions for engaging with a marketing program. We introduce both these sets of elements in the coming sections.

Critical Elements of Engagement Strategy

Irrespective of when, on what platform, and through which medium organizations implemented engagement strategies to influence the consumer, certain strategic elements were found to be essential in engaging the customer effectively. A thorough analysis of the field and the interview

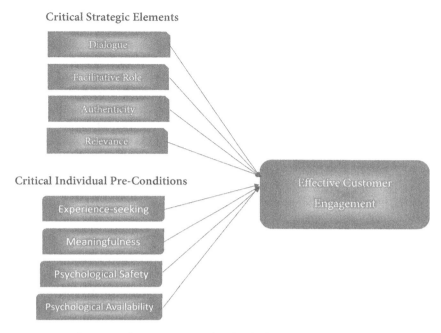

Fig. 2.1 Elements of CE strategy and individual preconditions

transcripts point to four important dimensions of any engagement marketing program: generate dialogue, encourage the facilitative role of the businesses, provide authentic connection, and offer relevance to customers (Fig. 2.1).

Although the extent of influence of each element may be moderated by several factors, for instance, the touchpoint offered, the nature of industry, and type of organization (Kumar and Pansari 2016), a successful engagement strategy will likely include all of these elements.

Dialogue Dialogue is an interaction which necessitates participation by all parties, emphasizes flexibility, interactivity, as well as the ability and willingness to let both sides act as equal partners. As the consumer transcends from being a passive receiver of communications and products, co-creation becomes the order of the day (Prahalad and Ramaswamy 2004). Co-creation is a function of organization-customer interactions where the customer creates the value as business facilitates such creation (Grönroos and Voima 2013) through varied opportunities such as mutually satisfying conversations, integrated value-chain management, recognition of the customer's voice, and value-in-use.

For example, creating an opportunity to co-create an experience, Deutsche Bahn RegioNetz Verkehrs GmbH (DB), conducted a dialogue-focused event in one of its existing train routes in Bavaria. To move away from the image of an old-world, large corporation, DB connected with people by inviting them to create awareness about the local region through local music, fun activities, and participation on the train and at the local stations. In this weekly summer event, local bands were encouraged to play traditional Bavarian music on the train and at major stops. The special event encouraged travelers and even non-traveling locals to join the experience at no extra cost to them. The music provided an environment for travelers to connect with each other as well as with the railway staff, trained to interact with the travelers, creating a journey that stood out from a typical mundane trip. While about a fifth of the interviewees pointed to some unease caused by the noise and distractions, they also felt that the firm paid attention to their suggested solutions to minimize the inconvenience. The popularity of this event produced significant increases in ticket sales (ticket sales increased by 15% in one station in the year following the event) (Fig. 2.2).

Events are a common marketing strategy to engage customers. Our interviewees argue that unlike past practices of communicating with them with traditional or modern media, effective programs that engage them can provide significant opportunities for multidirectional interactions, making customers feel comfortable and capable of influencing the design and flow of events through expressing opinions and sharing experiences. Sustained dialogue creates a participation-co-creation cycle that connects the customer with the engagement initiative in a flexible manner in contrast to a close-ended survey. Thus, the fluidity of an interaction with a salesperson, front-desk employee, or an online representative has the ability to engage the customer more (Baumann and Le Meunier-FitzHugh 2015). For example, one interviewee noted:

> I like it when it's a lot of interaction and not when somebody's lecturing, and you have to just sit there and listen. (Personal Interview, Heide, 34 years)

The organization's representatives should be knowledgeable enough to create an impressive dialogue while at the same time allowing customers to define their own role based on their interests. Substance in the content

Fig. 2.2 (a–c) Bands playing in the station and in the train

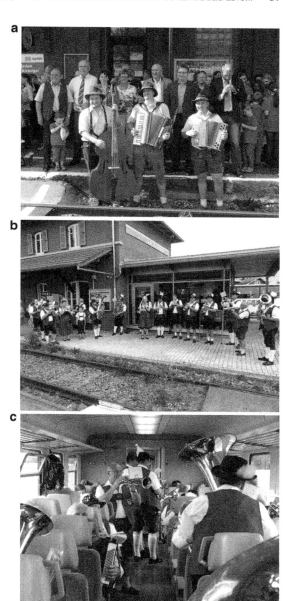

and context play an important role in creating and sustaining interaction. This process is facilitated by knowing the needs of the customer, ensuring their participation in the planning of the engagement initiatives, and allowing room for equal participation during the program. Instead of shifting work and responsibility onto customers as occurs in many self-service facilities, careful planning can create genuine opportunities for co-creation, just like DB did on its less traveled tourist-oriented train routes. We therefore propose:

Proposition 1 Introducing capability for multidirectional dialogue can increase the ability of a marketing program to engage customers.

Facilitative Role Engaging initiatives need to replace the highly structured marketing offerings of the past with customer-centric facilitation (Grönroos and Voima 2013). Effective marketing programs avoid leading, and instead facilitate participation, involving consumers in creating and carrying out the initiative. One of the interviewees explained this element using the example of American Express Members' project. Several years ago, American Express initiated a program to donate money to a cause through the Members' Project. Instead of offering a defined set of projects for customers to choose from, AmEx would announce the amount it would donate, but then let clients and even non-members propose, and vote on, the projects from around the world. The customers could then vote on which projects they wanted to see funded of those proposed and advocated by other customers. By creating an online platform for conversation, AmEx presented a successful model of facilitation in the nascent stages of social media in late 2000s.

Similarly, DB let passengers and locals select the programs they wanted the company to facilitate. DB facilitated traveler convenience by expanding ticket purchase options ranging from full-service ticket windows to self-service vending machines and opening cafes with expanded services for transit passengers on the previously deserted train stations. In response to customer wishes, expressed in a survey where 60% respondents proposed a café, the first expanded service café was opened in 2008. The cafés, operated by a local entrepreneur (a new concept for the German travelers), eased the wait for the train while providing a pleasant location selling trip essentials. Travelers could enjoy coffee and croissant or shop while waiting for the train. Following the first café in 2008, the concept was extended to six more stations in the following years.

Organizations have successfully incorporated facilitation through solution-focused customizable products that are not offered in final rigid forms. Instead, people are more engaged with customizable products not offered in a final form to them. Some examples include paintable cardboard cars in cereal boxes, smart phones, NikeiD's customizable shoes, or even loosely planned workshops for expectant fathers, providing them with an organized space and time to learn and share with each other and experts. However, not all levels of facilitation promote CE. Our participants reported that customizable products and services with backup support from experts are better received than are high-level, complex customization efforts with weak backup support. These complex customization efforts offer a challenge to customers beyond their comfort levels. This theme resonated with participating executives too. For example:

> We first offered an invite-to-invent environment but it was not well received. Customers thought it was intimidating......then we modified it to guided invention and it was a hit. (New Product Manager, 47 years, Electronics industry)

Thus, guidance could come from call centers or instant online chats where customers can get quick answers, expert customers or employees facilitated by the organization, or just very well-organized FAQ literation, all easily assessed. Keeping the challenge at the optimal level and supporting customers' confidence is critical to the process. When organizations let their customers decide on the level and nature of their involvement, it shows that they care, listen to, and empower their customers. Subsequently, as social exchange theory posits, consumers reciprocate to organizations who show an interest in them with interest in their offerings and programs (Homans 1958). Thus, customers will be more engaged when organizations entrust them to participate in and steer the direction of the company's engagement initiatives. One participant emphasized the importance of a facilitative role in a weight-loss program:

> They do not force a plan on me. I can make my own goals to suit my lifestyle, chart my own schedule. I meet with this other girl who has lost so much weight with her own plan, and I think she is awesome. (Personal Interview, Jessica, 27 years)

We therefore propose:

Proposition 2 Marketing initiatives that facilitate, rather than direct, customer participation are more likely to engage customers.

Authenticity "Marketing has become too artificial and construed, a bit like a sportsman who is trying too hard. We need to bring back authenticity to promise and ... deliver on that" (Gopalakrishnan 2008). Consumer empathy and intuition play a decisive role in making an engagement program effective. Before a successful program can be designed, organizations have to step into the consumer's shoes and understand what s/he needs, just as one participant describes:

> The way it deals with customers...the approach of Sony is not just price price price or doing things for the sake of doing things. They care for quality, and they care for the quality of life of their customers. They don't bug you with emails after emails. The company markets itself in a very discrete and sophisticated manner. (Personal Interview, Buns, 41 years)

It is crucial that the program be seen by the customer as genuinely concerned and caring about what s/he wants and is not viewed simply as a way to sell products or services. As long as the promotion serves as a means for attaining the stated objective of the program, it is not judged negatively by the consumers. Sephora generously provides samples of products that interest customers, but never pushes any specific items in the process. Due to this approach, customers view samples as an authentic means of helping them find solutions, rather than increasing the company's sales. Moreover, Sephora beauty consultations are not dependent on customers making purchases, which provides for a more authentic interaction (and engagement).

To reflect authenticity in their connection efforts, DB has been careful about staying in the background to facilitate connections among the locals through fun events. For instance, the "city-bet" challenges the mayor of a town to complete a specific task involving locals, such as, organizing a dance with 100 couples dressed in typical Bavarian costume. Such events, perceived as highly authentic attempts to connect the city with DB, are now an integral part of local tourism, positively impacting sales into future years. In one city, following the city-bet ticket sales increased in the corresponding months of the following 3 years by up to 9%.

Prahalad and Ramaswamy (2004) emphasize that consumers can also be convinced of authenticity through the organization's transparency. Conflict or differences in opinion among community members may be central to their engagement, leading to seemingly counterintuitive but successful strategies. For instance, Twitter users value negative reviews as being "more honest" than the positive ones (Hennig-Thurau et al. 2015). Similarly, new members in an online community take the presence of negative product feedback as proof of authenticity. Absence of information asymmetry (such as the removal of all negative product reviews) makes customers question the transparency and therefore the authenticity of the organization's efforts. Access to complete information can help customers assess the risk-benefit of their actions well in advance, which adds to the reflection of authenticity. We therefore propose:

Proposition 3 As an organization achieves higher transparency and authenticity in their engagement efforts with customers, CE levels will be higher.

Relevance Relevant information is that which is useful or pertinent to the decision-making process. Previous research establishes that for communication to be effective, it must be meaningful (Mohr and Spekman 1994). The information exchanged by marketers could offer task-related or functional relevance, or non-task-related or nonfunctional relevance. Martin and Clark (1996) clarify that task-related or functional encounters are related to the purchase and consumption of goods and services and include product-related learning and problem-solving, referrals, and product recommendations. Non-task-related information, however, is not directly related to the purchase and consumption of the product, for example, fun, finding community, pleasantries, and personal anecdotes.

Relevant information is useful in reducing customers' uncertainty and their risk perceptions involved in investing their time and effort. A consumer is more likely to participate if s/he finds an event or offering to be personally relevant. Our research analysis strongly points to the importance of achieving clarity in information sharing at every stage of engagement. Sharing clear information ahead of the moment of decision-making increases the individual's sense of relevance. Ambiguity in information sharing seems to send a strong message of lack of relevance, resulting in reduced involvement from the person. Our interviews indicated that events that provide personal relevance will engage consumers for longer durations and at higher levels than those seen as less relevant. One of the interviewees spoke about his attraction toward his church in terms of personal relevance.

It is multi-ethnicities and cultures, and I personally find different cultures very fascinating...these different cultures and these different people. That helps me to understand personally their point of view, and it helps me to understand my point of view better. (Personal Interview, Marc, 37 years)

In the process of being engaged, individuals assess relevance on a continuous basis. Even before committing their time to an offering or activity, relevance is judged through the communication made by the organization. Once an individual commits to participating, s/he will judge the relevance of the initiative through the atmosphere, as well as by an assessment of the extent to which the organization lived up to its promises made in its communication.

I went here with David to the baby talk, like after birth....but I didn't like that either... there were normally supposed to be 8 women, but normally between 2 or 3 showed up and like it was supposed to be one month or so up to three-year old kids...and the trainer prepared stuff for older children and then came three babies.....and they weren't very dynamic, like there were not enough women and sometimes I was just with David, myself and the leader there. (Personal Interview, Heide, 34 years)

DB has attempted to insure that travelers feel that their engagement efforts are relevant. While eliminating huge expenses on advertising or traditional marketing, the company experimented with providing more convenience to the customers on the platforms through additional facilities such as parcel shops and flower shops. With these shops situated in centrally located stations, with convenient hours, a pleasant atmosphere, and helpful staff, DB enables their customers to meet their diverse needs quickly and easily, subsequently simplifying their lives. The facility has been well received by customers, increasing footfall significantly.

Proposition 4 The more relevant the organization's programs and offerings are to their customers' broad range of needs, the higher the CE with the organization or its programs.

Customers may also find a program relevant if it serves as an anchor for customers to achieve an objective, or uses a common anchor to connect with the participant. For instance, one interviewee mentioned that she frequented mall events as well as visits to retail stores and that these events helped her bond with her children.

The necessary elements of dialogue, facilitation, authenticity, and relevance need to be present to increase customer engagement. But importantly individuals who are already preconditioned to these programs or efforts will be the ones most likely to engage. We now discuss the individual preconditions we discovered in our research.

Individual Preconditions

Even when an engagement strategy has all the elements of success, not all customers are likely to engage equally in an interaction with the organization. An analysis of interviews with customers as well as executives underlined individual differences in engagement and revealed four important individual preconditions which may influence the level of an individual's engagement. Besides experience-seeking, these preconditions include the psychological conditions proposed by Kahn (1990) for employee engagement—meaningfulness, psychological safety, and psychological availability. Each individual precondition is briefly discussed below along with proposals as to their influence on CE.

Experience-Seeking More than half a century ago, an economist emphasized the importance of consumer experiences, saying "What people really desire are not products but satisfying experiences. Experiences are attained through activities.....People want products because they want the experience-bringing services which they hope the products will render" (Abbott 1955, p. 40). Since the late 1990s, several authors have encouraged managerial attention to consumers' experiential needs, emphasizing that consumption is a holistic experience which involves the whole person (Pine and Gilmore 1999; Gentile et al. 2007). It is not the memorability of the staged events that sell, but the ability for the individual to live the experience, for which the organization can provide the right environment. Such experiences are highly personal and imply varying levels of individual involvement.

Experience-seeking is a composite of cognition-seeking, sensation-seeking, and novelty-seeking (Hirschman 1984). While some individuals might look for information due to their need for cognitive stimulation, others might seek sensory stimulation (sensation-seekers) in an attempt to stimulate one or more of their senses. Still others are novelty-seekers who are on the lookout for inherent innovativeness, for instance, by buying and using new products. Individuals may fall into one or more of these categories in general, but may use another category to enhance their primary search.

For instance, sensation-seekers might sometimes look for new information (cognition-seeking) to enhance their senses. Hirschman (1984) proposed that people genetically differ in their capacity to seek out experiences. This will differentiate each person's response to even the most effective engagement offerings. Thus, for engagement to occur, the individual must seek the experience to a certain degree.

Proposition 5 The higher the individual's experience-seeking, the higher his or her potential to be engaged by an organization or its programs.

Meaningfulness Meaningfulness has long been recognized as associated with engagement (Kahn 1990; May et al. 2004). Meaningfulness is defined as the value of a purpose, judged in relation to an individual's own ideals or standards (May et al. 2004). Our interviews support Kahn's (1990) statement that people find an activity worthwhile when they feel they can make a difference and are not being taken for granted. An engagement initiative may lack meaningfulness if an individual perceives it as one in which there will be little room to contribute, as well as to receive something of value. Although meaningfulness is judged in relation to one's personal standards, some program characteristics can affect an individual's perception of meaningfulness. Individuals may not find a program meaningful if they perceive it not to be authentic, or do not feel comfortable or relaxed in the setting or environment. Supporting Kumar and Pansari's (2016) framework of the influence of employee engagement on CE, our interviews indicate that for a program to be meaningful, the employees conducting the program should be perceived as knowledgeable and experts in the area. Thus, this finding suggests that employee engagement and program authenticity can increase perceptions of meaningfulness. As the following quote suggests, the presence of contradiction can also affect the perception of meaningfulness negatively.

> These classes didn't really help me....and the funniest thing was that in the breast-feeding classes they give you presents, like the advertisement thing, and we got formula, and that was ridiculous...kind of like really trying to encourage use of the formula. (Personal Interview, Heide, 34 years)

A program is perceived as more meaningful if the individual sees it as facilitating learning that s/he sees as challenging. Moreover, meaningful programs may provide opportunities to make a worthwhile difference in the lives of others. Providing autonomy to an individual is another source of meaning for the initiative (Kahn 1990). When an engagement initiative gives an individual the freedom to make a rational choice, it recognizes that the individual is capable of making an informed decision and in taking personal responsibility for his/her actions. Such a program may be perceived as more meaningful. One of the interviewees suggested that she expects marketing initiatives should be genuinely informative but then leave the decision up to her. Whatever the source of perceived meaningfulness, its presence increases an individual's engagement with the offering or program.

Proposition 6 Higher perceived meaningfulness of an organization's program(s) will produce higher CE.

Psychological Safety Psychological safety has also been previously identified as a precondition to engagement. The term "psychological safety" captures the degree to which people perceive that their environment is conducive to taking interpersonal risks (Edmondson 2002). In psychologically safe environments, people believe that if they make a mistake, ask silly questions, ask for help, information or feedback, others will not think less of them. The interviewees also suggested that they felt safe when they could trust the organization and the employees to be knowledgeable about issues of concern and to show they really cared. Also people feel more comfortable in programs where the organizers seem open to criticism. Moreover, the dynamics of the group in an engagement initiative involving other consumers or employees can also affect individuals' perceptions of safety as well as levels of interpersonal risk. Unequal roles of participants (e.g., where one party seems to be contributing more than the others) can produce an uncomfortable, less safe environment. We therefore propose the following:

Proposition 7 Greater perceptions of the psychological safety of a marketing program or initiative can positively engage a customer.

Psychological Availability The idea of psychological availability was first presented in the context of employee engagement. Kahn (1990) proposed that an employee's belief about his or her level of physical, emotional, and cognitive resources available to get involved in the workplace will influence his or her level of employee engagement. Given that individuals have limited discretionary resources to invest in organizations' marketing efforts, individuals will tend to do a cost-benefit analysis before investing their time, energy, or other resources in a marketing engagement opportunity. Our interviews highlighted the importance of an individual's readiness or confidence to engage with a marketing program. One participant said that he had always loved Mercedes automobiles, but could not afford to own one. However, as his income rose, his engagement with Mercedes' marketing overtures increased tremendously. Thus, his engagement with Mercedes' various marketing efforts became higher as his confidence in his ability to own a Mercedes grew (i.e., due to his increasing availability of financial resources). We argue that engagement can be a transitory state with its level greatly influenced by an individual's confidence in his or her available resources, such as money, time, and/or effort, to invest in the engagement offering.

Proposition 8 As one's psychological availability increases, so too does a customer's willingness to engage with a marketing program.

For example, Ashley et al. (2011) found a relationship between the organization's controllable factors (inconvenience and benefits) and a customer's receptiveness to joining a loyalty program. This individual cost-benefit analysis is subjective in nature. For example, the income threshold at which an individual feels financially able to buy a Mercedes automobile will vary across individuals, while the price of the car is set by the company and is outside of the control of an individual.

CONCLUSION

Recent trends indicate the importance of CE efforts in marketing programs. As noted in the introduction, CE strategies are those organizational strategies aimed at fostering closer connections and ties with the individual and involve some type of active participation by the consumer. These strategies are in contrast to "non-engagement" type marketing strategies, which are not aimed at making these connections or getting customers actively involved with the brand, program, or more generally with the organization. While it is not always easy to differentiate between the two types of strategies, an understanding of the organization's goals for the promotion or program will often provide a way to differentiate between them. For example, a strategy aimed at simply increasing sales or market share with no consideration as to making customers feel more connected or involved with the company would not be a CE strategy.

As academic research and practitioner strategies focus on measuring and defining CE, this paper seeks to illuminate what makes for success in CE program strategies, aimed at improving the overall performance of such programs. Our findings indicate that successful CE strategies involve several types of antecedents: those originating within the organization launching the marketing program and the internal tendencies of individuals. Those CE programs that are more successful in terms of customer connections and loyalty, as well as sales and positive word of mouth, will tend to involve more organizational efforts at facilitation or allowing the customer to be involved in the creation of the program, as well as making sure the programs are more authentic, relevant, and involve successful dialogue between the parties based on how the consumer wishes to communicate. Further, individuals are more likely to engage in programs if they are experience-seeking, feel psychologically safe about the program, perceive the program to be meaningful, and feel psychologically available to engage with the program or organization.

Successful CE relies on the presence of factors from both organizational and individual precondition categories. For example, one participant's perceived lack of authenticity in a pre-natal care workshop ultimately resulted in a negative overall impression of the hosting hospital. The deciding factor in this unsuccessful CE experience was related to the implementation of the organization's engagement strategy.

Conversely, another interviewee's CE experience was mitigated by his sense of psychological availability. Although he had a long-term engagement with Mercedes, the intensity of his engagement increased as his financial ability to commit to the brand became more viable. Therefore, the Mercedes CE program was appropriately engaging, but internal factors determined the individual's level of engagement with the brand and its marketing programs.

Our research is supported by both social exchange theory (Homans 1958) and the proposed theory of engagement (Kumar and Pansari 2016). Organizations need to take into consideration a number of important factors (as suggested here) to achieve successful engagement programs. Additionally, individuals need to be predisposed to absorb, or engage in, these programs as suggested here.

Managerial Implications

This study contributes to the understanding of marketing engagement strategies and their roles in achieving effective CE. Marketing scholars and practitioners have been aware of the experiential emphasis of modern consumers, resulting in a bevy of marketing program enrichment options. Despite the sheer variety of creative add-ons, many marketing programs fail to engage consumers, either because the program design was not conducive to CE or because the individuals were not truly receptive to being engaged, in the first place. By implementing and understanding the elements identified in this paper, organizations can increase their odds of creating customer engagement through their marketing efforts.

However, first, organizations need to understand the individuals they are targeting, as this will determine the levels of the various internal CE predictors they possess and which strategies will most successfully engage them. A segmentation of customers based on their preconditions can help management develop more effective engagement strategies aimed at the right individuals. As noted earlier, although strategy components are chosen by organizations, customer perceptions of those elements are subjective, such that an organization's attempts at authenticity may be rejected as opportunistic or insincere by some. Organizations need to understand their customer perceptions of their marketing efforts and programs so as to better implement their engagement strategies. Conveying relevance is also sometimes a challenge for organizations designing CE programs, requiring an understanding of the concerns and lifestyles of their consumers. For example, many of DB's engagement strategies focused on specific lifestyle elements important to local residents for both functional and symbolic reasons, often evoking community-wide experiences common across age groups.

The recent trend toward self-sufficient customer groups has increased the necessity for the facilitative role of the organization, as well as more dialogue between the parties. Studies show that customers value their inclusion in product development, service recovery, and self-service (Dong et al. 2008; Fang et al. 2008), although there is a fine line between facilitating customer self-sufficiency and overburdening customers with busy-work. One of the key elements of organizational facilitation of CE is a two-way dialogue. For example, as noted earlier, a closed-ended survey does not elicit the same response from a customer as the opportunity for them to speak directly to the organization through whatever mechanism is most convenient to them. When initiating a dialogue, what matters is that customers feel that their voices are being heard and responded to and that their opinions matter to the organization.

Overall, there is a definite move by organizations to develop customer relationships through creating better customer experiences that cannot be ignored. Understanding consumer perspectives and finding opportunities for co-creating experiences is often the most relevant path to a rewarding B2C relationship. It is important to keep in mind that insincere efforts can and will be rejected in an environment where multiple organizations and brands are clamoring for attention and engagement from overlapping consumer groups.

Limitations and Future Research Directions

Our study is a comprehensive attempt to understand elements of organizations' marketing programs aimed at engaging their customers. However, just as with any study, this exploratory attempt also has several limitations that can be addressed by future research. Based on the existing literature and qualitative interviews in this research, we have proposed an antecedent framework for successful CE. Although we studied Deutsche Bahn's (DB) regional experiments in the light of each proposed element and analyzed its impact on business outcomes, a rigorous and detailed quantitative analysis will present a more definitive picture. Future empirical work could include data collection on the critical elements of an engagement strategy, such as dialogue, facilitative role of the organization, and relevancy and authenticity. Data could also be collected on individual preconditions facilitating engagement with a product, service, or activity. Further, it will be interesting to evaluate competing hypotheses and the influence of demographic variables on the proposed model.

Additionally, we believe that interactions between the various organizational elements and customer preconditions should be considered and examined further. There may be a circle of relationships between the antecedent factors which could be explored by future work. Future research might also study the relationship moderators that may be found in customer demographics, brand category, product usage, and similar factors.

References

Abbott, L. (1955). *Quality and Competition.* New York: Columbia University Press.

Ashley, C., Noble, S. M., Donthu, N., & Lemon, K. (2011). Why Customers Won't Relate: Obstacles to Relationship Marketing Engagement. *Journal of Business Research, 64,* 749–756.

Baumann, J., & Le Meunier-FitzHugh, K. (2015). Making Value Co-creation a Reality – Exploring the Co-creative Value Processes in Customer-Salesperson Interaction. *Journal of Marketing Management, 31*(3–4), 289–316.

Brodie, R. J., Hollebeek, L., Jurić, B., & Ilić, A. (2011). Customer Engagement: Conceptual Domain, Fundamental Propositions, and Implications for Research. *Journal of Service Research, 14*(3), 252–271.

Corbin, J., & Strauss, A. (1990). Grounded Theory Research: Procedures, Canons and Evaluative Criteria. *Qualitative Sociology, 13*(1), 3–21.

Dong, B., Evans, K., & Zou, S. (2008). The Effects of Customer Participation in Co-created Service Recovery. *Journal of the Academy of Marketing Science, 36*(1), 123–137.

Edmondson, A. (2002). Managing the Risk of Learning: Psychological Safety in Work Teams. In M. West (Ed.), *International Handbook of Organizational Teamwork.* London: Blackwell.

Fang, E., Palmatier, R., & Evans, K. (2008). Influence of Customer Participation on Creating and Sharing of New Product Value. *Journal of the Academy of Marketing Science, 36*(3), 322–336.

Fournier, S., & Lee, L. (2009). Getting Brand Communities Right. *Harvard Business Review, 87*(4), 105–111.

Gentile, C., Spiller, N., & Noci, G. (2007). How to Sustain the Customer Experience: An Overview of Experience Components that Co-create Value with the Customer. *European Management Journal, 25*(5), 395–410.

Glaser, B., & Strauss, A. (1999). *The Discovery of Grounded Theory: Strategies for Qualitative Research.* New York: Aldine de Gruyter.

Gopalakrishnan, R. (2008). *Consumer Engagement Gives Way to Marketing Success.* http://www.financialexpress.com/archive/consumer-engagement-gives-way-to-marketing-success/280905. Date Accessed 22 Feb 2017.

Grönroos, C., & Voima, P. (2013). Critical Service Logic: Making Sense of Value Creation and Co-creation. *Journal of the Academy of Marketing Science, 41*(2), 133–150.

Hennig-Thuau, T., Wiertz, C., & Feldhaus, F. (2015). Does Twitter Matter? The Impact of Microblogging Word of Mouth on Consumers' Adoption of New Movies. *Journal of the Academy of Marketing Science, 43*(3), 375–394.

Higgins, E. T., & Scholer, A. (2009). Engaging the Consumer: The Science and Art of the Value Creation Process. *Journal of Consumer Psychology, 19*(2), 100–114.

Hirschman, E. C. (1984). Experience Seeking: A Subjectivist Perspective of Consumption. *Journal of Business Research, 12*(1), 115–136.

Hollebeek, L. (2011). Exploring Customer Brand Engagement: Definition and Themes. *Journal of Strategic Marketing, 19*(7), 555–573.

Hollebeek, L., Srivastava, R., & Chen, T. (2016). S-D Logic–Informed Customer Engagement: Integrative Framework, Revised Fundamental Propositions, and Application to CRM. *Journal of the Academy of Marketing Science*, first online 06 September 2016.

Homans, G. (1958). Social Behavior as Exchange. *American Journal of Sociology, 63*(6), 597–606.

Kahn, W. (1990). Psychological Conditions of Personal Engagement and Disengagement at Work. *Academy of Management Journal, 33*(4), 692–724.

Kumar, V., & Pansari, A. (2016). Competitive Advantage through Engagement. *Journal of Marketing Research, 53*(4), 497–514.

Marbach, J., Lages, C., & Nunan, D. (2016). Who Are You and What Do You Value? Investigating the Role of Personality Traits and Customer-Perceived Value in Online Customer Engagement. *Journal of Marketing Management, 32*(5–6), 502–525.

Martin, C., & Clark, T. (1996). Networks of Customer-to-Customer Relationships in Marketing: Conceptual Foundations and Implications. In D. Iacobucci (Ed.), *Networks in Marketing* (p. 342). New York: Sage Publications.

May, D., Gilson, R., & Harter, L. (2004). The Psychological Conditions of Meaningfulness, Safety and Availability and the Engagement of the Human Spirit at Work. *Journal of Occupational and Organizational Psychology, 77*, 11–37.

Mohr, J., & Spekman, R. (1994). Characteristics of Partnership Success: Partnership Attributes, Communication Behavior, and Conflict Resolution Techniques. *Strategic Management Journal, 15*(2), 135–152.

Pansari, A., & Kumar, V. (2016). Customer Engagement: The Construct, Antecedents, and Consequences. *Journal of Academy of Marketing Science*, first online June 11, 2016.

Pine, J. B., & Gilmore, J. H. (1999). *The Experience Economy*. Boston: Harvard Business Press.

Prahalad, C. K., & Ramaswamy, V. (2004). Co-creation Experiences: The Next Practice in Value Creation. *Journal of Interactive Marketing, 18*(3), 5–14.

Vivek, S., Beatty, S., & Morgan, R. (2012). Customer Engagement: Exploring Customer Relationships Beyond Purchase. *Journal of Marketing Theory and Practice, 20*(2), 122–146.

Vivek, S., Beatty, S., Dalela, V., & Morgan, R. (2014). A Generalized Multidimensional Scale for Measuring Customer Engagement. *Journal of Marketing Theory and Practice, 22*(4), 401–420.

CHAPTER 3

Measuring and Managing Customer Engagement Value Through the Customer Journey

Rajkumar Venkatesan, J. Andrew Petersen,
and Leandro Guissoni

INTRODUCTION

The relationships between a firm and its customers are ever evolving. Customers are now continually connected to other customers, firms, and consumers through the internet, mobile applications, e-commerce platforms, and social networks. Thus, customer engagement is now becoming a strategic imperative for many firms. As a result, some firms have found ways to provide customers with richer and more relevant information, more frequent interactions, and real-time personal experiences to create more customer engagement.

For instance, the public transportation system of Montréal (Société de Transport de Montréal (STM)), decided that it would be important to

R. Venkatesan (✉)
University of Virginia, Charlottesville, VA, USA

J.A. Petersen
Pennsylvania State University, State College, PA, USA

L. Guissoni
San Paulo School of Business Administration, Sao Paulo, Brazil

© The Author(s) 2018
R.W. Palmatier et al. (eds.), *Customer Engagement Marketing*,
DOI 10.1007/978-3-319-61985-9_3

53

engage customers before, during, and after they rode on buses and trains around the city. STM developed an app which uses real-time analytics to update customers about upcoming travel information before their rides. In addition, the app uses the geo-location on the customer's smartphone to provide relevant promotional offers to businesses that are along the route.[1] This has led to a significant increase in ridership for STM. This is not the only evidence that engaged customers are more profitable for the firm. A recent Gallup research study shows that engaged customers represent a 23% premium in terms of share of wallet, profitability, revenue, and relationship growth over the average customer across retail, consumer electronics, and hospitality industries.[2] However despite this evidence, only 58% of executives in a 2016 Convero survey claimed to have a formal customer engagement program in place. But, 74% of the executives from the same survey expected to increase spending on customer engagement over the subsequent year.[3]

Over the last decade several academic articles have defined customer engagement (Kumar et al. 2010a; van Doorn et al. 2010). As expected from a nascent field, there are multiple perspectives and definitions of customer engagement. Kumar et al. (2010a) define customer engagement as the value a customer provides a firm from its transactions, interactions with other customers, and knowledge they can share with a firm. Van doorn et al. (2010), on the other hand, define customer engagement as all the interactions of the customer with a firm outside of the customer's own transaction behavior. Irrespective of the definitions, the fundamental premise is that customers are valuable to a firm in multiple ways in addition to the traditional view of the value generated from the customer's own transaction behavior. This is also an evolution of the relationship marketing perspective wherein a customer's transactions with a firm is the base for a broader mutually beneficial relationship. For example, Oliver (1999) and Narayandas (2005) propose that customers first start transacting with a firm and then the relationship between the customer and the firm can slowly evolve toward the customers eventually investing in the firm.

Much of the discussion to this point in the literature about customer engagement is around how to extract value from customers (Lemon and Verhoef 2016). Recent studies by Pansari and Kumar (2016) also focus on how firms can begin to develop customer engagement. This is a first step in a very critical direction toward value creation for different customer types. The majority of the literature on value creation is around the customer experience or the customer journey.

We propose that researchers can benefit from combining these different research streams. Customer relationships evolve through different states that can be broadly categorized as acquisition, growth, retention, and win-back. They engage in repeated journeys with the firm and their social networks in each state. This synergy between short-term experiences and the accumulation of such experiences that lead to progression in relationship states leads to different levels of customer engagement. A lot is known about experiences from pre-purchase to post-purchase that can lead to repeated transactions and maximize. But the role of experiences in creating value for customers to advocate for a brand or provide information that can allow brands to develop better and newer products is unknown. Managing this multidimensional perspective on the customer experience and journey maps is exactly what is needed to develop customer engagement-based business models and processes.

In this chapter we develop a framework for developing a journey map-based view of customer engagement. We start with a review of the literature on customer relationships, customer journeys, and customer engagement. We then illustrate our framework, highlight the existing knowledge in the literature on this topic, and then identify avenues for research. We believe the framework we propose will be useful for managers also to develop an action plan to effectively manage customers with an engagement perspective. We illustrate some of these possible actions in the conclusion section.

Literature Review

Customer Journeys

Customer journey is described as "the process a customer goes through, across all stages and touch points, that makes up the customer experience" (Lemon and Verhoef 2016, p. 3). Changes in technology have allowed shoppers to go through a variety of touchpoints across online and offline media, channels, and devices on their paths to purchase (Kannan et al. 2016). These changes have led to new ways consumers use to research, buy, and recommend products. According to a quote from a McKinsey report "the funnel concept fails to capture all the touch points and key buying factors resulting from the explosion of product choices and digital channels" (Court et al. 2009, p. 1).

Therefore, industry experts have stated that the buying process is no longer linear and started to draw attention of the so-called consumer decision journey. This is considered as an improvement over the traditional funnel because "prospects don't come in the top and out the bottom, but move through an ongoing set of touchpoints before, during, and after a purchase" (Bonchek and France 2014, p. 2). However, the focus of this consumer decision journey is still on a given transaction instead of an experience (Bonchek and France 2014). Recently, studies have proposed to associate the customer decision journey with the goal of optimizing experience with individual touchpoints along the way (Edelman and Singer 2015).

Customer Management

Relationship marketing is then defined as the process and all marketing activities directed toward establishing, maintaining, enhancing, and when necessary terminating relationship with customers and other stakeholders (Morgan and Hunt 1994; Grönroos 2004). Its managerial relevance is to generate stronger customer relationships that enhance seller performance outcomes (Morgan and Hunt 1994; Palmatier et al. 2006). Some of the relationship marketing strategies can include communication, interaction frequency, and relationship investment such as time and resources focused on building a stronger relationship. These strategies can allow firms to optimize decisions such as customer acquisition and retention which have a direct impact on the customer engagement value (CEV). A previous study even highlights that relationships have the greatest influence on cooperation and word of mouth, suggesting that "firms that depend on WOM strategies for new customers should implement effective relationship marketing programs" (Palmatier et al. 2006, p. 151). In turn, word of mouth and cooperation, which leads to co-creation as consumers desire to play a greater role in the process of value creation (Hoyer et al. 2010), are important elements to enhance CEV and its components (i.e., customer lifetime value (CLV), customer influencer value (CIV), customer referral value (CRV), and customer knowledge value (CKV)). Consequently, relationship marketing should not be overlooked, especially in the context of more complex customer journeys (i.e., non-linear with multiple different touchpoints). In fact, such complex journeys make it even harder to establish and maintain relationships between companies and customers to create value.

Today the marketing literature emphasizes that customer value is a dual concept, describing that the purpose of a business is "first, to create value for customers and, second, to extract some of that customer value in the form of profit, thereby creating value for the firm" (Kumar and Reinartz 2016).

Customer management practices of companies are supported by four processes that allow them to get more value from these relationships (Kaplan and Norton 2006).

The first is the process of selecting customers based on the most attractive segments to the company based on its value proposition and this is important to reduce the chances of acquiring an unprofitable customer (Cao and Gruca 2005). Measures such as market share in targeted segments, percent of unprofitable customers, and customer surveys on brand awareness and preference further supported this process.

The second process is to acquire customers by converting prospects to customers. To that end, acquisition campaigns attempt to acquire prospects that resemble current best customers (Venkatesan 2015). Measures such as customer response rate to campaigns, percent of leads converted, cost per new customer acquired, and the estimated lifetime value of new customers acquired were suggested to support decisions through this process. The CLV, one dimension of CEV, can be also used as a metric for customer selection and resource allocation (Venkatesan and Kumar 2004).

The third is to retain customers and some questions are critical to that end (Venkatesan et al. 2012; Venkatesan 2015): is the customer–firm relationship "contractual" or "non-contractual"? When customers quit the relationship, are they "lost for good", or is there "always a share" that can be obtained from them? Contracts dominate B2B transactions, but several non-contractual situations also exist, such as the relationship between a firm and an office supplies vendor. Non-contractual situations often dominate B2C transactions, but several situations exist such as the subscription models (e.g., Netflix) and the consumer packaged goods (CPG) context. Regardless the type of relationship, the CEV measures such as CLV can be adjusted to analyze the engagement value (Sunder et al. 2016; Venkatesan et al. 2012). Further, companies realize that it is less expensive to retain customers than to continually add new ones to replace those who churned. Notwithstanding, customer win-back is a term that identifies the processes of firms revitalizing relationships with customers who have defected (Thomas et al. 2004a). Measures such as retention rate, number of referrals to new customers, number of new customers acquired from referrals by existing customers, number of suggestions, and feedback for company's improvements could be used during this stage.

Finally, the fourth process is to grow the relationship with customers. This means that companies can expand their share of the customers' purchase by cross-selling and up-selling. Companies can use some measures to track their performance during this stage, such as number of products per customers, revenue from post-sale services, share of wallet, and margin per customer.

Customer Relationship Management (CRM)

All of these four processes can be facilitated by the implementation of customer relationship management (CRM) that allows marketing practitioners to identify key activities and measures under the CEV perspective. Besides, in the context of more complex customer journeys, CRM implementations play an important role because it includes the building of a single view of the customer across all contact channels according to three dimensions: relationship initiation, maintenance, and termination (Reinartz et al. 2004). It is associated with "coordinating information across time and contact channels to manage the entire customer relationship systematically" (Reinartz et al. 2004, p. 294). Overall, CRM allows companies to use these data and analysis to support their understanding of how to manage customers. For example, firms use the information in CRM systems in order to acquire new customers, retain current customers, and enhance these relationships through customized communications and cross-selling (Boulding et al. 2005; Payne and Frow 2005; Thomas et al. 2004b). Indeed, information provided by the CRM systems and tools focused on managing customers can be useful to both measure and enhance CEV and its components. Thus, the influence of prior experiences on future customer expectations, the different treatment of each customer, and the value of long-term relationships between customers and firms have become fundamental aspects of CRM for selecting, acquiring, retaining, and growing (Grönroos 2004; Gummesson 1987; Boulding et al. 2005).

Customer Experiences and Customer Journeys

The increasing importance of customer experience has been a result of more complex customer journeys. The customer makes a purchase from the firm, which creates an experience (Pansari and Kumar 2016). Customer experience is the "evolution of a person's sensorial, affective, cognitive, relational, and behavioral responses to a firm or brand by living through a journey of touchpoints along pre-purchase, purchase, and post-purchase situations" (Homburg et al. 2016, p. 8). Firms should be able to continually renew customer experiences to sustain long-term customer loyalty. Thus, the touchpoint journey design, prioritization, monitoring, and adaptation are key identified firm capabilities (Day 2011; Homburg et al. 2016; Lemon and Verhoef 2016).

Lemon and Verhoef (2016) take an experience approach to the customer journey and identify a process model according to pre-purchase, purchase, and post-purchase stages and four categories of customer experience touchpoints: (i) brand-owned, managed by the firm and under the firm's control such as websites and elements of the marketing mix controlled by the firm; (ii) partner-owned, customer interactions during the experience that are jointly designed by the firm and its partners such as marketing agencies and distributors; (iii) customer-owned, which refer to touchpoints that the firm does not influence or control, but they are part of the customer experience; and (iv) social/external touchpoints that recognize the roles of others in the customer experience (e.g., other customers) that may influence the process.

Although customer experience is conceptualized as a customer's journey with a firm over time across multiple touchpoints, it does not reflect the customers' actions toward the firm, whereas, customer engagement reflects these actions toward the firm (Pansari and Kumar 2016). The customer engagement approach has been extended as customers become active co-producers or destroyers of value for firms, specifically because new technological developments have empowered customers to engage more with firms. However, firms should consider that behavioral manifestations of customer engagement can be positive and/or negative which makes it particularly challenging (Kumar et al. 2010a; Lemon and Verhoef 2016; Verhoef et al. 2010). Finally, as managing customers has evolved from a customer transaction orientation to engaging customers in all possible ways, we believe the customer journey perspective should go beyond experience to address engagement value.

Customer Engagement

Customer engagement is a vital component of relationship marketing and represents the intensity of an individual's participation in and connection with a company's offerings or activities (Vivek et al. 2012; Brodie et al. 2011). It is defined "as the mechanics of a customer's value addition to the firm, either through direct or/and indirect contribution" (Pansari and Kumar 2016). According to Kumar et al. (2010a), direct contributions consist of customer purchases, and indirect contributions consist of incentivized referrals that the customer provides. Further research described customer engagement as a firm's effort to motivate, empower, and measure customer contribution to the firm beyond the economic transaction (Harmeling et al. 2016). Ultimately, this has led to the belief that engagement marketing can reduce acquisition costs, promote customer-centric innovations, and improve post-purchase service quality (Harmeling et al. 2016). It can also capture more accurate measures of customer value (Kumar et al. 2010a; Kumar 2013a, b) beyond the traditional customer value measurement focus on customer acquisition, retention, and increasing customers' spending with a company over time. Engagement differs from traditional relational concepts (e.g., "participation" and "involvement") because it reflects the notion of interactive, co-creative experiences (Brodie et al. 2011).

According to Kumar et al. (2010a), the four components of a customer's engagement value (CEV) with a firm are: customer lifetime value (CLV), which is related to the customer's purchase behavior and it can be through repeated purchases or additional purchases; customer referral value (CRV), as it relates to the acquisition of new customers through a firm's incentivized referral programs; customer influencer value (CIV), which includes the customer's behavior to influence other acquired customers and/or prospects; and the customer knowledge value (CKV), the value added to the firm by feedback from the customer. Each of these measures, in turn, could be associated with specific stage of the customer journey.

Customer Engagement Value in the Context of the Customer Journey

Engagement components such as word-of-mouth (WOM) referrals can produce longer carryover effects and higher response elasticities than traditional marketing actions (Trusov et al. 2009). The engagement-based measures can help companies make better decisions from knowing the customer value that comes from direct and indirect contributions. It can also help companies on how to improve the CEV and (i) get new people to buy a product, (ii) make an existing customer to repurchase a product, (iii) encourage customers that have churned to make a new purchase from the firm, and (iv) get people to write product reviews or to participate in referral programs. In this article, we explore the four components of a customer's engagement value over time during the purchase cycle (i.e., pre-purchase, purchase, and post-purchase).

Once the buying process is no longer linear, each component of the CEV can be enhanced in a multitude of ways from the interaction between pre-purchase and post-purchase customers. This means that an existing customer can start a new journey from anywhere in the funnel and use different touchpoints to interact with a brand. At the same time, this customer can help bring new customers to the firm while interacting with other pre-purchase customers. This dynamic can generate changes in the company's total value extracted from CEV through the direct and indirect contributions that can cause an effect on CLV, CRV, CIV, and CKV. For example, during the pre-purchase stage, new potential customers of a firm can be influenced by the value generated from post-purchase customers through their reviews they post on social media and word of mouth. This situation could lead to an increase in both CLV from the pre-purchase customers who make a decision to purchase after reading the reviews and CIV of the post-purchase customers who wrote the reviews. At the same time, these post-purchase customers can bring a new customer into the firm through a referral program, which could help the company to increase the CLV of the new customer who purchased due to the referral and the CRV of the post-purchase customer who made the referral. Besides, they can sometimes share their knowledge with a firm from an experience they are having during the purchase stage and increase the CKV through the customer knowledge-sharing process. Finally, the post-purchase customer can increase his/her own purchases from this firm, leading to an increase in that customer's CLV. Thus, the customer lifetime value can be enhanced on both sides from a customer that moves through each stage of the funnel by interacting with new prospective customers and interacting with the firm and the market by means of different touchpoints.

Amazon's Initiatives Toward Customer Engagement Value
In order to review an example of how these dynamics can take place in a company, we highlight some initiatives from Amazon.com. With regard to improving CLV, the company launched the Amazon Dash in 2014 for quick consumer product reordering. It first started with a Wi-Fi device that allows consumers to build a shopping list by either scanning barcodes or saying products' name that are recognized by the device. Later, in 2015, the company had introduced The Dash Button, which is a Wi-Fi-connected device that can be placed anywhere in the house, and it is paired with a

product of a consumer's choice. When a product is running low in the house, consumers simply make reorders by pressing a button. Potentially, the Amazon Dash can have an effect on Amazon's share of wallet as a channel for a specific product, retention rate, and purchase frequency and thus on CLV. It can also allow a non-linear buying process during the funnel as consumers do not play a key role during the pre-purchase stage (e.g., searching information of a brand or considering other brands to satisfy a need). To improve CRV Amazon has already developed an initiative to generate customer referral value besides CLV. For example, when they offer "get $5 when your friends join prime"[4] or "Earn credit for every friend who joins Amazon Student: $10 for you, $10 for them".[5] Further, the company carries a program that was launched in 1996 called Amazon Associates.[6] This program allows participants to advertise products that are sold on Amazon.com, and they can earn up to 10% in referral fees if consumers make a purchase from their link. Since 2005, Amazon.com also offers a crowdsourcing internet marketplace called Amazon Mechanical Turk (mTurk) to improve CKV. In this marketplace, employers are able to post jobs, and workers can select jobs and complete them in exchange for monetary payment offered by the employer.[7] This is open to any company, but ultimately can help Amazon.com and its customers to gain knowledge value from the jobs that are offered. Customer's reviews are an integral part of the Amazon.com post-purchase experience that improve CIV. Some opinions on products that are sold through Amazon.com can play a role at the pre-purchase (e.g., making people to know more about the product's performance), purchase (e.g., influencing people to decide to purchase the product), or post-purchase (e.g., consumers willing to write reviews after their purchase and some experience with the product bought) stages. This example shows how Amazon's customers can not only interact with Amazon, but also directly and indirectly with other current and potential Amazon customers.

As practical relevance for Amazon and its network of sellers and consumers, these different forms of engagement (i) create value for the company which can be measured and managed within the CEV framework; and (ii) the Amazon example also illustrates the amount of possible data collected by the company's interaction with consumers that can be used to generate actionable insights during the interaction of customers with firms along the different purchasing stages.

In fact, as the CRM applications have evolved due to new technological tools, marketing scholars and practitioners have turned their attention to the use of large customer databases to help firms manage customer relationships across different channels and touchpoints consumers use during their journey. This is an important aspect to consider when companies target the CEV as objective function because the use of CRM systems can generate the following benefits that might enhance the CEV. First, it enables companies to automate all aspects of customer relationship cycle such as development of offering, sales, superior experience, retention, and win-back lost customers (Thomas et al. 2004a). Second, the CRM systems can enhance acquisition and retention of customers through a better resource allocation across different activities, selling channels, and touchpoints (Tanner et al. 2005). Actually, the development of a resource allocation strategy that fully utilized the individual customer-level information was identified as key factor that would determine the success of CRM investments (Venkatesan 2015). Third, it improves customization of products and marketing efforts to individual customers (Thomas et al. 2004b). Finally, it enhances customer knowledge and feedback, supports new product development, relational values, and ultimately it improves marketing overall effectiveness (Thomas et al. 2004b; Richards and Jones 2008). We conclude that companies should manage the interaction process during the various types of contacts between the firm and customers by means of CRM systems that take into account the customer lifecycle and long-term customer relationships through the process of acquisition, retention, growth, and win-back. In turn, it can support improvements in the calculation for each of the CEV elements and, consequently, actions taken by the company at the individual level driven by these results.

RESEARCH FRAMEWORK

Table 3.1 provides the organizing framework for putting customer engagement to action. In the columns of Table 3.1, we have the different stages of customer relationships: acquisition, growth, retention, and win-back. In the rows of Table 3.1, we have the different stages of a customer journey: pre-purchase, purchase, and post-purchase. Within each of the cells, we provide customer types to target for each combination of relationship state and customer journey. In addition to targeting, the framework also provides the objective of the customer experience for the combination of relationship state and customer type. For example, the pre-purchase phase experience for acquiring high-lifetime value customers would be different than the experience for acquiring high-influencer value customers. We next discuss

Table 3.1 Customer journeys, customer relationship management, and customer engagement value

	Acquisition	Growth	Retention	Win-back
Pre-purchase	CLV, CIV, CKV	CLV, CKV, CRV, CIV		SCLV, SCRV
Purchase		CLV, CKV, CIV	CLV	
Post-purchase		CRV, CKV	CRV	

All the CEV metrics in the table are meant to represent the net present value (NPV) of the potential value generated by a given customer through transactions (CLV), influence (CIV), knowledge sharing (CKV), and word of mouth/referrals (CRV)

what is known and what needs to be known for each relationship stage, where we take the perspective of the firm that needs to make decisions to manage current and potential customers using the four key metrics we have outlined that impact CEV.

Acquisition

What Is Known?
A firm's goal is to acquire customers who have a high potential to add value to the firm. The majority of research to this point has focused on the value that is derived from new customer purchase behavior (i.e., CLV of a potential customer). For instance, research has shown that firms can acquire customers with higher CLV depending on the channel of acquisition (Villanueva et al. 2008) or by leveraging current customer using referrals (Kumar et al. 2010b).

What Do We Need to Know?
However, relatively little research has addressed how firms can leverage CIV and CKV during customer acquisition efforts. To start with, can firms identify customers with potential for high CIV during the acquisition stage? For instance, can firms find potential customers who already have high degrees of influence (e.g., large social networks) as targets for acquisition? Are the customers with high degrees of influence in other situations or contexts the same customers that are likely to have a high degree of influence on customers for a different firm? Further, once these customers are identified, what are the best methods for acquiring these potential customers (e.g., discounts, samples, etc.)?

Similar questions are likely to arise regarding customer selection for acquisition efforts using CKV. Can firms predict the customers who are likely to provide high levels of knowledge value to other customers? While there is some literature related to the value of social influence (i.e., CIV), the literature related to the value of customer knowledge (i.e., CKV) is sparser. For instance, research does suggest that lead users can be great sources of new product innovation (Von Hippel 1986). However, it can be challenging to identify these potential customers before adoption.

Growth

What Is Known?
Once a customer is acquired, the next step by a firm to increase value comes from efforts to grow the customer relationship. This can include efforts to cross- and up-sell products to customers. To this point, the majority of research on customer growth has developed models to cross-sell products to current customers (e.g., Li et al. 2005) and identify drivers of cross-buying potential (e.g., Kumar et al. 2008).

What Do We Need to Know?
Recently many companies have made significant investments to improve their customers' experience (Senior et al. 2016) so as to improve the effectiveness of their cross-selling or up-selling activities. Related to the customer experience, an important open issue is the role customer experience plays in motivating customers to influence prospects directly through referrals or indirectly through sharing recommendations through social networks (i.e., increase CRV or CIV). Thus, would the growth of the relationship between the firm and customer (i.e., increase in cross-buying or up-buying) have different implications for the value provided by a firm to a high CLV customer vs. the value provided to a high CIV or CRV customer? Further, would the products and services that firms choose to cross- and up-sell be different when the firm is trying to increase CLV vs. CRV or CIV? For instance, customizing the experience of a CLV customer is likely to be aligned with products and services that are adjacent to their current product ownership. But, it is likely the case that increasing CIV might mean introducing customers to products which more broadly cover the entire set of offerings by the firm.

This is important because the firm would want CIV customers to be able to talk more about the firm and be able to fit the firm's products to many segments. Further, many consumers prefer user-generated content

(UGC) from their peers rather than the content only generated and com-municated directly by an industry. For example, Red Bull is also known for its extreme competition events and sponsored athletes. Because of the brand's content (e.g., events, videos, posts, website, articles on the news), these athletes are encouraged to talk about Red Bull on their social media with their own audience; thus, they are the influencers. Therefore, Red Bull's strategy on influencers and events is a good example of how to use social media to spread the reach through user-generated content to influence someone's peers. Another example includes fashion and apparel brands that sponsor fashion bloggers based on their number of followers. These brands believe that bloggers could use their own network to influence other cus-tomers instead of communicating directly to consumers. Even luxury brands such as Chanel rely on this type of initiative to optimize CIV, and the fol-lowing are some strategies[8]: gifting goods to most influential bloggers, sponsoring posts when bloggers are paid to publish content about a brand using their "own voice", and encouraging product reviews from bloggers.

Additionally, while CLV and CIV customers are likely to increase value when purchasing well-developed and tested products across categories, the CKV customers may be more valuable at the beta stage of new product development. For instance, one can think of these customers with high CKV being more valuable in the worlds of software development, new video games, and new services (say, ones that incorporate virtual reality in stores) or new store formats. Further, it would be important to under-stand how to best gather information from these customers with high CKV so that it is useful for firms in new product development. For instance, is it better to have these customers in isolation or as groups? An example of an online platform for idea generation to optimize CKV is provided by Starbucks and it is called "My Starbucks Idea".[9] This online crowdsourcing platform launched in 2008 allows people to submit their ideas according to some categories: products (e.g., coffee, food, new tech-nology, Starbucks card); experience (e.g., ordering, atmosphere, and loca-tions); and involvement (e.g., social responsibility). People can also vote and comment submitted ideas of others.

Retention

What Do We Know?
In addition to trying to grow the relationship with customers (as discussed in the previous section), firms need to also be aware of customers that might churn. To this point, most of the research on customer retention and

churn has focused on the models firms can use to predict which customers are likely to repurchase and which customers are likely to defect (e.g., Neslin et al. 2006). These models have helped most with identifying the drivers of customer retention and defection, mostly with the focus on maximizing customer duration and in turn, customer profitability (i.e., CLV).

What Do We Need to Know?

As noted, there is a lot of research which helps firms predict which customers are likely to repurchase or to churn. However, the link among customer retention, word of mouth (CRV), and influence (CIV) is less clear. What are the best mechanisms firms can use to enable customers to talk about their experiences? Would inviting customers to blog about their experiences work? What type of customers would be interested in different firm-initiated post-purchase activities, those with higher CRV or CIV?

There is significant research on the drivers of customers writing product reviews and how the aggregate measures of product reviews drive general customer purchase behavior. However, we do not know if there are certain types of reviews which are more or less valuable to driving future customer purchases. Further, we know that reviews are often more effective when there are several available, compared to only one. So, how is the CIV from a customer who writes product reviews affected by the other reviews that are available?

Additionally in network economies, a customer may be not as profitable but they add to the same and cross-side network effects. For example, Gmail is more valuable to customers if others also use it. So, even if a Gmail customer is not individually valuable to Google from a CLV perspective, they are important to create the same-side (and maybe even cross-side) network effects. Thus, it is important that we still try to better understand the value of a customer who makes no direct transactions (CLV) with the firm (Gupta and Mela 2008).

Still, the major open issue in the area of customer retention is to understand whether the models that predict churn based on CLV-related variables are also valuable in predicting how firms can retain customers which are valuable for knowledge (CKV), influence (CIV), and word of mouth (CRV). For instance, is it the case that the customer experience variables are more important in predicting customer retention for CKV, CIV, and CRV customers?

Win-Back

What Do We Know?

Once a customer leaves the firm, the firm needs to decide whether it is important to make an effort to reacquire the customer. To this point, customer reacquisition and win-back have been the least researched of the stages in the customer lifecycle. Those papers which have addressed the topic of win-back have focused on the type(s) of win-back offers which should be provided to customers (e.g., Tokman et al. 2007) as well as predicting the right customers to target based on their potential second customer lifetime value (SCLV) (Kumar et al. 2015).

What Do We Need to Know?

To this point, research on customer win-back is mainly concerned with the customer's potential second lifetime value (commonly notated as SCLV). What we still need to better understand is whether it is important for firms to also consider CKV, CRV, and CIV when thinking about which customers to attempt to win back. For example, the assumption here is likely that a customer with high CIV would continue to influence others even if they are no longer a customer. Would the influence still have the same impact on potential customers even after the customer leaves the firm?

Further, the strategies to win back customers are often based solely on the customer's expected second lifetime value (SCLV). What types of strategies can firms use to win back customers who have a high potential second customer referral value (SCRV)? Also, how do the values of the CEV metrics vary between the first and second lifetimes?

SUMMARY, MANAGERIAL IMPLICATIONS, AND FUTURE RESEARCH

The goal of this chapter was to better understand how customer engagement can create value for firms across the customer lifecycle including acquisition, growth, retention, and win-back. Part of that includes identifying the key research in those areas which has already addressed some of the CEV metrics of CLV, CIV, CKV, and CRV. The other part includes trying to identify fruitful areas of future research which can help researchers and managers better understand how and when to use the different aspects of CEV to make better customer management decisions. In order to help summarize the research opportunities, we provide a summary

Table 3.2 Summary of key research questions

Acquisition	*Growth*
Can firms identify potential customers who will have high influence (CIV) or knowledge (CKV)?	Are the cross-selling and up-selling strategies firms use to enhance CLV the same as those that will lead to increases in CIV, CKV, and CRV?
What types of acquisition strategies will be more effective in acquiring customers who will have high CIV or CKV?	Are certain CEV metrics more likely to create value earlier (e.g., CKV) vs. later (e.g., CIV) in the customer relationship?

Retention	*Win-back*
How do experiences during purchases drive different aspects of CEV?	How should firms use metrics such as CRV, CKV, and CIV in making decisions about which customers to win back?
How do actions by customers after purchases (e.g., writing a review or interacting with customers in a social network) impact other customers to make purchases?	Are the strategies to win back customers different based on the value that the customer provides to the firm?

table of questions which need to be addressed during each of the parts of the customer relationship lifecycle (see Table 3.2).

At a high level, answers to the research questions identified in Table 3.2 will help improve the average CLV of a firm's customers and improve the return on investment (ROI) of the firm's marketing actions. We propose that CLV will increase because measurement of CRV and CIV are based on the CLV of the customers acquired through referrals and influence. Further, CKV is higher if firms can develop better products and design better experiences that improve the CLV of other customers. An engagement perspective encourages a multidimensional perspective of customers which allows firms to improve relationships even with customers that have lower direct transactional value or CLV. The engagement perspective also increases the rigor of evaluating customer experience design options by focusing on customer-level financial metrics in addition to intermediate mind-set metrics such as satisfaction and delight. Such a focus on customer-level financial metrics can improve the ROI of the customer design efforts.

As firms begin to measure and manage customers across the different metrics of CEV, it is important to also note that they face several implementation challenges. A major outstanding challenge would be organizing to manage customers from a multidimensional perspective. A customer-centric organization is organized according to customers and a typical manifestation of this is key account management. In the traditional structure, the key accounts represent highly profitable customers who justify a dedicated team. In an engagement-oriented firm, separate key accounts teams need to be formed for high CLV, high CRV, high CIV, or high CKV customers. The structure, function, and communication among these different key account teams need to be researched. Further, the same customer can be part of multiple key account teams, and the experience of this customer needs to be consistent across these teams. This also raises the issue of coordinating communications to the customer across these teams. Even in CLV only customer-centric firms, sales teams that coordinate across product and service groups are expected to improve customer profits and relationship attitudes (Kumar et al. 2010a). This requires firms to systematically gather and share information about customers during pre-purchase, purchase, and post-purchase.

Econometric models as discussed in this article are well developed for predicting customer profits. But there is a dearth of predictive models for identifying high CRV, CIV or CKV customers. In addition to model frameworks, the information sources internal and external to an organization that can help with identifying the different customer types also need to be explored. Firms are also structured to send outbound communications that target high CLV customers and maximize their potential. Now this effort would require a multidimensional view that also accommodates for synergies (positive and negative) across these activities.

Communication and coordination of activities across silos is important because the success of an engagement-oriented approach lies in identifying synergies among the customer types to improve the firm's activities. For example, high CKV customers are important assets for developing new products and also designing effective customer experiences for high CLV, CRV, and CIV customers. High CKV and CIV customers are essential for reducing acquisition costs and also improving the ROI of acquisition activities by attracting high CLV or CKV customers.

Firms will be successful in their customer engagement strategy only if they can design and deliver personalized experiences for multiple customer preference and engagement segments. Big data, machine learning, Internet of Things, and artificial intelligence technologies are enabling companies such as Disney, Amazon, Netflix, and Google deliver such personalized experiences even in physical environments.

The engagement-oriented approach urges firms to co-create a wider range of activities with their customers. It also requires alliances between organizations that go deeper through their respective supply chains. The structure of organizations and their internal and external ecosystems in such an environment is still an open question.

NOTES

1. http://images.forbes.com/forbesinsights/StudyPDFs/SAP_Customer_ Engagement-REPORT.pdf
2. http://www.gallup.com/services/169331/customer-engagement.aspx
3. 2016 Convero customer engagement study; https://sessioncam.com/ customer-engagement-stats-2016/
4. https://www.amazon.com/gp/help/customer/display.html?node Id=201062980
5. https://www.amazon.com/gp/help/customer/display.html?node Id=201567080
6. https://affiliate-program.amazon.com
7. https://www.mturk.com/mturk/welcome
8. https://blog.hubspot.com/agency/collaborate-influential-bloggers#sm.0 000yeesdaszrd2npfx1vbnuvtnfd
9. MyStarbucksIdea.com

REFERENCES

Bonchek, M., & France, C. (2014, May 7). Marketing Can No Longer Rely on the Funnel. *Harvard Business Review.* https://hbr.org/2014/05/marketing-can-nolonger-rely-on-the-funnel

Boulding, W., Staelin, R., Ehret, M., & Johnston, W. J. (2005). A Customer Relationship Management Roadmap: What is Known, Potential Pitfalls, and Where to Go. *Journal of Marketing, 69*(October), 155–166.

Brodie, R. J., Hollebeek, L. D., Juric, B., & Ilic, A. (2011). Customer Engagement: Conceptual Domain, Fundamental Propositions, and Implications for Research. *Journal of Service Research, 14*(3), 252–271.

Cao, Y., & Gruca, T. S. (2005). Reducing Adverse Selection Through Customer Relationship Management. *Journal of Marketing, 69*(October), 219–229.

Court, D., Elzinga, D., Mulder, S., & Vetvik, O. J. (2009, June). The Consumer Decision Journey. *McKinsey Quarterly.* http://www.mckinsey.com/business-functions/marketing-andsales/our-insights/the-consumer-decision-journey

Day, G. S. (2011). Closing the Marketing Capabilities Gap. *Journal of Marketing, 75*(4), 183–195.

Edelman, D. C., & Singer, M. (2015, November). Competing on Customer Journeys. *Harvard Business Review*, 88–100.

Grönroos, C. (2004). The Relationship Marketing Process: Communication, Interaction, Dialogue, Value. *Journal of Business & Industrial Marketing, 19*(2), 99–113.

Gummesson, E. (1987). The New Marketing: Developing Long-Term Interactive Relationships. *Long Range Planning, 20*(4), 10–20.

Gupta, S., & Mela, C. F. (2008). What Is a Free Customer Worth? Armchair Calculations of Nonpaying Customers' Value Can Lead to Flawed Strategies. *Harvard Business Review, 86*(11), 102–109, 38.

Harmeling, C., Moffett, J. W., Arnold, M. J., & Carlson, B. D. (2016). Toward a Theory of Customer Engagement Marketing. *Journal of Academy of Marketing Science, 45*(3), 312–335.

Homburg, C., Jozié, D., & Kuehnl, C. (2016). Customer Experience Management: Toward Implementing an Evolving Marketing Concept. *Journal of Academy of Marketing Science, 45*(3), 377–401.

Hoyer, W. D., Chandy, R., Dorotic, M., Krafft, M., & Singh, S. S. (2010). Consumer Cocreation in New Product Development. *Journal of Service Research, 13*(3), 283–296.

Kannan, P. K., Reinartz, W., & Verhoef, P. C. (2016). The Path to Purchase and Attribution Modeling: Introduction to Special Section. *International Journal of Research in Marketing, 33*, 449–456.

Kaplan, R. S., & Norton, D. P. (2006). *Alignment: Using the Balanced Scorecard to Create Corporate Synergies.* Boston: Harvard Business Press.

Kumar, V. (2013a). *Profitable Customer Engagement: Concept, Metrics and Strategies.* Los Angeles: SAGE Publications.

Kumar, V. (2013b). *Customer Lifetime Value: The Path to Profitability.* Hanover: Now Publishers.

Kumar, V., & Reinartz, W. (2016). Creating Enduring Customer Value. *Journal of Marketing, 80*(November), 36–68.

Kumar, V., George, M., & Pancras, J. (2008). Crossbuying in Retailing: Drivers and Consequences. *Journal of Retailing, 84*(1), 15–27.

Kumar, V., Aksoy, L., Donkers, B., Venkatesan, R., Wiesel, T., & Tillmanns, S. (2010a). Undervalued or Overvalued Customers: Capturing Total Customer Engagement Value. *Journal of Service Research, 13*(3), 297–310.

Kumar, V., Petersen, J. A., & Leone, R. P. (2010b). Driving Profitability by Encouraging Customer Referrals: Who, When, and How. *Journal of Marketing, 74*(5), 1–17.

Kumar, V., Bhagwat, Y., & Zhang, X. (2015). Regaining "Lost" Customers: The Predictive Power of First Lifetime Behavior, the Reason for Defection, and the Nature of the Winback Offer. *Journal of Marketing, 79*(4), 34–55.

Lemon, K. N., & Verhoef, P. C. (2016). Understanding Customer Experience Throughout the Customer Journey. *Journal of Marketing, 80*(6), 69–96.

Li, S., Sun, B., & Wilcox, R. (2005). Cross-Selling Sequentially Ordered Products: And Application to Consumer Banking. *Journal of Marketing Research, 69*(4), 230–238.

Morgan, R. M., & Hunt, S. D. (1994). The Commitment–Trust Theory of Relationship Marketing. *Journal of Marketing, 58*(July), 20–38.

Narayandas, D. (2005, September). Building Loyalty in Business Markets. Tool Kit. *Harvard Business Review, 83*(9), 131–139.

Neslin, S. A., Gupta, S., Kamakura, W., Lu, J., & Mason, C. H. (2006). Defection Detection: Measuring and Understanding the Predictive Accuracy of Customer Churn Models. *Journal of Marketing Research, 43*(2), 204–211.

Oliver, R. L. (1999). Whence Consumer Loyalty? *The Journal of Marketing, 63*, 33–44.

Palmatier, R. W., Dant, R. P., Grewal, D., & Evans, K. R. (2006). Factors Influencing the Effectiveness of Relationship Marketing: A Meta-Analysis. *Journal of Marketing, 70*(October), 136–153.

Pansari, A., & Kumar, V. (2016). Customer Engagement: The Construct, Antecedents, and Consequences. *Journal of Academy of Marketing Science, 45*(3), 294–311.

Payne, A., & Frow, P. (2005). A Strategic Framework for Customer Relationship Management. *Journal of Marketing, 69*(October), 167–176.

Reinartz, W., Krafft, M., & Hoyer, W. D. (2004). The Customer Relationship Management Process: Its Measurement and Impact on Performance. *Journal of Marketing Research, 41*(August), 293–305.

Richards, K. A., & Jones, E. (2008). Customer Relationship Management: Finding Value Drivers. *Industrial Marketing Management, 37*, 120–130.

Senior, J., Springer, T., & Sherer, L. (2016, November 22). 5 Ways to Increase Your Cross-Selling. *Harvard Business Review.* https://hbr.org/2016/11/5-ways-to-increase-your-cross-selling

Sunder, S., Kumar, V., & Zhao, Y. (2016). Measuring the Lifetime Value of a Customer in the Consumer Packaged Goods Industry. *Journal of Marketing Research, 53*(December), 901–921.

Tanner, J. E., Ahearne, M., Leigh, T. W., Mason, C. H., & Moncrief, W. C. (2005). CRM in Sales-Intensive Organizations: A Review and Future Directions. *The Journal of Personal Selling and Sales Management, 25*(2), 169–180.

Thomas, J. S., Blattberg, R. C., & Fox, E. J. (2004a). Recapturing Lost Customers. *Journal of Marketing Research, 41*(February), 31–45.

Thomas, J. S., Reinartz, W., & Kumar, V. (2004b). Getting the Most of Your Customers. *Harvard Business Review, 82*, 116–123.

Tokman, M., Davis, L. M., & Lemon, K. N. (2007). The WOW Factor: Creating Value Through Win-Back Offers to Reacquire Lost Customers. *Journal of Retailing, 83*(1), 47–64.

Trusov, M., Bucklin, R. E., & Pauwels, K. (2009). Effects of Word-of-Mouth Versus Traditional Marketing: Findings from an Internet Social Networking Site. *Journal of Marketing, 73*, 90–102.

Van Doorn, J., Lemon, K. N., Mittal, V., Nass, S., Pick, D., Pirner, P., & Verhoef, P. C. (2010). Customer Engagement Behavior: Theoretical Foundations and Research Directions. *Journal of Service Research, 13*(3), 253–266.

Venkatesan, R. (2015). Customer Lifetime Value Based Resource Allocation. In V. Kumar & D. Shah (Eds.), *Handbook of Research on Customer Equity in Marketing*. Cheltenham: Edward Elgar.

Venkatesan, R., & Kumar, V. (2004). A Customer Lifetime Value Framework for Customer Selection and Resource Allocation Strategy. *Journal of Marketing, 68*(October), 106–125.

Venkatesan, R., Kumar, V., & Reinartz, W. (2012). Customer Relationship Marketing (CRM) in Business Markets. In G. Lilien & R. Grewal (Eds.), *Handbook of Business to Business Marketing*. Glos: Edward Elgar Publishing.

Verhoef, P. C., Reinartz, W. J., & Krafft, M. (2010). Customer Engagement as a New Perspective in Customer Management. *Journal of Service Research, 13*(3), 247–252.

Villanueva, J., Yoo, S., & Hanssens, D. M. (2008). The Impact of Marketing-Induced vs. Word-of-Mouth Customer Acquisition on Customer Equity Growth. *Journal of Marketing Research, 45*(1), 48–59.

Vivek, S. D., Beatty, S. E., & Morgan, R. M. (2012). Customer Engagement: Exploring Customer Relationships Beyond Purchase. *Journal of Marketing Theory and Practice, 20*(2), 122–146.

Von Hippel, E. (1986). Lead Users: A Source of Novel Product Concepts. *Management Science, 32*(7), 791–805.

CHAPTER 4

Customer Engagement Through Personalization and Customization

Alexander Bleier, Arne De Keyser, and Katrien Verleye

Customer engagement is rapidly becoming a key strategic focus for many companies (Pansari and Kumar 2016). In a world where customers are constantly connected to an abundance of at-the-ready information and intelligence, companies increasingly opt for individualized, instead of mass marketing efforts to engage them (Aguirre et al. 2016; Rust and Huang 2014). Today, an increasing number of (online) stores act as marketplaces for tailor-made products and services (Tedeschi 2005) which can—compared to standardized equivalents—significantly increase customers' loyalty to the brand or company (Spaulding and Perry 2013). Moreover, 38% of industry professionals across industries worldwide personalize their messages to individual customers (Statista 2015), with nine in ten consumers indicating it to positively impact their purchase journeys (Lindsay 2014). This shift from mass to individualized marketing efforts is enabled by (1) the increasing levels of (voluntary) customer input and control over the marketing process (Chan et al. 2010) and (2) the growing prevalence of

A. Bleier (✉)
Boston College, Boston, MA, USA

A. De Keyser
EDHEC Business School, Lille, France

K. Verleye
Ghent University, Gent, Belgium

© The Author(s) 2018
R.W. Palmatier et al. (eds.), *Customer Engagement Marketing*,
DOI 10.1007/978-3-319-61985-9_4

individual-level customer data allowing marketers to better serve individual needs (Wedel and Kannan 2016). Individualized marketing efforts should ultimately lead to higher customer value and long-term profitability, strengthening companies' competitive positions (Kumar and Pansari 2016).

To implement a corresponding engagement strategy, marketers need to decide in which individualized customer engagement practices to invest (Arora et al. 2008). Two broadly applied forms are customization and personalization. In customization, customers take on an active role to partly adapt the marketing mix according to their preferences (e.g., tailor products and services to their own tastes). By contrast, in personalization, companies take the lead and tailor marketing activities to individual customers (e.g., personalize messages to customers). The expected benefits of both approaches are a better-fitting marketing mix allowing to create deeper connections (Urban et al. 2014), charge premium prices, and foster customer loyalty (Valenzuela et al. 2009).

ENGAGEMENT GOALS ALONG THE CUSTOMER LIFECYCLE

A customer's relationship with a company typically evolves over three main stages—acquisition, retention/development, and attrition—that come with specific engagement goals (Kumar 2008). We next elaborate on these engagement goals along the customer relationship lifecycle, building on Pansari and Kumar (2016). In line with this work, we argue that companies opt for a *customer engagement strategy* that includes both direct and indirect customer contributions to the company (see also Fig. 4.1).

The *acquisition* stage begins with the first interaction between customer and company and proceeds through the first purchase. The main engagement goal is to spark a consumer's interest in the company's offerings such as to initiate a relationship through a first buying act (Pansari and Kumar 2016).

In the *retention/development* stage, the primary engagement goals are to foster direct customer engagement in the form of repeat purchases, cross-buying, and up-buying as well as indirect customer engagement in the form of referral, word of mouth, and feedback behaviors (Kumar 2008, 2013; Kumar et al. 2010). A referral is the acquisition of a new customer, who would not have been attracted through traditional marketing channels, by an existing customer that the company incentivized to this end (Kumar et al. 2010). Similar to incentivized referrals, spontaneous

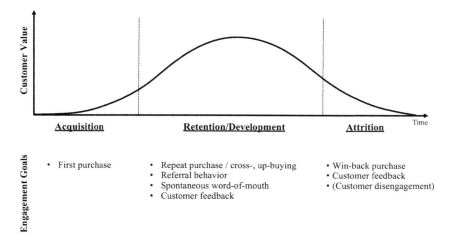

Fig. 4.1 Engagement goals along the customer lifecycle

word-of-mouth (WOM) behaviors can help attract new customers that are part of existing customer networks (Baker et al. 2016). Finally, customer feedback leads to a better understanding of customer preferences, desires, and needs which can help innovate and/or improve existing touchpoints and brand offerings (Joshi and Sharma 2004).

In the *attrition stage*, the customer-company relationship deteriorates and might eventually end over time. Attrition is either customer-initiated (Van den Poel and Larivière 2004) or company-initiated (Fournier and Avery 2012). In the former case, companies may try to reignite buying behaviors through churn prevention or win-back actions (Coussement and Van den Poel 2009; Kumar and Bhagwat 2015). They may also seek customer feedback to determine the reasons for ending the relationship in order to re-engage lost customers with adapted offerings, or as input for product and service improvements (Kumar and Bhagwat 2015). In the latter case, the company's goal is to disengage specific customers in order to avoid negative customer value from them.

Altogether, companies seek to enhance customer value throughout the lifecycle by fostering customers' direct (i.e., purchases, cross-buying, and up-buying) and indirect (i.e., referrals, WOM, and feedback behaviors) contributions to the company. We next elaborate on key customization and personalization approaches to achieve these engagement goals.

Reaching Engagement Goals Through Customization and Personalization

Customization

Customization is a process by which consumers adapt offerings to their own preferences (Valenzuela et al. 2009). A prototypical example is Dell (www.dell.com), allowing its customers to self-select the components of their computers. Demonstrating its ability to build computers to specific customer orders, Dell's revenues grew from $2 to $16 billion in 4 years (Byrnes 2003). To date, the combination of advanced engineering and rapid IT development has created nearly limitless customization opportunities (see www.configurator-database.com, for an overview of online customization projects) (de Bellis et al. 2016; Franke et al. 2009). In general, customization allows customers to (partly) adapt the marketing mix to their individual preferences (Arora et al. 2008). Importantly, approaches differ with respect to the level of control that customers may exercise over the marketing mix (Jimenez et al. 2013), or the amount of autonomy that is given to them. Under very high autonomy, customers get quasi to full sovereignty to determine their own marketing mix (Arora et al. 2008). At lower levels of autonomy, customization occurs within predetermined boundaries. Accordingly, customers are presented a specific set of options, the so-called solution space, which they can adjust to their preferences (Valenzuela et al. 2009). The number of options determines the flexibility customers have to tailor their own marketing mix. Next, we structure prominent customization options according to different marketing mix elements, summarized in Fig. 4.2.

Product Most attention in the area of customization has been devoted to the product part of the marketing mix. The level of autonomy that companies award customers shapes the form of each specific product-customization approach. The highest level of customer autonomy corresponds to *full customization*. Here, customers have (quasi) complete autonomy over any feature of the product (Jimenez et al. 2013). Although more common in B2B settings (e.g., the production of unique molds), there is a growing ability for consumers in B2C settings to fully customize specific offerings through technologies like 3D printing (Berman 2012), for instance, at Shapeways (www.shapeways.com). At lower levels of autonomy, we identify three common customization strategies. First,

	CUSTOMIZATION = individual customers co-determine their optimal marketing mix =			PERSONALIZATION = company determines optimal marketing mix for individual customers =	
Product	By-alternative customization	By-attribute customization Customization via starting solutions	Full customization	Segment-level product personalization	Individual-level product personalization
Price	Name-your-own-price		Pay-what-you-want	Segment-level price personalization	Individual-level price personalization
Promotion	Opting-in/out for company communication		Company communication needs specification	Segmented communication and/or online recommendations	Personalized communication and online recommendations
Place	Channel/facility/equipment choice		Channel/facility/equipment add-ons and specifications	Segment-level place adjustments	Automated place adaptations at the level of the individual
People	Choice of sales people and/or service provider		Sales people and/or service provider specification	Adjusting behaviors to segments (whether or not supported by information systems)	Adaptive behaviors at the level of individuals (whether or not supported by information systems)

Increased levels of autonomy for customer →   Increased levels of granularity for company →

Contingency factors	• Customer role readiness • Customer familiarity with the company	• Customer trait reactance • Company familiarity with the customer and trust

Fig. 4.2 Customization and personalization opportunities

under *by-attribute customization* (Valenzuela et al. 2009), customers can select specific product components from a predefined set of options. At Spreadshirt (www.spreadshirt.com), for instance, customers can design custom T-shirts by choosing fittings and colors as well as adding custom texts and uploading images to be imprinted. By contrast, under *customization via starting solutions* (Hildebrand et al. 2014), customers do not design the product from scratch. Rather, they start from a predefined product—the "starting solution"—and can then modify this to their needs by changing specific attributes. This type of customization allows companies to simplify the by-attribute customization process while maintaining large flexibility. For instance, Mix My Own (www.mixmyown.com) offers a wide array of breakfast cereal mixes that customers can refine by adding or removing certain ingredients. A final form of customization is *by-alternative customization* (Valenzuela et al. 2009). Here, customers select their most preferred option from a set of fully determined products—hence, limiting their flexibility and choice freedom compared to the previous alternatives. An example of this is Acer (www.acer.com), where customers can choose their favorite option from a number of fully specified configurations.

Customized products and services can increase customers' willingness to pay by 20% and lead to a 50% increase in their likelihood to recommend a brand or company (Spaulding and Perry 2013). As such, customization engages customers in purchasing products and services at premium prices as well as spreading positive WOM. In addition, firms can easily collect feedback about customer preferences through the customization process which they can then use for further product improvements (Kramer 2007).

Price Price customization is becoming more popular through participative pricing mechanisms. These schemes afford customers an active role in the pricing of products and services and come in two main forms: *pay-what-you-want pricing* and *name-your-own-price* (Hinterhuber and Liozu 2014).

Pay-what-you-want (PWYW) pricing implies maximum customer autonomy over the price setting for products and services. Customers can pay any price they deem fit (including nothing at all) which the seller has to accept (Kim et al. 2009). A famous example is the British rock band Radiohead that in 2007 sold its album *In Rainbows* online and let fans decide how much to pay for it. Although more people downloaded the album for free than paid for it, it was before its later physical release already more successful than the previous album (Lewis 2008). Humble Bundle (www.humblebundle.com), an online store for video games, took the PWYW model even further by allowing customers to not only name the price but also decide upon how they want to allocate payments among game developers, charities, and the Humble Bundle organization. This strategy generated $50 million in revenue for Humble Bundle in the first 3 years, of which $20 million were directed to charities (Bertini and Koenigsberg 2014).

Under a name-your-own-price (NYOP) scheme, customers have less autonomy over the final price. Here, they submit a bid which is accepted if it surpasses a threshold price set by the company and unknown to customers in advance (Shapiro 2011). Priceline (www.priceline.com), an online seller of travel services, demonstrated the viability of the NYOP pricing scheme with more than $2 billion sales revenues in 2005 (Amaldoss and Jain 2008). Another case is American Airlines where customers can request seating upgrades by naming their own price (Bertini and Koenigsberg 2014).

Due to their still rather uncommon application in practice, these pricing schemes generally spark customers' interest which oftentimes triggers trial purchase and stimulates WOM behaviors (Kim et al. 2009).

Promotion With companies moving toward more individual and interactive media channels like email and mobile text messages, customers increasingly gain control over the messages they receive from companies. Communications, such as newsletters, display advertisements, and other promotional offers are nowadays more and more permission based (Kumar et al. 2014). Kruidvat (www.kruidvat.nl), a Dutch drug store chain, launched an app where customers can indicate how often they want to be informed about specific types of special offers. Moreover, customers can activate special offers which helps the company to gather detailed feedback about individual preferences. Altogether, the customization of promotion ranges from simply opting-in/opting-out for company communications to specifying one's own communication needs in detail. These forms of active commitment lead to a higher effectiveness of company messages as they are less ignored and more deeply processed (Kumar et al. 2014). The corresponding engagement opportunities include cross- and up-buying behaviors, stimulated by more relevant and welcomed messages, and enhanced customer feedback through the establishment and stimulation of two-way communication.

Place Customization of place is related to the increasing number of options that customers have for shopping through various channels and the way they receive purchased goods. Many companies allow customers to choose between shopping offline, in traditional or pop-up stores, or online. Moreover, retailers offer mixed-channel solutions, such as Macy's (www.macys.com) where customers can shop online and pick their purchased items up in a physical store (Macy's 2016). Also, more and more brick-and-mortar stores offer home delivery, often providing customers even with control over the exact delivery time. For instance, Stop & Shop, a grocery chain on the US East Coast, offers a grocery delivery service (www.peapod.com) and allows customers to select a 2-hour window for home delivery that best suits their preferences. Customization of place also relates to providing customers with the ability to adapt the shopping environment. Nike's mobile app Nike+, for example, enables customers to set individual categories of interest that are then shown on the main shopping page as "shop favorites" (www.nikeplus.com.br). Not only the choice between multiple channels but also the customization of channel usage awards customers more flexibility, possibly stimulating increased purchase behaviors (Neslin et al. 2006).

People Companies can also provide customers with decision power over the salespeople and/or service provider. For example, the Belgian tailoring company Café Costume (www.cafecostume.com) permits its customers to choose the outfitter they want to meet when making an appointment. Similarly, customers can often book their favorite hair stylist at their hair salon. At the same time, customers increasingly act as "coordinators" of their own service delivery networks (Tax et al. 2013). For instance, in healthcare settings, patients with chronic diseases regularly participate actively in the treatment process, co-deciding upon the different parties involved (e.g., doctors, nurses, dieticians, personal trainer) and their designated activities (McColl-Kennedy et al. 2012). In this context, companies need to understand how customers view their role in the network, help them build a delivery network, and coordinate their activities with complementary providers to tailor offerings to their individual needs (Tax et al. 2013). Allocating decision power over salespeople, service providers, and/or service delivery networks allows both the customer and the company to develop a stronger relationship that should ultimately nurture purchase and other engagement behaviors such as customer referrals and positive WOM (Gremler et al. 2001).

Personalization

In contrast to customization where customers actively adapt the marketing mix, almost no effort on their behalf is required for personalization. Here, companies themselves determine the optimal marketing mix for individual customers (Arora et al. 2008). Industry studies show the adoption of a personalization strategy to be associated with a 26% increase in profitability and a 12% greater market capitalization (Lindsay 2014). Importantly, for personalization, companies decide upon the level of granularity they seek to apply. Overall, there are three main levels: mass, segment, and individual-level personalization (Zhang and Wedel 2009). Under *mass personalization*, companies offer the same marketing mix to all customers, tailored to inferences about their average preferences.[1] Under *segment-level personalization*, companies offer different customer groups, or segments, a marketing mix that is tailored to the group needs. Last, using *individual-level personalization*, companies tailor the marketing mix to each customer's individual needs, tastes, and behaviors. While these three levels of granularity are often seen as mutually exclusive, companies can easily combine them. As Wedel and Kannan (2016) note, the level of granularity for different elements of the marketing mix can differ. We next discuss available options, summarized in Fig. 4.2.

Product While product *customization* is still more common today, companies increasingly *personalize* product and service offerings to drive customer engagement mainly in the form of purchases. At low levels of granularity, international restaurant chains such as Burger King adjust their menus to the local tastes of specific countries. Product personalization, however, is increasingly moving toward the individual level, driven by detailed customer-level data and rapidly evolving predictive analytical techniques (Chung et al. 2016). The Nest self-learning thermostat (www.nest.com), for instance, is a device that automatically creates a personalized heating schedule for one's home, building on the individual habits and preferences of its users captured through integrated sensors and algorithms. Another online example is Sunfrog (www.sunfrog.com). The company captures names, birthplaces, and other information from individual Facebook profiles to then offer personalized garments with imprints such as "Keep calm and let Bleier handle it!" or "Zerkegem, Belgium, is where my story began." With this approach, companies aim to not only increase purchase likelihood but also stimulate WOM through the surprise of real-time dynamic personalization.

Price Price personalization builds on the idea that customers typically obtain different utility from products and services and are thus heterogeneous in their willingness to pay (Esteves and Resende 2016). Personalized pricing at a segment level is common practice, for example, in early-bird pricing, seasonal pricing, and location-based pricing. With regard to location-based pricing, Center Parcs (www.centerparcs.com), a Dutch operator of holiday villages, charges different prices for the same holiday, depending on the country from which customers access its booking page. Moreover, recent advances in technology are pushing price personalization toward more granular, individual-level pricing schemes (Sonnier 2014). Safeway's "Just for U" program, for instance, personalizes prices and promotions based on customers' individual shopping histories. Other retailers like Kroger, Home Depot, Sears, and Orbitz have been conducting pricing experiments along the same lines. Similarly, many insurance companies now offer personalized discounts. Progressive, for instance, (www.progressive.com) personalizes pricing for car insurance based on customers' driving behaviors. In general, personalized prices or discounts should lead to more purchase engagement.

Promotion The personalization of promotional efforts and the sales process has a longstanding tradition by which the growing availability of individual-level data has opened significant new opportunities (Wedel and Kannan 2016). Most popular in this realm are personalized communication and online recommendation systems.

Personalized communication refers to tailored messages in which content is based on past behaviors and inferred personal experiences and interests (Bleier and Eisenbeiss 2015a). An example from brick-and-mortar retailing is Target (www.target.com) that sends personalized promotional leaflets to its customers, building on observed purchase patterns. Online apps such as Tinder (www.gotinder.com) use personalized push notifications to revive inactive users, sending messages like "25 people liked you since you last checked Tinder." Moreover, after customers leave the online store of retailers such as Zalando (www.zalando.com) without purchase, they are shown banner ads featuring related products to those previously browsed on zalando.com. Finally, companies also send personalized messages to gain feedback. Jetblue (www.jetblue.com), for instance, personalizes its feedback form such that customers that indicate low satisfaction are further presented with a "what went wrong?" section, whereas high satisfaction scores are followed by a "thank you" message and a section where customers can share compliments (Bone et al. 2016).

Online recommendation systems focus on highlighting specific products that may be of interest to customers (Chung et al. 2009). These recommendations are either based on the similarity of a focal customer to other customers (collaborative filtering), attributes of previously viewed products (content filtering), or mixtures of both (hybrid filtering) (Adomavicius and Tuzhilin 2005). Amazon and Netflix are among the most successful companies relying on this technology. Making use of individual-level browsing and purchase data, they tailor recommendations to increase the relevance of their offerings.

In sum, personalized communication and online recommendation systems can foster customer engagement especially in the form of purchases, feedback, WOM, and referrals.

Place Today, many companies are turning toward online "morphing" practices that automatically adapt the look and feel of their websites to visiting customers. For instance, Trulia's website (www.trulia.com) automatically detects visitors' locations to show them available apartments in their proximity. Taking this even a step further are approaches to dynamically adapt websites based on customers' cognitive styles (Hauser et al. 2009). While this technology is still in its infancy, research has shown it to positively impact customer engagement—increasing click-through rates, brand consideration, and purchase intentions (Hauser et al. 2014).

People Many service companies routinely tailor personal encounters and encourage frontline employees to adjust their behaviors to subgroups (i.e., business people, elderly people, etc.) or even individual customers (Gwinner et al. 2005; Mittal and Lassar 1996). From referring to customers by name to proactively modifying offerings to accommodate individual needs, these practices occur both offline and online (Shen and Ball 2009). While employees' adaptive behaviors are often ad hoc in nature (Gwinner et al. 2005), companies also support them with corresponding information systems (Gremler et al. 2001). Specifically, customer relationship management software can help with recommendations or default choices, thereby reducing the number of decisions customers have to make to generate better customer experiences (Glushko and Nomorosa 2012) and consequently engage customers with the company beyond purchase.

CONTINGENCY FACTORS INFLUENCING THE APPLICABILITY OF CUSTOMIZATION AND PERSONALIZATION

So far, we focused on the opportunities and benefits of customization and personalization. Yet, it is important to note that these customer engagement strategies might also entail negative outcomes to customers and companies. For instance, customers might perceive certain customization processes as overly complex which can then decrease the utility they derive from a company's offerings (Dellaert and Stremersch 2005; Hildebrand et al. 2014). In the same vein, ill-informed customization decisions may lead to negative customer experiences (Franke et al. 2009). Also, customized offerings might generate only limited value if customers do not have stable preferences or experience information overload (Kramer 2007). To avoid these negative repercussions from customization, companies might opt for personalization, but customers are not always receptive to that either (Kramer 2007; Kramer et al. 2007). Personalized interactions may, for example, trigger defense mechanisms if customers believe that marketers attempt to manipulate their preferences (Simonson 2005) or if customers experience privacy concerns because companies collect and use their data

(Aguirre et al. 2016). Thus, to complete our discussion on customization and personalization opportunities, we will first elaborate on customer characteristics as general contingency factors that influence the applicability of certain tactics. Subsequently, we turn to relationship characteristics as contingency factors that vary over the duration of the customer-company relationship.

Customer Characteristics

With respect to customer characteristics as contingency factors, we examine customer role readiness as an important factor for customization and customer trait reactance as an important factor for personalization (see also Fig. 4.2).

Customer Role Readiness Despite the growing prevalence of *customization* applications, not all customers are eager to customize their own marketing mix. Recent findings indicate that only a small portion of customers actually use the full potential of customization systems (de Bellis et al. 2016). Some customers are simply unwilling to invest the necessary time to customize products and services (customer motivation). Others are unsure about what is expected from them (customer role clarity) or do simply not know how to customize offerings to their preferences (customer ability) (Simonson 2005; Verleye 2015). Consequently, the level of autonomy for customization strategies needs to be aligned with customers' role readiness, that is, their willingness and ability to actually make use of offered customization options (Verleye 2015). As a remedy for a lack of customer role readiness, Verleye (2014) suggests three managerial processes: (1) customer encouragement to increase customer motivation, (2) customer socialization to raise customer role clarity, and (3) customer support to augment customer ability. *Customer encouragement* relates to those activities that demonstrate customers the potential returns of customization. Aliveshoes (www.aliveshoes.com), for instance, uses the slogan "Shoes define your image, let's make sure that they speak about who you really are" to convince customers of the value received from customization. *Customer socialization* involves clarifying to customers what is expected from them in order to boost successful customization efforts. The website of Lego's Digital Designer (www.ldd.lego.com) highlights the customer's designer role through the slogan "Build Freely and Share with the World." *Customer support* entails all company efforts to explain how the customization procedure works, for example, through "how to" videos and FAQ pages. Nike, for example, has developed a clear step-by-step customization procedure for its Nike ID project which generated a revenue growth close to 30% (Trefis 2015). Additionally, customer support relates to initiatives that help customers better understand their preferences, for instance, through preference measurement methods (Kramer 2007).

Customer Trait Reactance As a personal characteristic, some customers dislike being told what to do and react negatively to such efforts. This reactance (Brehm 1966) occurs when customers believe their freedom of choice is restricted due to attempted manipulations of their preferences (Simonson 2005). Obviously, companies should prevent their *personalization* endeavors to be considered inappropriate and ensure that their applied level of granularity for personalization strategies is in line with customers' trait reactance. One tactic to this end is to increase the perceived fit between an offering and a customer's preferences while also justifying how the use of personal information is relevant to the offering (White et al. 2008). Amazon, which rigorously measures customers' preferences, explains customers the reasons behind specific recommendations, thereby helping them to recognize their value (Kramer 2007). Another tactic involves companies giving customers more control over their personally identifiable information to reduce reactance (Tucker 2014).

Relationship Characteristics

The depth of the customer-company relationship is reflected in the extent to which customer and company know and are familiar with each other (Tam 2008). In this section, we posit that *customer familiarity* with the company is important for the application of customization across the customer lifecycle, whereas *company familiarity* with the customer in combination with trust matters for personalization across the customer lifecycle (see Fig. 4.2).

Customer Familiarity with the Company During the acquisition stage, customers are typically less familiar with a company and its offerings. Prior knowledge often stems only from promotional company efforts or input from peers. As they progress from the acquisition to the retention/development stage, customers' familiarity with the company and its offerings increases to reach its maximum in the attrition stage (Alba and Hutchinson

1987). This monotonically increasing evolution of familiarity over the course of the customer lifecycle has important implications for the way in which companies should manage their *customization* strategies. Customers with little familiarity might find it difficult to take full advantage of customization offers with very high autonomy due to (1) uncertainty about their preferences for a company's offerings or their inability to express these preferences (Simonson 2005), (2) the number of choices they have to make, and (3) the amount of information they have to process in order to make an informed decision (Valenzuela et al. 2009). Thus, it might be advisable to simplify the customization process at first by either limiting the number of options for new customers (i.e., restricting the solution space) or by offering starting solutions that simplify the interaction (Hildebrand et al. 2014). For more experienced customers in the retention/development stage, offering higher levels of autonomy should be a promising strategy. These customers already know how to benefit from the company's offerings and should appreciate more sophisticated options.

Company Familiarity with the Customer and Trust A similar monotonically increasing evolution occurs for the familiarity of a company with its customers, referring to the amount and quality of individual-level data acquired. This familiarity has important implications for *personalization* strategies. In the acquisition phase, companies have little detailed information about customers, a condition referred to as the cold start problem (Wei et al. 2017). Here, data is oftentimes limited to demographic and panel-based variables (e.g., lifestyles) that are obtained from list vendors or initial information about online behaviors (e.g., shopping behavior on companies' websites tracked by Google Analytics). In these situations, personalization opportunities at the segment level, such as changing website content based on locational data, might be preferable. In the meanwhile, companies can benefit from helping customers understand their own preferences in this stage to develop a long-term relationship (Kramer 2007). As the relationship continues and develops over time, more detailed customer-level data becomes available to the company. More data implies additional options for more granular personalization efforts (Chung et al. 2009). More granular approaches, however, only hold value when customers' trust in the company is high. Under low trust, highly granular personalization might merely trigger privacy concerns and encourage customers to behave counter to the intention of the personalization action (Bleier and Eisenbeiss 2015b). Trust typically increases from the acquisition to the retention/development stage, due to positive and satisfying interactions between the customer and the company. However, with further progression to the attrition stage, customer satisfaction likely decreases which should go along with reductions in trust (Luo 2002). Given this inverted U-shaped evolution, in the attrition stage it may be advisable to personalize merely at the segment level, although a company here holds the richest data about a customer.

CONCLUDING THOUGHTS

Even though customer engagement has become a strategic imperative for many companies, managers continue to struggle with its implementation. In this chapter, we shed light on this very issue and discuss two possible engagement strategies: customization and personalization. While both approaches hold great potential to achieve customer engagement goals across the customer lifecycle, we delineate that the level of autonomy for customization strategies and the level of granularity for personalization strategies need to be aligned with customer characteristics as well as characteristics of the customer-company relationship (see Fig. 4.3). Since the level of familiarity and trust in the customer-company relationship varies across the customer lifecycle, companies need to tailor their customization and personalization strategies accordingly. In particular, companies benefit from low-level customization strategies and segment-level personalization strategies in the acquisition and attrition stages, whereas high-level customization and individual-level personalization strategies appear preferable in the retention/development stage. Overall, we hope to strengthen both academic and managerial insight into customization and personalization as strategies to help companies engage customers. Further

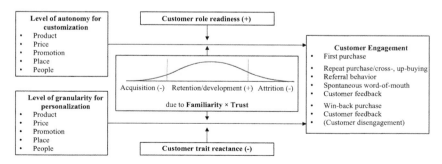

Fig. 4.3 Customer engagement implications of customization and personalization

research, however, is needed to specifically assess the relative importance of different customization and personalization options to generate customer engagement value.

NOTES

1. Given its broad nature, we do not consider mass personalization as a true company effort to enhance the personal relevance of its products and services. In what follows, we therefore only discuss segment-level and individual-level personalization.

REFERENCES

Adomavicius, D., & Tuzhilin, A. (2005). Personalization Technologies: A Process-Oriented Perspective. *Communications of the ACM, 48*(10), 83–90.

Aguirre, E., Roggeveen, A. L., Grewal, D., & Wetzels, M. (2016). The Personalization–Privacy Paradox: Implications for New Media. *Journal of Consumer Marketing, 33*(2), 98–110.

Alba, J. W., & Hutchinson, J. W. (1987). Dimensions of Consumer Expertise. *Journal of Consumer Research, 13*(March), 411.

Amaldoss, W., & Jain, S. (2008). Joint Bidding in the Name-Your-Own-Price Channel: A Strategic Analysis. *MIT Sloan Management Review, 54*(10), 1685–1699.

Arora, N., Dreze, X., Ghose, A., Hess, J. D., Iyengar, R., Jing, B., Joshi, Y., Kumar, V., Lurie, N., Neslin, S., Sajeesh, S., Su, M., Syam, N., Thomas, J., & Zhang, Z. J. (2008). Putting One-to-One Marketing to Work: Personalization, Customization, and Choice. *Marketing Letters, 19*(3–4), 305–321.

Baker, A. M., Donthu, N., & Kumar, V. (2016). Investigating How Word-of-Mouth Conversations About Brands Influence Purchase and Retransmission Intentions. *Journal of Marketing Research, 53*(2), 225–239.

de Bellis, E., Sprott, D. E., Herrmann, A., Bierhoff, H. W., & Rohmann, E. (2016). The Influence of Trait and State Narcissism on the Uniqueness of Mass-Customized Products. *Journal of Retailing, 92*(2), 162–172.

Berman, B. (2012). 3-D printing: The New Industrial Revolution. *Business Horizons, 55*(2), 155–162.

Bertini, M., & Koenigsberg, O. (2014). When Customers Help Set Prices. *MIT Sloan Management Review, 55*(4), 57–64.

Bleier, A., & Eisenbeiss, M. (2015a). Personalized Online Advertising Effectiveness: The Interplay of What, When, and Where. *Marketing Science, 34*(5), 669–688.

Bleier, A., & Eisenbeiss, M. (2015b). The Importance of Trust for Personalized Online Advertising. *Journal of Retailing, 91*(3), 390–409.

Bone, S. A., Lemon, K. N., Voorhees, C. M., Liljenquist, K. A., Fombelle, P. W., DeTienne, K. B., & Money, R. B. (2016). Mere Measurement 'Plus': How Solicitation of Open-Ended Positive Feedback Influences Customer Purchase Behavior. *Journal of Marketing Research, 54*(1), 156–170.

Brehm, J. W. (1966). *A Theory of Psychological Reactance.* New York: Academic Press.

Byrnes, J. (2003). http://hbswk.hbs.edu/archive/3497.html. Date Accessed 10 Jan 2017.

Chan, K. W., Yim, C. K., & Lam, S. S. K. (2010). Is Customer Participation in Value Creation a Double-Edged Sword? Evidence from Professional Financial Services Across Cultures. *Journal of Marketing, 74*(3), 48–64.

Chung, T. S., Rust, R. T., & Wedel, M. (2009). My Mobile Music: An Adaptive Personalization System for Digital Audio Players. *Marketing Science, 28*(1), 52–68.

Chung, T. S., Wedel, M., & Rust, R. T. (2016). Adaptive Personalization Using Social Networks. *Journal of the Academy of Marketing Science, 44*(1), 66–87.

Coussement, K., & Van den Poel, D. (2009). Improving Customer Attrition Prediction by Integrating Emotions from Client/Company Interaction Emails and Evaluating Multiple Classifiers. *Expert Systems with Applications, 36*(3), 6127–6134.

Dellaert, B. G. C., & Stremersch, S. (2005). Marketing Mass-Customized Products: Striking a Balance Between Utility and Complexity. *Journal of Marketing Research, 42*(2), 219–227.

Esteves, R.-B., & Resende, J. (2016). Competitive Targeted Advertising with Price Discrimination. *Marketing Science, 35*(4), 576–587.

Fournier, S., & Avery, J. (2012). Firing Your Best Customers—How Smart Firms Destroy Relationships using CRM. In S. Fournier, M. Breazeale, & M. Fetscherin (Eds.), *Consumer-Brand Relationships: Theory and Practice* (pp. 301–316). London: Routledge/Taylor & Francis Group.

Franke, N., Keinz, P., & Steger, C. J. (2009). Testing the Value of Customization: When Do Customers Really Prefer Products Tailored to Their Preferences? *Journal of Marketing, 73*(5), 103–121.

Glushko, R. J., & Nomorosa, K. J. (2012). Substituting Information for Interaction: A Framework for Personalization in Service Encounters and Service Systems. *Journal of Service Research, 16*(1), 21–38.

Gremler, D. D., Gwinner, K. P., & Brown, S. W. (2001). Generating Positive Word-of-Mouth Communication Through Customer-Employee Relationships. *International Journal of Service Industry Management, 12*(1), 44–59.

Gwinner, K. P., Bitner, M. J., Brown, S. W., & Kumar, A. (2005). Service Customization Through Employee Adaptiveness. *Journal of Service Research, 8*(2), 131–148.

Hauser, J. R., Urban, G. L., Liberali, G., & Braun, M. (2009). Website Morphing. *Marketing Science, 28*(2), 202–223.

Hauser, J. R., Liberali, G. G., & Urban, G. L. (2014). Website Morphing 2.0: Switching Costs, Partial Exposure, Random Exit, and When to Morph. *Management science, 60*(6), 1594–1616.

Hildebrand, C., Haeubl, G., & Herrmann, A. (2014). Product Customization via Starting Solutions. *Journal of Marketing Research (JMR), 51*(6), 707–725.

Hinterhuber, A., & Liozu, S. M. (2014). Is Innovation in Pricing Your Next Source of Competitive Advantage? *Business Horizons, 57*(3), 413–423.

Jimenez, F. R., Voss, K. E., & Frankwick, G. L. (2013). A Classification Schema of Co-Production of Goods: An Open-Systems Perspective. *European Journal of Marketing, 47*(11–12), 1841–1858.

Joshi, A. W., & Sharma, S. (2004). Customer Knowledge Development: Antecedents and Impact on New Product Performance. *Journal of Marketing, 68*(4), 47–59.

Kim, J.-Y., Natter, M., & Spann, M. (2009). Pay What You Want: A New Participative Pricing Mechanism. *Journal of Marketing, 73*(1), 44–58.

Kramer, T. (2007). The Effect of Measurement Task Transparency on Preference Construction and Evaluations of Personalized Recommendations. *Journal of Marketing Research (JMR), 44*(2), 224–233.

Kramer, T., Spolter-Weisfeld, S., & Thakkar, M. (2007). The Effect of Cultural Orientation on Consumer Responses to Personalization. *Marketing Science, 26*(2), 246–258.

Kumar, V. (2008). *Managing Customer for Profit: Strategies to Increase Profits and Build Loyalty.* Philadelphia: Wharton School Publishing.

Kumar, V. (2013). *Profitable Customer Engagement: Concept, Metrics, and Strategies.* India: Sage Publications.

Kumar, V., & Bhagwat, Y. (2015). Regaining Lost Customers: The Predictive Power of First-Lifetime Behavior, the Reason for Defection, and the Nature of the Win-Back Offer. *Journal of Marketing, 79*(July), 34–55.

Kumar, V., & Pansari, A. (2016). Competitive Advantage Through Engagement. *Journal of Marketing Research, 53*(4), 497–514.

Kumar, V., Aksoy, L., Donkers, B., Venkatesan, R., Wiesel, T., & Tillmans, S. (2010). Undervalued or Overvalued Customers: Capturing Total Customer Engagement Value. *Journal of Service Research, 13*(3), 297–310.

Kumar, V., Zhang, X. (. A.)., & Luo, A. (2014). Modeling Customer Opt-In and Opt-Out in a Permission-Based Marketing Context. *Journal of Marketing Research, 51*(4), 403–419.

Lewis, H. (2008). http://www.businessinsider.com/2008/10/radiohead-s-innovative-approach-paid-off-or-did-it-?IR=T. Date Accessed 10 Jan 2017.

Lindsay, K. (2014). https://blogs.adobe.com/digitalmarketing/personalization/personalization-payoff-roi-getting-personal/. Date Accessed 10 Jan 2017.

Luo, X. (2002). Trust Production and Privacy Concerns on the Internet: A Framework Based on Relationship Marketing and Social Exchange Theory. *Industrial Marketing Management, 31*(2), 111–118.

Macy's. (2016). http://www.macys.com/ce/splash/buy-online-pickup-in-store/index. Date Accessed 24 Oct 2016.

McColl-Kennedy, J. R., Vargo, S. L., Dagger, T. S., Sweeney, J. C., & van Kasteren, Y. (2012). Health Care Customer Value Cocreation Practice Styles. *Journal of Service Research, 15*(4), 370–389.

Mittal, B., & Lassar, W. M. (1996). The Role of Personalization in Service Encounters. *Journal of Retailing, 72*(1), 95–109.

Neslin, S. A., Grewal, D., Leghorn, R., Shankar, V., Teerling, M. L., Thomas, J. S., & Verhoef, P. C. (2006). Challenges and Opportunities in Multichannel Customer Management. *Journal of Service Research, 9*(2), 95–112.

Pansari, A., & Kumar, V. (2016). Customer Engagement: The Construct, Antecedents, and Consequences. *Journal of the Academy of Marketing Science, 45*(3), 294–311.

Rust, R. T., & Huang, M.-H. (2014). The Service Revolution and the Transformation of Marketing Science. *Marketing Science, 33*(2), 206–221.

Shapiro, D. (2011). Profitability of the Name-Your-Own-Price Channel in the Case of Risk-Averse Buyers. *Marketing Science, 30*(2), 290–304.

Shen, A., & Ball, A. D. (2009). Is Personalization of Services Always a Good Thing? Exploring the Role of Technology-Mediated Personalization (TMP) in Service Relationships. *Journal of Services Marketing, 23*(2), 79–91.

Simonson, I. (2005). Determinants of Customers' Responses to Customized Offers: Conceptual Framework and Research Propositions. *Journal of Marketing, 69*(1), 32–45.

Sonnier, G. P. (2014). The Market Value for Product Attribute Improvements Under Price Personalization. *International Journal of Research in Marketing, 31*(2), 168–177.

Spaulding, E., & Perry, C. (2013). http://www.bain.com/publications/articles/making-it-personal-rules-for-success-in-product-customization.aspx. Date Accessed 10 Jan 2017.

Statista. (2015). https://www.statista.com/statistics/451761/reasons-use-marketing-personalization-worldwide/. Date Accessed 10 Jan 2017.

Tam, J. L. M. (2008). Brand Familiarity: Its Effects on Satisfaction Evaluations. *Journal of Services Marketing, 22*(1), 3–12.

Tax, S. S., McCutcheon, D., & Wilkinson, I. F. (2013). The Service Delivery Network (SDN): A Customer-Centric Perspective of the Customer Journey. *Journal of Service Research, 16*(4), 454–470.

Tedeschi, B. (2005). http://www.nytimes.com/2005/08/08/technology/to-internet-stores-its-all-about-the-personal-touch.html?_r=0. Date Accessed 10 Jan 2017.

Trefis. (2015). http://www.forbes.com/sites/greatspeculations/2015/07/09/how-nikeid-is-helping-nikes-push-for-greater-profits/#4ddab71f48b7.Date Accessed 10 Jan 2017.

Tucker, C. E. (2014). Social Networks, Personalized Advertising and Privacy Controls. *Journal of Marketing Research, 51*(5), 546–562.

Urban, G. L., Liberali, G. G., Macdonald, E., Bordley, R., & Hauser, J. R. (2014). Morphing Banner Advertising. *Marketing Science, 33*(1), 27–46.

Valenzuela, A., Dhar, R., & Zettelmeyer, F. (2009). Contingent Response to Self-Customization Procedures: Implications for Decision Satisfaction and Choice. *Journal of Marketing Research, 46*(6), 754–763.

Van den Poel, D., & Larivière, B. (2004). Customer Attrition Analysis for Financial Services Using Proportional Hazard Models. *European Journal of Operational Research, 157*(1), 196–217.

Verleye, K. (2014). Designing Service Interfaces for Customer Engagement in the Creation of Value. In J. Kandampully (Ed.), *Customer Experience Management: Enhancing Experience and Value Through Service Management* (pp. 73–97). Dubuque: Kendal Hun Publisher.

Verleye, K. (2015). The Co-Creation Experience from the Customer Perspective: Its Measurement and Determinants. *Journal of Service Management, 26*(2), 321–342.

Wedel, M., & Kannan, P. K. (2016). Marketing Analytics for Data-Rich Environments. *Journal of Marketing, 80*(6), 97–121.

Wei, J., He, J., Chen, K., Zhou, Y., & Tang, Z. (2017). Collaborative Filtering and Deep Learning Based Recommendation System for Cold Start Items. *Expert Systems with Applications, 69*, 29–39.

White, T. B., Zahay, D. L., Thorbjornsen, H., & Shavitt, S. (2008). Getting too Personal: Reactance to Highly Personalized Email Solicitations. *Marketing Letters, 19*(1), 39–50.

Zhang, J., & Wedel, M. (2009). The Effectiveness of Customized Promotions in Online and Offline Stores. *Journal of Marketing Research, 46*(4), 190–206.

CHAPTER 5

Managing Product Returns Within the Customer Value Framework

Alec Minnema, Tammo H.A. Bijmolt,
J. Andrew Petersen, and Jeffrey D. Shulman

INTRODUCTION

Marketing scientists and practitioners acknowledge that it is essential to measure and manage customer value (Petersen and Kumar 2015). Customers can create value to the firm by purchasing products, not returning these products, recommending products to other potential customers, influencing other customers, and providing feedback to the company (Kumar et al. 2010a). Importantly, these customer behaviors will be interrelated. For example, product returns may affect future purchases, product returns, and engagement behaviors—which all affect customer value. Hence, customer value goes beyond customer purchase behavior, and customer value management should also include customer engagement behavior and customer product return behavior (Van Doorn et al. 2010; Kumar et al. 2010a).

A. Minnema (✉) • T.H.A. Bijmolt
University of Groningen, Groningen, Netherlands

J.A. Petersen
Pennsylvania State University, State College, PA, USA

J.D. Shulman
University of Washington, Seattle, WA, USA

© The Author(s) 2018
R.W. Palmatier et al. (eds.), *Customer Engagement Marketing*,
DOI 10.1007/978-3-319-61985-9_5

First, customer engagement involves customer behaviors that are not directly purchase-related behavior. Van Doorn et al. (2010, p. 253) define customer engagement behaviors as "the customer's behavioral manifestations toward a brand or a firm, beyond purchase, resulting from motivational drivers". This behavioral dimension of customer engagement incorporates writing reviews and customer referrals. Customers can create value to the firm by writing reviews. A recent meta-analysis demonstrates that product reviews affect sales, where more reviews and more positive reviews lift sales (Babic et al. 2016). In addition, product reviews have an impact on product returns (Minnema et al. 2016). Hence, academic research examined customer referral behavior and demonstrated its impact on firm profit (Kumar et al. 2010b).

Second, including product returns in customer value management is critical because product returns can be a substantial economic cost for retailers. Return rates reportedly vary between 10% and 50%, with substantial profit impact (Banjo 2013; Forrester 2015). Annually, US customers return $264 billion worth of products (Kerr 2013). Product returns not only result in lost sales but also lead to other costs such as shipping fees, often paid by the retailer, and remanufacturing costs such as repackaging the product (Guide et al. 2006). Consequently, Gartner (2014) labels product returns "the ticking time bomb of multichannel retailing".

The large financial impact of product returns has spurred academic research in several fields. For instance, one solution to reduce the costs of product returns is to make the reverse logistics more efficient, a problem that has been addressed extensively in the operations literature (Dekker et al. 2004). However, the focus of this chapter is on managing product returns from a marketing perspective, which we cluster around three major topics. First, we discuss how product returns and engagement behaviors should be included in the customer value framework (see Fig. 5.1). Second, we discuss the antecedents of a customer's product return decision. These include the impact of product return policies and the effect of information provision at the moment of purchase on purchase and return decisions. We also discuss the impact of customer and product characteristics on product return decisions. Third, we focus on the consequences of product returns. We discuss the effect of product returns on future purchase and product return behavior, as well as on customer engagement behaviors. Thus, the aim of this chapter is to support both researchers and practitioners through a comprehensive, research-based synthesis of current knowledge on antecedents and consequences of product returns and how this relates to measuring and managing customer value (Fig. 5.1).

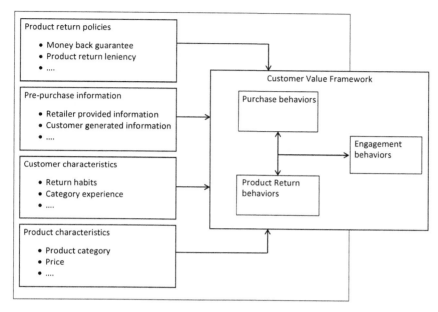

Fig. 5.1 Antecedents and consequences of customer product return behavior within a customer value framework

THE RELATIONSHIP BETWEEN PRODUCT RETURNS AND CUSTOMER VALUE

A customer's decision to return a product has an immediate economic impact on a firm's profitability, both in terms of the loss in the profit margin from the customer's original purchase of that product as well as the cost the firm bears to process the product return. Because of this many firms still treat product returns as an economic cost that needs to be managed (and often minimized). At a minimum some firms try to manage these costs at the aggregate level given that product returns are such a substantial cost for firms (Blanchard 2007). They do this by setting return policies that try to minimize the number of products returned by providing disincentives for customers to return products (e.g., a restocking fee or offering only a limited time window to return a product) or by attempting to streamline the reverse supply chain to reduce the average costs of product returns (see Dekker et al. 2004).

Some firms have even taken it a step further by implementing strategies which are responsive to an individual customer's product return behavior. For instance, research has shown that some firms actually reduce marketing expenditures to customers that return products in the hopes that these return-prone customers will make fewer future purchases that have the potential to be returned (Petersen and Kumar 2009). However, managing customers based on their product return behavior does not seem to be a common practice by retailers as of yet. A recent survey suggests that many retailers (over 60% of those surveyed) did not consider an individual customer's product return behavior when determining optimal marketing resource allocation decisions (Petersen and Kumar 2015). This seems shortsighted as recent research has shown that there could be positive consequences that arise out of customer product returns (e.g., improving future customer relationships).

This leads to the question of what firms should do to better manage customers accounting for the relationship between purchases, product returns, engagement behaviors, and profitability. It is important for firms to adjust their processes for customer management and optimal marketing resource allocation. From a customer management perspective, this should start by including customer product return and engagement behaviors in the customer value framework. Based on recent work by Kumar et al. (2010a) and Petersen and Kumar (2015), we propose that customer value can be measured in the following way:

$$CV_{i,t=0} = CLV_{i,t=0} + \sum_{t=1}^{T} \pi_3 \left(\text{Engagement}_{it}\right) \tag{5.1}$$

$$CLV_{i,t=0} = P\left(\text{Relationship}_{i,t=1}\right) * \sum_{t=1}^{T} \frac{\pi_1\left(\text{Purchases}_{it}\right) - \pi_2\left(\text{Returns}_{it}\right) - \text{Marketing}_{it}}{\left(1+r\right)^t} \tag{5.2}$$

$$\pi_2\left(\text{Returns}_{it}\right) = \text{Returns}_{it}{}^* \left(\text{ReverseLogistics} + \text{Price}_{it}\right) \tag{5.3}$$

where:
   $CV_{i,t=0}$ = Customer value for customer i at time $t = 0$
   $CLV_{i,t=0}$ = Customer lifetime value for customer i at time $t = 0$
   $\pi_1(\text{Purchases}_{it})$ = Expected profit from purchases by customer i in time t

$\pi_2(\text{Returns}_{it})$ = Expected profit lost and costs incurred from returns by customer i in time t

$\pi_3(\text{Engagement}_{it})$ = Expected profit from engagement behaviors by customer i in time t

Marketing_{it} = Expected marketing costs spent on customer i in time t

Returns_{it} = Expected number of returns by customer i in time t

ReverseLogistics = Expected reverse logistics costs per return

Price_{it} = Expected average price per returned purchase by customer i in time t

r = Discount rate (Approximately 3.56% by quarter—or 15% annually)

n = All customers in the sample

T = Number of time periods in the prediction horizon

$P(\text{Relationship}_{i,t=1})$ = The probability customer i is active in the relationship at $t = 1$

First, scholars argued that customer engagement behaviors, such as providing referrals and writing reviews, should be included when measuring customer value (Kumar et al. 2010a). Hence, customers can create value through engagement behaviors, as shown in Eq. (5.1). Second, a recent study by Petersen and Kumar (2015) adapted the traditional customer value framework to include the cost of product returns when measuring customer lifetime value (CLV). By measuring CLV as in Eq. (5.2), it is clear that customers can increase value to the firm by making more purchases but also by returning fewer products. It is important to include return behavior in Eq. (5.2) because the traditional CLV model may prefer selecting a customer who has purchased a lot even if that customer has returned the majority of products purchased. In fact, Petersen and Kumar (2015) found that the correlation between customer selection based on the traditional CLV framework and a CLV framework which includes product returns was only weak (0.27).

Product returns are a relatively new addition to the customer value framework, and the question becomes how much the inclusion can improve a firm's marketing resource allocation decisions. Petersen and Kumar (2015) ran a field experiment and found that allocating resources on the value framework including product returns can lead to significant benefits to the firm relative to the resource allocation strategy based on the traditional customer value model. The study was able to increase the profit from purchases by 18.1%, decrease the profit lost from product returns by 30.7%, and decrease the marketing costs to the firm by 29.7%. This lead to an increase in short-term average customer profit by 28.5% and long-term average customer profit by 19.7%. Thus, product returns play a significant role in the value of the customer to the firm which indicates that product returns should be taken into account.

Equation 5.3 shows that profit or loss due to product returns depends on both the number of returns and the reverse logistics costs. The focus of the next section is on antecedents of customer product return decisions which is directly related to the number of returns.

ANTECEDENTS OF CUSTOMER PRODUCT RETURN DECISIONS

For today's retailers it is important to understand the drivers of customer return decisions because product returns affect profitability considerably and thereby form a key component of customer value management as explained in Section "The Relationship Between Product Returns and Customer Value". Extant literature defines the customer journey in three stages, namely, pre-purchase, purchase, and post-purchase (Lemon and Verhoef 2016). A mix of behavioral and empirical research has examined various antecedents of product returns at each stage of the customer journey. Prior research can be clustered around how product return decisions are affected by the seller's decisions influencing the pre-purchase stage of the customer journey, seller decisions targeted toward the post-purchase stage, customer characteristics, and product characteristics. In the following sections, we review the key findings of these streams of research.

SELLER'S DECISIONS DURING PRE-PURCHASE STAGE

Sellers often take actions in the pre-purchase stage to avoid the substantial cost of product returns. In the pre-purchase stage, the customer collects information about the products that could be purchased. Typically, this information does not reveal the product at full and so customers make their purchase decisions on imperfect information (Shulman et al. 2015). When customers are allowed to return purchases, consumers follow the pre-purchase stage with two additional stages in the customer journey: the customer decides to purchase the product (purchase stage) and next the customer decides to keep or return the purchased product (post-purchase stage) (Anderson et al. 2009a; Minnema et al. 2016). In the post-purchase stage, the customer inspects the product and ultimately the product will be revealed at full (Wood 2001). If the product does not meet the expectations formed in the pre-purchase stage, the customer will be dissatisfied and hence is more likely to return the product (Bechwati and Siegal 2005). Therefore, the information provided pre-purchase will affect both the purchase and return decision.

Especially when purchasing online, customers have limited ability to evaluate and test products before purchasing them (Shulman et al. 2015). As a consequence, retailers offer multiple sources of information on their website to inform customers, such as product specifications, product pictures, and online customer reviews. These information sources will affect the customer's expectations regarding the product.

Prior studies show that there is a tension in the effect of information on purchase and product return decisions (Shulman et al. 2015). On the one hand, more information may prevent customers from purchasing the product if there is a poor fit between the product and the customer. Without additional information, the customer might have purchased the product which he would probably have returned due to the poor fit: the purchase prevention effect. On the other hand, providing more information may increase customer expectations which leads to more purchases and more returns because the product does not meet these expectations: the marginal loss aversion effect. Thus, information at the moment of purchase affects the decision to return or keep a purchased product.

To provide more detailed product information, retailers invested in web technologies such as zoom features and alternative pictures to help customers to make better decisions (De et al. 2013). In general, zoom technology allows customers to see finer product details such as fabric and small decorative features which conveys mainly factual product information. When a customer gains more factual information, the customer expectations will be more realistic and hence, use of zoom technologies lowers product returns (De et al. 2013) due to less product uncertainty (Hong and Pavlou 2014). A second web technology to convey product information is the alternative photo technology, which enables the customer to see the focal products rotation but also the contextualization. The contextualization provides mainly impression-based information because in clothing this contains models wearing the product. Impression-based information may be more ambiguous and hard to verify, which may lead customers form unrealistic expectations which results in higher product returns and more importantly, lower net sales (i.e., purchases—returns) (De et al. 2013). Thus, web technologies can either help or hurt retailers in reducing product return rates and increasing net sales, all depending on the type of information provided.

The presentation of products also affects the decision to return the product. When products are simultaneously presented, customers generate many comparative thoughts. In contrast, when products are sequentially presented, this will result in more non-comparative thoughts (Bechwati and Siegal 2005). Hence, when customers are faced with an alternative not in the initial choice set after they decided to purchase, they are more likely to remain with their initial choice when the products are sequentially presented. They do so because their non-comparative thoughts regarding the product are still valid to defend their initial purchase decision.

An additional source of information that is available on many retailers' websites is formed by online customer reviews (OCRs), which are the result of customer engagement behavior. OCRs complement retailer-provided information (Chen and Xie 2008) and make other information available on the retailer's website less important (Kostyra et al. 2016). Online customer reviews may help to form pre-purchase expectations about a product, and thus may affect return decisions, next to customer purchase decisions (Babic et al. 2016). Review valence (i.e., average product rating) helps to form or alter product expectations at the moment of purchase. If reviews are *overly positive* (i.e., valence is higher than the long-term product average), this leads to high expectations about the product which increases the purchase probability. After the purchase, the high expectations due to overly positive reviews are not met, which results in negative expectation disconfirmation and consequently increases return probability as well (Minnema et al. 2016). The effect of overly positive reviews is—more notable—negative for a retailer's financial performance because of the high reverse logistics costs associated with product returns. The other OCR characteristics (volume and variance) mainly affect purchase decisions, and have little to no effect on product returns. Thus, a substantial body of research shows that information provided at the moment of purchase affects both the decision to purchase and the decisions to return the product.

SELLER RETURN POLICY IN POST-PURCHASE STAGE

The firm's product return policy may have an impact on customer purchase behavior as well as on their return behavior, and hence on customer value (Fig. 5.1). One might think that firms with a lenient product return policy will just have to process more product returns which can lead to costs spiraling out of control potentially outweighing the benefits of increases in future purchase behavior (Eq. 5.2). However, the effect of the return policy on purchases and product returns may depend on specific dimensions of that policy. A meta-analytic review study classifies return policy leniency along five dimensions (Janakiraman et al. 2016): monetary leniency, time leniency, effort leniency, scope leniency, and exchange leniency (see Table 5.1). The results of the meta-analysis indeed indicate that different return policy dimensions have different effects on purchase and return decisions. In what follows, we provide a more detailed overview of the literature along dimensions of leniency.

Monetary Leniency

A key dimension of product return policies is whether a firm asks a restocking fee or refunds the full monetary amount paid (monetary leniency). A large body of literature provides guidance as to when a firm should offer a money-back guarantee. A general rule of thumb is that a retailer should accept returns if it can earn greater value from salvaging the returned item than the customer's cost of returning the item. This rule of thumb established in Davis et al. (1995) holds when the retailer sells on a consignment agreement with the manufacturer (Hu et al. 2014), when the retailer sets inventory levels with demand uncertainty (Akcay et al. 2013), and when accounting for reduced clearance prices intended to clear inventory (Altug and Aydinliyim 2016). One concern with a money-back guarantee is that customers may decide to rent for free by buying and then returning. Davis et al. (1995) shows that if customers experience a transaction cost smaller than their trial value obtained from free renting, then a money-back guarantee is less profitable.

Building on the general rule of thumb, research provides guidance about how the quality of the product affects the decision to offer a money-back guarantee. The suggestions depend on whether or not quality is known by the customers. If product quality is unobservable, then high-quality sellers should offer a money-back guarantee to signal quality, but low-quality sellers will find such an offer too costly (Moorthy and Srinivasan 1995). If quality is observable, product returns arise because of uncertainty about product fit rather than because of quality. In this case, the low-quality seller has a greater gain as a result of offering a money-back guarantee than the high-quality retailer, though both retailers should allow returns.

Table 5.1 Antecedents of purchase and return decisions

Dimension	Description	Purchase	Return	Key study
Return policy				
Monetary leniency	**Effect of a lenient policy on** Whether a retailer asks for a restocking fee or allows for the refund of the full monetary amount paid (lenient)	+	0	Bower and Maxham (2012)
Time leniency	Whether a retailer allows short deadlines or long deadline (lenient) in the return policy	0	–	Janakiraman and Ordóñez (2012)
Effort leniency	Whether a retailer creates "hassle" for customers who aim to return the product, such as requiring the original receipt and product package; no effort is regarded as more lenient	+	0	Janakiraman and Ordóñez (2012)
Scope leniency	Whether a retailer considers all items "return-worthy" or restrict customers to return sales items, no restriction is regarded as more lenient	0	+	Wood (2001)
Exchange leniency	Whether a retailer offers cash refunds or only allows product exchange or store credit, cash refund is regarded as more lenient	0	–	Janakiraman et al. (2016)
Web technologies	**Effect of web technologies on**	**Purchase**	**Return**	
Zoom features	Zoom technology allows customers to see some finer product details such as fabric and small decorative features	0	–	De et al. (2013)
Alternative photo technology	Alternative photo technology allows customers to see the focal product in rotation by models wearing the product	+	+	De et al. (2013)

Online customer reviews (OCR)	Effect of OCRs on	Purchase	Return	
Valence	The average star rating of reviews posted for the product	+	–	Minnema et al. (2016)
Volume	The number of reviews posted for the product	+	0	Minnema et al. (2016)
Variance	Variance in star rating of reviews posted for the product	–	0	Minnema et al. (2016)
Customer characteristics	Effect of customer characteristics on	Purchase	Return	
Income	The income of the customer	0	0	Petersen and Kumar (2009)
Married	Whether the customer is married	0	0	Petersen and Kumar (2009)
Age	The age of the customer	+	0	Minnema et al. (2016)
Experience	The experience of the customer in the category	N.A.	–	Petersen and Kumar (2009)
Product characteristics	Effect of product characteristics on	Purchase	Return	
Search vs. experience products	Whether the product is a search product (vs. experience)	N.A.	–	Hong and Pavlou (2014)
Durable vs. consumable	If focal product is a durable product (vs. consumable)	+	0	Janakiraman et al. (2016)
Sale item	Whether the item is on sale (vs. regular item)	+	–	Petersen and Kumar (2009)

+ is a positive significant effect, – is negative significant effect, 0 is no significant effect, NA is not applicable

A variety of factors have been shown to affect a company's optimal restocking fee. The greater importance customers place on how well a product matches their needs, the higher the restocking fee should be (Shulman et al. 2009). The higher return penalty ensures that customers keep their purchase when they would otherwise return it without subsequently exchanging for another product. Competition can actually increase restocking fees because firms want to dissuade customers from making a return in order to buy from the competition (Shulman et al. 2011). Moreover, a more generous return policy attracts customers who are less likely to keep their purchase, thereby increasing the company's cost disadvantage relative to its competitor.

Product quality also affects the optimal restocking fee, though there is no consensus in the academic literature on exactly how. Gu and Tayi (2015) find that a monopolist should have a tightened return policy if the product value is high as a means to encourage consumers to mend the product to improve fit. In contrast, Inderst and Tirosh (2015) find that when quality is observable and customers vary both in their ex ante appreciation of quality and their ex post evaluations, high-quality retailers will be more generous in their refund than their low-quality competitors. This is consistent with the empirical finding of Bonifield et al. (2010) that in practice return leniency increases as the ratings of e-tailer quality increases. There is apparently room for further research to resolve the discrepancies between findings and develop a unifying theory of when the high-quality seller will be more or less generous in its refund.

Manufacturers often cannot set the return policy retailers offer to customers, but can influence these policies with their contract to the retailer. Research has found that the manufacturer should accept returns from the retailer at an overly generous refund in order to incentivize the retailer to offer an efficient refund to customers, thereby boosting sales (Shulman et al. 2010). Additionally, Su (2009) shows that a manufacturer can improve profitability with a differentiated buy-back contract that pays the retailer different rates for returned units than units the retailer was unable to sell. However, when this is not possible, a manufacturer can use a sales rebate contract to achieve the same channel profits.

A monetary lenient product return policy (no restocking fee) leads to increases in purchases (Bower and Maxham 2012). For the return decision, the results are mixed: economic models indicate that monetary lenient return policies increase returns (e.g., Shulman et al. 2009).

An analytic review study based on experimental and field studies find a positive, albeit insignificant effect of a monetary lenient return policy on costumer return decisions (Janakiraman et al. 2016). Hence, more research is needed to conclude on the impact of monetary lenient return policies on product return decisions.

TIME LENIENCY

Return deadlines (time leniency) have little to no impact on purchase decisions, but do affect customer return decision: when offering more lenient return deadlines (longer deadlines), customers have a lower likelihood to return the product. This happens because a customer may postpone the returning decision and next forgets to return the product or starts to appreciate the product more, the so-called endowment effect (Janakiraman and Ordóñez 2012).

SCOPE LENIENCY

Some stores restrict the items they consider "return-worthy", and some retailers do not allow customers to return sales items (low scope leniency). Scope leniency mainly influences the return decision: if a retailer does not allow customers to return items on sale, purchases probability is not affected, but customer return rates decrease. Hence, higher scope leniency increases the product return probability.

EFFORT LENIENCY

Companies can make decisions that impact the effort required to return a product. For instance, some retailers create "hassle" for customers who aim to return the product, such as requiring the original receipt and that the product package should be retained (low effort leniency). Higher effort leniency, where the retailer reduces the hassle to customers, increases the purchase probability, but does not influence customer return decision (Janakiraman and Ordóñez 2012). Research shows that companies should impose a greater hassle for returns when the product's benefits can be consumed in a short period of time (Davis et al. 1998). This will reduce the number of customers who get "free rent" by buying and returning after use.

Exchange Leniency

The final leniency factor studied is exchange leniency. Some retailers offer cash refunds whereas others only allow product exchange or store credit. Having a lenient exchange policy does not have an impact on purchase probabilities, but does result in lower return probabilities; a potential explanation is that customers with minor product complaints are more likely to exchange products when exchange clauses are more salient (Janakiraman et al. 2016), and hence a more strict exchange policy results in more returns.

Summary of Return Leniency

A less lenient return policy is one way to reduce the costs of product returns. However, there is an inherent trade-off in that such a cost-reducing policy will also reduce revenue due to its negative impact on demand. For example, in women's footwear category, allowing returns generates $15 in value to the customer per purchase (Anderson et al. 2009a). Hence, a key decision firms have to make to handle product returns is to set product return policies.

There is a large and growing body of academic research (see Janakiraman et al. 2016) to help managers as they decide whether to accept returns, how much of a refund to offer for returns, and how long to allow a customer to hold the product before making the return. The effectiveness of these decisions, at both the retailer and manufacturer level, interacts with customer-level factors, the firm's cost structure, and the competitive landscape. Yet, overall, the impact of a more lenient return policy on purchase decisions outweighs the impact on return decisions. In engaging customers to make a purchase and to manage returns, managers should recognize the strategic and cost implications of their return policy as well as the revenue implications.

Customer Characteristics

Most studies found non-significant effects of customer demographics on product returns, but some differences exist across studies. So far, research did not find significant effects on return likelihood for income, marital status, education, and age (Hong and Pavlou 2014; Petersen and Kumar 2009). The effects for gender are mixed: Minnema et al. (2016) found that males have lower return rates in electronics and furniture category, whereas Hong and Pavlou (2014) found no significant difference in return rate between males and females for online auctions at Taobao and eBay. In addition, customers who are new in the category tend to have higher return rates (Petersen and Kumar 2009). When customers purchase for the first time in a category, they have higher levels of uncertainty and are therefore more likely to return purchased products.

Return rates may also vary depending on specific contextual settings. Schulze and Srinivasan (2016) find that return rates vary from country to country. They argue that this between-country variation is not driven by variation in customer characteristics but by variation in the efficiency of the postal system between countries. Customers may purchase products as gifts, which are given to a recipient and hence do carry both economic value reflected in the product price but also have an added value from a social dimension. Because returning a gift can cause tension in the relationship between the gift giver and the recipient, products purchased as gift are returned less compared to when the customers purchased the product not as a gift (Petersen and Kumar 2009).

PRODUCT CHARACTERISTICS

Product return rates vary considerably across product categories. For categories such as fashion and footwear, return rates are reportedly higher than for categories such as electronics and furniture (Mollenkopf et al. 2007; Minnema et al. 2016). A major difference between categories is the degree to which it is difficult for customers to assess the fit between the product and their own preferences (fit uncertainty; Hong and Pavlou 2014). Customers perceive higher fit uncertainty for experience products compared to search products, and hence we observe higher return rates for experience products. However, prior studies did not find differences in return likelihood between durable and consumable products, where consumable products are immediately consumed or last a short period of time (Janakiraman et al. 2016). For more expensive products, customers are more critical, and hence more likely to return a product that lacks fit (Anderson et al. 2009b; Hess and Mayhew 1997). This also holds for the temporary price differences; the return rate for items on sale is lower because if the product is less expensive, customers are not as critical (Petersen and Kumar 2009). Multiple studies suggest that average review valence can be used as a proxy for average perceived product quality

(De Langhe et al. 2016). For products with higher average valence, product return rates are lower which suggests that for higher perceived quality, lower return rates are observed (Minnema et al. 2016; Sahoo et al. 2016).

CONSEQUENCES OF CUSTOMER RETURNS ON TRANSACTIONAL AND NON-TRANSACTIONAL BEHAVIORS

In this section, we review the key findings of research related to the consequences of product returns. Specifically, we discuss the impact of product returns on future purchase and return behavior and the impact on customer engagement behaviors.

IMPACT ON FUTURE PURCHASE AND RETURN BEHAVIOR

For firms it is important to understand the relationship between contemporary customer product returns and the future purchase and return behavior, and in this way account for the indirect effect of product returns on customer value.

First, a study by Petersen and Kumar (2009) with a catalog retailer that has a lenient product return policy empirically showed that increases in a customer's product returns led to increases in that customer's future purchase behavior relative to customers that did not return products. In fact, a simulation in this study found that the optimal product return rate which generated the highest profit for the retailer was around 13% at which the costs of product returns outweighed the benefits of increases in future purchases. Other studies confirm this finding, so does improved refund speed help to improve total relationship value (Griffis et al. 2012) and can increase total spending at the retailer by 158%–457% after customers have experienced a free return (Bower and Maxham 2012). In addition, a higher proportion of returned items result in longer relations with the firm. This is explained by the positive encounter with the firm's service representatives which enhance loyalty to the firm (Reinartz and Kumar 2003). Thus, firms need to think about creating strategies that might encourage customer behaviors (e.g., cross-buying) that also lead to increases in product returns when customers have not returned many (or any) products in the past. However, retailers should be cautious in asking customers a fee to return the purchased product when the retailers perceive that the customer is at fault (equity-based return policy). When customers perceive this policy as unfair, their post-return spending decreases by 75%–100% at the retailer (Bower and Maxham 2012).

Second, contemporary purchase and return behavior also influences future return behavior. In general, customers who purchase more products, return more products (Petersen and Kumar 2009) because customers must buy products in order to return them. However, there are significant differences based on previous return behavior. Some customers consistently return previously purchased products, whereas 20% of the customers did not exhibit any incidence of return behavior (Shah et al. 2014). Also other studies reported higher return rates for customers who returned in the past (Petersen and Kumar 2009; Minnema et al. 2016). Therefore, habitual returners are more likely to be unprofitable cross- category buyers (Shah et al. 2012) and are likely to contribute negatively by their CLV to the firm, see Eqs. (5.1, 5.2 and 5.3) in Section "The Relationship Between Product Returns and Customer Value" (Shah et al. 2014). Hence, examining product returns becomes even more critical in customer value management, because of a positive indirect effect through increasing future purchases and a negative indirect effect through increasing future returns.

Impact on Customer Engagement Behaviors

Customer value is not limited to the value of the transaction itself, but also comprises behavioral manifestations after a purchase (Van Doorn et al. 2010). Customers can help acquire new customers by providing referrals and can influence customers by, for example, writing reviews (Kumar et al. 2010a). Hence, ignoring non-transactional behavior may not provide the complete impact of product return behavior, see Eq. (5.1). A study by Petersen and Kumar (2010) ran a field experiment with a retailer which changed its return policy from being somewhat strict (only allowing product returns when products are defective or the wrong products have been shipped) to a more lenient return policy (allowing product returns at any point after purchase). The results of this field experiment showed that product return leniency did result in an increase in product returns, but the increase in purchase behavior was significantly larger, leading to a beneficial effect on net sales. Additionally, the study found that there were additional indirect benefits from this change in product return policy—a significant increase in customer referrals. When customers have a product return experience that is low in hassle due to a lenient product return policy, this leads to an increase in profitability due to purchases outpacing product returns, and it also has a positive indirect effect on firm profitability through mechanisms such as increases in customer referral behavior.

The effort in returning the product has similar consequences: higher effort in the customer product return experience negatively influences customer satisfaction with the return process which lowers the loyalty intentions toward the firm (Mollenkopf et al. 2007). Although a satisfactory return process between customer and retailer creates positive attitudes toward the retailer, customers are obviously less satisfied with the product. Hence, product return behavior also influences the arrival of customer reviews for the returned product. Customers are less likely to write a review for a product they have returned, and if customers do write a review, the expected star rating is lower (Minnema et al. 2016). Given the profit impact of nontransaction behaviors such as referrals and customer reviews, it is important for firms to take these behaviors into account (Kumar et al. 2010a).

To conclude this section, the existing literature on the consequences of product returns provides the following insights. First, product returns are not just an economic cost that needs to be minimized. A satisfactory product return experience between a customer and a firm can actually lead to future benefits for the firm in several ways. It can lead to a decrease in the customer's perceived risk to purchase in the future, making the customer more likely to engage in future purchases with the firm. The positive interaction can also lead to increases in a customer's attitude toward the firm which can lead to increases in positive word of mouth and/or referrals. However, the customer may also learn from a product return and have a higher probability to return future purchases, which has a negative impact on customer value.

Conclusion and Discussion

In this chapter, we have discussed product returns and its relation with purchase and customer engagement behavior, within the customer value framework. Product returns form a key component of customer value and one of the main drivers of profitability for today's retailers. In the past decade, we have observed a growing stream of research on product returns, due to the increasing use of distant channels for purchasing and associated higher return rates that are observed for these channels. One of the most important findings is that product returns are not a necessary evil in the exchange process: product returns have positive consequences on

Table 5.2   Ten main findings on product returns

Managing product return behavior

1. Incorporating customer product return behavior in customer value models improves a firm's marketing resource allocation and profit
2. Return policy leniency increases with the perceived quality of the retailer
3. Manufacturers should accept returns from the retailer at an overly generous refund in order to incentivize the retailer to offer an efficient refund to customers to boost sales

Antecedents of product returns

4. Return policies that offer monetary and/or effort leniency lead to an increase in purchases whereas longer deadlines reduce return rates
5. The information provided at the moment of purchase can either increase or decrease product return likelihood: return rates increase when information leads to higher product expectations and decrease when information mainly reduces uncertainty in expectations
6. Return rates are higher for experience products compared to search products, because customers perceive more fit uncertainty in the former case.
7. Return rates are higher for more expensive products and lower for products on sale, because customers are more critical for more expensive products

Consequences of product returns

8. Customers who experience a satisfactory return process are likely to increase their future spending at the retailer because of the lower perceived risk in making a purchase
9. Product return behavior is a habit; some customers consistently return purchased products, whereas others do not exhibit any incidence of return behavior
10. Product returns affect non-transactional behaviors. Customers who experience a low-hassle return process are more likely to provide positive referrals to the firm. When customers return, they are less likely to write a product review and the provided review is more negative

the future purchase behavior and help to foster loyalty and engagement toward the retailer. A large body of studies showed that retailers have instruments to manage product returns, such as customer relationship management tools, effective product return policies, and information provision at the moment of purchase. Based on extent research, we provide ten important findings on product returns (see Table 5.2).

This synthesis also helps to provide guidance in the identification of important areas for future research on product returns. Although research related to product returns spurred during the last decade, we believe that research can contribute to further improve understanding. One of the main directions for future research deals with examining under which conditions and for what type of firms, products, and customers a more or less lenient return policy is called for, and how this is different for the five dimensions of the return policy. For example, one could develop a unifying theory of when the high-quality seller should be more or less generous in its return policy compared to a low-quality retailer. Although studies showed the positive impact of return policy leniency dimensions (Janakiraman et al. 2016), future research should examine how this effect is contingent on retailer quality and product characteristics.

A second direction for future research is related to the *antecedents* of product returns. A substantial body of research showed the impact of pre-purchase information on product return decisions (Shulman et al. 2015). With respect to the customer engagement behaviors, extant research shows that reviews affect returns (Minnema et al. 2016). However, future research could examine the impact of the other behavioral dimensions of customer engagement on product returns. For example, when customers discuss their return behavior in (electronic) word of mouth, what is the social influence of these behaviors on the return behavior of other customers?

A third direction for future research is related to the *consequences* of product return decisions. Kumar et al. (2010a) propose four core dimensions of customer engagement value (CEV): (1) customer purchasing behavior, (2) customer referral behavior, (3) customer influencer behavior, and (4) customer knowledge behavior. Prior studies showed that product returns have a positive effect on customer purchase (Petersen and Kumar 2009), referral behavior (Petersen and Kumar 2010), and customer information value (Minnema et al. 2016). However, research on the impact on customer knowledge behavior is lacking. A positive relation between product return behavior and customer knowledge behavior can be expected. Customers who return a product can provide the firm of very valuable feedback regarding the information provision that may have caused the misfit or can help firms better understand for what kind of customer the product fits best. More broadly, the consequences of product returns on customer engagement behaviors are not completely clear as of yet. Recent managerial research discusses the "loyalty loop" (see Court et al. 2009), which suggests that in the post-purchase stage, a trigger may either strengthen the bond with the retailer or that customers may consider alternative retailers (Lemon and Verhoef 2016). A positive return experience results in more purchases and referrals but future research should examine the long-term impact on these relations.

This overview aims to provide readers a better understanding of product returns and how product returns should be managed and be taken into account in customer value management. In addition, we hope this overview fuels research on the important topics related to product returns, in particular in retailing and in customer relationship management.

REFERENCES

Akcay, Y., Boyaci, T., & Zhang, D. (2013). Selling with Money-Back Guarantees: The Impact on Prices, Quantities, and Retail Profitability. *Production and Operations Management, 22*(4), 777–791.

Altug, M. S., & Aydinliyim T. (2016). Counteracting Strategic Purchase Deferrals: The Impact of Online Retailers' Return Policy Decisions. *Manufacturing & Service Operations Management, 18*(3), 376–392.

Anderson, E. T., Hansen, K., & Simester, D. (2009a). The Option Value of Returns: Theory and Empirical Evidence. *Marketing Science, 28*(3), 405–423.

Anderson, E. T., Hansen K., Simester D., & Wang L. K. (2009b). *How Price Affects Returns: The Perceived Value and Incremental Customer Effects* (Working paper). Kellogg School of Management, Northwestern University.

Babic, A., Sotgiu, F., de Valck, K., & Bijmolt, T. H. A. (2016). The Effect of Electronic Word of Mouth on Sales: A Meta-Analytic Review of Platform, Product, and Metric Factors. *Journal of Marketing Research, 53*(3), 297–318.

Banjo, S. (2013, December 22). Rampant Returns Plague E-retailers. *The Wall Street Journal.* http://online.wsj.com/news/articles/SB1000142405270230 4773104579270260683155216. Last Accessed 23 June 2014.

Bechwati, N. N., & Siegal, W. S. (2005). The Impact of the Prechoice Process on Product Returns. *Journal of Marketing Research, 42*(3), 358–367.

Blanchard, D. (2007). Supply Chains also Work in Reverse. *Industry Week.*

Bonifield, C., Cole, C., & Schultz, R. L. (2010). Product Returns on the Internet: A Case of Mixed Signals? *Journal of Business Research, 63*(9), 1058–1065.

Bower, A. B., & Maxham, J. G., III. (2012). Return Shipping Policies of Online Retailers: Normative Assumptions and the Long-Term Consequences of Fee and Free Returns. *Journal of Marketing, 76*(5), 110–124.

Chen, Y., & Xie, J. (2008). Online Consumer Review: Word-of-Mouth as a New Element of Marketing Communication Mix. *Management Science, 54*(3), 477–491.

Court, D., Elzinga, D., Mulder, S., & Vetvik, O. J. (2009). The Customer Decision Journey. *McKinsey Quarterly, 3*, 96–107.

Davis, S., Gerstner, E., & Hagerty, M. (1995). Money Back Guarantees in Retailing: Matching Products to Consumer Tastes. *Journal of Retailing, 71*(1), 7–22.

Davis, S., Hagerty, M., & Gerstner, E. (1998). Return Policies and the Optimal Level of "Hassle". *Journal of Economics and Business, 50*(5), 445–460.

De, P., Hu, Y., & Rahman, M. S. (2013). Product-Oriented Web Technologies and Product Returns: An Exploratory Study. *Information Systems Research, 24*(4), 998–1010.

De Langhe, B., Fernbach P. M., & Lichtenstein D. R. (2016). Navigating by the Stars: Investigating the Actual and Perceived Validity of Online User Ratings. *Journal of Consumer Research,* forthcoming.

Dekker, R., Fleischmann M., Inderfurth K., & van Wassenhove L. N. (2004). *Reverse Logistics: Quantitative Models for Closed-Loop Supply Chains.* Berlin/New York: Springer.

Forrester. (2015, March 2). *Forrester Research: The State of Retailing Online 2015: Key Metrics, Initiatives, and Mobile Benchmarks, Media Release* (Accessed 25 May 2016). https://www.apteligent.com/wp-content/uploads/2015/10/The_State_Of_Retailing_On-1.pdf. Last Accessed 26 February 2016.

Gartner. (2014). *Returns—The Ticking Time-Bomb of Multichannel Retailing.* https://www.gartner.com/doc/2849018/returns--ticking-time-bomb. Last Accessed 25 May 2016.

Griffis, S. E., Rao, S., Goldsby, T. J., & Niranjan, T. T. (2012). The Customer Consequences of Returns in Online Retailing: An Empirical Analysis. *Journal of Operations Management, 30*(4), 282–294.

Gu, Z. J., & Tayi, G. K. (2015). Consumer Mending and Online Retailer Fit-Uncertainty Mitigating Strategies. *Quantitative Marketing and Economics, 13*(3), 251–282.

Guide, V., Daniel, R., Souza, G. C., Van Wassenhove, L. N., & Blackburn, J. D. (2006). Time Value of Commercial Product Returns. *Management Science, 52*(8), 1200–1214.

Hess, J. D., & Mayhew, G. E. (1997). Modeling Merchandise Returns in Direct Marketing. *Journal of Direct Marketing, 11*(2), 20–35.

Hong, Y., & Pavlou, P. A. (2014). Product Fit Uncertainty in Online Markets: Nature, Effects, and Antecedents. *Information Systems Research, 25*(2), 328–344.

Hu, W., Li, Y., & Govindan, K. (2014). The Impact of Consumer Return Policies on Consignment Contracts with Inventory Control. *European Journal of Operations Research, 233*(2), 398–407.

Inderst, R., & Tirosh, G. (2015). Refunds and Returns in a Vertically Differentiated Industry. *International Journal of Industrial Organization, 38*(1), 44–51.

Janakiraman, N., & Ordóñez, L. (2012). Effect of Effort and Deadlines on Consumer Product Returns. *Journal of Consumer Psychology, 22*(2), 260–271.

Janakiraman, N., Syrdal, H. A., & Freling, R. (2016). The Effect of Return Policy Leniency on Consumer Purchase and Return Decisions: A Meta-Analytic Review. *Journal of Retailing, 92*(2), 226–235.

Kerr, J. C. (2013, August 12). Buyers Beware: Retailers Track Serial Returners. *NBC Today.* http://www.today.com/money/serial-returners-beware-retailers-are-tracking-you-6C10900265. Last Accessed 20 Mar 2016.

Kostyra, D. S., Reiner, J., Natter, M., & Klapper, D. (2016). Decomposing the Effects of Online Customer Reviews on Brand, Price and Product Attributes. *International Journal of Research in Marketing, 33*(1), 11–26.

Kumar, V., Aksoy, L., Donkers, B., Venkatesan, R., Wiesel, T., & Tillmanns, S. (2010a). Undervalued or Overvalued Customers: Capturing Total Customer Engagement Value. *Journal of Service Research, 13*(3), 297–310.

Kumar, V., Petersen, J. A., & Leone, R. P. (2010b). Driving Profitability by Encouraging Customer Referrals: Who, When, and How. *Journal of Marketing, 74*(5), 1–17.

Lemon, K. N., & Verhoef, P. C. (2016). Understanding Customer Experience Throughout the Customer Journey. *Journal of Marketing, 80*(6), 69–96.

Minnema, A., Bijmolt, T. H. A., Gensler, S., & Wiesel, T. (2016). To Keep or Not to Keep: Effects of Online Customer Reviews on Product Returns. *Journal of Retailing, 92*(3), 253–267.

Mollenkopf, D. A., Rabinovich, E., Laseter, T. M., & Boyer, K. K. (2007). Managing Internet Product Returns: A Focus on Effective Service Operations. *Decision Sciences, 38*(2), 215–250.

Moorthy, S., & Srinivasan, K. (1995). Signaling Quality with a Money-Back Guarantee: The Role of Transaction Costs. *Marketing Science, 14*(4), 442–466.

Petersen, J. A., & Kumar, V. (2009). Are Product Returns a Necessary Evil? Antecedents and Consequences. *Journal of Marketing, 73*(3), 35–51.

Petersen, J. A., & Kumar, V. (2010). Can Product Returns Make You Money? *MIT Sloan Management Review, 51*(3), 85–89.

Petersen, J. A., & Kumar, V. (2015). Perceived Risk, Product Returns, and Optimal Resource Allocation: Evidence from a Field Experiment. *Journal of Marketing Research, 52*(2), 268–285.

Reinartz, W. J., & Kumar, V. (2003). The Impact of Customer Relationship Characteristics on Profitable Lifetime Duration. *Journal of Marketing, 67*(1), 77–99.

Sahoo, N., Dellarocas, C., & Srinivasan, S. (2016). The Impact of Online Product Reviews on Product Returns. *MSI Working Paper Series,* 16–101.

Schulze, C., & Srinivasan, S. (2016). *Managing Product Returns for Multinational Online Retailers.* Paper Presented at the 2016 Informs Marketing Science Conference.

Shah, D., Kumar, V., Yingge, Q., & Chen, S. (2012). Unprofitable Cross-buying: Evidence from Consumer and Business Markets. *Journal of Marketing, 76*(3), 78–95.

Shah, D., Kumar, V., & Kim, K. H. (2014). Managing Customer Profits: The Power of Habits. *Journal of Marketing Research, 51*(6), 726–741.

Shulman, J. D., Coughlan, A. T., & Canan Savaskan, R. (2009). Optimal Restocking Fees and Information Provision in an Integrated Demand-Supply Model of Product Returns. *Manufacturing & Service Operations Management, 11*(4), 577–594.

Shulman, J. D., Coughlan, A. T., & Canan Savaskan, R. (2010). Optimal Reverse Channel Structure for Consumer Product Returns. *Marketing Science, 29* (6), 1071–1085.

Shulman, J. D., Coughlan, A. T., & Canan Savaskan, R. (2011). Managing Consumer Returns in a Competitive Environment. *Management Science, 57* (2), 347–362.

Shulman, J. D., Cunha, M., Jr., & Saint Clair, J. K. (2015). Consumer Uncertainty and Purchase Decision Reversals: Theory and Evidence. *Marketing Science, 34*(4), 590–605.

Su, X. (2009). Consumer Returns Policies and Supply Chain Performance. *Manufacturing & Service Operations Management, 11*(4), 595–612.

Van Doorn, J., Lemon, K. N., Mittal, V., Nass, S., Pick, D., Pirner, P., & Verhoef, P. C. (2010). Customer Engagement Behavior: Theoretical Foundations and Research Directions. *Journal of Service Research, 13*(3), 253–266.

Wood, S. L. (2001). Remote Purchase Environments: The Influence of Return Policy Leniency on Two-Stage Decision Processes. *Journal of Marketing Research, 38*(2), 157–169.

CHAPTER 6

Multi-tier Loyalty Programs to Stimulate Customer Engagement

Tammo H.A. Bijmolt, Manfred Krafft, F. Javier Sese, and Vijay Viswanathan

Stimulating Customer Engagement

As firms have moved from a product-driven management approach to a customer-centric, service-oriented approach, their focus has shifted from stimulating transactions to building and maintaining relationships with customers (Kumar and Reinartz 2016; Sheth and Parvatiyar 1995). In managing customer relationships, customer engagement has become a central theme, where customer engagement is defined as the customers' behavioral manifestation toward a brand or firm, beyond purchase, resulting from attitudinal drivers (Brodie et al. 2011; Van Doorn et al. 2010). Firms can affect customer engagement behaviors by providing rewards and other incentives

T.H.A. Bijmolt (✉)
University of Groningen, Groningen, Netherlands

M. Krafft
University of Münster, Münster, Germany

F.J. Sese
University of Zaragoza, Zaragoza, Spain

V. Viswanathan
Northwestern University, Chicago, IL, USA

© The Author(s) 2018   119
R.W. Palmatier et al. (eds.), *Customer Engagement Marketing*,
DOI 10.1007/978-3-319-61985-9_6

to their customers for purchase behaviors. In addition, they can provide incentives for non-purchase behaviors that are beneficial for the firm, such as online product reviews, referrals, and other types of word of mouth, using specific channels for transacting and communicating with the firm and so on. When making decisions on the nature and extent of these rewards, firms often distinguish between (segments of) customers.

Parallel to the general developments in marketing management, loyalty programs (LPs) are changing from being purely transaction-oriented toward integrated systems that truly support building and maintaining customer relationships (see also Bijmolt and Verhoef 2017). Modern LPs are often-times based on digital and mobile technology which facilitates better tar-geted communication with individual customers. Such technological advances allow for highly individualized elements in the LP design and communication, throughout the individual-specific customer journey. New LPs are designed along these developments, and existing LPs are being redesigned to include these modern features. One of the important devel-opments in the area of LPs is the rise of multi-tier loyalty programs (MTLPs). A MTLP allows for an explicit way to accommodate prioritization of cus-tomer groups by means of a hierarchical tier structure (e.g. Silver, Gold, Platinum). Customers in different tiers of the MTLP are provided increas-ing levels of tangible rewards and intangible benefits based on their past purchase behavior. As such, MTLPs are potentially powerful instruments to stimulate customer engagement in terms of a range of purchase and non-purchase customer behaviors. Is this chapter, we will discuss whether, why, and how MTLPs are effective (or not) in influencing customer behavior, thereby enhancing customer engagement and financial performance.

MULTI-TIER LOYALTY PROGRAMS: DEFINITION AND EXAMPLES

Definition of Multi-tier Loyalty Programs

A loyalty program is an integrated system of structured and customized marketing actions designed to build customer loyalty among profitable customers (Bijmolt et al. 2010). Among these programs, the type of design that we focus on in this chapter, the MTLP, has become very popular in recent years as a means to enhance loyalty among the best customers and to promote engagement behaviors (Berry 2015; Boston Retail Partners 2015). A MTLP can be defined by the following dimen-sions (Bijmolt et al. 2010; Viswanathan et al. 2017a, b):

- The main purpose of a MTLP is to *manage and foster behavioral and attitudinal loyalty of customers and thereby improve the financial performance of the firm.* The behavioral loyalty includes traditional purchase-related behavior, measured by metrics like sales, customer retention and share of wallet (SOW), and *customer engagement* behavior, measured by metrics like word-of-mouth intention.
- A MTLP has a predefined *structure, rules, and procedures.* A key element of a MTLP is the *hierarchical structure of customer tiers.* Customers are categorized into these tiers based on their past purchase behavior. The rules used by the MTLP to assign customers to different tiers are predetermined and often publicly available. Typically, the tier to which a customer currently belongs is communicated to him, and this tier membership is reevaluated periodically, often per year.
- A MTLP *rewards* customers on the basis of their past, current, or future value to the firm. MTLP provides customers with material or tangible rewards. For example, customers are rewarded for their purchase behavior with points that can be redeemed for certain aspirational goods and services. MTLPs also provide customers with symbolic rewards including preferential treatment and special privileges. These benefits include rights and privileges such as lower waiting times, access to VIP areas or special events, or personal assistance by courteous personnel. In a MTLP, the rewards and benefits for the customers increase for customers in higher tiers. Customers are frequently made aware of the benefits in various tiers.
- A customer must become a member of the MTLP to collect points, acquire status, redeem rewards, and obtain other benefits. In addition, the firm *can identify each individual MTLP member* and use this to manage the customer relationship.
- A MTLP is a *long-term investment* and should not be abandoned as firms may suffer more from dispossessing customers of privileges than from not offering an MTLP at all. In other words, firms planning to introduce MTLPs have to anticipate the long-term costs and benefits before making this decision.

Examples of Multi-tier Loyalty Programs

MTLPs are omnipresent in many countries and industries. Our overview of selected programs in Table 6.1 shows that MTLPs are used in services such as aviation, banking, car rentals, and hospitality. Interestingly, loyalty

Table 6.1 Examples and characteristics of multi-tier loyalty programs

Firm (country), name of program	Industry	No. of tiers	Tier labels	Thresholds	Currency	Change of status	Selection of special rewards and benefits
Breuninger (Germany), *Breuninger Card*	Retailer	Two	Breuninger Card; Breuninger Platinum Card	No requirements; ≥ € 7500 within 2 consecutive years	Spending level	Biannually	Birthday voucher, special offers and events for members, no shipping costs, fashion news, paying without cash. For Platinum members: 10% discount on all purchases on 1 day each year, luxury gift wrapping, special parking areas, own service hotline
Starbucks (USA), *My Starbucks Rewards*	Coffee shop	Two	Green; Gold	Five Stars; 30 Stars	One Star per purchase	Annually	For the first star: free beverage on birthday. Green level: one espresso shot for free, refill of coffee and tea, drink for free when buying coffee beans; Gold level: free drink every 15 stars, special offers
Lufthansa (Germany), *Miles and More*	Airline	Four	Participant; frequent traveler (FTV); Senator; Hon Circle	One mile; 35,000 miles or 30 flights; 100,000 miles; 600,000 miles in 2 years	Miles or number of flights	Biannually	Additional miles; FTV, Senator, and Hon Circle: upgrade vouchers, advance miles, booking guarantee, lounge access, waiting list priority, priority check-in, free luggage, service hotline. Priority luggage treatment; Hon Circle: transfer service, personal assistance
Best Western (USA), *Best Western Rewards*	Hotels	Five	Blue; Gold; Platinum; Diamond; Diamond Select	Nil; 10 nights/7 stays/10,000 points; 15/10/15,000;30/20/30,000;50/40/50,000	Number of nights, number of stays, or points	Annually	Special offers, worldwide free nights from 8000 points, bonus points [−, 10%, 15%, 30, 50%], exclusive reservation hotline; Platinum and higher: room upgrades, welcome present

Company	Industry	Number of tiers	Tier names	Thresholds	Basis	Timing	Benefits
Caesars Entertainment Corp. (USA), *Total Rewards*	Casino	Four	Gold; Platinum; Diamond; Seven Stars	Nil; 5000;15,000; 150,000	Points	Annually	Discounts, special offers, turn reward credits into free plays, presale access to shows, priority check-in; Diamond and Seven Stars: access to Diamond lounges, VIP reservations hotline, guaranteed room, 15% off on rooms and suites, no resort fees, discounts at golf courses, celebration dinner. Seven Stars: complimentary room, upgrade to best available room, complimentary early check-in/late check-out, companion card, invitation to signature events
Hertz (USA), *Hertz Gold Plus Rewards*	Car rentals	Three	Gold Plus Rewards; Five Star; President's Circle	No requirement; > 6 rentals; > 19 rentals	Number of rentals	Annually	Special offers, free additional driver, discounts on children's seats; Five Star or President's Circle: Upgrade to next car category, 10% bonus points, 900 bonus points after every tenth rental, events; President's Circle: Guarantee of car availability or free upgrade, 25% bonus points
Bank of America (USA), *Platinum Privileges*	Banking	Three	Gold; Platinum; Platinum Honors	$ 20,000; $ 50,000; $ 100,000	Investment accounts	Annually	Interest rate booster [5%; 10%; 20%], rewards bonus [25%; 50%; 75%], preferred rewards mortgage benefits [$ 200; $ 400; $ 600], interest rate discount [0.25%, 0.35%, 0.50%], priority service, select free banking services, free non-Bank of America ATM transactions [–, up to 12/year, unlimited]
Bayer (Germany), *Premeo*	Agriculture (B2B)	Four	Standard; Silver; Gold; Platinum	0-30%; >30-45%; >45-65%; >65%	Share of wallet	Annually	Receive bonus points [0%, 10%, 25%, 50%] at the end of the year; Gold and Platinum: access to VIP areas at events and agricultural trade fairs

programs with multiple tiers are increasingly used in B2B as well, as the example of Bayer clarifies. The overview also shows that MTLPs are characterized by financial rewards and preferential treatments with more pronounced benefits for higher status levels. As the example of the MTLP of Hertz clarifies, most hierarchical programs use the total volume as a key metric to assign program members to tiers. Limited benefits such as a free additional driver or special offers serve as an incentive for members in base levels, while premium customers receive free upgrades, bonus points, or benefits with higher certainty than lower-tier members.

Mechanisms to Stimulate Customer Engagement

As emphasized in the previous sections, multi-tier loyalty programs are introduced by firms with the aim to enhance customer engagement and thereby improve financial performance. In this section, we focus our discussion on identifying the ways through which a MTLP promotes and sustains desired customer behaviors. We distinguish between the static effects of a MTLP, that is, the effect of a customer having a certain tier in the MTLP, and the dynamic effects of a MTLP, that is, the effect of changes in the tier level of a customer (promotion, no change, or demotion) and/or the effect of a customer aiming to reach a higher tier. In addition, we identify the following routes by which a MTLP may stimulate customer engagement:

1) Monetary and non-monetary rewards (instrumental benefits)
2) Status (symbolic benefits)
3) Customer-company identification (emotional benefits)
4) Consumer learning (cognitive benefits)

Figure 6.1 offers a graphical representation of the four routes by which MTLPs lead to customer engagement. In the next subsections, we discuss each of these routes in turn, and identify the psychological mechanisms that underlie the impact on customer behavior.

Monetary and Non-monetary Rewards (Instrumental Benefits)

Multi-tier loyalty programs are designed to provide rewards to their members, and these rewards are worth more in higher tiers. The rewards can be monetary (e.g. presents or price discounts) or non-monetary (e.g. additional service or a customer magazine), but each reward represents a rather

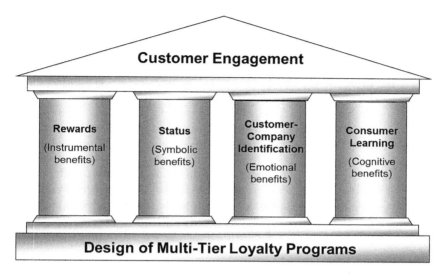

Fig. 6.1 Routes to customer engagement in multi-tier loyalty programs

direct, instrumental benefit. Hence, obtaining these rewards enhances the *economic utility* of the offering (Henderson et al. 2011) under the economic principle of utility maximization (Kumar and Reinartz 2016). However, rewards operate in additional ways to influence behavior, above and beyond the economic utility argument. As has been shown, "customers possess voracious appetites for rewards" (Drèze and Nunes 2011, p. 268). When presented with an opportunity to earn a reward, customers often alter their purchase behavior to gain access to these benefits (Taylor and Neslin 2005; Liu 2007). Taylor and Neslin (2005) theoretically propose and empirically demonstrate that customers experience a "*points pressure*" *effect*, that is, a motivational impulse to increase purchases in anticipation of the reward. Kivetz et al. (2006) demonstrate that the "goal-gradient hypothesis" is present in the human psychology of rewards, particularly in the context of loyalty programs: the closer the customer gets to the reward, the stronger the effort exerted toward achieving it.

Rewards can also impact behavior once the customer has received the reward, through the "*rewarded behavior*" *effect* (Taylor and Neslin 2005). This could occur through the positive reinforcement to the performed behavior that a reward produces, as demonstrated by work in "operant conditioning" (Skinner 1974). Thus, the rewarded behavior is more likely to persist and be repeated in the future. Another way is through the positive emotions that obtaining the reward produces for the customer, such as excitement, joy, and gratitude. Customers in the top tier who received a higher reward perceive the MTLP to be more fair, while second-tier customers are not negatively affected when explicitly exposed to the fact that they have been denied these rewards (Colliander et al. 2016). Another mechanism stems from the *reciprocity norm* of the social exchange theory, that is, a customer who receives a (high) reward feels the need to repay the company for the benefits received through gratitude-driven changes in purchase behavior (Palmatier et al. 2009; Wetzel et al. 2014). This may lead to a variety of desired outcomes, such as higher purchase volume, positive word of mouth, and willingness to co-create. Thus, the rewards offered by a MTLP stimulate customer engagement behaviors both before the reward is received due to a point pressure to earn the reward, and after it has been received due to the economic value of the rewards and due to positive emotions and a reinforcement of the performed behavior. Instrumental benefits are present in all examples provided in Table 6.1.

Status (Symbolic Benefits)

As noted before, MTLPs are accessible to all customers and provide increasing levels of symbolic benefits such as recognition, preferential treatment, and special privileges (Drèze and Nunes 2009) to customers in higher tiers. Receiving such symbolic benefits enhances the *perception of status* among customers in higher tiers (Brashear-Alejandro et al. 2016). MTLPs frequently label customer tiers using status-laden precious metals (e.g. bronze, silver, gold, platinum) in order to reinforce the notion of a hierarchy among customers and provide observable indicators of status (Berger et al. 1972; Chaabane and Pez Perard 2014; Drèze and Nunes 2009; Melnyk and Van Osselaer 2012). Thus, by including this stratification, MTLPs aim to leverage the power of status, widely recognized as a strong motivator of human behavior (Anderson et al. 2001; Frank 1985; McFerran and Argo 2014). This happens because individuals are socially sensitive, and they have an intrinsic motivation to evaluate their situation by engaging in comparisons with others (social comparison theory; Festinger 1954). In particular, customers in the top tiers perform downward comparisons that favor self-enhancement and feelings of exclusivity, by differentiating them from less prestigious groups (Drèze and Nunes 2009).

The effectiveness of the top of the tier hierarchy (e.g. Gold or Platinum) on customer behavior may depend on the size of this group. Research on customer perceptions of exclusivity suggests that the desirability of a position in society increases with its scarcity (e.g. Gierl and Huettl 2010). Henderson et al. (2011) suggest that consumers prefer being conferred high status when the elite group is small. Consistent with this, Drèze and Nunes (2009) demonstrate that the attractiveness of an elite-status group decreases with an increasing number of individuals who are granted elite status. Arbore and Estes (2013) also find that perceived status in the top tier increases as the number of customers in the top tier decreases, and as the number of tiers increases. A recent study conducted in a B2B setting finds that elite-status members can also influence new enrollments. However, an increase in the number or fraction of elite-status members can have a detrimental effect on the speed of adoption (Viswanathan et al. 2017b). This effect is most likely to be observed in an industry with high perceived exclusivity (airlines), and not in an industry with low perceived exclusivity (supermarkets). With regard to intermediate tiers, it has been shown that customers in these tiers are more concerned about their status and more susceptible to social contagion (Hu and Van den Bulte 2014). Finally, even low-tier members, while receiving limited preferential treatment and fewer special privileges, often favor programs with elite tiers despite not qualifying to becoming members of these top categories (Drèze and Nunes 2009), although they may resent members in higher status categories (see Section The Dark Side of MTLPs). Consistent with social comparison theory (Festinger 1954), an individual's level of aspiration is often greater than their level of performance and, thus, customers in the MTLP will perform upward social comparisons that will motivate them to improve their status in the program. Therefore, symbolic benefits such as status are a powerful force to promote favorable behaviors among program members. In Table 6.1, all programs offer some degree of status, though symbolic benefits are almost non-existent in the MTLP offered by Starbucks, and less pronounced in Bank of America's Platinum Privileges.

Customer-Company Identification (Emotional Benefits)

Multi-tier loyalty programs, by stratifying the membership base into different customer groups, provide a sociological context which enhances customer-company bonding in two ways and may therefore stimulate customer engagement. First, social identity theory proposes that the groups to which an individual belongs, or aspires to be part of, are a central element to the self-concept as they provide the basis to form a *social identity* (Tajfel and Turner 1979). Similarly, literature on group connectedness indicates that consumers tend to use brands whose images match the groups to which they belong, which enhances the association with those groups (Escalas and Bettman 2005; Winterich et al. 2009). Individuals strive to achieve a positive social identity and to bolster their self-image, which promotes aspirations to belong to elevated-status groups (Henderson et al. 2011). If the rewards and benefits of the MTLP are visible to other customers, for example, in the form of exclusive lounge access for high-tier members, the MTLP becomes more salient to customers and enables members to identify each other as part of the in-group (Esmark et al. 2016). Thus, by creating an in-group context ("the Gold members of firm X") in which its members share a number of experiences and benefits, a MTLP helps individual customers to define who they are and enhance their self-image and self-esteem (Brashear-Alejandro et al. 2016).

Second, a MTLP may enhance *connectedness to the firm* itself (Tanford 2013). For example, Brashear-Alejandro et al. (2016) demonstrate that the symbolic benefits (e.g. recognition, preferential treatment) provided by an LP promote a strong and deep identification with the company, which may be particularly strong for the high-tier groups of a MTLP. Drèze and Nunes (2009) further demonstrate that these programs impact a customer's perceived feelings of superiority, which are central to help individuals fulfill their self-definitional needs, including the need for self-enhancement and self-distinctiveness (Tajfel and Turner 1979). Satisfying these self-definitional needs motivates the development of identification with the company, which becomes "the primary psychological substrate for the kind of deep, committed, and meaningful relationships" with the firm (Bhattacharya and Sen 2003, p. 76). Clearly, firms need to utilize these findings and enable consumers to identify themselves with their brands. Digital technologies such as mobile applications can be extremely useful in this regard since there is increasing empirical evidence that such digital initiatives have a long-term effect on customers' purchase and reward redemption behaviors and vice versa (Viswanathan et al. 2017a, b). Thus, multi-tier loyalty programs offer customers an important source of value through the formation of a social identity, which enhances the importance of the customer-firm relationship and promotes the development of positive attitudes such as trust, commitment, involvement, or loyalty, that ultimately result in customer engagement (Brodie et al. 2011).

As an example of very pronounced emotional benefits, consider Breuninger's Platinum-tier customers. Interestingly, many Platinum members do not value the Platinum card the most, but the special bag that only Platinum customers receive for their purchased goods at the check-out. It is clearly visible to others, and within midsize cities in Southern Germany, most women exactly know what this bag implies. It also serves to define members of the in-group, and the out-group.

Consumer Learning (Cognitive Benefits)

Over time, individual customers derive valuable information from a MTLP which becomes the basis for acquiring, modifying and reinforcing their knowledge, preferences, and behaviors (Kopalle et al. 2012). This dynamic learning process is important, because it can have a profound impact on customer behaviors, including customer engagement (Brodie et al. 2011). Drèze and Nunes (2011) identify three different types of learning that can have different implications for the understanding of how customer behavior in a loyalty program evolves over time: procedural learning, learning from experience, and self-learning. *Procedural learning* refers to the process by which individuals gain knowledge about how they should proceed in order to derive benefits from the loyalty program (e.g. spend $ 1,000 in company products during a calendar year to become Gold member). *Learning from experience* occurs when individuals gain knowledge about something after experiencing it. For example, when a customer has been upgraded to a higher tier, he learns about the rewards and symbolic benefits that members of that tier receive (e.g. privileges such as lower waiting times, access to VIP areas or special events, or personal assistance by courteous personnel). *Self-learning* refers to the process by which individuals gain knowledge about their abilities to perform specific activities or actions. Individual customers invest resources and direct action to yield the rewards and symbolic benefits provided by the MTLP (Wang et al. 2016). In principle, customers feel a drive to look up (upward comparison), which motivates them toward greater achievements in the future and being promoted to a higher tier (Henderson et al. 2011). When a customer achieves or fails to achieve those goals or when a customer is successful at moving up one tier, he reassess the perceptions of his ability to execute these actions and determines the motivation and effort needed to invest in subsequent attempts (Drèze and Nunes 2011; Taylor and Neslin 2005). In contrast, when a customer fails to achieve the reward-contingent goals, motivation to invest to achieve the rewards may decrease (Wang et al. 2016).

Another type of learning that occurs in the context of MTLPs is *associative learning* (Sheth and Parvatiyar 1995), a process by which individuals learn an association between a stimulus (e.g. a reward) and a behavior (e.g. purchases). Importantly, this type of learning in an MTLP promotes the development of recursive customer purchases and other customer engagement behaviors (Shah et al. 2014) and thus may lead to the development of habits (Liu and Tam 2013; Henderson et al. 2011). Hence, by repeatedly offering increasing levels of rewards and symbolic benefits to customers, MTLPs induce different customer learning processes that condition and determine future engagement behaviors. An effective way of reinforcing such learning happens by explicitly reporting points acquired or money saved on check-out receipts or booking summaries, or providing MTLP members the choice of an immediate rebate instead of collecting points.

THE DARK SIDE OF MTLPs

As discussed in the previous section, a MTLP stimulates customer engagement in a variety of ways. This may suggest that such programs are efficacious by definition, and all firms should seriously consider to introduce a MTLP. However, this is not always the case. Depending on the type of firm, customers, and market conditions, a MTLP may have negative (side) effects. In this section, we identify a number of potential ways through which MTLP can negatively impact the development of customer engagement behaviors and their ultimate impact on financial performance.

Expectations and Entitlement In the general framework of expectation-confirmation theory, customer satisfaction will depend critically on the pre-experience expectations. If a firm explicitly acknowledges to some of its customers that they are the "best" customer by classifying them as Gold member of the MTLP, this may cause an upward shift in their expectations: "I'm a Gold member so I'm entitled to receive excellent service". A potential discrepancy between perceived performance and expectations may have a strong negative effect on customer satisfaction; the "satisfaction trap". Consistent with this line of reasoning, Von Wangenheim and Bayón (2007) show that a negative incident has a substantial detrimental impact on customer satisfaction of high-tier customers, whereas it hardly affects customers in the lower tiers. Returning to our Breuninger example, demoting Platinum customers to a standard status means they lose many benefits they have got used to, such as the "platinum bag" or parking in select, reserved spots. Even worse, losing these visible benefits will probably be recognized by others as well. Conversely, the effect of a positive critical incident is stronger for low-tier customers than for high-tier customers. Wetzel et al. (2014) also reflect on the perils of customer prioritization strategies by noting that customers with a high standing in the company's hierarchy will feel entitled to demand efforts and services from the supplier commensurate with their standing. In practice, it may be hard or even impossible to circumvent such increased expectations of high-tier customers. Hence, a MTLP should be carefully managed and the products, service, rewards, and so on should be of high quality and meet the expectations of the customers in different tiers.

Customer Heterogeneity A MTLP distinguishes between customers of a firm where customers in the higher tiers receive discretionary preferential treatment in an attempt to stimulate desired engagement behaviors (see previous section). A customer may observe these differential treatments and compare the way he is treated with reciprocity norms, with how other customers are treated, and with norms based on input-outcome ratios (Steinhoff and Palmatier 2015). In addition, some customers do not like to be treated differently. Butori and De Bruyn (2013) show that preferential treatment may delight one customer but enrage or embarrass another. The effect depends on the degree of justification, imposition, visibility, and surprise. In general, customers prefer preferential treatments that are justified, imposed by the firm, visible to other customers, and a surprise to the recipients. However, a substantial proportion of customers may feel embarrassed if the preferential treatment is visible and if the imposed treatment creates a disadvantage for other customers. Customers' preference for preferential treatment depends among others on their gender and age (Butori and De Bruyn 2013; Melnyk and Van Osselaer 2012). For example, Melnyk and Van Osselaer (2012) find that male customers value MTLP-induced status more positively than female customers, especially if the high-tier level and symbolic benefits are highly visible to other customers. In addition, Steinhoff and Palmatier (2015) find significant "bystander" effects: the relationships with low-tier customers who observe others' preferential treatment are harmed considerably. Accommodating such customer heterogeneities is a major challenge in the design and management of a MTLP. Although visibility is valued by many customers, firms should not overdo this. Furthermore, to increase the perception of fairness and justification, the MTLP could be open and explicit in the rules and procedures to become a member of the high-tier groups. The MTLPs mentioned in Table 6.1 typically communicate the tier thresholds and other regulations explicitly on their websites.

Customer Promotions and Demotions Over time, customers may also change their tier membership. In other words, customers may get promoted to a higher tier or demoted to a lower tier. These dynamics may cause specific effects due to an increase or decrease of the MTLP rewards and benefits for the customer, as discussed in the previous section. Prospect theory (Kahneman and Tversky 1979) predicts that customers are more sensitive to losses than to gains of similar magnitude. Consequently, a drop in MTLP rewards can be more damaging to the customer-firm relationship than a corresponding increase. Wagner et al. (2009) demonstrate that individuals are more sensitive to tier losses (demotions) than to tier gains (promotions) of an equivalent magnitude, leading to lower customer engagement among customers who experience an upgrade followed by a downgrade (or the other way around) than among customers who never experience a change in tier level in the first place. A similar asymmetric pattern of demotion versus promotion is found for the effect on trust, commitment, and loyalty (Van Berlo et al. 2014). Interestingly, the negative effect of a demotion is particularly strong with an external locus of causality, rather than with an internal or situation locus. In the former case, the customer may blame the firm for the demotion and consider the demotion as unfair or due to opportunistic behavior of the firm (Van Berlo et al. 2014). Not only demotions can produce negative effects. The study by Eggert et al. (2015) shows that the practice of endowing customers who do not meet the requirements with upgrades in the hierarchy of status can produce negative behavioral responses. In contrast to achieved status, endowed status may be interpreted as a persuasion attempt by the firm and prompt an external attribution, which can lead to potential negative emotional reactions in the form of skepticism ultimately affecting loyal behaviors. However, this negative effect can largely be circumvented by targeting customers who are already close to the threshold requirement of the promotion and allowing the customer to choose whether he wants to be promoted or not. Thus, firms should be careful with demoting and promoting customers and weigh the benefits and costs of changing the tier membership of customers. In some cases, the outcomes are more beneficial if the firm does not change tier membership of a customer although he no longer meets the requirements. Keeping MTLP status levels for 2 or more years is a policy going in this direction. In Table 6.1, Breuninger and Lufthansa represent such examples.

MTLP Design A firm running a MTLP will need explicit criteria to classify its customers into the hierarchical structure of tiers. It is a priori not obvious which criteria should be used for this purpose. Metrics based on absolute purchase levels will favor customers with high category expenditures, whereas metrics based on relative purchase levels, for example, share of wallet, may favor customers with low category expenditures. Which customer should be treated as a "better" customer, as member of a higher tier: customer A, who spends 60 out of 100 euro at our firm, or customer B, who spends 40 out of 50 euro at our firm? Some customers may have a very high attitudinal loyalty and high share of wallet, but do not meet profitability requirements for a high tier as set by the firm, simply because their category expenditures are low, for example, grocery expenditures by a single-person household. This may lead to frustration and reactance against the MTLP (Wendlandt and Schrader 2007). The decision as to which criteria should be used to grant status needs to be consistent with the strategic objectives of the organization as well as the nature and characteristics of the market in which it operates. One of the companies in Table 6.1, Bayer (Premeo program), assigns status based on relative purchase levels (i.e. share of wallet). This company operates in a B2B context, where purchases from multiple vendors are common "to ensure supply and competition among vendors to keep prices in check" (Bowman and Narayandas 2004, p. 436) and, thus, gaining customer loyalty is a particularly difficult task (Wathne et al. 2001). Using share of wallet to grant status helps the firm promote loyalty among their customers, and, if share of customer can be increased for many customers, a firm's market share will be increased as well. Altering the thresholds for different tiers after the program has been rolled out can also result in frustration and disappointment. The perceived legitimacy of preferential treatment and thereby the effects of the MTLP on satisfaction, customer engagement, and so on may depend heavily on the customer's perception of his tier level, rather than actual tier level granted by the firm (Pez et al. 2015). To prevent negative consequences, the firm running a MTLP should aim to match the structure of granting tier levels to the perceived status or customer value to the firm.

CONCLUSION

To summarize, a MTLP is a long-term marketing investment designed to strengthen the relationship between the firm and its customers. Numerous firms providing a range of service and product offerings have introduced MTLPs for their customers. A key success factor for a MTLP is to communicate the benefits associated with different tiers of a loyalty program and thus clearly differentiate themselves from competition. Some firms even brand their MTLPs to achieve this objective. Consequently, some customers have learnt over time to evaluate the costs and benefits associated with different loyalty programs and then enroll in one that offers the maximum value. In the event that customers are unable to evaluate the differences between different programs, they might enroll in multiple MTLPs, which lowers the effectiveness of each program.

MTLPs can differentiate themselves by clearly stating how customers would be rewarded with tangible benefits or rewards and intangible benefits such as status for purchasing the firms' products over time. As customers gain rewards and achieve higher status, they gradually develop a stronger sense of belonging with the firm. Eventually, these customers become invaluable not just because of their purchases but also because of their goodwill for the firm. For instance, this goodwill is often translated into positive word of mouth or referrals and helps the firms acquire new customers. Due to the principle of homophily, it is quite likely that these new customers are also potentially of high value to the firm (Viswanathan et al. 2017a, b). Another exemplification of this goodwill is co-creation. High-value customers have immense knowledge and experience of the firm's products and can therefore provide rich insights on how firms can improve their market offerings. These insights could enable firms to enhance the value of their services and thus sustain their advantage over competition in the marketplace.

The marketing landscape is changing, and this holds true also for the area of loyalty programs (see also, Bijmolt and Verhoef 2017). At least two major developments are particularly relevant for MTLPs. First, digitalization and the proliferation of using mobile technology allows faster and more targeted (in terms of message, location, timing, and personalization) communication within the MTLP. Instead of sending a weekly direct mail to a selection of its customers, a firm can contact any number of specifically selected LP members at any point in time, even depending on the location of the customer. When being in close proximity to the store, a program member could receive a personal message on her or his mobile with a discount or other interesting offer, which would result in a higher status, for example, becoming a Gold member. This communication approach could be very effective, but could also be perceived as obtrusive. Research is needed on the message, customer, and context factors that strengthen or harm the effectiveness of MTLPs. Second, while MTLPs originally have been managed and studied fairly independent of other marketing mix decisions of the firm, integration is taking place in practice. Customers perceive the MTLP as strongly connected to other components of the firm, and decisions made within the MTLP management affect and will be affected by general decisions on communication, pricing, assortment, and so on. For example, the degree to which Gold status in the MTLP is valued by customers will depend on the image of the firm and on its products, customer service, price level, and location. Hence, future research should examine MTLP within the context of other marketing instruments.

While firms can benefit immensely from MTLPs, they should not lose sight of the costs associated. Moreover, they have to be cognizant of the fact that these benefits accrue over a period of time. Hence, short-term measures of success and even metrics such as ROI may be difficult to not only attain but also measure. The latter may be particularly true in cases when a firm has multiple touchpoints with a customer, a MTLP being one of them. MTLPs can raise expectations and evoke negative emotions such as anger and frustration among certain customers and stretch the resources of the firm. Nevertheless, as explained in this chapter, when designed and executed properly, a MTLP can help identify the most valuable customers for a firm and subsequently help the firm increase both customer engagement and firm profitability in the long term.

REFERENCES

Anderson, C., John, O. P., Keltner, D., & Kring, A. M. (2001). Who Attains Social Status? Effects of Personality and Physical Attractiveness in Social Groups. *Journal of Personality and Social Psychology, 81*(1), 116–132.

Arbore, A., & Estes, Z. (2013). Loyalty Program Structure and Consumers' Perceptions of Status: Feeling Special in a Grocery Store? *Journal of Retailing and Consumer Services, 20*, 439–444.

Berger, J., Cohen, B. P., & Zelditch, M., Jr. (1972). Status Characteristics and Social Interaction. *American Sociological Review, 37*(3), 241–255.

Berry, J. (2015, February). The 2015 Colloquy Loyalty Census. Big Numbers, Big Hurdles. *Colloquy.*

Bhattacharya, C. B., & Sen, S. (2003). Consumer–Company Identification: A Framework for Understanding Consumers' Relationships with Companies. *Journal of Marketing, 67*(2), 76–88.

Bijmolt, T. H. A., & Verhoef, P. C. (2017). Loyalty Programs: Current Insights, Research Challenges, and Emerging Developments. In B. Wierenga & R. van der Lans (Eds.), *Marketing Decision Models.* New York: Springer.

Bijmolt, T. H. A., Dorotic, M., & Verhoef, P. C. (2010). Loyalty Programs: Generalizations on Their Adoption, Effectiveness and Design. *Foundations and Trends in Marketing, 5*(4), 197–258.

Boston Retail Partners. (2015). *Loyalty Programs—Rewarding the Customer Experience.* BRP Special Report.

Bowman, D., & Narayandas, D. (2004). Linking Customer Management Effort to Customer Profitability in Business Markets. *Journal of Marketing Research, 41*(4), 433–447.

Brashear-Alejandro, T., Kang, J., & Groza, M. D. (2016). Leveraging Loyalty Programs to Build Customer–Company Identification. *Journal of Business Research, 69*(3), 1190–1198.

Brodie, R., Hollebeek, L. D., Jurić, B., & Ilić, A. (2011). Customer Engagement: Conceptual Domain, Fundamental Propositions, and Implications for Research. *Journal of Service Research, 14*(3), 252–271.

Butori, R., & De Bruyn, A. (2013). So You Want to Delight Your Customers: The Perils of Ignoring Heterogeneity in Customer Evaluations of Discretionary Preferential Treatments. *International Journal of Research in Marketing, 30*(2013), 358–367.

Chaabane, A. M. & Pez Perard, V. (2014). Towards a Better Understanding of Perception and Consequences of Status in Hierarchical Loyalty Programs. In *The 13th International Research Conference in Service Management*, La Londe les Maures, France.

Colliander, J., Söderlund, M., & Szugalski, S. (2016). Multi-Level Loyalty Program Rewards and Their Effects on Top-Tier Customers and Second-Tier Customers. *Journal of Consumer Marketing, 33*(3), 162–171.

Drèze, X., & Nunes, J. C. (2009). Feeling Superior: The Impact of Loyalty Program Structures on Consumer's Perceptions of Status. *Journal of Consumer Research, 35*(6), 890–905.

Drèze, X., & Nunes, J. C. (2011). Recurring Goals and Learning: The Impact of Successful Reward Attainment on Purchase Behavior. *Journal of Marketing Research, 48*(2), 268–281.

Eggert, A., Steinhoff, L., & Garnefeld, I. (2015). Managing the Bright and Dark Sides of Status Endowment in Hierarchical Loyalty Programs. *Journal of Service Research, 18*(2), 210–228.

Escalas, J. E., & Bettman, J. R. (2005). Self-Construal, Reference Groups, and Brand Meaning. *Journal of Consumer Research, 32*(3), 378–389.

Esmark, C. L., Noble, S. M., & Bell, J. E. (2016). Open Versus Selective Customer Loyalty Programmes. *European Journal of Marketing, 50*(5/6), 770–795.

Festinger, L. (1954). A Theory of Social Comparison Processes. *Human Relations, 7*(2), 117–140.

Frank, R. H. (1985). *Choosing the Right Pond: Human Behavior and the Quest for Status.* New York: Oxford University Press.

Gierl, H., & Huettl, V. (2010). Are Scarce Products Always More Attractive? The Interaction of Different Types of Scarcity Signals with Products' Suitability for Conspicuous Consumption. *International Journal of Research in Marketing, 27*(3), 225–235.

Henderson, C. M., Beck, J. T., & Palmatier, R. W. (2011). Review of the Theoretical Underpinnings of Loyalty Programs. *Journal of Consumer Psychology, 21*(3), 256–276.

Hu, Y., & Van den Bulte, C. (2014). Nonmonotonic Status Effects in New Product Adoption. *Marketing Science, 33*(4), 509–533.

Kahneman, D., & Tversky, A. (1979). Prospect Theory: An Analysis of Decision Under Risk. *Econometrica, 47*(2), 263–292.

Kivetz, R., Urminsky, O., & Zheng, Y. (2006). The Goal-Gradient Hypothesis Resurrected: Purchase Acceleration, Illusionary Goal Progress, and Customer Retention. *Journal of Marketing Research, 43*(1), 39–58.

Kopalle, P. K., Sun, Y., Neslin, S. A., Sun, B., & Swaminathan, V. (2012). The Joint Sales Impact of Frequency Reward and Customer Tier Components of Loyalty Programs. *Marketing Science, 31*(2), 216–235.

Kumar, V., & Reinartz, W. (2016). Creating Enduring Customer Value. *Journal of Marketing, 80*(6), 36–68.

Liu, Y. (2007). The Long-Term Impact of Loyalty Programs on Consumer Purchase Behavior and Loyalty. *Journal of Marketing, 71*(4), 19–35.

Liu-Thompkins, Y., & Tam, L. (2013). Not All Repeat Customers Are the Same: Designing Effective Cross-Selling Promotion on the Basis of Attitudinal Loyalty and Habit. *Journal of Marketing, 77*(5), 21–36.

McFerran, B., & Argo, J. J. (2014). The Entourage Effect. *Journal of Consumer Research, 40*(5), 871–884.

Melnyk, V., & van Osselaer, S. M. J. (2012). Make Me Special: Gender Differences in Consumers' Responses to Loyalty Programs. *Marketing Letters, 23*(3), 545–559.

Palmatier, R. W., Burke Jarvis, C., Bechkoff, J. R., & Kardes, F. R. (2009). The Role of Customer Gratitude in Relationship Marketing. *Journal of Marketing, 73*(5), 1–18.

Pez, V., Butori, R., & de Kerviler, G. (2015). Because I'm Worth It: The Impact of Given Versus Perceived Status on Preferential Treatment Effectiveness. *Journal of Business Research, 68*, 2477–2483.

Shah, D., Kumar, V., & Hannah Kim, K. (2014). Managing Customer Profits: The Power of Habits. *Journal of Marketing Research, 51*(6), 726–741.

Sheth, J. N., & Parvatiyar, A. (1995). Relationship Marketing in Consumer Markets: Antecedents and Consequences. *Journal of the Academy of Marketing Science, 23*(4), 255–271.

Skinner, B. F. (1974). *About Behaviorism*. New York: Knopf.

Steinhoff, L., & Palmatier, R. W. (2015). Understanding Loyalty Program Effectiveness: Managing Target and Bystander Effects. *Journal of the Academy of Marketing Science, 44*(1), 88–107.

Tajfel, H., & Turner, J. (1979). An Integrative Theory of Intergroup Conflict. In W. G. Austin & S. Worchel (Eds.), *The Social Psychology of Intergroup Relations* (pp. 138–182). Monterey: Wadsworth.

Tanford, S. (2013). The Impact of Tier Level on Attitudinal and Behavioral Loyalty of Hotel Reward Program Members. *International Journal of Hospitality Management, 34*, 285–294.

Taylor, G. A., & Neslin, S. A. (2005). The Current and Future Sales Impact of a Retail Frequency Reward Program. *Journal of Retailing, 81*(4), 293–305.

Van Berlo, G., Bloemer, J., & Blazevic, V. (2014). Customer Demotion in Hierarchical Loyalty Programmes. *The Service Industries Journal, 34*(11), 922–937.

Van Doorn, J., Lemon, K. N., Mittal, V., Nass, S., Pick, D., Pirner, P., & Verhoef, P. C. (2010). Customer Engagement Behavior: Theoretical Foundations and Research Directions. *Journal of Service Research, 13*(3), 253–266.

Viswanathan, V., Tillmanns, S., Krafft, M., & Asselmann, D. (2017a). *Counting on Recommendations: The Roles of Extroversion and Opinion Leadership in Customer Engagement*. Working Paper.

Viswanathan, V., Sese, F. J., & Krafft, M. (2017b). *The Role of Elite Members in Influencing Loyalty Program Adoption*. Working Paper.

Von Wangenheim, F., & Bayón, T. (2007). Behavioral Consequences of Overbooking Service Capacity. *Journal of Marketing, 71*(October), 36–47.

Wagner, T., Hennig-Thurau, T., & Rudolph, T. (2009). Does Customer Demotion Jeopardize Loyalty? *Journal of Marketing, 73*(3), 69–85.

Wang, Y., Lewis, M., Cryder, C., & Sprigg, J. (2016). Enduring Effects of Goal Achievement and Failure Within Customer Loyalty Programs: A Large-Scale Field Experiment. *Marketing Science, 35*(4), 565–575.

Wathne, K. H., Biong, H., & Heide, J. (2001). Choice of Supplier in Embedded Markets: Relationship and Marketing Program Effects. *Journal of Marketing, 65*(2), 54–66.

Wendlandt, M., & Schrader, U. (2007). Consumer Reactance Against Loyalty Programs. *Journal of Consumer Marketing, 24*(5), 293–304.

Wetzel, H. A., Hammerschmidt, M., & Zablah, A. R. (2014). Gratitude Versus Entitlement: A Dual Process Model of the Profitability Implications of Customer Prioritization. *Journal of Marketing, 78*(2), 1–19.

Winterich, K., Mittal, V., & Ross, W. T. (2009). Donation Behavior Toward In-Groups and Out-Groups: The Role of Gender and Moral Identity. *Journal of Consumer Research, 36*(2), 199–214.

CHAPTER 7

Happy Users, Grumpy Bosses: Current Community Engagement Literature and the Impact of Support Engagement in a B2B Setting on User and Upper Management Satisfaction

Sander F.M. Beckers, Sterling A. Bone, Paul W. Fombelle, Jenny van Doorn, Peter C. Verhoef, and Kristal R. Ray

INTRODUCTION

Co-creating value is a widely acknowledged concept on how firms and customers work together to create value. Beyond creating products and solutions that might be more tailored to specific customer needs, it may also increase the engagement of customers. Researchers have acknowledged that customer co-creation is a specific element of customer engagement (i.e., "the customer's behavioral manifestations that have a brand of firm

S.F.M. Beckers (✉) • J. van Doorn • P.C. Verhoef
University of Groningen, Groningen, Netherlands

S.A. Bone • K.R. Ray
Utah State University, Logan, UT, USA

P.W. Fombelle
Northeastern University, Boston, MA, USA

© The Author(s) 2018
R.W. Palmatier et al. (eds.), *Customer Engagement Marketing*,
DOI 10.1007/978-3-319-61985-9_7

focus, beyond purchase, resulting from motivational drivers", Van Doorn et al. 2010, p. 254). Customers may not only co-create value in the product or service delivery but may also be engaged in the after-sales support specifically through online support communities. In these support communities, customers not only receive support service from other customers but they also engage with others in an effort to solve other community member problems (Wiertz and de Ruyter 2007). This type of community engagement takes over the service functions traditionally provided by the host firm, often times with little cost to the firm (Bone et al. 2015).

Offering support services is a critical component of successful business relationships (e.g., El Sawy and Bowles 1997; Karpen et al. 2015). In line with marketing literature, we define service support as customer assistance in learning about the product and its usage opportunities and solving product-related issues (e.g., Das 2003; Dholakia et al. 2009). Given technological advancements, delivering customer support is evolving from traditional one-to-one support *service requests* (i.e., logging a formal service demand on a one-to-one basis, for instance, through phone consults) toward one-to-many web-based support services, which can be both passive *online knowledge consultation* (i.e., consulting a static online knowledge repository, such as a frequently asked questions section) and *active community support* (i.e., participating in an interactive online support community, for instance, by posting questions) (Dholakia et al. 2009; Nambisan 2002).

Managerial interest in organizing and facilitating web-based support services, online communities in particular, to deliver support is thriving (Nambisan and Baron 2010), triggered by the possibility to invest in customer relationships and to obtain cost advantages (Algesheimer et al. 2005). Recent research suggests that online community support is cheaper to deliver than traditional support (Dholakia et al. 2009; Rosenbaum 2008), and also reduces the usage of more costly traditional support through service requests (Bone et al. 2015). Also, community usage is documented to lead to stronger customer relationships, such as increased likelihood to recommend (Gruen et al. 2006). While set in a brand community, Bruhn et al. (2013) demonstrate that the quality of customer-to-customer (C2C) interactions in B2B brand communities positively impacts the functional, experiential, and symbolic brand community benefits. Online communities tailored to customer support but, also in general, are heavily studied recently.

In this chapter we contribute to the literature by providing an overview of community research. From this overview we conclude that online community research is a mature field and studies cover a wide range of settings (e.g., B2B as well as B2C) and phenomena (e.g., brand-building communities as well as sharing communities). Nonetheless, we notice that all current studies are always investigated at the level of the individual user, even in B2B settings (e.g., Bone et al. 2015). However, we argue that for engagement to have an impact in a B2B setting, it is important that decision-makers are incorporated into the model. Therefore, we con-ducted an empirical illustrative study to investigate whether there is value to look beyond the individual users when studying online communities. B2B organizations have multiple organizational layers, as the individual who uses the support services (which is not necessarily the individual who uses the functional product for which support is requested) is often dis-tinct from the individual(s) responsible for purchase decisions. Therefore, for support usage in a B2B setting to have an effect on beneficial and last-ing corporate relationships, the benefits of obtained support (e.g., increased knowledge or efficient problem solving) and/or awareness of benefits must transfer from the individual support user to the decision-maker within the customer organization. This is illustrated by quotes from the business press documenting that in order to reach engagement in B2B set-tings, you must know your audience and reach multiple individuals within an account (Gletcher 2016). In additional, popular press quotes that it is imperative to understand that users need to do their job and as community owner, you must "think about how you can make them look like rockstars in front of their peers and managers" (Mashable 2011). Accordingly, our second contribution to literature is to take service support research beyond the individual user[1] by investigating the effect of different types of service activity (i.e., service requests, consulting online knowledge database, and active community support) on the customer satisfaction of users as well as its influence on upper management decision-makers.

Literature Overview

In Table 7.1 we provide an overview of selected and exemplary literature on community. We do not claim that our overview is exhaustive (given the contemporary interest in online communities as a research topic such an overview would be virtually impossible to provide), yet we included the most-cited exemplary papers within the domain, and we complemented these key papers with some of the most recent work. We classified the study based on the type of community that is investigated, which setting is investigated, and the unit of analysis. We also show the main findings of

Table 7.1 Exemplary overview of community literature

Study	Type of community		Setting		Unit of analysis		Main finding
	Brand advocacy (social)	Product support (informative)	B2C	B2B	Individual user	Upper management decision-maker	
Algesheimer et al. (2005)	✓		✓		✓		Community engagement, on the positive side, leads to participation, continuation, and recommendation intentions. But on the negative side community engagement leads to normative pressure and ultimately reactance
Algesheimer et al. (2010)	✓		✓		✓		Community usage makes customers more efficient and conservative; they, for instance, spend less money
Bagozzi and Dholakia (2006)		✓	✓		✓		Participation in online support community leads to intentions of additional positive behaviors (e.g., spending money, co-creation) toward the company
Bone et al. (2015)		✓		✓	✓		Usage of online community support decreases usage of the more costly traditional offline customer support
Brodie et al. (2013)		✓	✓		✓		Customer engagement leads to connection and emotional bonding, customer empowerment, customer loyalty and satisfaction, trust, and commitment
Bruhn et al. (2013)		✓		✓	✓		Brand trust positively impacts brand community trust

Source					Description
Chan et al. (2015)	✓	✓		✓	If customers submitted ideas in a community before their interaction with the company, operating the community becomes more important and interaction with other customers becomes less important
De Almeida et al. (2014)	✓	✓		✓	Community diversity facilitates learning and hinders social identification, whereas freedom of expression only facilitates learning
De Valck et al. (2009)	✓	✓		✓	Virtual communities among others serve as reference groups that have a more heterogeneous character than traditional reference groups
Dholakia et al. (2009)	✓	✓	✓	✓	Functional and social benefits can be derived from community participation
Homburg et al. (2015)	✓	✓		✓	Consumers respond with diminishing returns to active firm engagement in an online community, in particular for conversations addressing functional needs
Khansa et al. (2015)	✓	✓		✓	Community participation is determined by incentives, membership characteristics, and past behavior
Krush et al. (2015)	✓	✓		✓	Sharing in online communities is a form of positive marketing. Sharing can occur without feelings of caring and without individual-level reciprocity
Leal et al. (2014)	✓	✓		✓	Communities can act as a strong reference group

(continued)

Table 7.1 (continued)

Study	Type of community		Setting		Unit of analysis		Main finding
	Brand advocacy (social)	Product support (informative)	B2C	B2B	Individual user	Upper management decision-maker	
Lee and Van Dolen (2015)		✓	✓		✓		Community company owner's management style influences collective sentiment in the community. Counterintuitively, growing positive sentiment decreases future participation, whereas growing negative sentiment increases it
Manchanda et al. (2015)	✓	✓	✓		✓		Customers that are active within communities spend more, especially those customers that contribute content by posting and those with more social ties in the community
Mathwick et al. (2008)		✓	✓	✓	✓		Social capital determines the informational and social value is derived from a community, which in turn impacts community commitment
McAlexander et al. (2002)	✓		✓		✓		Brandfest participation positively impacts attitude toward the brand, the company, and fellow customers
Nambisan and Baron (2007)		✓	✓	✓	✓		Customers' interactions in communities (which can be both positive and negative) influence their perceptions of the firm
Porter and Donthu (2008)	✓		✓		✓		Fostering membership embeddedness is the most fruitful way for firms to operate a community, but this can be a double-edged sword

					Description
Schau et al. (2009)	✓		✓		Brand communities have 12 common practices through which value is created
Thompson and Sinha (2008)	✓		✓		Brand community participation decreases adoption of new products from competing brands
Zhou et al. (2012)	✓		✓		Brand attachment fully mediates the relationship between brand community commitment and brand commitment
Zhou et al. (2013)	✓		✓		Viewing community posts leads to community participation intention
Zhu et al. (2012)		✓	✓		Online community participants make riskier financial decisions than non-participants
This Project		✓	✓	✓	

each study. We will not elaborate on each of the studies, but the overview table clearly shows strong attention for communities in marketing and that researchers have studied multiple processes and outcomes.

Based on Table 7.1 we can draw a number of conclusions regarding the current status of community engagement literature. The field is heavily studied, and therefore it is unsurprising that community engagement is investigated in various settings (in B2B as well as B2C environments) and the communities studied have various purposes (product support as well as brand communities). Studies show primarily positive, but somewhat mixed outcomes (e.g., social value, but also normative pressure). We also conclude that current outcomes of community engagement are always investigated at the level of the individual user, even in B2B settings (e.g., Bone et al. 2015).

However, we argue that for engagement to have an impact in a B2B setting, it is important that decision-makers are incorporated into the model. Therefore, we next conducted conceptual development (including hypotheses) and an empirical study to investigate whether there is value to look beyond the individual users when studying online communities.

CONCEPTUAL DEVELOPMENT AND HYPOTHESES

In our empirical part, we investigate support community engagement in a B2B community on user and upper management satisfaction. Next to the impact of active community support usage, we seek to understand the impact of traditional service requests and online knowledge consultation on customer satisfaction. Although customers might use alternative support channels (e.g., Google search), we focus our attention on the support channels which are directly under the control of the focal service provider. Thus, we relate three distinctive types of service activity (i.e., traditional service requests, online knowledge consultation, and active community support) to customer satisfaction and argue that these relationships vary across individuals working at the user versus management levels, influenced by job function relevance. See Fig. 7.1 for our conceptual framework.

Sources of Service Support

Service Requests Traditionally, support has been delivered to customers on a one-to-one basis through service requests, in which the customer reports a problem to the company and a member of the company's support staff works together with the customer to solve this problem. A service request occurs when a customer contacts the service department of a service

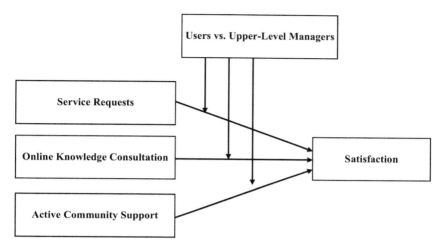

Fig. 7.1   Conceptual framework

supplier, thereby logging a formal service request. Typical methods to do so include calling the helpdesk and receiving phone consults, email support, and onsite visits (Wiertz and De Ruyter 2007). This labor-intensive way of delivering customer support is costly since there is a great deal of repetitiveness due to solutions being distributed on an individual basis (Bone et al. 2015) and obtained solutions still need to be disseminated further throughout the customer organization. On the other hand, from the receiving customer organization's perspective, more labor-intensive customer support might be yielding better service quality, due to involvement of support staff that understands the customer organization's nuances and thereby tailoring solutions (Rust and Huang 2012). Research has argued that support users will perceive the service provider's staff members (in comparison to peer customers) to be the highest experts and to provide the most reliable answers (Dholakia et al. 2009). However, research also documents that the mere act of having to log a service request is often not liked by customers, since it typically indicates a service failure (e.g., Bitner et al. 1994; Challagalla et al. 2009). The non-performance of a supplied product can lead to significant losses (Markeset and Kumar 2005); potential system downtime due to service failures leads to a significant reduction in B2B company revenues (CA Technologies 2011). Not surprisingly given the undesirable atmosphere they are in, customers typically have a negative mind-set when (needing to) contacting the service provider (Challagalla et al. 2009) and thus evaluate the service requests negatively. This type of engagement takes the least effort on the customer's part, but still requires them to connect to the firm, clearly articulate their problem, and work with the firm to find a solution.

Online Knowledge Consultation Technological advancements have altered the traditional way support is delivered to customers (Rust and Huang 2012). Information technology made it possible to go from a one-to-one support model toward one-to-many web-based support services (Wiertz and De Ruyter 2007). Instead of on an individual basis, solutions are disseminated on a global basis by making them visible and accessible to other customers. Customers in turn can be passively or actively involved in one-to-many web-based support. On the passive side, they can go to the company's online knowledge base to solve their product issues. Instead of contacting a support employee, customers can browse a web-based support portal containing a static knowledge repository, which "can only be searched and accessed for support service but cannot be added to, changed, or altered" (Bone et al. 2015, p. 25) (e.g., searching for key terms, reading the frequently asked questions section of the service provider). As such, online knowledge consultation is a self-service channel in which customers can obtain service support without the service provider's direct interference (Negash, et al. 2003). From the service provider's perspective, this is a lower-cost support channel due to savings on support staff costs (Dholakia et al. 2009; Rosenbaum 2008). From the customer organization's perspective, this support channel has the potential to solve problems in a timely manner, since recurring problems do not have to be solved from scratch and/or individually by a staff member of the service provider (El Sawy and Bowles 1997). In addition, besides problem resolution, online knowledge consultation also enables learning about the product and its usage opportunities (Bone et al. 2015). Through static knowledge repositories, service providers can transfer knowledge and provide more timely dissemination of information to stakeholders (e.g., their customers). In static knowledge repositories, solutions to previous problems are ubiquitous, so that support users can access them again and hence gain in flexibility of solution implementation (Piccoli et al. 2001) and do not require much internal information dissemination throughout the customer organization. Also, the customer organization can learn about and prevent new unanticipated issues. Therefore, consulting online knowledge does not necessarily mean that a customer organization already faces a service failure. Contrary to service request activity, online knowledge consultation offers faster problem resolution and learning opportunities (Bone et al. 2015), which make customers likely more positive toward online knowledge consultation. However, there are also some innate drawbacks to this support model. For instance, solutions might not be fine-tuned to the customer's situation, may be out-of-date, difficult to navigate, or may take considerable time investments to search for the correct solution (Bone et al. 2015). Further, more complex problems often found in B2B situations are not easily solved via simple online knowledge repositories.

Active Community Support Usage To overcome some of the limitations associated with passive web support, customers can actively be involved in peer-to-peer problem solving communities. In such communities, they can ask questions and/or reply to questions of others. Similar to online knowledge consultation, active community support usage offers faster problem resolution. An online support community has the potential to offer real-time solutions for new problems (Dholakia et al. 2009). For instance, for novel problems other support channels might not be available or updated, yet community users could already be a few steps ahead in problem resolution. A support community enables users to tap into a large knowledge network (i.e., wisdom of the crowd) at any point in time (Bone et al. 2015). However, factors such as low response rate or contradictory answers could hamper this positive impact. In addition, community support not only allows learning opportunities but also goes a step further by allowing dynamic and interactive learning. A support community facilitates active exchange with the 'teacher' (be it a peer customer or a staff member of the service provider) (Piccoli et al. 2001). Contrary to static knowledge repositories, active involvement allows shared understanding and thereby greater insights (Porter et al. 2011), which is often necessary for effective learning with respect to problem resolution and prevention (Nambisan and Baron 2010). Because of this active involvement, support community usage goes beyond self-servicing toward customer co-creation in service support (Bone et al. 2015). In comparison to alternative means of obtaining support, customers have to perform more tasks on their own and thereby make more investments to obtain support (Wiertz and De Ruyter 2007). However, since customers co-create value with the company, they gain additional control over support and have the ability to improve the service offering (Chan et al. 2010). Furthermore, besides providing mere utilitarian value, active community support allows participants, particularly in a high-involvement setting, to experience additional benefits from the co-creating experience, such as social status gains (e.g., Bruhn et al. 2013; Karpen et al. 2015). Such an exceptional service experience will positively impact customer retention (Bolton et al. 2006). Hence, active community support engagement offers even further increased efficiency of problem resolution, interactive learning opportunities, and a favorable service experience. Due to this favorable experience, customers likely evaluate active support community usage positively; recent research indicates a wide variety of positive effects of active community usage, such as increased recommendation likelihood (Gruen et al. 2006) and repurchase intentions (Bagozzi and Dholakia 2006).

Job Function Heterogeneity

As apparent from our previous reasoning, each distinctive support channel operated by a focal service provider (i.e., service requests, online knowledge consultation, and active community support) has its own inherent benefits and drawbacks. In general, service requests are negatively evaluated, since they typically indicate a service failure (e.g., Challagalla et al. 2009). In contrast, online knowledge consultation and active community support usage are typically valued due to increased efficiency and, especially for community usage, the offering of a favorable service experience (e.g., Dholakia et al. 2009). As we will argue next, we expect that job function influences the evaluation of the distinctive benefits and drawbacks of various ways of obtaining support. Users need to solve their customer organization's support issues, whereas upper-level managers need to manage, supervise, and oversee their staff members' behavior (Eisenhardt 1989). Upper-level managers will primarily pursue the customer organization's interest, whereas their staff members (i.e., users) will primarily pursue their own (job function) interest.[2] Upper-level managers should make sure that the interests of the customer organization and the individual users are aligned. These job functions have implications regarding how both users and upper-level managers perceive the various ways of obtaining support, which we will discuss next.

Users User's core need is solving their customer organization's support needs fast and adequate (Van der Heijden et al. 2013). They thereby likely employ a short-term orientation toward support by focusing on day to day issues. Due to this short-term orientation, users may trade quality for speed when dealing with their customer organization's support issues. They need to solve the actual issues and would like to do this quickly. Since increased efficiency of problem resolution is a prime benefit of web-based support (e.g., Nambisan and Baron 2010; Rust and Huang 2012), users will positively evaluate web-based support. In contrast, service request may yield higher perceived quality due to involvement of supplier support staff (Dholakia et al. 2009; Rust and Huang 2012), yet may be less efficient. Since users are the ones actually dealing with their organization's support issues, users will experience the negative mind-set associated with having to log a service request.

In addition, besides their core job task, individual users are also interested in their own personal values and needs, which can be considered non-task jobs (Webster and Wind 1972). In particular active community support yields the ability to satisfy the users' own personal values and needs, by providing the opportunity to obtain side benefits from customer support. Users have to invest resources (e.g., time, effort) in order to participate in and contribute to the community (e.g., by helping other customers), without this aiding them directly in their core job. However, in return for their community investments, users not only gain technological knowledge but also psychological (e.g., emotional) and/or social benefits (e.g., by gaining community status) (Hoyer et al. 2010). As such, active community usage not only delivers purely informational value but also a favorable service experience (Mathwick et al. 2008; Nambisan and Baron 2007). This benefits the individual user, but not necessarily the customer organization he or she is working for.

Upper-level manager/s. In contrast to users, upper management is typically not directly involved in daily and regular service support and problem resolution. Instead of directly experiencing the benefits of customer support, employees operating at higher levels simply need to know that support channels are helpful for his or her staff in order to assess whether investments are paying off, especially given the predominant contractual nature of B2B problem resolution (Bone et al. 2015). Given their different functions within the customer organization, the core benefits upper-level managers are looking for in support are different from the core benefits users are looking for. Whereas users might primarily want fast solutions, upper-level managers additionally also want solutions that are meeting future business needs at a profitable cost level, reflecting a tension between short-term (which are more likely pursued by users) and long-term (which are more likely pursued by upper management) goals (Katzenbach and Santamaria 1999).

As stated before, within the typical trade-off between automated and fast support on the one hand, and high-quality support on the other hand (Rust and Huang 2012; Van der Heijden et al. 2013), community support leans toward the former, rather than the latter (Dholakia et al. 2009). In contrast, traditional service requests might be more time-consuming, yet yield higher perceived quality of support, due to the involvement of supplier support staff understanding the customer organization's particularities, sensitivities, and future needs (Dholakia et al. 2009; Rust and Huang 2012). Since upper-level managers are typically not the ones solving their organization's actual support issues, they will not personally experience the negativities and frustration of having to deal with service request issues. They are therefore neutral toward this aspect of service requests, yet their quality perceptions may be lowered. Although we think that upper-level managers will evaluate service requests less negatively, we do not think this goes as far as upper-level managers evaluating service requests positively. The general principle, however, still holds that service requests typically are surrounded by negative connotations and are thought of as service failures (e.g., Bitner et al. 1994; Challagalla et al. 2009), such that upper-level managers will still evaluate service requests negatively.

With respect to active community usage, since upper-level managers do not personally experience additional (psychological and social) benefits from customer support, they are likely attaching less value to these benefits. In fact, upper-level managers might even perceive potential dark sides of active support community usage. First, their staff members (i.e., users) invest valuable company resources (e.g., their time) in order to obtain side benefits of community support, while these investments have no direct or tangible payoffs for the customer organization. Since the job of upper management is to oversee the customer organization's interest (e.g., Eisenhardt 1989), upper-level managers will attach less or even negative value to citizenship behavior in the support community. While a manager may see value in their employees receiving support from the community, they may not see value in their employees engaging in helping behavior for those in the community but not likely from the firm. From a rational customer organization perspective, such behavior has a negative cost-benefit trade-off, due to potential knowledge leakage, waste of time, and even leakage of human capital. Upper management may treat their knowledge as proprietary goods (i.e., intellectual capital) and therefore be reluctant to knowledge spoilage in web-based support (Wasko and Faraj 2000). In addition, upper management may, correctly or not, regard their employees' community activity as "socializing and detracting from work" (Wasko and Faraj 2000, p. 171) and believe that time spent taking up additional service roles could be better spent on more important tasks for the customer organization (Van der Heijden et al. 2013). Also, in extreme cases, highly qualified staff members may reveal their qualifications and may become susceptible to competitive job offers.

Hypotheses

To recap, given their different job functions and reflecting a classic principal-agent tension, users and upper-level managers employ different perspectives on customer support. In light of the above arguments, we hypothesize the following (see Table 7.2 for an overview of types of support, their definition, and anticipated effects):

H1a: *The effect of service request activity on satisfaction is negative for users.*
H1b: *The effect of service request activity on satisfaction is negative for upper-level managers.*
H2a: *The effect of online knowledge consultation on satisfaction is positive for users.*

Table 7.2 Overview of types of support and anticipated effects

Kind of support	Definition	Hypothesized effect on users/reasoning	Hypothesized effect on upper-level managers/reasoning
Service requests	Logging a formal service demand on a one-to-one basis, for instance, through phone consults	– / Service requests are typically indications of service failure and other negativities	– / Service requests are typically indications of service failure and other negativities
Online knowledge consultation	Consulting a static online knowledge repository, such as a frequently asked questions section	+ / Problems can be solved quickly	– / Obtained solutions might be of lesser quality
Active community support usage	Participating in an interactive online support community, for instance, by posting questions	+ / Problems can be solved quickly and side benefits (such as status gains) can be obtained	– / Obtained solutions might be of lesser quality and side benefits benefit the entire firm

H2a: *The effect of online knowledge consultation on satisfaction is negative for upper-level managers.*

H3a: *The effect of active community support usage on satisfaction is positive for users.*

H3b: *The effect of active community support usage on satisfaction is negative for upper-level managers.*

An Illustrative Example

We conducted an empirical study to test our hypotheses and present it here as an illustrative example of how both users and upper management value the various ways their organization obtains customer support. We use the overall customer organization as the unit of analysis and relate, through multiple regression equations, a customer organization's support usage to satisfaction outcomes of employees operating at various corporate levels within the organizational hierarchy of the customer organization (i.e., individual users and upper-level managers).

Data and Sample

Data were collected in partnership with a large Fortune 100 supplier of high-tech services and merged from multiple sources over a longitudinal period of time. The data covers a representative group of 7865 customer organizations, all with access to each distinct support channel offered by the Fortune 100 high-tech service company, operating in a wide variety of industries and using various products and services offered by the Fortune 100 company. Data include behavioral activities, aggregated over all individuals working within the same customer company, regarding the support activity of these customer organizations and survey data regarding their satisfaction. Using a common identifier, we merged service request logs (captured from the service provider's log files), the customer organizations' online knowledge consultation (captured from clickstream data), the customer organizations' active support community usage (also captured from clickstream data), and a customer relationship survey. Since we relate support behavioral data to survey outcomes, we preclude common method bias problems.

The customer relationship survey, which contains our dependent variable, is targeted at employees operating at various corporate levels performing various job roles within the organizational hierarchy of the customer organization. We classified those who self-reported their job level as individual contributor (i.e., functional and technical users) or as manager (who at least used support themselves once) as users and those who indicated their job level as director or as manager (but did not use support themselves at least once) as upper-level managers. Discussions with the Fortune 100 high-tech service company revealed that respondents who classify themselves as managers can be either lower-level managers seeking service or community support themselves or upper-level managers who do not do so. We therefore distinguished between managers that used or did not use support at least once. In addition, we excluded those who indicated their job level as executive (they are, according to the Fortune 100 high-tech service company, too far removed from daily operations) from our sample. Although the Fortune 100 company administers the customer relationship survey on a biquarterly basis, their basic sampling policy is to survey one job role per customer organization and to survey each customer organization only once, in order to reduce burden on their customers. Therefore, to ensure a representative and substantial sample, we pooled multiple time periods by relating support activity of 2–3-month time frames (Q3 2011 or Q1 2012) to satisfaction outcomes measured in the succeeding 3-month time frame (Q4 2011 or Q2 2012). These time periods were selected on the basis of the start of the online community. Note that in order to test causal relationships, we measured support activity in one time period (t_1) and measured satisfaction outcomes in a subsequent time period (t_2).

Measures

Dependent Variable Our dependent variable is customer satisfaction (with the firm). Customer satisfaction is measured with a survey item on a 10-point scale. Since customer satisfaction is a straightforward construct, we used a single-item survey measure (cf. Rossiter 2002).

Independent Variables Our independent variables are captured with behavioral data and reflect the various ways of obtaining customer support. We measured *service requests* with a single-item measure: the total number of opened and closed service requests. We measured *online knowledge consultation* with three items (which we combined into factor scores): the number of search queries, the number of community logins, and the number of note reads. We also used a multi-item scale to measure *active community support*. This scale contained the following items (we also combined these items into factor scores): number of threads started in the support community, number of questions asked in the support community, and number of replies given in the support community.

Table 7.3 Summary of measures

Construct	Measure	Time period	Level
Satisfaction	Survey item ("Overall, how satisfied are you with company X as a provider?") on a 10-point scale	Q4 of 2011 and Q2 of 2012	Upper-level managers
Service request	Number of opened and closed service requests (log-transformed)	Q3 of 2011 and Q1 of 2012	Customer organization
Online knowledge consultation	Number of search queries (log-transformed)	Q3 of 2011 and Q1 of 2012	Customer organization
	Number of note reads (log-transformed)	Q3 of 2011 and Q1 of 2012	Customer organization
	Number of community logins (log-transformed)	Q3 of 2011 and Q1 of 2012	Customer organization
Active community support	Number of threads started (log-transformed)	Q3 of 2011 and Q1 of 2012	Customer organization
	Number of replies given (log-transformed)	Q3 of 2011 and Q1 of 2012	Customer organization
	Number of questions asked (log-transformed)	Q3 of 2011 and Q1 of 2012	Customer organization

We log-transformed all behavioral items, since they were non-normally distributed (we do this for means of normality, which is amongst others a requirement for the factor analysis we perform later on; Byrne 2001).[3] An overview of all measures and associated data sources appears in Table 7.3; the overview of the descriptive statistics and correlations of variables is in Table 7.4.

Modeling Approach

To test our hypotheses, we make use of a three-step approach. First, we use factor analysis using oblique rotation to develop and verify a multi-item scale for online knowledge consultation and a multi-item scale for active community support usage.[4] Second, we estimate a pooled regression equation relating a customer organization's service request activity, online knowledge consultation, and active community support usage to customer satisfaction. Third, after determining using a Chow test that it is not justified to pool over job levels, we estimate two separate regression equations for the two job level groups: one regression for the user group (with a sample size of 4323 customer organizations) in which we relate a customer

Table 7.4 Descriptive statistics and correlation matrix

	Mean	SD	1.	2.	3.	4.
1. Satisfaction	6.83	1.86	1.00			
2. Service request	−1.20	4.76	−0.10***	1.00		
3. Online knowledge consultation	0.00	1.00	−0.09***	0.83***	1.00	
4. Active community support	0.00	1.00	0.01	0.19***	0.17***	1.00

The mean and standard deviation for online knowledge consultation and active community support usage are 0 and 1, respectively, since these scales are based on Z-scores

***$p < 0.01$

organization's support usage to their users' satisfaction and another regression for the upper-level manager group (with a sample size of 3542 customer organizations) in which we relate a customer organization's support usage to their upper-level managers' satisfaction.

RESULTS

Factor Analysis

By means of a factor analysis with oblimin rotation, we reduced the dimensionality of our online knowledge consultation and active community usage scales. The factor analysis with good Kaiser-Meyer-Olkin (KMO) scores confirmed our scales; all items loaded substantially on their target factor (average factor loading 0.97, minimum factor loading 0.89) and did not load on their nontarget factor (all cross-factor loadings below 0.30) (see Table 7.5). Cronbach's α indicates that our scales are "excellent" (Cronbach's $\alpha_{\text{online knowledge consultation}} = 0.99$; Cronbach's $\alpha_{\text{active community usage}} = 0.94$). We used factor scores for online knowledge consultation and active community usage in our subsequent analyses.

Regression Results

We pooled our sample over users and upper-level managers and estimated a pooled regression equation relating a customer organization's service request activity, online knowledge consultation, and active community support usage to customer satisfaction. Results in Table 7.6 indicate that

Table 7.5   Multi-item scale validity and factor loadings

Scale (Cronbach's α)	Items	Item loading
Online knowledge consultation (Cronbach's α = 0.99)	Number of search queries (log-transformed)	0.99
	Number of note reads (log-transformed)	0.99
	Number of community logins (log-transformed)	0.98
Active community usage (Cronbach's α = 0.94)	Number of threads started (log-transformed)	0.98
	Number of replies given (log-transformed)	0.88
	Number of questions asked (log-transformed)	0.98

a customer organization's service request activity significantly decreases satisfaction ($\beta = -0.04$, $p < 0.01$), a customer organization's online knowledge consultation does not significantly impact satisfaction ($\beta = -0.02$, n.s.), and a customer organization's active community support usage increases satisfaction ($\beta = 0.06$, $p < 0.01$). A Chow test indicates that the effects of service request activity, online knowledge consultation, and active community support usage differ between users and upper-level managers (Chow F statistic $(4, 7857) = 18.10$ $p < 0.01$).

Therefore, we estimated separate regression equations for users and upper-level managers. As can be seen from Table 7.6, a customer organization's service request activity significantly decreases user satisfaction ($\beta = -0.05$, $p < 0.01$), in support of H_{1a}. Supporting H_{1b}, service request activity also significantly decreases satisfaction of upper-level managers ($\beta = -0.03$, $p < 0.05$). We also formally compared the coefficients of service request activity for users and upper-level managers by means of a χ^2-difference test.[5] Results indicate that the satisfaction implications of service request activity do not differ significantly between users and upper-level managers ($\Delta\chi^2 (1) = 1.65$, n.s.). With respect to online knowledge consultation, surprisingly, a customer organization's online knowledge consultation does not increase user satisfaction, although the coefficient is in the hypothesized direction ($\beta = 0.03$, n.s.) (contrary to H_{2a}). However, online knowledge consultation significantly decreases upper management satisfaction ($\beta = -0.13$, $p < 0.05$), in support of H_{2b}. Furthermore, users and upper-level managers

Table 7.6 Impact of customer organization's support channel usage on satisfaction

	Pooled sample	User group	Upper-level managers
Independent variables			
Service request activity	−0.040 (0.008)***	−0.049 (0.010)***	−0.028 (0.012)**
Knowledge consultation	−0.021 (0.037)	0.031 (0.050)	−0.128 (0.056)**
Active community usage	0.064 (0.021)***	0.066 (0.028)**	0.069 (0.033)**
Intercept	6.783 (0.023)***	6.922 (0.030)***	6.601 (0.036)***
Number of observations	7865	4323	3542
R^2	0.012	0.013	0.018
Adjusted R^2	0.012	0.012	0.017
F-value	31.778***	18.620***	21.167***

Notes: Parameter estimates (standard errors). Two-sided tests are used for all effects. The dependent variable is customer satisfaction; for pooled sample this is overall satisfaction, for user group this is the satisfaction of users, and for upper-level managers group, this is the satisfaction of upper-level managers.

*$p < 0.10$; **$p < 0.05$; ***$p < 0.01$

differ significantly in their reaction toward their customer organization's online knowledge consultation ($\Delta\chi^2$ (1) = 4.23, $p < 0.05$). Finally, as predicted in H_{3a}, a customer organization's active support community usage significantly increases user satisfaction ($\beta = 0.07$, $p < 0.05$). For upper management, active support community usage also increases upper management satisfaction, opposite to the direction predicted in H_{3b} ($\beta = 0.07$, $p < 0.05$). Users and upper-level managers do not differ significantly in their reaction toward their customer organization's service request activity ($\Delta\chi^2$ (1) = 0.01, n.s.).

Robustness Checks

To add further robustness to our findings, we investigate alternative explanations of our findings and an alternative estimation method. By collecting additional data, we could not find evidence that age differences between upper-level managers and employees might explain our results. We also aimed to assess whether the sequence of usage of service channels would explain some of our findings. Based on some additional data collection, no evidence was found for that. Finally, we used structural equation modeling instead of regression analysis. The results are very similar. More details on these alternative explanations can be requested from the authors.

DISCUSSION

Communities have become of great interest in marketing and are a very relevant topic within customer engagement. In this chapter we first documented the current status of online community literature and noticed that all studies take the individual user as unit of analysis. Next, we argued that to capture effects in a B2B setting also, upper management decision-makers should be taken into account. To see whether there is value in going beyond the individual user we present an illustrative example wherein we investigate how both users and upper management value various ways of obtaining customer support (i.e., through traditional service requests, online knowledge repositories, and active community support). The main insight of our research is that we show that when studying the effectiveness of various support channels within a B2B setting, it is imperative to not only look at implications for users (they that obtain the actual support) but also at the implications for upper-level managers (they that are primarily responsible for contract renewal, contract upgrading, and the like). Our key insight and results have important theoretical and managerial implications.

Theoretical Implications

The effectiveness (in terms of customer satisfaction) of various types of customer support behavior varies significantly across employees operating at various corporate levels. Those in upper management become satisfied from active community support and dissatisfied from service support employees spending time and resources solving their problems in online knowledge databases or using traditional service requests. It seems that managers in general dislike that their customer organization has to use support, but that active community usage buffers this negative effect. The surprisingly positive effect for upper management satisfaction of active community usage could be because upper-level managers see upsides in networking with other customer organizations, benefitting from the wisdom of the crowd, and solution richness when obtaining advice from peer customers who can include context from using the product (e.g., Mathwick et al. 2008). Conversely, as predicted, those actually involved in support activity (i.e., users) appear to attach satisfaction to more engaged types of support (i.e., active community support) over traditional support (i.e., service requests). Therefore, we can conclude that "one size does not fit all". We take service support research in a B2B setting beyond the individual user and show the relevance of investigating individuals operating at various job roles within the customer organization.

Managerial Implications

We provide managers valuable insight in the performance implications of offering various support channels in a B2B context and the underlying processes. Our key findings point at the crucial role of understanding your audience in service support, especially since in typical B2B relationships and organizational buying centers, multiple individuals are involved taking up various roles and responsibilities (e.g., Anderson and Narus 1990).

Our findings can provide an answer to the following central question managers nowadays face (e.g., Wiertz and De Ruyter 2007): Can you (partially) delegate support to customers? Difference in the effectiveness of online knowledge consultation versus active community support allows us to provide an answer to this question. Our results show that self-service in customer support appears to not be accepted, since users do not become more satisfied from their customer organization's online knowledge consultation, while upper-level managers become less satisfied. In contrast, customer co-creation in support seems more appropriate, for both users and upper-level managers, since for both of them active support community usage has a positive effect on satisfaction. For the service provider, online support is a low-cost alternative to deliver support (Dholakia et al. 2009; Rosenbaum 2008), yet key players become less satisfied from solving problems through online knowledge databases (even in comparison to other types of support). Our results indicate that upper-level managers hold the insight that obtaining solutions through online knowledge consultation might not be exactly fine-tuned to the customer's individual situation and might highly dependent on the effectiveness of their staff members' search skills and the completeness of the knowledge database, whereas active support community usage allows customer organizations to have more control over support, gain the opportunity to improve the service offering they receive, and actively discuss problems with peer customers (Bone et al. 2015; Chan et al. 2010). Therefore, it appears that upper-level managers, within the emerging web-based support services, do not fear for a dark side of community rather they fear for a dark side of static knowledge consultation.

The above insights bring inherent channel guidance recommendations. Support service providers could create a win-win situation by steering away support users from traditional service requests. This traditional model is usually costly for the service provider (Bone et al. 2015), and our results show that both service users and upper-level managers become dissatisfied from using this support option. In addition, with respect to web-based support service, service providers should aim to activate customers instead of having them only lurk in communities, since online knowledge consultation decreases upper management satisfaction and active community support usages increases upper management satisfaction. An alternative approach is that service providers could highlight the benefits of and aim to create leverage for passive web-based support services among upper-level managers. While upper-level managers may hold the view that in web-based support active engagement is a prerequisite (upper management might want solutions rather than just reading and browsing), service providers should inform them that mere lurking also provides value and is not a waste of company resources.

Further Research Opportunities

While this study did take the unit of analysis past the individual level, there are a variety of other job functions in a firm that we did not examine. Future research should shed light on how other various job functions view and use online support communities. Given the field nature of our study, we were not able to identify any mediating or moderating factors in our study. It would be interesting if researchers could experimentally test these findings in order to identify some of the underlying mechanisms explaining our findings. Hereby one could consider the role of perceived benefits and costs, leakage of information, reduced on increased effectiveness and efficiency, and so on. Further, future research should study the net effect of operating web-based support, as called for by Libai et al. (2010). Finally, we emphasize that while our study provides an illustrative example of how diferent community support activities create satisfaction in a Fortune 500 company, more research is required with richer data.

NOTES

1. To be concise throughout this manuscript, we use the term "user" to denote the customer support user. In a B2B setting, the support user is not necessarily the product user. It occurs that product users contact an internal support department within their customer organization, which in turn contacts (i.e., uses the support of) the service provider.
2. In practice both users and upper-level managers will (partially) pursue their organization's interest and (partially) their own job function and career interest. Despite this communality the main insight here is that upper-level managers and users have different job functions bearing different responsibilities: an important part of upper-level managers' job function is to have a long-term

strategic focus and make sure their staff members are acting in their organization's best interest. In contrast, an important part of the users' job function is to have a short-term, day-to-day orientation and solve daily support issues.

3. Since we log-transformed our independent variables we essentially estimated a level-log model. We also re-estimated our model after log-transforming our dependent variable and hence investigated a log-log model. Results of the log-log model are substantially very similar to the results of the reported level-log model.

4. We also estimated our model with an orthogonal rotation method. Results are similar, only exception is the diminished significance (from 5% to 10% significance level) of the effect of active community usage on upper management satisfaction.

5. We also compared whether the satisfaction implications of various support channels differ between users and upper-level managers by means of a pooled regression with interaction effects between job level and support channel. Results indicate that upper-level managers do not differ in their reaction towards service request activity ($\beta_{\text{service requests * upper-level managers}} = 0.02$, n.s.), become dissatisfied instead of satisfied from online knowledge consultation ($\beta_{\text{online knowledge consultation * upper-level managers}} = -0.16$, $p < 0.05$), and do not differ in their reaction towards active community support usage ($\beta_{\text{active community usage * upper-level managers}} = -0.04$, n.s.)

References

Algesheimer, R., Dholakia, U. M., & Herrmann, A. (2005). The Social Influence of Brand Community: Evidence from European Car Clubs. *Journal of Marketing, 69*(3), 19–34.

Algesheimer, R., Borle, S., Dholakia, U. M., & Singh, S. S. (2010). The Impact of Customer Community Participation on Customer Behaviors: An Empirical Investigation. *Marketing Science, 29*(4), 756–769.

Anderson, J. C., & Narus, J. A. (1990). A Model of Distributor Firm and Manufacturer Firm Working Partnerships. *Journal of Marketing, 54*(1), 42–58.

Bagozzi, R. P., & Dholakia, U. M. (2006). Open Source Software User Communities: A Study of Participation in Linux User Groups. *Management Science, 52*(7), 1099–1115.

Bitner, M.-J., Booms, B. H., & Mohr, M. S. (1994). The Service Encounter: Diagnosing Favorable and Unfavorable Incidents. *Journal of Marketing, 54*(1), 71–84.

Bolton, R. N., Lemon, K. N., & Bramlett, M. D. (2006). The Effect of Service Experiences Over Time on a Supplier's Retention of Business Customers. *Management Science, 52*(12), 1811–1823.

Bone, S. A., Fombelle, P. W., Ray, K. R., & Lemon, K. N. (2015). How Customer Participation in B2B Peer-to-Peer Problem-Solving Communities Influences the Need for Traditional Customer Service. *Journal of Service Research, 18*(1), 23–38.

Brodie, R. J., Ilic, A., Juric, B., & Hollebeek, L. D. (2013). Consumer Engagement in a Virtual Brand Community: An Exploratory Analysis. *Journal of Business Research*, *66*(1), 105–114.

Bruhn, M., Schnebelen, S., & Schäfer, D. (2013). Antecedents and Consequences of the Quality of e-Customer-to-Customer Interactions in B2B Brand Communities. *Industrial Marketing Management*, *43*, 164–176.

Byrne, B. M. (2001). *Structural Equation Modeling with AMOS: Basic Concepts, Applications, and Programming*. Mahwah: Lawrence Erlbaum Associates.

CA Technologies. (2011). *The Avoidable Cost of Downtime*. Available at: http://www.ca.com/~/media/Files/SupportingPieces/acd_report_110110.ashx. Accessed 4 Dec 2014.

Challagalla, G., Venkatesh, R., & Kohli, A. K. (2009). Proactive Postsales Service: When and Why Does It Pay Off? *Journal of Marketing*, *73*(2), 70–87.

Chan, K. W., Yim, C. K., & Lam, S. S. K. (2010). Is Customer Participation in Value Creation a Double-Edged Sword? Evidence from Professional Financial Services Across Cultures. *Journal of Marketing*, *74*(3), 48–64.

Chan, K. W., Yiyam, S., & Zhu, J. J. (2015). Fostering Customer Ideation in Crowdsourcing Community: The Role of Peer-to-Peer and Peer-to-Firm Interactions. *Journal of Interactive Marketing*, *31*, 42–62.

Das, A. (2003). Knowledge and Productivity in Technical Support Work. *Management Science*, *49*(4), 416–431.

De Almeida, S. O., Dholakia, U. M., Hernandex, J. M. C., & Mazzon, J. A. (2014). The Mixed Effects of Participant Diversity and Expressive Freedom in Online Peer-to-Peer Problem Solving Communities. *Journal of Interactive Marketing*, *28*, 196–209.

De Valck, K., Van Bruggen, G. H., & Wierenga, B. (2009). Virtual Communities: A Marketing Perspective. *Decision Support Systems*, *47*, 185–203.

Dholakia, U. M., Blazevic, V., Wiertz, C., & Algesheimer, R. (2009). Communal Service Delivery: How Customers Benefit from Participation in Firm-Hosted Virtual P3 Communities. *Journal of Service Research*, *12*(2), 208–226.

Eisenhardt, K. M. (1989). Agency Theory: An Assessment and Review. *The Academy of Management Review*, *14*(1), 57–74.

El Sawy, O. A., & Bowles, G. (1997). Redesigning the Customer Support Process for the Electronic Economy: Insights from Storage Dimensions. *MIS Quarterly*, *21*(4), 457–483.

Gletcher, A. (2016). *5 Steps to Build an Impressive B2B Account-Based Marketing Framework*. http://www.business2community.com/b2b-marketing/5-steps-build-impressive-b2b-account-based-marketing-framework-01476070#G34T SSJXmxiu01qd.97. Accessed 18 Feb 2017.

Gruen, T. W., Osmonbekov, T., & Czaplewski, A. C. (2006). eWOM: The Impact of Customer-to-Customer Online Know-How Exchange on Customer Value and Loyalty. *Journal of Business Research*, *59*, 449–456.

Homburg, C., Ehm, L., & Artz, M. (2015). Measuring and Managing Consumer Sentiment in an Online Community Environment. *Journal of Marketing Research, 52*(5), 629–641.

Hoyer, W. D., Chandy, R., Dorotic, M., Krafft, M., & Singh, S. S. (2010). Consumer Co-creation in New Product Development. *Journal of Service Research, 13*(3), 283–296.

Karpen, I. O., Bove, L. L., Lukas, B. A., & Zyphur, M. J. (2015). Service-Dominant Orientation: Measurement and Impact on Performance Outcomes. *Journal of Retailing, 91*(1), 89–108.

Katzenbach, J. R., & Santamaria, J. A. (1999). Firing up the Frontline. *Harvard Business Review, 77*(3), 107–117.

Khansa, L., Ma, X., Linginlal, D., & Kim, S. S. (2015). Understanding Members' Active Participation in Online Question-and-Answer Communities: A Theory and Empirical Analysis. *Journal of Management Information Systems, 32*(2), 162–203.

Krush, M. T., Pennington, J. R., Fowler, A. R., III, & Mittelstaedt, J. D. (2015). Positive Marketing: A New Theoretical Prototype of Sharing in an Online Community. *Journal of Business Research, 68*, 2503–2512.

Leal, G. P. A., Hor-Meyll, L. F., & De Paula Pessôa, L. A. G. (2014). Influence of Virtual Communities in Purchasing Decisions: The Participants' Perspective. *Journal of Business Research, 67*, 882–890.

Lee, H. M., & Van Dolen, W. (2015). Creative Participation: Collective Sentiment in Online Co-creation Communities. *Information & Management, 52*, 951–964.

Libai, B., Bolton, R. N., Bügel, M. S., De Ruyter, K., Götz, O., Risselada, H., & Stephen, A. T. (2010). Customer to Customer Interactions: Broadening the Scope of Word of Mouth Research. *Journal of Service Research, 13*(3), 267–282.

Manchanda, P., Packard, G., & Pattabhiramaiah, A. (2015). Social Dollars: The Economic Impact of Customer Participation in a Firm-Sponsored Online Customer Community. *Marketing Science, 34*(3), 367–387.

Markeset, T., & Kumar, U. (2005). Product Support Strategy: Conventional Versus Functional Products. *Journal of Quality in Maintenance Engineering, 11*(1), 53–67.

Mashable. (2011). *10 Tips for Better B2B Community Management.* http://mashable.com/2011/07/11/b2b-community-management/#Do4jBlaab8qH. Accessed 18 Feb 2017.

Mathwick, C., Wiertz, C., & De Ruyter, K. (2008). Social Capital Production in a Virtual P3 Community. *Journal of Consumer Research, 34*(6), 832–849.

McAlexander, J. H., Schouten, J. W., & Koenig, H. F. (2002). Building Brand Community. *Journal of Marketing, 66*(1), 38–54.

Nambisan, S. (2002). Designing Virtual Customer Environments for New Product Development: Toward a Theory. *Academy of Management Review, 27*(3), 392–413.

Nambisan, S., & Baron, R. A. (2007). Interactions in Virtual Customer Environments: Implications for Product Support and Customer Relationship Management. *Journal of Interactive Marketing, 21*(2), 42–62.

Nambisan, S., & Baron, R. A. (2010). Different Roles, Different Strokes: Organizing Virtual Customer Environments to Promote Two Types of Customer Contributions. *Organization Studies, 21*(2), 554–572.

Negash, S., Ryan, T., & Igbaria, M. (2003). Quality and Effectiveness in Web-Based Customer Support Systems. *Information and Management, 40*(8), 757–768.

Piccoli, G., Ahmad, R., & Ives, B. (2001). Virtual Learning Environments: A Research Framework and a Preliminary Assessment of Effectiveness in Basic IT Skills Training. *MIS Quarterly, 25*(4), 401–426.

Porter, C. E., & Donthu, N. (2008). Cultivating Trust and Harvesting Value in Virtual Communities. *Management Science, 54*(1), 113–128.

Porter, C. E., Donthu, N., MacElroy, W. H., & Wydra, D. (2011). How to Foster and Sustain Engagement in Virtual Communities. *California Management Review, 53*(4), 80–110.

Rosenbaum, M. S. (2008). Return on Community for Consumers and Service Establishments. *Journal of Service Research, 11*(2), 179–196.

Rossiter, J. R. (2002). The C-OAR-SE Procedure for Scale Development. *International Journal of Research in Marketing, 19*, 305–335.

Rust, R. T., & Huang, M.-H. (2012). Optimizing Service Productivity. *Journal of Marketing, 76*(2), 47–66.

Schau, H. J., Muñiz, A. M., Jr., & Arnould, E. J. (2009). How Brand Community Practices Create Value. *Journal of Marketing, 73*(5), 30–51.

Thompson, S. A., & Sinha, R. K. (2008). Brand Communities and New Product Adoption: The Influence and Limits of Oppositional Loyalty. *Journal of Marketing, 72*(6), 65–80.

van der Heijden, G. A. H., Schepers, J. J. L., Nijssen, E. J., & Ordanini, A. (2013). Don't Just Fix It, Make It Better! Using Frontline Service Employees to Improve Recovery Performance. *Journal of the Academy of Marketing Science, 41*(5), 515–530.

Van Doorn, J., Lemon, K. N., Mittal, V., Naß, S., Pick, D., Pirner, P., & Verhoef, P. C. (2010). Customer Engagement Behavior: Theoretical Foundations and Research Directions. *Journal of Service Research, 13*(3), 253–266.

Wasko, M. M., & Faraj, S. (2000). It Is What One Does: Why People Participate and Help Others in Electronic Communities of Practice. *Journal of Strategic Information Systems, 9*, 155–173.

Webster, F. E., Jr., & Wind, Y. (1972). A General Model for Understanding Organizational Buying Behavior. *The Journal of Marketing, 36*, 12–19.

Wiertz, C., & Ruyter, D. (2007). Beyond the Call of Duty: Why Customers Contribute to Firm-Hosted Commercial Online Communities. *Organization Studies, 28*(3), 347–376.

Zhou, Z., Zhang, Q., Su, C., & Zhou, N. (2012). How Do Brand Communities Generate Brand Relationships? Intermediate Mechanisms. *Journal of Business Research, 65*, 890–895.

Zhou, Z., Wu, J. P., Zhang, Q., & Xu, S. (2013). Transforming Visitors into Members in Online Brand Communities: Evidence from China. *Journal of Business Research, 66*, 2438–2443.

Zhu, R., Dholakia, U. M., Chen, X., & Algesheimer, R. (2012). Does Online Community Participation Foster Risky Financial Behavior? *Journal of Marketing Research, 49*(3), 394–407.

PART II

Consequences of Customer Engagement

CHAPTER 8

Customer Engagement and Employee Engagement: A Research Review and Agenda

Vikas Mittal, Kyuhong Han, and Robert A. Westbrook

Customers and employees are among the two most important stakeholders that create value for a firm. While customers are the primary source of cash flow for a firm (Gupta and Zeithaml 2006), employees create customer value by transforming raw materials and other inputs into products and services that satisfy customer needs (Heskett et al. 1994; Loveman 1998). Ongoing customer and employee engagement enables firms to create sustainable competitive advantage (Groening et al. 2016; Homburg et al. 2009a).

A Gallup meta-analysis reports that US work units with high employee engagement (i.e., in the top quartile) outperform those with low employee engagement (i.e., in the bottom quartile) by 21% in productivity and 22% in profitability. In the United States, the cost of active employee disengagement is estimated to be between $450 billion and $550 billion per year (O'Boyle and Harter 2013). Concurrently, Gallup suggests that engaged customers generate a premium of 23% for firms in terms of profitability and revenue.[1] An emerging body of academic research has examined the association between customer engagement and employee engagement and their effect on firm financial performance (Brodie et al. 2011; Hogreve et al. 2016; Kumar and Pansari 2016). In this chapter, we review extant research, highlight key issues that scholars and managers should consider, and develop a framework (see Fig. 8.1) for understanding and implementing engagement initiatives in firms.

V. Mittal (✉) • K. Han • R.A. Westbrook
Rice University, Houston, TX, USA

© The Author(s) 2018
R.W. Palmatier et al. (eds.), *Customer Engagement Marketing*,
DOI 10.1007/978-3-319-61985-9_8

173

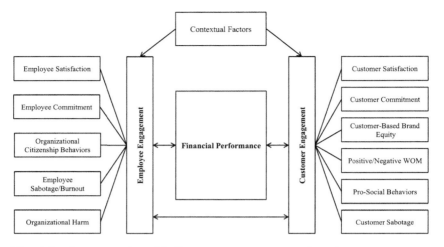

Fig. 8.1   A conceptual model of customer engagement and employee engagement

HOW CUSTOMERS AND EMPLOYEES AFFECT ORGANIZATIONAL PERFORMANCE

The exchange perspective (Bagozzi 1975) examines how customers and employees affect organizational performance. In exchange for goods and services that satisfy their needs, customers provide a firm with monetary and nonmonetary value. Monetary value accrues to the firm in the form of the price customers pay for the goods or services. Nonmonetary value accrues in the form of referrals and recommendations to others, positive reviews, and other behaviors that strengthen the firm's ability to increase revenues from other customers (Van Doorn et al. 2010). Employees, in exchange for wages and benefits, provide value to the firm by creating products and performing services that satisfy customer needs (Payne and Webber 2006). In other words, firms are able to satisfy their customers' needs based on the activities of their employees.

A large number of studies separately measure the association of customer engagement and employee engagement with organizational performance. Regarding customer engagement, research shows several customer-related constructs that are positively associated with increased firm performance, including customer satisfaction (Anderson et al. 1994, 2000; Morgan and Rego 2006), customer commitment (Keiningham et al. 2015), customer-based brand equity (Rego et al. 2009), and customer word of mouth (Chevalier and Mayzlin 2006). Similarly, employee-based constructs associated with firm performance include employee satisfaction (Harter et al. 2002), employee engagement (Saks 2006), and employee commitment (Arthur 1994). Surprisingly, however, very few studies show a direct impact of employee-based constructs on a firm's financial performance. Some studies show that a firm's financial performance affects job satisfaction among employees (e.g., Bagozzi 1980), and still others show that employee-related constructs are associated with firm performance through customer-related constructs (e.g., Evanschitzky et al. 2012b; Homburg et al. 2009b). The latter set of studies suggests that employee engagement may be associated with firm performance only in the presence of customer engagement.

CUSTOMER ENGAGEMENT AND EMPLOYEE ENGAGEMENT: DEFINITION

Van Doorn et al. (2010) differentiate customer engagement from related constructs, such as brand engagement and customer commitment. Taking a behavior-based perspective, the authors define customer engagement as

> the customers' behavioral manifestation toward a brand or firm, beyond purchase, resulting from motivational drivers. CEBs *(customer engagement behaviors)* include a vast array of behaviors including word-of-mouth (WOM) activity, recommendations, helping other customers, blogging, writing reviews, and even engaging in legal action. (Van Doorn et al. 2010, p. 253, italics added)

Van Doorn and colleagues acknowledge that customer engagement is a consequence of motivational drivers, such as customer satisfaction, customer trust/commitment, and brand performance.

Regarding employee engagement, there is considerable confusion about its definition and measurement. Saks (2006) notes that employee engagement is often confused with constructs such as commitment, organizational citizenship behavior (the opposite of job burnout), and so forth. Robinson et al. (2004) express surprise at the lack of academic research, both theoretical and empirical, on a topic with such high managerial relevance. Harter et al. (2002, p. 269) define employee engagement as "the individual's involvement and satisfaction with as well as enthusiasm for work." Differentiating employee engagement from employee satisfaction, they use

12 items to measure various aspects of employee engagement, with the caveat that each of the items is actionable by an employee's supervisor. More recently, Kumar and Pansari (2016, p. 498) have defined customer and employee engagement with a broader conceptualization of engagement:

> Engagement ...represents cocreation, interaction, solution development, and so on, all of which depend on the attitude that drives the behavior of customers and employees toward a firm. We define engagement as the attitude, behavior, the level of connectedness (1) among customers, (2) between customers and employees, and (3) of customers and employees within a firm.

According to this definition, behavior is a foundational element of engagement, with the explicit acknowledgment that the behaviors are causally driven by customers' and employees' attitudes toward a firm. Thus, engagement *may* be measured using attitudinal metrics such as satisfaction, but it *must* be conceptualized in terms of behaviors. As such, the ideal scale would tap into key behaviors that emanate from specific attitudes toward a firm.

This review recognizes that engagement is a qualitatively different construct from satisfaction or loyalty. Yet it includes studies that measure both to provide a better understanding of pertinent issues that can be addressed in future research.

THEORETICALLY INTEGRATING CUSTOMER ENGAGEMENT AND EMPLOYEE ENGAGEMENT

Customer engagement and employee engagement are driven by motivational forces based on attitudinal constructs such as satisfaction (Anderson et al. 2000; Harter et al. 2002), commitment (Keiningham et al. 2015), attachment (Schau et al. 2009), and identification (Homburg et al. 2009b). By definition, engagement is a behavioral construct, with an exchange-based component. Thus, a specific customer or a specific employee is engaged with an entity, such as a brand, a firm, and/or stakeholders associated with the brand or firm. In many instances, a specific customer or a specific employee may be simultaneously engaged with multiple exchange partners. For example, the items in the Gallup's employee engagement survey measure how employees engage with multiple entities, such as the workplace, their supervisor, their associates, fellow employees, and the company (see Table 8.1 in Harter et al. 2002, p. 269).

Similarly, customer engagement behaviors of a specific customer are likely to involve multiple entities, such as service employees, colleagues, friends, family, other customers, competitor companies, and the brand (Van Doorn et al. 2010). In the case of customer engagement, there are also multiple behaviors directed toward and performed by these different entities. For example, a focal customer's colleagues, friends, and family may become instrumental in engagement by being involved in word-of-mouth and social media activities. Similarly, competitor brands, through comparison shopping, may provide a forum and an opportunity to increase or decrease a customer's level of engagement.

Earlier research on this issue is rooted in the service-profit chain (SPC) paradigm, according to which employee effort is considered an input to customer satisfaction and customer satisfaction is considered an input to customer loyalty as well as firm financial outcomes (e.g., Kamakura et al. 2002). Most of the empirical research using the SPC paradigm generally confirms the positive association between customer satisfaction and downstream firm outcomes, though the association of employee satisfaction with customer satisfaction and firm financial outcomes is tenuous (Frennea et al. 2013). The SPC paradigm may be limiting in terms of understanding engagement because it is based on a systems approach that is more mechanistic than organic. Within a mechanistic approach, most relationships are unidirectional, with little or no room for contingent associations (Frennea et al. 2013).

Two theoretical perspectives are important for further understanding the interplay between customer engagement and employee engagement. From a macro-perspective, stakeholder theory explains how different levels of engagement by two key stakeholders—customers and employees—can affect financial consequences for a firm (Donaldson and Preston 1995). Recent empirical evidence shows that simultaneously achieving positive outcomes for customers and employees can increase firm value in the long run (Groening et al. 2016). Thus, engaging customers and employees should not be viewed as a zero-sum game. Rather, there is a symbiotic and mutually reinforcing association between fulfilling both customers' *and* employees' interests.

The micro-foundations for understanding the interplay between customer engagement and employee engagement can be traced to generalized exchange theory or GET (Bearman 1997; Marshall 1998; Molm et al. 2007). GET goes beyond dyadic exchanges and examines three or more

Table 8.1   Customer engagement, employee engagement, and financial performance

Paper	Data type	Industry (unit of analysis)	Sample	Matched employees and customers	Lag between EE and CE	Analysis
Bernhardt et al. (2000)	Cross-sectional	Restaurant (store)	3009 employees 342,308 customers 8 waves (12 months) From 382 stores (employee) and 432 stores(customer)			Correlation analysis
Bettencourt and Brown (1997)	Cross-sectional	Bank (branch)	50 managers 232 tellers From 50 branches	✓[b]		Correlation analysis
Brown and Chin (2004)	Cross-sectional	Manufacturing (individual)	248 employees 3926 customers	✓		Partial least squares
Brown and Lam (2008)	Meta-analysis	(Research paper)	22 papers			Meta-analysis SEM
Brown and Mitchell (1993)	Cross-sectional	Bank (branch)	93 employees 5490 customers from 52 branches			Correlation analysis
Chi and Gursoy (2009)	Cross-sectional	Hotel (hotel)	2023 employees 3346 customers From 250 hotels			SEM
Chuang et al. (2012)	Cross-sectional	Services (individual)	55 managers 214 employees 210 customers From 52 stores	✓[b]		HLM
Evanschitzky et al. (2011)	Cross-sectional	Retail (individual)	50 owner–franchisees 933 employees 20,742 customers From 50 outlets			SEM HLM

Effect size of EE–CE[a]	Mediator of EE–CE	Moderator of EE–CE	Relationship of EE and CE with financial performance[a]
ES–CS (r = .53, p < .05)			CS(t)–Profit(t)/Sales(t) (r = 0.04, n.s./r = 0.05, n.s.) ES(t)–Profit(t)/Sales(t) (r = 0.05, n.s./r = 0.07, n.s.) ΔCS(t − 1)–ΔProfit(t)/ΔSales(t) (r = 0.42, p < 0.05)
ES–CS (r = −0.05, n.s.)			
ES → CS (b = .07, n.s.)	Employee-perceived service performance Customer-perceived service quality		
ES–CS (r = 0.23, p < 0.05)	Customer-perceived service quality	Personal vs. nonpersonal service Encounter vs. relationship business B2B vs. B2C contexts Level of analysis (individual vs. organizational unit) Timing sequence of surveys (employee first vs. concurrent) Measurement scales (global ES vs. ES by job facet)	
ES–CS (n.s.)			
ES → CS (b = 0.34, t = 5.93)			CS → Financial performance [Profitability/ROI/Net profit] (b = 0.24, t = 6.30) ES → Financial performance (b = 0.09, n.s.) ES → CS → Financial performance (b = 0.08, t = 4.40)
ES → CS (b = .28, p < .01)	Service performance		
ES → CS (b_{SEM} = 0.24, p < 0.01; b_{HLM} = 0.07, p < 0.05)			

(*continued*)

Table 8.1 (continued)

Paper	Data type	Industry (unit of analysis)	Sample	Matched employees and customers	Lag between EE and CE	Analysis
Evanschitzky et al. (2012a)	Cross-sectional	B2B bank (individual)	18 employees 188 customers	✓		HLM
Evanschitzky et al. (2012b)	Panel	Retail (outlet)	7668/6040/2755 employees 44,965/100,351/161,922 customers 3 periods (year) From 119 outlets		✓c	3SLS
Frey et al. (2013)	Experiment Field study: Cross-sectional	B2B services (individual)	Experiment: 172 MBA students Field study: 112 dyads of professional services employees and clients	✓		Experiment: MANOVA Field study: SEM
Gazzoli et al. (2013)	Cross-sectional	Restaurant (individual)	186 employees 1117 customers From 11 restaurants	✓		Correlation analysis
Gounaris and Boukis (2013)	Cross-sectional	Bank (individual)	183 employees 604 customers From 15 branches			HLM path analysis
Grandey et al. (2011)	Cross-sectional	Warehouse retail (store)	328 stores		✓	Regression analysis
Harter et al. (2002)	Meta-analysis	Multi-industry (business unit)	Employee: 42 studies (198,514 employees from 7939 business units in 36 companies) Customer: 24 studies (20 companies) Performance: 3–28 studies			Correlation analysis
Hogreve et al. (2016)	Meta-analysis	(Research paper)	518 studies (576 independent datasets with 1591 correlations)			Meta-analytic SEM
Homburg and Stock (2004)	Cross-sectional	B2B manufacturing and services (individual)	164 employees 328 customers	✓		SEM
Homburg and Stock (2005)	Cross-sectional	B2B manufacturing and services (individual)	164 employees 328 customers	✓		SEM

Effect size of EE–CE[a]	Mediator of EE–CE	Moderator of EE–CE	Relationship of EE and CE with financial performance[a]
ES → CS (b = 0.205, t = 2.921)			
ES → CS (b = .218, t = 3.20)			CS(t − 1) → Operating profit(t) (b = 66,513.17, t = 5.96) CS(t) → Operating profit(t) (b = 12,219.02, n.s.) ES(t − 1) → Operating profit(t) (b = −21,403.43, n.s.)
Experiment: CS → ES (b = 0.66, p < 0.01) Field study: CS → ES (b = 0.34, p < 0.01)	Perceived appreciation	Employee–client attitudinal congruency	
ES–CS (r = 0.10, p < 0.05)			
ES → CS (b = 0.50, p < .001)		Branch size Employee age	
ES → CS (b = 0.25, p < 0.01)	Employee responsiveness	Store busyness	
EE–CS (r = 0.16)			EE–Profitability (r = 0.10) EE–Productivity (r = 0.15)
ES → CS (b = 0.081, p < 0.01)		Service intangibility	• CS → Profitability (b = 0.105, p < 0.01) ES → Profitability (b = −0.014, p < 0.01)
ES → CS (b = 0.24, p < 0.05)	Quality of customer interaction	• Frequency of customer interaction • Intensity of customer integration into the value-creating process Product/service innovativeness	
ES → CS (b = 0.34, t = 8.53)	Employee's customer orientation	Employee empathy Employee expertise Employee reliability Customer trust Customer price consciousness Customer importance of product/service	

(*continued*)

Table 8.1 (continued)

Paper	Data type	Industry (unit of analysis)	Sample	Matched employees and customers	Lag between EE and CE	Analysis
Homburg et al. (2009)	Cross-sectional	Travel agency (individual)	258 employees 597 customers From 109 travel agencies	✓		HLM path analysis
Hur et al. (2015)	Cross-sectional	Senior care service (individual)	282 employees 282 customers	✓		SEM
Jeon and Choi (2012)	Cross-sectional	Private education (individual)	277 employees 277 customers	✓		SEM
Koys (2001)	Panel	Restaurant (store)	64/79 managers 774/693 employees 5565/4338 customers 2 periods (year)		✓	Regression analysis
Kumar and Pansari (2016)	Panel	Multi-industry (firm)	120 public firms 2 periods (year)		✓c	HLM
Loveman (1998)	Cross-sectional	Bank (branch)	409–955 branches			Regression analysis
Namasivayam et al. (2014)	Cross-sectional	Restaurant (unit)	238 employees 2915 customers From 40 units			SEM
Netemeyer et al. (2010)	Cross-sectional	Clothing and accessories (individual)	306 managers 1615 employees 57,656 customers From 306 stores	✓		HLM path model
Ostroff (1992)	Cross-sectional	School (school)	13,808 teachers 24,874 students From 193–298 schools			Correlation analysis

Effect size of EE–CE[a]	Mediator of EE–CE	Moderator of EE–CE	Relationship of EE and CE with financial performance[a]
ES → CS (b = 0.024, t = 0.79)	Customer orientation		CS–Financial performance [sales per employee] (r = −0.06, n.s.) ES–Financial performance [sales per employee] (r = −0.07, n.s.)
ES → CS (b = 0.34, p < 0.01)			
ES → CS (b = 0.133, t = 2.660) CS → ES (b = 0.051, t = 0.439)		Employee self-efficacy Employee cooperative orientation Employee perceived fairness Employee perceived supervisory support	
• ES(t1) → CS(t2) (b = 0.62, p < .01) CS(t1) → ES(t2) (b = 0.39/0.34, n.s.).			ES(t1) → Profit(t2)/Profit-to-sales(t2) (b = 0.06, n.s./b = 0.15, n.s.)
ΔEE → ΔCE (b = 0.510, p < 0.001)		B2B vs. B2C firms Manufacturing vs. services firms Employee empowerment	ΔEE → ΔRevenue/ΔNet income (b = 0.377, p < 0.001/b = 0.352, p < 0.001) ΔCE → ΔRevenue/ΔNet income (b = 0.631, p < 0.001/b = 0.622, p < 0.001)
ES with company → CS (b = 1.9, p < 0.05) ES with job → CS (b = 1.3, p < 0.05) ES → CS (b = 0.42, p < 0.01)			
Manager satisfaction → CS (b = 0.30, t = 5.29) ES → CS (b = 0.17, t = 2.93)			• Manager satisfaction → Average customer transaction value (b = 0.29, t = 5.39) ES → Average customer transaction value (b = 0.04, n.s.) CS → Average customer transaction value (b = 0.13, t = 2.43)
Teacher satisfaction– student satisfaction with the teachers (r = 0.24) Teacher satisfaction– student overall satisfaction (r = 0.44)			

(continued)

Table 8.1   (continued)

Paper	Data type	Industry (unit of analysis)	Sample	Matched employees and customers	Lag between EE and CE	Analysis
Pantouvakis and Bouranta (2013)[d]	Cross-sectional	Shipping (individual)	168 employees			SEM
Payne and Webber (2006)	Cross-sectional	Hairstylists (individual)	249 employees 249 customers	✓		Correlation analysis
Pritchard and Silvestro (2005)	Cross-sectional	Home improvement store (store)	Number of employees not reported Over 24,000 customers From 75 stores			Correlation analysis
Reynierse and Harker (1992)	Cross-sectional	Bank (branch)	145 customer service representatives 322 tellers 4065 customers From 79 branches			Correlation analysis
Ryan et al. (1996)	Panel	Finance (branch)	142 branches 2 periods (year)	✓		SEM
Schlesinger and Zornitsky (1991)[d]	Cross-sectional	Insurance (individual)	1277 employees 4269 customers			Correlation analysis
Siddiqi and Sahaf (2009)	Cross-sectional	Bank (Branch)	211 employees 630 customers From several branches of 4 banks	✓		Regression analysis
Silvestro and Cross (2000)	Cross-sectional	Grocery retail (store)	6 stores			Correlation analysis
Steinke (2008)[d]	Cross-sectional	Emergency department (individual)	180 nurses			SEM

Effect size of EE–CE[a]	Mediator of EE–CE	Moderator of EE–CE	Relationship of EE and CE with financial performance[a]
ES → CS (b = 0.24, t = 3.35)	Interactive service feature		
ES–CS (r = 0.137, p = 0.031)		Employee affective commitment	
ES–CS (r = −0.044, n.s.)			ES–Revenue growth/Profit (r = 0.279, p < .02/r = 0.131, n.s.) ES–Sales per staff/Sales per square foot (r = −0.268, p < 0.05/ r = 0.097, n.s.) CS–Revenue growth/Profit (r = −0.038, n.s./r = −0.016, n.s.) CS–Sales per staff/Sales per square foot (r = −0.079, n.s./r = −0.312, p < .01)
ES–CS (r = +, p < 0.05)			
ES(t1)–CS(t2) (r = 0.19, p < .05) ES(t2)–CS(t2) (r = 0.18, n.s.) ES–CS (r = 0.18, p < 0.01)			
ES → CS (b = .37, p < 0.001)			
ES–CS (r = −0.64, n.s.)			ES–Profit margin (r = −0.87, p < 0.05) ES–Sales per square foot (r = −0.61, n.s.) CS–Profit margin (r = 0.70, n.s.) CS–Sales per square foot (r = 0.59, n.s.)
ES–CS (r = 0.31, p < 0.01)			

(continued)

Table 8.1 (continued)

Paper	Data type	Industry (unit of analysis)	Sample	Matched employees and customers	Lag between EE and CE	Analysis
Subramony et al. (2008)	Cross-sectional	Manufacturing and services (firm)	1530 employees From 126 companies	✓		SEM
Tornow and Wiley (1991)	Cross-sectional	Computer (business unit)	667 employees 633 customers From 30 business units			Correlation analysis
Ugboro and Obeng (2000)[d]	Cross-sectional	Multiple industries	250 employees			Correlation analysis
Wangenheim et al. (2007)	Cross-sectional	DIY retail (outlet)	1659 employees 53,645 customers From 99 outlets			SEM
Whitman et al. (2010)	Meta-analysis	(Unit-team, branch, organization)	60 articles (5849 units)			Correlation analysis
Wiley (1991)	Cross-sectional	Retail (store)	4854 employees 158,878 customers From 56 stores			Correlation analysis
Zablah et al. (2016)	Panel	Retail (individual)	1470 employees 49,242 customers 2 waves (year)	✓	✓	SEM

Notes: *B2B* business-to-business, *B2C* business-to-consumer, *CS* customer satisfaction, *CE* customer engagement, *ES* employee satisfaction, *EE* employee engagement, *HLM* hierarchical linear model, *MANOVA* multivariate analysis of variance, *ROI* return on investment, *SEM* structural equation model, and *3SLS* three-stage least squares, *DIY* do it yourself, *n.s.* not significant

[a]r indicates the correlation coefficient, b indicates the path/regression coefficient; direct effects are reported. For studies that do not provide significance levels, only effect sizes are reported. For studies that do not provide effect sizes, only the sign of the effects are reported

[b]Bettencourt and Brown's (1997) sample has matched tellers–customer service managers; however, customers are not matched with these employees

[c]Evanschitzky et al. (2012b) have time lags between the measurement of constructs but not between ES and CS. Kumar and Pansari (2016) measure the constructs as changes rather than as levels

[d]Pantouvakis and Bouranta (2013), Schlesinger and Zornitsky (1991), Steinke (2008), and Ugboro and Obeng (2000) measure employees' perceived level of customer satisfaction

[e]Whitman et al. (2010) measure of productivity includes various financial (e.g., ROI, sales, financial growth) and nonfinancial (e.g., academic competency, innovation rate) measures

Effect size of EE–CE[a]	Mediator of EE–CE	Moderator of EE–CE	Relationship of EE and CE with financial performance[a]
ES → CS (b = 0.34, p < 0.01)			
ES with company–CS (r = +, p < 0.05) ES with job–CS (r = +, p < 0.05) ES–CS (r = 0.60, p = 0.00 for manufacturing firms; r = 0.67, p = 0.00 for service firms)		Manufacturing vs. service firms	CS–Gross profit (r = n.s.) ES with company–Gross profit (r = n.s.) ES with job–Gross profit (r = n.s.)
ES → CS (b = 0.27, p < 0.01)		Employee group (storeroom workers, cashiers, services and sales employees)	
ES–CS (r = 0.34, p < 0.05)			ES–Productivity[c] (r = 0.29, p < 0.05)
ES–CS (r = +, p < 0.01)			CS–Net sales/Net income (r = −, p < 0.01/r = −, p < 0.01)
ES(t1) → CS(t2) (b = 0.05, p < 0.01) CS(t1) → ES(t2) (b = 0.14, p < 0.01)			

actors who engage in a chain of indirect and reciprocal transfers among each other. Different from bilateral exchanges, such as those between a customer and an employee, GET recognizes the reality and importance of multilateral exchanges, such as those among the focal customer, other customers, service employees, and even potentially the managers of the service employees.

Evanschitzky et al. (2011) use GET to examine the reciprocal association between satisfaction levels of three actors in a do-it-yourself retailer context. They examine the relationships among customer satisfaction, customer loyalty (purchase intentions), frontline employee satisfaction, and employer/manager satisfaction. The results show a complex association among these constructs. Specifically, the association between employer satisfaction and customer satisfaction was fully mediated by frontline employee satisfaction. Frontline employee satisfaction not only directly affected customer satisfaction but also moderated the relationship between customer satisfaction and customer loyalty, such that customer satisfaction had a stronger association with customer loyalty when frontline employee satisfaction was relatively high than when it was relatively low.

In summary, supplementing the SPC model with stakeholder theory and with GET can provide a framework for better understanding the association between customer engagement and employee engagement. This approach also articulates the larger nomological and contextual network of constructs needed to understand customer engagement and employee engagement.

CUSTOMER ENGAGEMENT AND EMPLOYEE ENGAGEMENT: EMPIRICAL ASSESSMENT

Table 8.1 summarizes studies that simultaneously examine both customer engagement and employee engagement. For each study, the table describes the research setting (data, industry, sample size, unit analysis), methodological details (method of analysis, matched samples of employees and customers, lags between constructs), contingent factors (mediators and moderators), and the association of employee engagement and customer engagement with firm financial performance. Several important observations can be distilled from Table 8.1:

- Most studies, whether cross-sectional or longitudinal, support a statistically significant and positive association between employee engagement and customer engagement. However, the magnitude of the association varies substantially across studies. This may be due to potential moderators of the relationship at the individual, firm, and industry levels.

- Virtually all the studies support a strong, direct, and positive association between customer engagement and firm financial outcomes.
- There are divergent findings with regard to the association between employee engagement and firm financial outcomes. Table 8.1 includes 13 studies that investigate 22 associations between employee engagement and firm financial outcomes. Among these 22 associations, 13 are statistically nonsignificant, 6 are statistically significant and positive, and the remaining 3 are statistically significant and negative.
- Among these studies, 72.7% show a negative or nonexistent association between employee engagement and firm financial performance. Only 27.3% of the studies support the widely held lay belief that higher levels of employee engagement are financially beneficial for a firm.
- Overall, these empirical results suggest that theoretically the association between employee engagement and firm financial outcomes may best be conceptualized as being mediated by customer engagement.
- With the exception of Kumar and Pansari (2016) and Subramony et al. (2008), most of the studies in Table 8.1 are conducted within a single firm.
- Most studies are conducted in the business-to-consumer (B2C) context rather than the business-to-business (B2B) context (exceptions include Evanschitzky et al. 2012a; Frey et al. 2013; Homburg and Stock 2004, 2005).

Finally, it is notable that virtually all of the studies have taken a monovalent and unidirectional view of customer engagement and employee engagement. Specifically, it is assumed that engagement ranges from a person being disengaged to a person being positively engaged. However, as the literature on negative word of mouth (Luo 2009; Richins 1983), employee burnout (Jackson et al. 1986), and organizational sabotage by both customers (Reynolds and Harris 2009) and employees (Harris and Ogbonna 2006), shows active negative engagement is a reality. It is important to note here that negative engagement is not exactly the opposite of positive engagement. An asymmetry exists between the negative and the positive aspects of engagement (Singh and Sirdeshmukh 2000). The nature and magnitude of the antecedents and consequences of negative engagement are likely to differ from those associated with positive engagement. There are also likely to be differences among the interrelationships in positive and negative disengagement, both within and between customer engagement and employee engagement. Thus, measuring both the positive and negative domain of engagement should be a key priority for future research.

CUSTOMER ENGAGEMENT AND EMPLOYEE ENGAGEMENT: CONTINGENT FACTORS

Most studies examining employee engagement and customer engagement have been conducted within the context of a single firm, with a focus on ascertaining the focal relationships. As such, few, if any, studies have examined the moderated nature of the key relationships.

In a recent study, Kumar and Pansari (2016) examine the moderating effect of a firm's business type (B2B vs. B2C, manufacturing vs. services) on the association of employee engagement with customer engagement and firm financial performance. The authors find a positive association in both cases. Furthermore, they show that the effect of employee engagement on customer engagement and firm performance becomes stronger (1) for firms operating in a service (vs. manufacturing) sector and (2) for B2B (vs. B2C) firms.

Groening et al. (2016, p. 2) examine the role of firm business scope, defined as "the number of business segments in which a firm competes." They find that the joint effect of a firm's activities designed to affect customers and employees on firm value is stronger for firms with a narrower business scope than for those with a broader business scope. At a more granular level, Grandey et al. (2011) demonstrate that the relationship between employee satisfaction and customer satisfaction is stronger in busier than in slower stores.

Aspects of employee–customer relationships have also been examined as contingent factors. Wangenheim et al. (2007) find a moderating role of customer contact, such that the association of employee engagement with customer engagement is stronger for employees who have more direct contact with customers (e.g., service and sales employees). In a similar context, Homburg and Stock (2004) show that salespeople's job satisfaction has a stronger association with customer satisfaction when there are higher levels of interaction between the salesperson and the customer. Frey et al. (2013) show that attitudinal congruence between customers and employees strengthens the employee engagement–customer engagement association.

Studies also examine the moderating role of employee and customer perceptions on the association between employee engagement and customer engagement. Kumar and Pansari (2016) show that the association is stronger when employees are more empowered. Homburg and Stock (2005) find that employee empathy, expertise, and reliability as well as customer trust strengthen the association, whereas customer price consciousness weakens the association between the two constructs. Jeon and Choi (2012) demonstrate that employees' levels of self-efficacy and cooperative orientation strengthen the employee satisfaction–customer satisfaction relationship.

Many other psychological and sociological factors should be examined as potential moderators in future studies. These may include firm-level constructs, such as organizational identity (Homburg et al. 2009b), or individual-level constructs, such gender identity (Winterich et al. 2009), local–global identity (Gao et al. 2017), political identity (Winterich et al. 2012), and moral identity (Reed et al. 2007). For example, studies show that customers and employees with a stronger moral identity may be more willing to engage in prosocial behaviors, which in turn can improve a firm's financial outcomes (Bove et al. 2009; Shao et al. 2008). However, it is also possible that an increase in prosocial behaviors will distract employees from performing certain core functions designed to increase customer engagement. These are just some examples of potential moderating influences. There are many other possibilities for researchers to consider.

OUTCOMES OF CUSTOMER ENGAGEMENT AND EMPLOYEE ENGAGEMENT

As Table 8.1 shows, studies of employee engagement and customer engagement have focused on financial performance metrics, such as sales, revenue, and profit. A broader set of metrics—especially behavioral metrics—should be examined in future research.

In addition to separately measuring the positive and negative domain of engagement, research should also ascertain the outcomes of positive and negative engagement. Likely, they are not mere opposites of each other. In terms of positive customer engagement, a variety of consequences beyond customer loyalty could be examined. These may include prosocial customer behaviors, such as donating to charitable organizations associated with the firm or the brand (Varadarajan and Menon 1988). Do more engaged customers also display more environmentally friendly and sustainable behaviors, such as recycling and reusing? In contexts such as healthcare and education, would positive customer engagement result in higher levels of compliance and consequent outcome gains among patients and students? In contrast, negatively engaged customers (Harris and Reynolds 2003) can exhibit behaviors such as harming and mistreating employees and service providers (Reynolds and Harris 2006; Skarlicki et al. 2008), cheating and stealing from the firm (e.g., shoplifting; Babin and Babin 1996), and providing misleading and false feedback to other customers in social media forums (Tuzovic 2010).

Regarding employee engagement, research suggests that positively engaged employees may demonstrate extra-role behaviors in their jobs. According to McNeely and Meglino's (1994) definition, these extra-role behaviors include being receptive to new ideas, tolerating temporary inconveniences, using organizational resources judiciously, helping plan social events in the office, bringing food and gifts for coworkers, or donating to community organizations and charities (see also Van Dyne and LePine 1998). Mittal et al. (2007) suggest that more satisfied employees are better able to assess customer satisfaction because the gap between employee and customer perceptions of service quality is smaller for more satisfied employees. In terms of negative employee engagement, a substantial body of research shows that negatively engaged employees may indulge in service sabotage (Harris and Ogbonna 2006), customer sabotage (Skarlicki et al. 2008), and other acts of organizational harm (Ambrose et al. 2002).

Regarding firm performance, research should investigate the longitudinal effects of customer and employee engagement on firm's financial outcomes. As Evanschitzky et al. (2012b) argue, the consequences of customer and employee engagement may be realized in the long run rather than in the short run; as a result, making future investments based on short-term outcomes may backfire. Bernhardt et al. (2000) suggest patience in implementing customer and employee engagement programs because their impact may manifest only over a longer period of time. A major obstacle to conducting such studies would be the difficulty of collecting longitudinal data. An alternative approach would be linking these constructs to long-term financial performance metrics, such as firm value (Srinivasan and Hanssens 2009).

In summary, customer and employee engagement should be understood in terms of both positive and negative engagement. Initially, qualitative and inductive research methodologies will be required to address this issue

(Deshpande 1983), which may be followed by measuring constructs using formalized scales and then causally testing hypotheses through field and experimental studies. Investigating their long-term effects—financial and nonfinancial, positive and negative—should also be a research priority.

METHODOLOGICAL ISSUES IN EXAMINING CUSTOMER ENGAGEMENT AND EMPLOYEE ENGAGEMENT

The majority of the studies in Table 8.1 take a cross-sectional approach to quantify the association between customer engagement, employee engagement, and their outcomes. Most studies are conducted within the context of a single firm and rely only on survey data. Although some studies use matched samples of employees and customers to infer more accurate relationships between the constructs, such an approach—that is, single period, single firm, and an exclusive reliance on survey data—can preclude the ability to make strong causal conclusions. At the same time, obtaining organizational cooperation to collect multiperiod data that combines surveys and secondary data is time consuming and resource intensive. To this end, we advocate the use of traditional approaches used in consumer behavior research—namely, small-scale, randomized experiments conducted with consumers and employees that enhance the internal validity of key conclusions.

Kumar and Pansari (2016) are an exception to the traditional approach based on cross-sectional data from a single firm. They use data from multiple firms and multiple periods and combine survey data (on customer and employee engagement) and nonsurvey data (on financial performance). Their approach also enables an assessment of firm-level moderators of the key relationships. Future research should build on Kumar and Pansari's (2016) methodological paradigm. This may require larger research teams to gain the cooperation of many firms. If such large-scale data collection is possible, and with executive cooperation, there may be the possibility of conducting field experiments to better explicate cause-and-effect relationships.

It would also be useful to develop measures and indices of customer engagement and employee engagement that can correlate with secondary measures of the constructs. For example, Groening et al. (2016) find a positive association between survey-based measures of customer and employee satisfaction and secondary measures of customer- and employee-based achievements, obtained through Kinder, Lydenberg, Domini, & Co. More generally, academics and practitioners will benefit from continued tracking of customer engagement and employee engagement at the firm level by a neutral third party. Such data exist with regard to other constructs, such as customer satisfaction (e.g., the American Customer Satisfaction Index[2]) and brand equity (e.g., Harris Poll EquiTrend, Young & Rubicam's BrandAsset Valuator, YouGov's BrandIndex[3]). Sources of secondary measures of negative customer engagement can also be found. These include customer complaints compiled by regulatory agencies such as the US Department of Transportation[4] (for airline travel complaints) and the Consumer Financial Protection Bureau[5] (for complaints against financial institutions).

There is also a need to further clarify the underlying constructs and adopt measures that are widely accepted by all. Consistency and consensus with regard to construct definition and measurement can significantly improve programmatic empirical research that can guide theory and practice. In this regard, we point to the explosion of research in areas such as service quality (Cronin and Taylor 1992; Parasuraman et al. 1988), customer equity (Reinartz and Kumar 2000), and brand equity (Aaker 1996).

Conclusion

Customers and employees enable firms to achieve sustained competitive advantage. Engaged customers and employees, in many ways, are the fundamental determinants of managerial success versus firm failure. Given the complex, reciprocal, and multilateral relationships between the related constructs, understanding the joint association of customer engagement and employee engagement and their effects on firm performance is critical for marketing scholars and managers alike. An improved understanding of these dynamics will provide firms with more concise guidance with regard to formulating appropriate marketing strategies and will enable firms to induce synergistic associations among customers, employees, and the management.

The current chapter has reviewed extant research on the association between customer engagement and employee engagement and the relationship of these two constructs with firm performance. The review suggests the need to develop clearer measures of customer engagement and employee engagement that tap the core concepts, to apply a theoretical perspective that may combine existing perspectives on the links between these constructs, and to generalize previous findings in different contexts to find important boundary conditions and moderators of these links. We also call for alternative approaches to data collection that lead to more consistent measures and stronger causal inferences. We encourage marketing scholars to further investigate these issues to enhance this classic, yet timeless, research area.

NOTES

1. See http://www.gallup.com/services/169331/customer-engagement.aspx
2. See http://www.theacsi.org/
3. EquiTrend:http://www.theharrispoll.com/equitrend-information/; BrandAsset Valuator: http://www.yr.com/BAV; BrandIndex: http://www.brandindex.com/
4. See https://www.transportation.gov/airconsumer/
5. See http://www.consumerfinance.gov/data-research/consumer-complaints/

REFERENCES

Aaker, D. A. (1996). Measuring Brand Equity Across Products and Markets. *California Management Review, 38*(3), 102–120.

Ambrose, M. L., Seabright, M. A., & Schminke, M. (2002). Sabotage in the Workplace: The Role of Organizational Injustice. *Organizational Behavior and Human Decision Processes, 89*(1), 947–965.

Anderson, E. W., Fornell, C., & Lehmann, D. R. (1994). Customer Satisfaction, Market Share, and Profitability: Findings from Sweden. *Journal of Marketing, 58*(3), 53–66.

Anderson, E. W., Fornell, C., & Mittal, V. (2000). Strengthening the Satisfaction-Profit Chain. *Journal of Service Research, 3*(2), 107–120.

Arthur, J. B. (1994). Effects of Human Resource Systems on Manufacturing Performance and Turnover. *Academy of Management Journal, 37*(3), 670–687.

Babin, B. J., & Babin, L. A. (1996). Effects of Moral Cognitions and Consumer Emotions on Shoplifting Intentions. *Psychology and Marketing, 13*(8), 785–802.

Bagozzi, R. P. (1975). Marketing as Exchange. *Journal of Marketing, 39*(4), 32–39.

Bagozzi, R. P. (1980). Performance and Satisfaction in an Industrial Sales Force: An Examination of Their Antecedents and Simultaneity. *Journal of Marketing, 44*(2), 65–77.

Bearman, P. (1997). Generalized Exchange. *American Journal of Sociology, 102*(5), 1383–1415.

Bernhardt, K. L., Donthu, N., & Kennett, P. A. (2000). A Longitudinal Analysis of Satisfaction and Profitability. *Journal of Business Research, 47*(2), 161–171.

Bettencourt, L. A., & Brown, S. W. (1997). Contact Employees: Relationships Among Workplace Fairness, Job Satisfaction and Prosocial Service Behaviors. *Journal of Retailing, 73*(1), 39–61.

Bove, L. L., Pervan, S. J., Beatty, S. E., & Shiu, E. (2009). Service Worker Role in Encouraging Customer Organizational Citizenship Behaviors. *Journal of Business Research, 62*(7), 698–705.

Brodie, R. J., Hollebeek, L. D., Jurić, B., & Ilić, A. (2011). Customer Engagement: Conceptual Domain, Fundamental Propositions, and Implications for Research. *Journal of Service Research, 14*(3), 252–271.

Brown, K. A., & Mitchell, T. R. (1993). Organizational Obstacles: Links with Financial Performance, Customer Satisfaction, and Job Satisfaction in a Service Environment. *Human Relations, 46*(6), 725–757.

Brown, S. P., & Chin, W. W. (2004). Satisfying and Retaining Customers Through Independent Service Representatives. *Decision Sciences, 35*(3), 527–550.

Brown, S. P., & Lam, S. K. (2008). A Meta-Analysis of Relationships Linking Employee Satisfaction to Customer Responses. *Journal of Retailing, 84*(3), 243–255.

Chevalier, J. A., & Mayzlin, D. (2006). The Effect of Word of Mouth on Sales: Online Book Reviews. *Journal of Marketing Research, 43*(3), 345–354.

Chi, C. G., & Gursoy, D. (2009). Employee Satisfaction, Customer Satisfaction, and Financial Performance: An Empirical Examination. *International Journal of Hospitality Management, 28*(2), 245–253.

Chuang, A., Judge, T. A., & Liaw, Y. J. (2012). Transformational Leadership and Customer Service: A Moderated Mediation Model of Negative Affectivity and Emotion Regulation. *European Journal of Work and Organizational Psychology, 21*(1), 28–56.

Cronin, J. J., & Taylor, S. A. (1992). Measuring Service Quality: A Reexamination and Extension. *Journal of Marketing, 56*(3), 5–68.

Deshpande, R. (1983). 'Paradigms Lost': On Theory and Method in Research in Marketing. *Journal of Marketing, 47*(4), 101–110.

Donaldson, T., & Preston, L. E. (1995). The Stakeholder Theory of the Corporation: Concepts, Evidence, and Implications. *Academy of Management Review, 20*(1), 65–91.

Evanschitzky, H., Groening, C., Mittal, V., & Wunderlich, M. (2011). How Employer and Employee Satisfaction Affect Customer Satisfaction: An Application to Franchise Services. *Journal of Service Research, 14*(2), 136–148.

Evanschitzky, H., Sharma, A., & Prykop, C. (2012a). The Role of the Sales Employee in Securing Customer Satisfaction *European Journal of Marketing. 46*(3/4), 489–508.

Evanschitzky, H., Wangenheim, F. V., & Wunderlich, N. V. (2012b). Perils of Managing the Service Profit Chain: The Role of Time Lags and Feedback Loops *Journal of Retailing. 88*(3), 356–366.

Frennea, C., Mittal, V., & Westbrook, R. A. (2013). The Satisfaction Profit Chain. In R. T. Rust & M.-H. Huang (Eds.), *Handbook of Service Marketing Research* (pp. 182–218). Northampton: Elwood Elgar.

Frey, R.-V., Bayón, T., & Totzek, D. (2013). How Customer Satisfaction Affects Employee Satisfaction and Retention in a Professional Services Context. *Journal of Service Research, 16*(4), 503–517.

Gao, H., Zhang, Y., & Mittal, V. (2017). How Does Local-Global Identity Affect Price Sensitivity? *Journal of Marketing,* forthcoming, doi: 10.1509/jm.15.0206.

Gazzoli, G., Hancer, M., & Kim, B. C. (2013). Explaining Why Employee-Customer Orientation Influences Customers' Perceptions of The Service Encounter. *Journal of Service Management, 24*(4), 382–400.

Gounaris, S., & Boukis, A. (2013). The Role of Employee Job Satisfaction in Strengthening Customer Repurchase Intentions. *Journal of Services Marketing, 27*(4), 322–333.

Grandey, A. A., Goldberg, L. S., & Douglas Pugh, S. (2011). Why and When Do Stores With Satisfied Employees Have Satisfied Customers? The Roles of Responsiveness and Store Busyness. *Journal of Service Research, 14*(4), 397–409.

Groening, C., Mittal, V., & Anthea Zhang, Y. (2016). Cross-Validation of Customer and Employee Signals and Firm Valuation. *Journal of Marketing Research, 53*(1), 61–76.

Gupta, S., & Zeithaml, V. (2006). Customer Metrics and Their Impact on Financial Performance. *Marketing Science, 25*(6), 718–739.

Harris, L. C., & Ogbonna, E. (2006). Service Sabotage: A Study of Antecedents and Consequences. *Journal of the Academy of Marketing Science, 34*(4), 543–558.

Harris, L. C., & Reynolds, K. L. (2003). The Consequences of Dysfunctional Customer Behavior. *Journal of Service Research, 6*(2), 144–161.

Harter, J. K., Schmidt, F. L., & Hayes, T. L. (2002). Business-Unit-Level Relationship Between Employee Satisfaction, Employee Engagement, and Business Outcomes: A Meta-Analysis. *Journal of Applied Psychology, 87*(2), 268–279.

Heskett, J. L., Jones, T. O., Loveman, G. W., Earl Sasser, W., Jr., & Schlesinger, L. A. (1994). Putting the Service-Profit Chain to Work. *Harvard Business Review, 72*(2), 164–174.

Hogreve, J., Iseke, A., Derfuss, K., & Eller, T. (2016). The Service–Profit Chain: A Meta-Analytic Test of a Comprehensive Theoretical Framework. *Journal of Marketing,* forthcoming, doi:10.1509/jm.15.0395.

Homburg, C., & Stock, R. M. (2004). The Link Between Salespeople's Job Satisfaction and Customer Satisfaction in a Business-to-Business Context: A Dyadic Analysis. *Journal of the Academy of Marketing Science, 32*(2), 144–158.

Homburg, C., & Stock, R. M. (2005). Exploring the Conditions Under Which Salesperson Work Satisfaction Can Lead to Customer Satisfaction. *Psychology and Marketing, 22*(5), 393–420.

Homburg, C., Wieseke, J., & Bornemann, T. (2009a). Implementing the Marketing Concept at the Employee–Customer Interface: The Role of Customer Need Knowledge *Journal of Marketing. 73*(4), 64–81.

Homburg, C., Wieseke, J., & Hoyer, W. D. (2009b). Social Identity and the Service–Profit Chain *Journal of Marketing. 73*(2), 38–54.

Hur, W.-M., Moon, T.-W., & Jung, Y. S. (2015). Customer Response to Employee Emotional Labor: The Structural Relationship Between Emotional Labor, Job Satisfaction, and Customer Satisfaction. *Journal of Services Marketing, 29*(1), 71–80.

Jackson, S. E., Schwab, R. L., & Schuler, R. S. (1986). Toward an Understanding of the Burnout Phenomenon. *Journal of Applied Psychology, 71*(4), 630–640.

Jeon, H., & Choi, B. (2012). The Relationship Between Employee Satisfaction and Customer Satisfaction. *Journal of Services Marketing, 26*(5), 332–341.

Kamakura, W. A., Mittal, V., de Rosa, F., & Mazzon, J. A. (2002). Assessing the Service-Profit Chain. *Marketing Science, 21*(3), 294–317.

Keiningham, T. L., Frennea, C. M., Aksoy, L., Buoye, A., & Mittal, V. (2015). A Five-Component Customer Commitment Model: Implications for Repurchase Intentions in Goods and Services Industries. *Journal of Service Research, 18*(4), 433–450.

Koys, D. J. (2001). The Effects of Employee Satisfaction, Organizational Citizenship Behavior, and Turnover on Organizational Effectiveness: A Unit-Level, Longitudinal Study. *Personnel Psychology, 54*(1), 101–114.

Kumar, V., & Pansari, A. (2016). Competitive Advantage Through Engagement. *Journal of Marketing Research, 53*(4), 497–514.

Loveman, G. W. (1998). Employee Satisfaction, Customer Loyalty, and Financial Performance: An Empirical Examination of the Service Profit Chain in Retail Banking. *Journal of Service Research, 1*(1), 18–31.

Luo, X. (2009). Quantifying the Long-Term Impact of Negative Word of Mouth on Cash Flows and Stock Prices. *Marketing Science, 28*(1), 148–165.

Marshall, K. P. (1998). Generalized Exchange and Public Policy: An Illustration of Support for Public Schools. *Journal of Public Policy & Marketing, 17*(2), 274–286.

McNeely, B. L., & Meglino, B. M. (1994). The Role of Dispositional and Situational Antecedents in Prosocial Organizational Behavior: An Examination of the Intended Beneficiaries of Prosocial Behavior. *Journal of Applied Psychology, 79*(6), 836–844.

Mittal, V., Rosen, J., Govind, R., Degenholtz, H., Shingala, S., Hulland, S., Rhee, Y. J., Kastango, K. B., Mulsant, B. H., Castle, N., Rubin, F. H., & Nace, D. (2007). Perception Gap in Quality-of-Life Ratings: An Empirical Investigation of Nursing Home Residents and Caregivers. *The Gerontologist, 47*(2), 159–168.

Molm, L. D., Collett, J. L., & Schaefer, D. R. (2007). Building Solidarity Through Generalized Exchange: A Theory of Reciprocity. *American Journal of Sociology, 113*(1), 205–242.

Morgan, N. A., & Rego, L. L. (2006). The Value of Different Customer Satisfaction and Loyalty Metrics in Predicting Business Performance. *Marketing Science, 25*(5), 426–439.

Namasivayam, K., Guchait, P., & Lei, P. (2014). The Influence of Leader Empowering Behaviors and Employee Psychological Empowerment on Customer Satisfaction. *International Journal of Contemporary Hospitality Management, 26*(1), 69–84.

Netemeyer, R. G., Maxham, J. G., III, & Lichtenstein, D. R. (2010). Store Manager Performance and Satisfaction: Effects on Store Employee Performance and Satisfaction, Store Customer Satisfaction, and Store Customer Spending Growth. *Journal of Applied Psychology, 95*(3), 530–545.

O'Boyle, E., & Harter, J. (2013). *State of the American Workplace: Employee Engagement Insights for US Business Leaders*. Washington, DC: Gallup.

Ostroff, C. (1992). The Relationship Between Satisfaction, Attitudes, and Performance: An Organizational Level Analysis. *Journal of Applied Psychology, 77*(6), 963–974.

Pantouvakis, A., & Bouranta, N. (2013). The Interrelationship Between Service Features, Job Satisfaction and Customer Satisfaction: Evidence from the Transport Sector. *TQM Journal, 25*(2), 186–201.

Parasuraman, A., Zeithaml, V. A., & Berry, L. L. (1988). SERVQUAL: A Multiple-Item Scale for Measuring Consumer Perceptions of Service Quality. *Journal of Retailing, 64*(1), 12–40.

Payne, S. C., & Webber, S. S. (2006). Effects of Service Provider Attitudes and Employment Status on Citizenship Behaviors and Customers' Attitudes and Loyalty Behavior. *Journal of Applied Psychology, 91*(2), 365–378.

Pritchard, M., & Silvestro, R. (2005). Applying the Service Profit Chain to Analyse Retail Performance: The Case of The Managerial Strait-Jacket? *International Journal of Service Industry Management, 16*(4), 337–356.

Reed, A., II, Aquino, K., & Levy, E. (2007). Moral Identity and Judgments of Charitable Behaviors. *Journal of Marketing, 71*(1), 178–193.

Rego, L. L., Billett, M. T., & Morgan, N. A. (2009). Consumer-Based Brand Equity and Firm Risk. *Journal of Marketing, 73*(6), 47–60.

Reinartz, W. J., & Kumar, V. (2000). On the Profitability of Long-Life Customers in a Noncontractual Setting: An Empirical Investigation and Implications for Marketing. *Journal of Marketing, 64*(4), 17–35.

Reynierse, J. H., & Harker, J. B. (1992). Employee and Customer Perceptions of Service in Banks: Teller and Customer Service Representative Ratings. *Human Resource Planning, 15*(4), 31–47.

Reynolds, K. L., & Harris, L. C. (2006). Deviant Customer Behavior: An Exploration of Frontline Employee Tactics. *Journal of Marketing Theory and Practice, 14*(2), 95–111.

Reynolds, K. L., & Harris, L. C. (2009). Dysfunctional Customer Behavior Severity: An Empirical Examination. *Journal of Retailing, 85*(3), 321–335.

Richins, M. L. (1983). Negative Word-of-Mouth by Dissatisfied Consumers: A Pilot Study. *Journal of Marketing, 47*(1), 68–78.

Robinson, D., Perryman, S., & Hayday, S. (2004). *The Drivers of Employee Engagement*. Brighton: Institute for Employment Studies.

Ryan, A. M., Schmit, M. J., & Johnson, R. (1996). Attitudes and Effectiveness: Examining Relations at an Organizational Level. *Personnel Psychology, 49*(4), 853–882.

Saks, A. M. (2006). Antecedents and Consequences of Employee Engagement. *Journal of Managerial Psychology, 21*(7), 600–619.

Schau, H. J., Muñiz, A. M., Jr., & Arnould, E. J. (2009). How Brand Community Practices Create Value. *Journal of Marketing, 73*(5), 30–51.

Schlesinger, L. A., & Zornitsky, J. (1991). Job Satisfaction, Service Capability, and Customer Satisfaction: An Examination of Linkages and Management Implications. *Human Resource Planning, 14*(2), 141–149.

Shao, R., Aquino, K., & Freeman, D. (2008). Beyond Moral Reasoning: A Review of Moral Identity Research and Its Implications for Business Ethics. *Business Ethics Quarterly, 18*(4), 513–540.

Siddiqi, M. A., & Sahaf, M. A. (2009). Customer Orientation of Service Employees and Organizational Performance: Empirical Evidence from Indian Banking. *Decision, 36*(2), 133–153.

Silvestro, R., & Cross, S. (2000). Applying the Service Profit Chain in a Retail Environment: Challenging the 'Satisfaction Mirror'. *International Journal of Service Industry Management, 11*(3), 244–268.

Singh, J., & Sirdeshmukh, D. (2000). Agency and Trust Mechanisms in Consumer Satisfaction and Loyalty Judgments. *Journal of the Academy of Marketing Science, 28*(1), 150–167.

Skarlicki, D. P., van Jaarsveld, D. D., & Walker, D. D. (2008). Getting Even for Customer Mistreatment: The Role of Moral Identity in the Relationship Between Customer Interpersonal Injustice and Employee Sabotage. *Journal of Applied Psychology, 93*(6), 1335–1347.

Srinivasan, S., & Hanssens, D. M. (2009). Marketing and Firm Value: Metrics, Methods, Findings, and Future Directions. *Journal of Marketing Research, 46*(3), 293–312.

Steinke, C. (2008). Examining the Role of Service Climate in Health Care: An Empirical Study of Emergency Departments. *International Journal of Service Industry Management, 19*(2), 188–209.

Subramony, M., Krause, N., Norton, J., & Burns, G. N. (2008). The Relationship Between Human Resource Investments and Organizational Performance: A Firm-Level Examination of Equilibrium Theory. *Journal of Applied Psychology, 93*(4), 778–788.

Tornow, W. W., & Wiley, J. W. (1991). Service Quality and Management Practices: A Look at Employee Attitudes, Customer Satisfaction, and Bottom-Line Consequences. *Human Resource Planning, 14*(2), 105–115.

Tuzovic, S. (2010). Frequent (Flier) Frustration and the Dark Side of Word-of-Web: Exploring Online Dysfunctional Behavior in Online Feedback Forums. *Journal of Services Marketing, 24*(6), 446–457.

Ugboro, I. O., & Obeng, K. (2000). Top Management Leadership, Employee Empowerment, Job Satisfaction, and Customer Satisfaction in TQM Organizations: An Empirical Study. *Journal of Quality Management, 5*(2), 247–272.

Van Doorn, J., Lemon, K. N., Mittal, V., Nass, S., Pick, D., Pirner, P., & Verhoef, P. C. (2010). Customer Engagement Behavior: Theoretical Foundations and Research Directions. *Journal of Service Research, 13*(3), 253–266.

Van Dyne, L., & LePine, J. A. (1998). Helping and Voice Extra-Role Behaviors: Evidence of Construct and Predictive Validity. *Academy of Management Journal, 41*(1), 108–119.

Varadarajan, P. R., & Menon, A. (1988). Cause-Related Marketing: A Coalignment of Marketing Strategy and Corporate Philanthropy. *Journal of Marketing, 52*(3), 58–74.

Wangenheim, F. V., Evanschitzky, H., & Wunderlich, M. (2007). Does the Employee–Customer Satisfaction Link Hold for All Employee Groups? *Journal of Business Research, 60*(7), 690–697.

Whitman, D. S., Van Rooy, D. L., & Viswesvaran, C. (2010). Satisfaction, Citizenship Behaviors, and Performance in Work Units: A Meta-Analysis of Collective Construct Relations. *Personnel Psychology, 63*(1), 41–81.

Wiley, J. W. (1991). Customer Satisfaction: A Supportive Work Environment and Its Financial Cost. *Human Resource Planning, 14*(2), 117–121.

Winterich, K. P., Mittal, V., & Ross, W. T. (2009). Donation Behavior Toward In-Groups and Out-Groups: The Role of Gender and Moral Identity. *Journal of Consumer Research, 36*(2), 199–214.

Winterich, K. P., Zhang, Y., & Mittal, V. (2012). How Political Identity and Charity Positioning Increase Donations: Insights from Moral Foundations Theory. *International Journal of Research in Marketing, 29*(4), 346–354.

Zablah, A. R., Carlson, B. D., Todd Donavan, D., Maxham, J. G., III, & Brown, T. J. (2016). A Cross-Lagged Test of the Association Between Customer Satisfaction and Employee Job Satisfaction in a Relational Context. *Journal of Applied Psychology, 101*(5), 743–755.

CHAPTER 9

The Disruptive Impact of Customer Engagement on the Business-to-Consumer Sales Force

Bryan W. Hochstein and Willy Bolander

INTRODUCTION

Customer engagement (CE) is an increasingly studied topic in marketing that relates to the attitudes, behaviors, and connectedness of customers to a firm and to the firm's other customers (i.e., the marketplace; see Kumar et al. 2010; Kumar and Pansari 2016; Van Doorn et al. 2010). CE has become an important topic because it reflects the increased ease with which business-to-consumer (B2C) customers (largely empowered by new technology) can engage with firms and other customers outside of face-to-face interactions. Overall, this is seen as a positive change—firms want better access to, and deeper relationships with, customers, and technology-driven CE facilitates this (Kumar and Pansari 2016). However, this development brings with it uncertainty regarding the future of B2C salespeople and the organizations that employ them because, traditionally, the sales force has been a firm's primary method of engaging customers. Research by Beatty

B.W. Hochstein (✉)
University of Alabama, Tuscaloosa, AL, USA

W. Bolander
Florida State University, Tallahassee, FL, USA

© The Author(s) 2018
R.W. Palmatier et al. (eds.), *Customer Engagement Marketing*,
DOI 10.1007/978-3-319-61985-9_9

and Smith (1987), for example, showed that in the past the bulk of a customer's external information search came from in-person sales interactions. However, more recent work suggests that this is no longer the case, as customers now enter sales interactions much later (57–70% of the way through decision) and after considerable prior engagement (Microsoft 2015). With customers now entering sales interactions highly engaged and informed, the question is, where does this leave the B2C salesperson?

While research is limited on this issue, industry reports have predicted that firms' newfound focus on CE outside of sales interactions is contributing to the demise of direct selling. For example, a report by Forrester Research suggests that one million, mostly order taker, sales jobs will be lost by 2020 (Hoar 2015). This decline is predicted because customers can now self-educate and make decisions separate from the sales interaction, which is precipitating a move of their purchasing activities to e-commerce sources. This point is further emphasized by a McKinsey report that reveals that car shoppers today visit only 1.6 dealerships before making a purchase decision (compared to 5 dealerships just a few years ago; Economist 2015). Figure 9.1 visually represents changes to how customers engage, within and external to sales interactions. The issue addressed by this chapter, how CE outside the direct sales interaction impacts CE inside the interaction, is important for reasons far beyond academic interest. If these doomsday prophets are correct, success in encouraging CE external to the sales interaction is ushering in the end of direct selling. While this may be a goal for some firms, we contend that diminishing direct CE also portends a decrease in the quality consumer decisions (i.e., decreased value) that has traditionally been a benefit of in-person sales interactions.

In order to explore this important and timely issue, we held a focus group with executives in the retail jewelry industry on the topic of the challenges involved in selling to engaged customers. The themes developed from this focus group run counter to suggestions in the literature that salespeople who act as "knowledge brokers" will be successful in creating value with their customers. In fact, the findings indicate that for customers highly engaged outside the sales interaction, a salesperson's efforts to engage within the face-to-face interaction may actually impede, rather than create, value. Thus, in the remainder of this chapter, we start by reporting the key themes that emerged from our focus group study. Concurrently, we introduce literature related to each theme and then propose a conceptual, literature-based solution to these key challenges by drawing upon research on CE, personal selling, and psychology. A summary of the main literature referenced is detailed in Table 9.1.

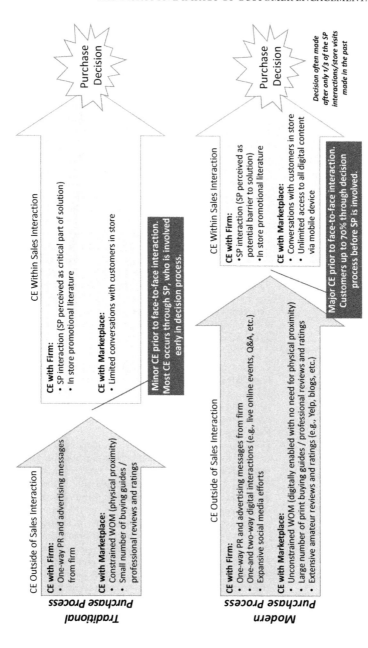

Fig. 9.1   Customer engagement (CE) in traditional versus modern purchases

Table 9.1   Literature relevant to chapter

Article	Importance to chapter
Customer engagement (CE)	
Kumar et al. (2010)	CE occurs within transactions (e.g., can include salespeople) and also external to transactions (e.g., does not require salespeople). Firms realize that value comes from direct CE actions (e.g., purchases and referrals) and indirect CE (customer influence on others and feedback to the firm). We focus on how external CE impacts CE within transactions as the basis for this chapter.
Van Doorn et al. (2010)	CE dimensions of valence, form/modality, and scope occur beyond purchase. The form/modality dimension describes CE activities such as word-of-mouth, recommendations, interaction with other external customers, blogging, writing reviews, co-creation of firm offerings, seeking information, and complaints. We consider how these CE activities impact salesperson–customer engagement.
Kumar and Pansari (2016)	Includes a focus on CE between customers and employees. This approach to CE differs from Van Doorn et al., but is the basis of our study that focuses on CE that occurs between customers and salespeople (firm employees).We focus on how external CE impacts CE within transactions as the basis for this chapter.
Sales & knowledge brokers	
Verbeke et al. (2011)	Concludes that drivers of sales performance indicate knowledge brokerage by salespeople is the key to sales success. This is important to the current chapter because brokering knowledge starts by developing a holistic understanding of the customer, which the comments of our focus group indicate CE impedes.
Dixon and Tanner (2012)	Discusses that the process of sales is changing and points to the new focus of sales, which is value creation through buyer–seller exchange. This research informs this chapter by further developing how salespeople need to develop a well-rounded view of their customer's situation and apply salient knowledge and solutions.
Zhu and Meyers-Levy 2007	Customers can adopt either promotion (on a mission) or prevention (seeking input) focus to decision-making. Prevention-focused customers are less open to new information, unless the information is highly salient and item-specific to their decision criteria, or determinant attributes. Our focus group participants described engaged customers in ways consistent with a prevention focus.

FOCUS GROUP AND LITERATURE REVIEW: KEY CHALLENGES IN SELLING TO ENGAGED CUSTOMERS

To begin our investigation of how CE impacts B2C sales interactions, a focus group was held with seven top-level executives of firms competing in the retail jewelry industry (e.g., rings, diamonds, etc.) and one industry expert/consultant. The leaders and firms were chosen based on the criteria that their firms must (1) sell predominantly through trained salespeople who interact directly with customers and (2) have customers that engage with their firm, as evidenced through social media and firm-initiated CE activities outside of the face-to-face interaction. Participants were specifically invited to interview while in attendance at an international conference of jewelers. The discussion developed from a set of open-ended questions, which was structured, yet adaptable to the conversation. The resulting recorded comments were analyzed to identify themes referenced by multiple participants. Specifically, three interrelated themes emerged, which we describe, and compare to salient existing research, below.

Theme 1: Customer and Salesperson Incongruence

The first theme suggests that customers with higher levels of engagement, specific to the firm or marketplace, do not view the salesperson as a participant in their decision process. These customers often disengage if they feel a salesperson does not have a similar understanding of, and engagement with, the product, even in situations where the salesperson is well-trained, knowledgeable, and professional. The theme was troubling to our focus group, as comments indicated concern over how CE outside the sales interaction has a negative effect at the point of purchase when salespeople are not perceived as "worthy" of the customer's business (e.g., lost sale, negative word of mouth, etc.). Some quotes from our focus group participants that embody this theme include:

> "When customers engage with our salespeople it seems that our employee has to pass a test of sorts with the customer to demonstrate their 'street cred' in the area, which bears more weight than a more professional approach." Rich M., nine retail locations

> "Our salespeople know a lot about our products and what's going on in the marketplace, but customers these days seem to discount a lot of that and will get frustrated and leave if the salesperson doesn't 'validate' them." Mike R., three retail locations

To develop this theme, we next look to literature that suggests that to be effective, salespeople should "broker knowledge" to their customers (e.g., Verbeke et al. 2011). In broad terms, knowledge brokering (i.e., being a knowledge broker, or KB) is defined as a process of translation, coordination, and alignment of perspectives in an effort to link and facilitate transactions between parties (Wenger 1998, p. 109). Inherent in brokering efforts is the potential for a salesperson to leverage their unique expertise to participate with customers in the value creation process. In sales, empirical support for the importance of the KB role is found in the Verbeke et al. (2011) update of the classic meta-analysis by Churchill et al. (1985) of sales performance drivers. The updated meta-analysis found that the most important driver of performance is selling-related knowledge, which is defined as "the depth and width of knowledge base that salespeople need to size up situations, classify prospects, and select appropriate sales strategies for clients" (Leong et al. 1989, p. 164). The second most important driver of performance is adaptiveness, which is defined as "the altering of sales behaviors during and across consumer interactions based on perceived information about the selling situation" (Weitz et al. 1986, p. 175). Verbeke et al. (2011) conclude that in the current knowledge economy, salespeople will be most effective in value creation when acting as KBs who leverage their selling-related knowledge to adapt to different customers.

Combining the literature with the first theme from our focus group raises a serious concern for the KB concept in practice. Specifically, our contributors explained that higher levels of external, pre-interaction customer engagement create situations where the salesperson's input is not valued and that she/he is, therefore, not viewed as a participant in the value creation process. In other words, our focus group seems to suggest that external CE has taken the role of the salesperson in value co-creation. This view runs contrary to the new definition of selling as the "human-driven interaction between and within individuals and organizations in order to bring about economic exchange within a value-creation context" (Dixon and Tanner 2012). So while managers and scholars alike believe that the salesperson *should* play a critical boundary spanning role in value co-creation (Blocker et al. 2012), our focus group indicates that in a B2C setting, engaged customers are closed off to the salesperson's inputs.

Two additional and related themes emerged from our focus group, which we detail in the next sections. However, given the importance of this identified problem, we now report that the final section of this chapter is devoted to developing a conceptual solution to this misalignment.

Theme 2: Customer's Minds Are Made Up

The second, and related, theme suggests that salespeople have difficulty selling to engaged customers because customer minds are already made up when they finally enter the face-to-face interaction with a salesperson. While we might expect salespeople to appreciate this phenomenon, our focus group suggested that it often leads customers to choose an inferior product. This notion is evidenced by customers that simply do not want further information, regardless of the salesperson's worthiness. In essence, the salesperson doesn't really get a chance to prove themselves, let alone participate in value co-creation, as customers are quickly frustrated by the process and simply want to "get it over with." Efforts by salespeople to find out more about the customer (i.e., by performing a general needs analysis as recommended in virtually all sales-training methodologies; e.g., Bolander et al. 2014; Rackham 1988) exacerbate, rather than help, the situation. In other words, and again, external CE disrupts attempts to engage in CE during the face-to-face interaction. Some quotes from our focus group participants that embody this theme include:

> "Most of our customers tell us exactly what they want and expect that we will provide no input into the decision." Dylan T., five retail locations

> "It is like they are shocked that salespeople have something to say, their friend told them they could get X for Y and that is the end of the story." Eric N, eleven retail locations

We again introduce literature as a basis to inform this theme. Several salient theories could be utilized to address this topic (e.g., involvement, consumer knowledge, information processing, etc.). However, to inform our study we turn to regulatory focus theory (Crowe and Higgins 1997), which tells us that consumers pursue pleasure and avoid pain in the pursuit of a goal (like making a purchase) and adopt one of two regulatory foci (prevention vs. promotion) during goal pursuit (Liberman et al. 1999). A prevention focus characterizes one who views goals as obligations or duties (Carver and Scheier 1998) and would lead a customer to become apprehensive when they feel deterred from fulfilling their duty and/or when interference is suspected (e.g., when they perceive that a salesperson is trying to change their mind). Alternatively, a promotion focus characterizes one who is focused on advancement and attainment of new information (Xie and Kahle 2014) and instead of leading a customer to protect their pre-made decision, would lead them to learn all they can to ensure an optimal decision in the future. We suggest that customers with higher engagement levels tend to adopt a prevention focus, while less engaged customers tend to adopt a promotion focus.

Bringing together the literature and our B2C sales setting, we suggest that salesperson messages congruent with the customer's goal pursuit produce pleasure (getting closer to goal attainment, or making a correct purchase), while those not in agreement cause pain (getting further from goal attainment, or delaying/redirecting purchase). Incongruent salesperson messages (i.e., those which cause pain in the form of confusion, doubt, etc.) can lead a customer to depart the sales interaction altogether. Further, regulatory focus proposes that the consumer's interpretation of the rightness or wrongness of an influence attempt will lead to strong judgments (Vaughn et al. 2009), which strengthens their resolve to depart an interaction when pressured.

These points culminate in the idea that because a customer is engaged externally, and before any in-person interaction, the efforts of salespeople to engage during the interaction are greatly undermined. To illustrate, consider a customer who is highly engaged and has made up their mind before meeting with a salesperson (recall that industry reports reveal that consumers are entering sales interactions as much as 70% of the way through the decision-making process (e.g., Microsoft 2015). The customer has drawn upon different engagement touchpoints to identify important decision criteria, or determinant attributes, and has formed a decision. This customer enters the sales interaction with a strong willingness to buy the predetermined product, which can be viewed as a duty or obligation to be accomplished (i.e., prevention focus). The next step in goal attainment is to purchase the product (not spend time talking to, or being persuaded by, a salesperson). As a result, the customer's prevention focus limits the salesperson's ability to act as a KB and co-create value because attempts to influence the customer will be viewed as a threat to goal attainment and engender a strong negative response.

With his or her mind made up, and prevention focus activated, the engaged customer would prefer a salesperson who functions as an order taker, not a KB. Of course, firms need to justify employing relatively highly paid salespeople as opposed to lower paid cashiers or even simply using an online store. So we see an interesting conflict where firms want their salespeople to be value-adding KBs, while customers (at least highly engaged ones) want the salesperson to get out of the way and let them fulfill their intended purchase. This theme provides some support for the doomsday prophets mentioned at this chapter's outset. If increased means of engaging customers external to the sales interaction are leading customers to adopt a prevention focus, why do we need the salesforce? Or, from a positive perspective, what are the behaviors that might allow a salesperson to perform the KB role even with highly engaged customers? As previously foreshadowed, we will later explore this issue as part of our conceptual solution.

Theme 3: Customers Believe Themselves to Be Well-Informed

The third theme that emerged from the focus group suggests that customers who are more engaged with the firm and its stakeholders consider themselves well informed concerning market offerings from both the focal firm and its competitors, yet often are not. The participants indicated that, despite their engagement with the firm and marketplace, most customers typically overestimated their knowledge of the actual product. In addition, many customers were also described as having errors and/or omissions in their knowledge, which caused problems for salespeople. Some quotes invoking this theme include:

> "Customers think they know everything from a few hours online and they assume that this 'knowledge' is more credible than a salesperson's five or ten years working with the product." George P., industry expert

> "Customers come in and say things like, 'I was watching this YouTube and it said that clarity (as one example) isn't important.' But, we know they are wrong, we've seen the video too – the video guy is selling a bad product. Doesn't matter, the customer is always right, right – not!" Stacey L., five retail locations

This theme shows that not only are customer's minds made up concerning their decision (as detailed in Theme 2), but also that they often overestimate their knowledge. According to our participants, engaged customers largely do not recognize knowledge deficiencies, resulting in problems for salespeople. They also stated that attempts to correct any deficiencies seem to threaten and further drive engaged customers away from the sales interaction.

This theme is highly related to the previous and, we suggest, also results from the prevention focus of the highly engaged customer. This point is also related to the salesperson KB concept and we suggest that it impedes a salesperson's ability to act in the role of KB. Specifically, the KB role requires a salesperson to develop an understanding of their customer's expressed and unexpressed needs, interpret them in regard to knowledge bases, and then present knowledge scarce to the customer. Scarce knowledge is characterized as information that consumers do not have access to (Verbeke et al. 2011). In other words, KBs add value to the sales interaction by knowing more than the EC, despite the latter's prior engagement and information gathering, which is used to provide relevant missing information to customers. Scarce knowledge can also address knowledge that the customer has that either is factually incorrect, or being interpreted incorrectly. For this type of scarce knowledge, the KB can provide correction for erroneous customer information (e.g., an incorrect mpg estimate in a car purchase situation). Or, consistent with the "Challenger Sales" model (Dixon and Adamson 2011) and/or "Provocation-Based" selling (Lay et al. 2009), the KB can provide correction intended to change or improve interpretation of information (i.e., challenge thinking). However, the prevention focus of customers with high levels of engagement impedes information exchange required for KB salespeople to effectively impart scarce knowledge.

In summary, our contributors expressed that customers highly engaged outside of the sales interaction have a sense of "entitlement" when they come to the retail location, based on their prior behaviors in regard to the firm. By entitlement we mean that higher levels of CE typically result in the customer having a specific purchase in mind when they enter the sales interaction. For these customers, when a salesperson has a credible recommendation for a superior product/service, it is often ignored by the customer in favor of the customer's pre-interaction product choice. Recommendations are ignored largely because the customer thinks they know more than the salesperson, and hence the salesperson is perceived as irrelevant, or worse, a threat. This notion was unanimously viewed as a negative aspect of customer engagement, as the customer's purchase of the inferior choice often leads to negative CE with other customers (e.g., negative reviews) and the firm (e.g., complaints) soon after purchase. Efforts to determine positive ways that salespeople could overcome this problem provided some interesting responses, but no clear theme emerged as a consistent solution.

For B2C firms that rely on salespeople, the phenomenon described poses an obvious problem. On one hand, the leaders we interviewed desire to propagate CE as a positive way to co-create value with customers. On the other, their salespeople seem hindered by high levels of it. So, despite what might be expected, our focus group comments indicate, and we suggest, that for B2C complex product sales, CE outside of the transaction has a dark side in need of a solution. In response, we use the three themes developed by our focus group to develop a theoretical basis to help remedy this problem.

PROPOSED SOLUTION

The themes described by our focus group participants do not bode well for salespeople of firms that promote CE outside of the sales interaction. Yet, most agree that promoting CE behaviors is positive for firm performance. And, regardless of if a firm actively promotes CE, most agree that customers will seek out engagement with the marketplace, if not the firm directly. Thus, we conclude this chapter by proposing some solutions to this dilemma. But first, we add that the comments provided by our focus group likely reflect a larger issue in sales, which simply put is that B2C sales interactions are rapidly changing. Many firms that experienced positive results from sales activities in the past are not assured that those same approaches will be effective today. Thus, our proposed solutions are theoretically based on the mechanisms that underlie the current problem. As identified, we suggest that in B2C sales, the regulatory focus of customers is the main underlying theme. Thus, we focus specifically on how a salesperson performing the KB role can address these problems based on regulatory focus theory.

Research on prevention- focused customers indicates that while those with a prevention focus are not interested in new, general information, they will elaborate on, and be receptive to, item-specific information (Zhu and Meyers-Levy 2007). Item-specific information addresses the few determinant attributes that the customer used to arrive at a decision. We suggest that this element of regulatory focus theory is directly related to how the salesperson, acting as a KB, can impart relevant scarce knowledge that addresses item-specific, determinant attributes. The issue is that attempts to uncover the determinant attributes of prevention-focused customers are counter-productive and will deter these customers from their goal, which may cause them to depart the sales interaction. Thus, we turn to a brief discussion of a new approach to needs analysis that we expect to be effective for prevention-focused customers.

We begin by suggesting that the KB task of "discovering expressed and unexpressed needs" is too general of an approach in a B2C sales interaction.

There is no dispute that it is important to understand the needs of the customer (Moncrief and Marshall 2005). In fact, for frontline employees, this understanding is critical because the needs of customers are varied (di Mascio 2010; Plouffe et al. 2016) and can be the difference between success and failure (Homburg et al. 2009). To gain an understanding of needs, salespeople are trained to conduct needs analysis (Bolander et al. 2014). However, the current study argues that assessing customer needs through a "traditional" needs analysis is not an optimal starting point for consumers that are highly engaged with a firm. Rather, we suggest that needs analysis is *precisely* the area where KBs need to change their sales approach. For highly engaged customers, who have largely identified their needs prior to entering a sales interaction, we expect that needs analysis will threaten customers and cause their premature departure from the sales interaction (Zhu and Meyers-Levy 2007). Thus, we propose that KBs should conduct *determinant attribute analysis*, which we define as "developing a holistic understanding of customer prioritized and self-identified determinant attributes, *which reflect their needs.*"

This enhancement and clarification of the KB concept—to include the task of determinant attribute analysis—is consistent with the "sales profile" of a KB outlined by Dixon and Tanner (2012). They suggest that KBs need to take a global view of the customer's situation to develop an understanding of their needs and *information about those needs.* In a traditional needs analysis, the salesperson may use a process, such as SPIN Selling (Rackham 1988), that starts with a general needs assessment that narrows through different question types to determine more specific needs. In settings where customers are unsure of their needs, or the potential solutions to those needs, this approach has proven merit. However, we propose that in settings where the customer perceives their level of awareness of alternatives/outcomes to be high, resulting in a predetermined solution choice, a more concise method is required. In this situation, we suggest that a salesperson essentially dispense with the niceties and quickly "cut to the chase." Of course, "cutting to the chase" must be done using selling-related knowledge (i.e., in a tactful way). For salespeople, it is important to determine if the customer is actually an expert, or simply informed. Often, customers think they understand a complex situation with greater depth than they actually have (Rozenblit and Keil 2002). In these situations, it is suggested that salespeople ask customers what they know about the product and to explain what attributes are most important to them. This simple approach is in response to the comments of our focus group, which indicated that customers want to be validated, understood, and listened to, but not sold. This approach also allows for quick identification of knowledge gaps and misinterpretations. We propose that an attribute analysis approach is a means to quickly get to the core of the customer's needs, and information about those needs, that will increase the potential for value to be created.

But, quickly understanding the determinant attributes of a customer with high levels of engagement is just the start. After identifying determinant attributes of this type of customer, the KB manifests his or her understanding by providing only *attribute-specific* information back to the customer (i.e., building "street cred") because such messages will be considered for their underlying merit by highly engaged, prevention-focused customers. To illustrate, consider a customer who enters a sales interaction to purchase a smartphone. Like most complex products, smartphones have many technical elements that can be considered during purchase decisions. Assume the customer's determinant attributes concern battery life, image quality, and charging time. Using a general approach, the salesperson who spends time talking about data download speeds, pricing plans, and extended warranties will simply irritate, and perhaps drive-away, the customer. But, if the KB first develops an understanding of the customer's determinant attributes, then information specific to these attributes can be adaptively articulated and presented (as per Spiro and Weitz 1990). According to regulatory focus theory, this approach allows for the potential of customer value creation and firm value appropriation. We, therefore, propose that providing attribute-specific information, determined from an attribute analysis, is the first step for a salesperson to not only act as a KB, but also to be effective in creating value with highly engaged customers, as represented by ongoing engagement behaviors and purchase.

We next turn to the idea of scarce knowledge and suggest that KBs are most likely to create *additive* value when they present not only attribute-specific information, but also scarce knowledge. We define additive value as being realized when the customer accepts a KB's recommendation (specifically, a recommendation counter to their initial choice). To elaborate, no scarce knowledge is presented when a KB determines the customer has complete information in comparison to her/his knowledge base (i.e., there is no scarce knowledge to add). In this scenario, value may exchange (i.e., order taking) but is not expected to be increased (i.e., persuasive, value-added selling). In other words, the customer purchases what she/he intended and, while not derailing the exchange, the salesperson doesn't add any marginal value. However, when the KB determines that the customer has deficient information, we suggest that salespeople can create additive value by providing attribute-specific *and* scarce knowledge. Thus, we propose that scarce knowledge acts as a moderator of the relationship between attribute-specific information and engagement outcomes. This interaction should result in acceptance of KB recommendations and higher levels of engagement outcomes (e.g., word of mouth, etc.).

To illustrate this moderating effect, recall the customer purchasing a smartphone. The KB has determined that battery life, image quality, and charging time are the customer's key determinant attributes. Next, the KB digs deeper by exchanging information to determine missing or incorrect information concerning the attributes. Assuming that missing or incorrect information is present, the KB can then present scarce knowledge that is attribute-specific. The culmination of such information exchange is likely a product/service recommendation, which draws upon the attribute-specific holes in the customer's knowledge. We expect that this interaction is the best way for salespeople to be effective as KBs, allowing them to co-create value with highly engaged customers. Thus, firms that can train their salespeople to "cut to the chase," "get specific," and "fill gaps" with the information they exchange are likely to overcome the negative phenomenon outlined in this chapter.

The key challenges and proposed solution outlined in this chapter should be considered an important starting point for advancements in this area. Other engagement outcomes of KB activities should be examined such as cognitive dissonance (increases or reductions), perceptual changes in relation to the firm's other CE activities (i.e., positive vs. negative), brand allegiance and/or switching, and, of course, sales performance. Additional moderators should also be considered, such as consumer persuasion knowledge, firm positioning of salespeople (e.g., Apple's "genius bar"), and/or traditional salesperson characteristics that affect performance (e.g., gender, likeability, etc.). Also, important topics, such as how price differences, information types, and perceived risk affect acceptance of KB recommendations, should also be studied. Continued research in this area is encouraged because the prevalence of highly engaged customers, and their impact on sales interactions, is expected to intensify as engagement opportunities become even more ubiquitous for firms and customers.

REFERENCES

Beatty, S. E., & Smith, S. M. (1987). External Search Effort: An Investigation Across Several Product Categories. *Journal of Consumer Research, 14*(1), 83–95.

Blocker, C. P., Cannon, J. P., Panagopoulos, N. G., & Sager, J. K. (2012). The Role of the Sales Force in Value Creation and Appropriation: New Directions for Research. *Journal of Personal Selling & Sales Management, 32*(1), 15–27.

Bolander, W., Bonney, L., & Satornino, C. (2014). Sales Education Efficacy Examining the Relationship Between Sales Education and Sales Success. *Journal of Marketing Education, 36*(2), 169–181.

Carver, C. S., & Scheier, M. F. (1998). *On the Self-Regulation of Behavior.* Cambridge, UK: Cambridge University Press.

Churchill, G. A., Jr., Ford, N. M., Hartley, S. W., & Walker, O. C., Jr. (1985). The Determinants of Salesperson Performance: A Meta-Analysis. *Journal of Marketing Research, 22*(2), 103–118.

Crowe, E., & Tory Higgins, E. (1997). Regulatory Focus and Strategic Inclinations: Promotion and Prevention in Decision-Making. *Organizational Behavior and Human Decision Processes, 69*(2), 117–132.

di Mascio, R. (2010). The Service Models of Frontline Employees. *Journal of Marketing, 74*(4), 63–80.

Dixon, M., & Adamson, B. (2011). *The Challenger Sale: Taking Control of the Customer Conversation.* New York: Penguin.

Dixon, A. L., & Tanner, J. F., Jr. (2012). Transforming Selling: Why It Is Time to Think Differently About Sales Research. *Journal of Personal Selling & Sales Management, 32*(1), 9–13.

Economist. (2015). *Death of a Car Salesman.* Available at http://www.economist.com/news/business/21661656-no-one-much-likes-car-dealers-changing-system-will-be-hard-death-car-salesman. Accessed 14 Sept 2015.

Hoar, A. (2015). *Death of a (B2b) Salesman.* Available at http://www.forbes.com/sites/forrester/2015/04/15/death-of-a-b2b-salesman/#708d38ed4e44. Accessed 12 Aug 2016.

Homburg, C., Wieseke, J., & Bornemann, T. (2009). Implementing the Marketing Concept at the Employee-Customer Interface: The Role of Customer Need Knowledge. *Journal of Marketing, 73*(4), 64–81.

Kumar, V., & Pansari, A. (2016). Competitive Advantage Through Engagement. *Journal of Marketing Research, 53*(4), 497–514.

Kumar, V., Aksoy, L., Donkers, B., Venkatesan, R., Wiesel, T., & Tillmanns, S. (2010). Undervalued or Overvalued Customers: Capturing Total Customer Engagement Value. *Journal of Service Research, 13*(3), 297–310.

Lay, P., Hewlin, T., & Moore, G. (2009). In a Downturn, Provoke Your Customers. *Harvard Business Review, 87*(3), 48–56.

Leong, S. M., Busch, P. S., & John, D. R. (1989). Knowledge Bases and Salesperson Effectiveness: A Script-Theoretic Analysis. *Journal of Marketing Research, 26*(2), 164–178.

Liberman, N., Idson, L. C., Camacho, C. J., & Tory Higgins, E. (1999). Promotion and Prevention Choices Between Stability and Change. *Journal of Personality and Social Psychology, 77*(6), 1135–1145.

Microsoft. (2015). *Always Be Closing: The Abc's of Sales in the Modern World.* Available at www.microsoft.com/en-us/dynamics/always-be-closing. Accessed 18 Feb 2016.

Moncrief, W. C., & Marshall, G. W. (2005). The Evolution of the Seven Steps of Selling. *Industrial Marketing Management, 34*(1), 13–22.

Plouffe, C. R., Bolander, W., Cote, J. A., & Hochstein, B. (2016). Does the Customer Matter Most? Exploring Strategic Frontline Employees' Influence of Customers, the Internal Business Team, and External Business Partners. *Journal of Marketing, 80*(1), 106–123.

Rackham, N. (1988). *Spin Selling.* New York: McGraw-Hill.

Rozenblit, L., & Keil, F. (2002). The Misunderstood Limits of Folk Science: An Illusion of Explanatory Depth. *Cognitive Science, 26*(5), 521–562.

Spiro, R. L., & Weitz, B. A. (1990). Adaptive Selling: Conceptualization, Measurement, and Nomological Validity. *Journal of Marketing Research, 27*(1), 61–69.

Van Doorn, J., Lemon, K. N., Mittal, V., Nass, S., Pick, D., Pirner, P., & Verhoef, P. C. (2010). Customer Engagement Behavior: Theoretical Foundations and Research Directions. *Journal of Service Research, 13*(3), 253–266.

Vaughn, L. A., Hesse, S. J., Petkova, Z., & Trudeau, L. (2009). "This Story Is Right On": The Impact of Regulatory Fit on Narrative Engagement and Persuasion. *European Journal of Social Psychology, 39*(3), 447–456.

Verbeke, W., Dietz, B., & Verwaal, E. (2011). Drivers of Sales Performance: A Contemporary Meta-Analysis. Have Salespeople Become Knowledge Brokers? *Journal of the Academy of Marketing Science, 39*(3), 407–428.

Weitz, B. A., Sujan, H., & Sujan, M. (1986). Knowledge, Motivation, and Adaptive Behavior: A Framework for Improving Selling Effectiveness. *Journal of Marketing, 50*(4), 174–191.

Wenger, E. (1998). *Communities of Practice: Learning, Meaning, and Identity.* Cambridge, UK: Cambridge University Press.

Xie, G. X., & Kahle, L. R. (2014). Approach or Avoid? The Effect of Regulatory Focus on Consumer Behavioural Responses to Personal Selling Attempts. *Journal of Personal Selling & Sales Management, 34*(4), 260–271.

Zhu, R., & Meyers-Levy, J. (2007). Exploring the Cognitive Mechanism That Underlies Regulatory Focus Effects. *Journal of Consumer Research, 34*(1), 89–96.

PART III

Application Context of Customer Engagement

CHAPTER 10

Creating Stronger Brands Through Consumer Experience and Engagement

Bobby J. Calder, Linda D. Hollebeek,
and Edward C. Malthouse

There is a general consensus that marketing is evolving in the way firms view customers. This evolution can be characterized as movement from a transactional point of view in which activity by the firm is directed toward influencing when, how often, and how much a consumer purchases, to an engagement point of view in which activity of the customer toward the firm is the focus (Pansari and Kumar 2017; Viswanathan et al. 2017). This evolution has important, though neglected, consequences for approaching the critical marketing activity of branding. In short, we need to move from a transactional approach to branding to an engagement approach (Harmeling et al. 2016; Venkatesan 2017). As we will show, this entails treating brands as experiences, not merely as things that consumers can be persuaded to buy and use. An experientially engaging brand is one that consumers find meaningful (not just useful) as part of their life, and

B.J. Calder (✉) • E.C. Malthouse
Northwestern University, Chicago, IL, USA

L.D. Hollebeek
University of Auckland, Auckland, New Zealand

© The Author(s) 2018
R.W. Palmatier et al. (eds.), *Customer Engagement Marketing*,
DOI 10.1007/978-3-319-61985-9_10

221

therefore mentally and behaviorally actively incorporate the brand into their lives in a larger way—hence, the term *experimentally engaging brand*. *We elaborate on the distinction between transactional and experientially engaging brands by considering several questions.*

How Are Brands Evolving?

With the goal of fostering a common language in marketing, a *brand* has been defined as a "name, term, design, symbol, or any other feature that identifies one seller's good or service as distinct from those of other sellers (AMA 2016)," thereby emphasizing that the purpose of branding is to communicate the uniqueness of a product that might otherwise be seen as similar to other products. In practice, marketers highlight brand benefits that are superior to those of other products. As articulated in the brand's "positioning statement" (Calder 2010), marketers focus on how their product better satisfies target consumers' product-related goals relative to competing offerings. The positioning statement specifies the brand's benefit and the product goal it satisfies in order to guide all marketing activities.

Branding has traditionally focused on the intrinsic value that a brand offers consumers, which is the extent to which the brand fulfills a product-related goal. The benefit is intrinsic to purchasing and using the branded product. This does not mean that the benefit/goal must be utilitarian in a narrow sense. The brand's benefit may be functional (e.g., "the smoothest shave"), but it can also be emotional or social identification as well (e.g., "The best shave a man can get"). Classic examples such as the Oreo brand are legendary successes in that, over time, they have "laddered" from the functional level to the emotional/social level. For a segment of adults, the Oreo brand is a cookie (compared to other products) that provides a chance to nibble, lick, and twist in a moment of escape and child-like fun.

At a higher conceptual level, this classical conception of branding can be viewed as clearly materialistic, part of a transactional marketing paradigm. It is materialistic in the very sense that branding identifies consumption with the qualities that intrinsically satisfy what the consumer wants in the product itself. It is part of a transactional paradigm in that it is focused on marketing mix management of product, price, promotion, and so on to attract and satisfy consumers (Coviello et al. 2002, p. 34). Customers are paying for the product benefit as optimized to their goal. Newer tools such as database marketing merely extend this transactional focus to further customization.

Although this materialistic/transactional view of branding has long been dominant, there is a growing realization that there is another view that should be recognized, not so much as an alternative, but as a potentially new way of making brands even more attractive from a marketing, consumer, and even societal point of view. It is characterized by the organization's strategic intent to develop customer experiences with their brands and brand-related *contact* or *touch points* ranging from direct marketing channels to indirect brand-related social media (Verhoef et al. 2010).

This new view of branding can best be characterized, in contrast to the materialistic/transactional view, as what we call *experientially engaging branding*. We also explore why experientially engaging brands might perform better, their role in social media, and derive key future implications. Our purpose here is to articulate this emerging point of view and to offer a theory of how it works and why it promises not only marketing effectiveness but increased consumer happiness.

WHAT IS AN EXPERIENTIALLY ENGAGING BRAND?

The current impetus for viewing experiences and engagement as a new basis for branding has emerged out of both marketing practice and academic research. (Table 10.1 provides a summary overview of some of this work.) In marketing practice, the pioneers Pine and Gilmour (1998, 1999) described experiences as memorable "events that engage individuals in a personal way." They suggested that experiences occur when services are used as a stage to engage consumers. Over the next several years, the notion of surrounding products with services to create an engaging experience was expanded. There has been an increasing focus in incorporating of interactive and/or service-based elements into focal offerings, in an attempt to render these more engaging and experiential (Brodie et al. 2011; Hollebeek et al. 2017a). The widely propounded Advertising Research Foundation (ARF) definition put it this way: "Engagement is turning on a prospect to a brand idea enhanced by the surrounding context (Elliott 2006)." It is how the consumer gets connected in a larger way with the brand. An example at the time was Pepsi's use of ring tones:

What is this non-nuptial form of engagement? Dawn E. Hudson, president and chief executive of Pepsi-Cola North America, offered an example. In six weeks, Pepsi plans to begin an advertising and promotional campaign that will offer consumers customized ring tones for cellphones, which can be downloaded from the Internet with codes found under soft drink bottle caps.

Table 10.1   Conceptual overview – CE, CX, and "experientially engaging brand"

Concept	Definition
Customer engagement (CE)	
Brodie et al. (2011, p. 260)	"A psychological state that occurs by virtue of interactive, cocreative customer experiences with a focal agent/object (e.g., a brand) in service relationships."
Kumar and Pansari (2015)	"CE comprises customer purchasing behavior, customer referral behavior, customer influencer behavior and customer knowledge behavior" (Kumar et al. 2010, p. 299).
Pansari and Kumar (2017, p. 2)	"The mechanics of a customer's value addition to the firm, either through direct and/or indirect contribution."
Hollebeek et al. (2017b, p. 6)	"A customer's motivationally driven, volitional investment of focal operant resources (including cognitive, emotional, behavioral, and social knowledge and skills), and operand resources (e.g. equipment) into brand interactions in service systems."
Malthouse et al. (2016a, p. 4)	"A psychological state that occurs by virtue of interactive, cocreative experiences with a focal agent/object (e.g. a brand)."
Customer experience (CX)	
Meyer and Schwager (2007, p. 2)	"The internal and subjective responses that consumers have to any direct or indirect contact with the brand."
De Keyser et al. (2015, p. 23)	"The customer's cognitive, emotional, sensory, and/or social responses to *any* interaction with a particular stimulus."
Lemon and Verhoef (2016, p. 71)	"A multidimensional construct focusing on a customer's cognitive, emotional, behavioral, sensorial, and social responses to a firm's offerings during the customer's entire purchase journey."
Brakus et al. (2009, p. 53)	"Subjective, internal consumer responses... evoked by brand-related stimuli that are part of a brand's design, identity, packaging, communications, and environments."
Conceptual association of CE/CX	
Calder et al. (2013, p. 4)	"The experiential nature of engagement is what distinguishes it from seemingly similar constructs, such as involvement and loyalty. For example, one may be highly involved in selecting a new home security system, but this involvement does not necessarily entail the kind of rich experiences at the heart of the engagement construct... Engagement flows from experiencing a product as something that leads to a larger personal goal."
Brakus et al. (2009, p. 54); Hollebeek et al. (2017b, p. 3)	"Brand experience...differs from motivational concepts, such as involvement" and CE; that is, in contrast to CE, "brand experience does not presume a motivational state."
Experientially engaging brand	
This study	A brand in which consumers make specific cognitive, emotional, and behavioral investments for the purpose of gaining a valued experience from interacting with the brand (Hollebeek et al. 2017b; Brakus et al. 2009).

Note: Selected table components adapted from Hollebeek et al. (2017b), and author's working paper

"Whenever the phone rings, you'll think you got that from Pepsi," said Ms. Hudson, whose company is part of PepsiCo. That engagement with Pepsi products and that "depth of brand experience," she said is far superior to what can be achieved with a "quick, passing message" like a TV commercial. (Elliott 2006)

Experiences thus came to be thought of as the internal and subjective responses that consumers have to all contacts with the brand (Meyer and Schwager 2007). Some academics began to identify engagement as a qualitative experience of the meaning of consuming a product, where this meaning comes from the larger context of the brand in the consumer's life. An "experientially engaging brand" is one in which consumers make specific cognitive, emotional, and behavioral investments for the purpose of gaining a valued experience from interacting with the brand (Hollebeek et al. 2017b; Brakus et al. 2009; Hollebeek 2013). Each brand-related touch point or contact provides an opportunity for creating meaningful experiences, which in turn foster further motivational engagement with the brand (Calder and Malthouse 2008; Calder et al. 2009). As Homburg et al. (2017) put it, engagement is "the evolvement of a person's sensorial, affective, cognitive, relational and behavioral responses to a firm or brand by living through a journey of touchpoints along prepurchase, purchase, and postpurchase situations and continually judging this journey against response thresholds of co-occurring experiences." Brodie et al. (2011) similarly view engagement as a psychological state created by context-dependent experiences (Brodie and Hollebeek 2011). Correspondingly, a 2013 Marketing Science Foundation (MSI) report stated that:

> The experiential nature of engagement is what distinguishes it from seemingly similar constructs such as involvement and loyalty. For example, one may be highly involved in selecting a new home security system, but this involvement does not necessarily entail the kind of rich experiences at the heart of the engagement construct. As another example, one might be very loyal to a particular airline without having the sort of experiences that result in engagement. Engagement flows from experiencing a product as something that leads to a larger personal goal. (Calder et al. 2013, p. 4)

In a recent MSI report reviewing the literature, De Keyser et al. (2015) endorsed such a process-oriented view of consumer experiences (CX). In contrast to CX, the user experience (UX) is one of using the product materially. It is more mundane, ordinary, and everyday. CX is richer and embedded within a larger experiential environment. At this point, there is clarity around the general concept of a brand that is experiential and engaging. A material, transactional-paradigm brand is defined by its consumer benefit relative to a product goal and is associated with a UX that may be more or less complex but is defined entirely by product usage. Consumers can, however, regard a brand as more than this, as part of a larger context. This context includes consumers' networks (Vargo and Lusch 2016) and any brand-related contacts or touch points, physical or vicariously mediated, through which the consumer experiences the brand as relevant to some life goal or personal value (Breidbach et al. 2014; Hollebeek and Brodie 2016). The brand has a value that is extrinsic to the product per se. It becomes part of a larger purpose or goal that is not limited to the benefit and product goal that the brand satisfies (Higgins and Scholer 2009).

The concept of an experientially engaging brand will be more concrete if we can measure the strength of particular brands in this regard. The above discussion implies that experiential brands, by definition, must be understood as highly qualitative in their nature (Holbrook and Hirschman 1982), which, in turn, renders the development of quantitative metrics for experiential engagement somewhat of a challenge. However, recent attempts at measurement add clarity to the concept of an experientially engaging brand.

Brakus et al. (2009) sought to indirectly quantify experiential engagement with four general dimensions: sensory, intellectual, affective, and behavioral. Consumers rate descriptions of the brand on each dimension, such as "I find this brand interesting in a sensory way" (sensory), "I engage in a lot of thinking when I encounter this brand" (intellectual), and "The brand is an emotional brand" (affective). Hence, the experience is being described according to beliefs about these four abstracted dimensions. Note that this approach does not attempt to assess the qualitative nature of the consumer's experience. We also observe that Brakus et al.'s (2009) "brand experience" measure overlaps with Hollebeek et al.'s (2014) "consumer brand engagement" scale. Both identify cognitive (intellectual), emotional (affective), and behavioral dimensions of CE, and CX, respectively. Sample items of Brakus et al.'s scale include the following: "I engage in a lot of thinking when I encounter this brand" (intellectual), and "The brand is an emotional brand" (affective). Sample items of Hollebeek et al. (2014) scale include "I think about [brand] a lot when I'm using it" (cognitive), and "Using [brand] makes me happy" (emotional).

In contrast, Calder et al. (2016a) measure consumers' context-specific beliefs about the extent to which a brand is associated with qualitatively defined life goals or personal values. They do this with context-specific beliefs about the extent to which a brand is associated with qualitatively defined life goals or personal values. In the case of a newspaper brand and the experience of socially interacting with other people as a goal, consumers rate the brand on beliefs, such as "I commonly bring up things I've read in this newspaper in conversations with others." Another example is the extent to which the brand is experienced as part of the consumer's goal of community and civic responsibility (Calder and Malthouse 2004).

This qualitative model of brand engagement can be further illustrated with a study conducted with the Chicago Jazz Festival, a branded summer event held in an outdoor venue (Calder et al. 2016a). As shown in Table 10.2, preliminary qualitative work indicated that three experiences were particularly important for the Festival, labeled Social, Discovery, and Transportation. Table 10.2 also shows the beliefs (items) that combine to describe these experiences. These experiences, as measured via the beliefs, were found to combine to yield a measure of overall engagement that was a weighted combination of the three experiences (cf. Fig. 10.1). A confirmatory factor analysis supported this model.

Table 10.2 Experiences and belief descriptions for the Chicago Jazz Festival Brand

Experience	Belief description items rated by consumers	Standardized loading
Social ($\alpha = .71$)	It made me feel more connected to other people and the community	.75
	I enjoyed talking with someone else about it	.76
	I enjoyed going to it with family and friends	.42
	I felt personally involved with it	.64
Discovery ($\alpha = .81$)	It motivated me to listen more jazz and learn more about it	.85
	It gave me a broader, richer perspective	.74
	I learned about what kind of jazz I like best	.68
Transportation ($\alpha = .83$)	I liked to imagine myself being on the stage	.95
	It made me think of actually playing an instrument or singing myself	.75

Weights are parameter standardized loading estimates from the confirmatory factor analysis measurement model; α indicates the extent to which the experience is unidimensional or pure, highest value = 1

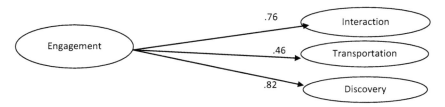

Fig. 10.1 Engagement as a weighted combination of the three experiences of the Chicago Jazz Festival Brand (second-order confirmatory factor analysis standardized loadings)

Regardless of whether an indirect or a qualitatively direct measurement approach is used, the objective is to measure the strength of experientially engaging brands. The stronger these experiences are across abstracted dimensions or across specific goal-defined qualitative types of experiences, the greater the engagement with the brand. So from a measurement point of view, engagement is a higher-order construct that arises out of lower-order constructs spanning all brand-related touch points (Calder et al. 2009).

Is Experiential Engagement Different from Traditional Constructs and Metrics?

We have mentioned that experiential engagement is a consequence of consumer touch points with the brand. Recently, Lemon and Verhoef (2016) have addressed this in a comprehensive manner. They emphasize that experience resides in the entire context of prepurchase, purchase, and postpurchase contacts that entail touch points both created by the brand and by partners (such as channels and agencies) and consumers themselves. Experience is a function of interactions with all of these relevant touch points. Lemon and Verhoef rightly point out that these experiences have traditionally been thought of in terms of constructs such as service quality and satisfaction. Their view seems to be that the construct of experience provides a more comprehensive perspective on the totality of the consumer's journey across the entire range of touch points, and that traditional constructs are incorporated into this as ways of analyzing experiences.

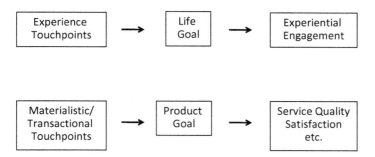

Fig. 10.2 Contrasting antecedents and consequences of materialistic/transactional and experientially engaging branding

While we agree that this framework is valuable in that it puts consumer experience into perspective, our view is different in that we emphasize that experiential engagement is not just the ordinary "experience" of service quality, satisfaction, or the like. Our view is that experiential engagement is exceptional. The consumer may be quite satisfied with a materialistic/transactional brand, but this is not experiential engagement. Engagement arises from the consumer's mental and behavioral response to the brand as being meaningful in their lives in a way that transcends an ordinary product goal-related benefit. This difference is not captured or measured by conventional ways of thinking. It requires the sort of analysis and measurement illustrated in our Jazz Festival example (Fig. 10.2).

One could of course choose to view experience in the broader sense of any and all of the consumer's responses to the brand. This is especially tempting with so many customer–brand interactions occurring in digital environments where every behavior is recorded. Thus, engagement is often equated with behaviors such as clicks, likes, shares, views, time in a branded environment, and so on. In our view, however, this would obscure the added power of experiential engagement in creating stronger brands.

Do Experientially Engaging Brands Perform Better?

Based on the conceptual distinction of brands from an experientially engaging versus transactional marketing perspective, a key question is whether (and to what extent) these brands impact consumers differently. Current research indicates that this is the case.

Relevant research has mainly addressed the question of how consumers respond differently to brands that are *perceived* by them to be more experiential versus more materialistic or transactional in nature. Originating with Van Boven and Gilovich (2003, p. 1194), consumers are assumed to be able to distinguish between material (i.e., tangible product) and experiential (e.g., intangible or phenomenological service) purchases. Consistent with our discussion, while material purchases are typically made for utilitarian purposes, experiential purchases tend to be made to acquire specific desired (life) experiences. This distinction, however, can be fuzzy because both may, to some extent, co-exist. For example, while having one's car serviced appears utilitarian, exceptional service may be experiential in nature. While we return to this fuzziness below, we assume that this perceived distinction exists in consumers' minds, and that they are able to apply it when classifying purchases as either transactional or experiential.

Using this distinction to have consumers classify different purchases, a variety of studies, as reviewed by Dunn et al. (2011), show that the consumption of experiences tends to generate greater happiness than the consumption of more transactional offerings. For example, Van Boven and Gilovich (2003) had people classify their most recent purchase over $100 as either material or experiential. Survey participants indicated more happiness with experiential purchases. In another study, they had people think of buying the same item as a material or as an experiential purchase. Thinking about buying the product as experiential was associated with elevated happiness. The book *Happy Money: The Science of Happier Spending* (Dunn and Norton 2013) surveys recent research and even recommends buying experiences as a self-help strategy for consumers.

This research supports the hypothesis that experiential brands are more powerful than material brands. Further, it is consistent with the notion that experiential brands are different because they link consumer life goal(s) or personal value(s) to the purchase of particular experiences. For example, experiences provide scope for the importance of social connections and ties among people, as well as self-identity. It has even been found that if experiences are too unusual to be shared (i.e., not connected to a larger social purpose), they can actually lower happiness (Cooney et al. 2014). Moreover, the impact of experiential purchases is not limited to the amount of money spent. Spending more time with an experiential activity increases happiness in the same way as spending money (Aaker et al. 2011; Vohs and Baumeister 2011). Relatedly, if one does not focus on the experience itself, the impact on happiness decreases (Killingsworth and

Gilbert 2010). In sum, there is more to the experiential brand than monetary, transactional, or material value.

There are, however, limitations to this line of research (Dunn and Norton 2013; Gilovich et al. 2015). Negative experiences do not lead to unhappiness (Nicolao et al. 2009), though, interestingly, regrets about experiential purchases tend to focus on lost opportunities rather than dissatisfaction (Rosenzweig and Gilovich 2012). Importantly, there are other reasons why a perceived experiential purchase could generate greater happiness, thus rendering a need to take care around inferring causality in this area. It may be that brands classified as experiential by consumers may, in their own right, be more idiosyncratic and memorable, rendering these less subject to comparison with other brands or offerings.

The underlying distinction in these studies between experiential and material/transactional purchases remains fuzzy (Gilovich et al. 2015). Perceptions are likely to be confounded with many other things associated with the product purchase (Schmitt et al. 2015). Going out to dinner inherently has more things associated with it than buying a disposable pen at an office supply store. Because materialistic and experiential purchases, by definition, differ in a number of ways, the classification of any purchase as one or the other is ambiguous in that it is difficult to ascertain the exact difference between the two. While the distinction has been useful in stimulating research on the consequences of consumption, these findings are currently effects without real attempts at explanation.

Any way in which purchases differ is a candidate for explaining the greater impact of experiential purchases, relative to materialistic ones. Research could, as Dun and Weidman (2015) put it, simply embrace the fuzziness of the distinction, although this would deny the need for an explanatory theory to guide further research and practice.

A better research strategy is to move beyond classifying purchases to build on previous work showing that consumers can classify a purchase as *either* materialistic or experiential if they are motivated to look at the purchase one way or the other (Van Boven and Gilovich 2003). A consumer can look at any purchase as either materialistic or experiential, depending on their focus. Consumers can approach a purchase either as buying something to satisfy utilitarian purposes or, alternatively, as buying something to have a positive life experience. Creating the perception of relevance to a life goal or value is indeed the rationale for experientially engaging brands. However, a better understanding of this process is needed, and we address this next.

WHY MIGHT EXPERIENTIALLY ENGAGING BRANDS PERFORM BETTER?

Research clearly indicates that experientially engaging brands can have a greater impact on consumers than a brand perceived as materialistic/transactional. To advance research and practice, we need a better explanation of why this occurs. Building on a suggestion by Calder et al. (2016b) and the literature on perceived experiential versus materialistic purchases, we propose a model of positive, as well as negative, self-control for this purpose.

Negative self-control has been examined extensively (Baumeister and Tierny 2011). The issue posed by negative self-control arises with the conflict between short- and long-term goals. For example, while a consumer may have a long-term goal of eating right and feeling healthier, the individual can face short-term temptations such as being offered a rich dessert like a piece of chocolate cake. What determines whether the consumer resists the cake in favor of the long-term goal or gives in to the short-term desire for the cake? Research has found that consumers have a capacity for self-control, but this capacity is limited. If consumers have depleted the capacity by recently exercising self-control (even in areas unrelated to eating, such as suppressing emotional responses), then they will be less able to resist. Conversely, practicing self-control may increase the capacity to self-regulate. Kotabe and Hoffman (2015) were able to summarize this research with an integrative self-control theory.

We can restate the Kotobe and Hoffman model as follows with respect to brands: the co-activation of a short-term, brand-related goal with a benefit that is incompatible with the consumer's higher-order goal triggers the exercise of self-control, which is limited by the individual's motivation and the capacity for self-control. If these factors are insufficient, the goal conflict will be resolved in favor of the brand (through negative self-control). If not, the brand is avoided in favor of the life goal taking precedence.

This theory can readily be further translated into brand practice. If a materialistic, transactional brand's product goal/benefit is consistent with the consumer's higher-order life goal(s), or at least is not inconsistent, there is no goal conflict. However, if there is a goal conflict, a failure of self-control may still result in consumers buying and using the materialistic/transactional brand. Yet, and this is critical to our proposed explanation, buying the materialistic brand in the case of conflict will have consequences. One is that the consumer may well be satisfied with the brand since it has provided the promised benefit and satisfied the product goal. The additional consequence, however, will be that the consumer experiences guilt or another negative experience associated with the violation of the higher-order life goal or personal value. In other words, the consumer is satisfied with the material brand but unhappy about the sacrifice of the higher-order goal. Hence:

> Implication 1: A materialistic/transactional brand that is *inconsistent* with a consumer's higher-order goal will be weaker by virtue of having more negative consequences if purchased/consumed than a materialistic brand that does not conflict with the individual's higher-order goal.

Now consider the case of an experientially engaging brand. Here, the brand is, by definition, consistent with the consumer's relevant higher-order goal. This consistency, and lack of any goal conflict, will increase the consumer's happiness because it is meaningful and gives some sense of purpose in the consumer's life. Thus, the experientially engaging brand has an impact that transcends the merely materialistic/transactional brand. Hence:

> Implication 2: An experientially engaging brand that is *consistent* with a consumer's higher-order goal will be stronger than a materialistic/ transactional brand that is not relevant to the consumer's higher-order goals.

A materialistic brand can also be an experientially engaging. Consequently, the distinction with experiential brands ought not to be viewed as mutually exclusive, but rather as theoretical poles along a continuum. To the extent that a materialistic/transactional brand has a strong benefit relevant to a product goal, it should produce satisfaction with the brand. The key point is that, if the brand is consistent with a higher-order goal, then, as an experientially engaging brand, it will increase the consumer's happiness (and avoid any unhappiness due to goal conflict). It is also possible that a brand can be weak in a materialistic way and can still lead to consumer happiness, if not so much materialistic satisfaction (think raspberries for dessert). Hence:

> Implication 3: A brand that is *consistent* with a consumer's lower-order product goal *and* a higher-order goal will be stronger than either separately. And, corollary, an experientially engaging brand may be strong even if it is less consistent with the consumer's lower-order product goal.

Our explanation for the superior performance of experientially engaging brands requires testing in research and practice. We view such work as the next stage in thinking about creating experientially engaging brands and their value. However, we can offer some preliminary evidence in support of this explanation by returning to the Chicago Jazz Festival brand. The brand experience and engagement measures reported earlier were correlated not only with consumers' intentions to attend the festival in the following year but also with a behavioral measure of category-level intentions to attend classical music concerts, art museums, dance performances, and jazz concerts. This finding supports the notion that an experientially engaging brand that is experientially engaging has an impact beyond that of the specific material product benefit (in this case enjoying the festival).

A related study of newspaper brands is also instructive (Calder et al. 2016a). Here, we included a measure of brand satisfaction as well as the measure of experiential engagement described earlier. Note that newspaper brands have been declining for years in terms of material product goal benefits. The study indeed found that experiential engagement predicted overall newspaper consumption (i.e., time spent, frequency, and completeness of usage) over and beyond the effects of mere consumer brand satisfaction (Mersey et al. 2012). In fact, part of the relationship between the consumer satisfaction measure and consumption was produced by experiential engagement. We view this as a case of a weaker materialistic/transactional brand having an impact on consumer behavior, not through satisfaction with a product-related goal, but through a larger consistency with higher-order life goal experiences.

CAN ALL BRANDS BE EXPERIENTIALLY ENGAGING?

Our discussion implies that no product is inherently either a materialistic/transactional or an experientially engaging brand. In principle, any product can be branded in an engaging way. It might seem that the Chicago Jazz Festival would naturally be engaging because music is inherently experiential. But what about an ordinary commodity-type product?

Consider the case of Coca-Cola. One might think that in the last decade or so, with the proliferation of all types of beverages, Coca-Cola could at best be positioned around a unique benefit such as taste. But the company was successful in branding Coca-Cola around the experience of being happy by making others happy. Any number of touch points were created for this purpose, from handing out Coca-Cola flags in Copenhagen (resembling the Danish flag) that consumers could use to welcome home friends and family (this sort of welcome being a local custom) to placing a special Coke machine in public places that dispensed fun gifts that turned routine vending into a happy occasion for everyone around.

This is not to say that creating experientially engaging brands is easy. Recently, Coca-Cola has found it increasingly difficult, given concerns about sugar use, to brand experientially. In fact, it has recently returned to materialist/transactional branding around taste.

Nor is it the case that a product necessarily lends itself to experiential engagement. It might be thought that a luxury product, for instance, would automatically be engaging. But we have only to look at the recent problems of a brand such as Ralph Lauren to see that luxury alone does not make for experiential engagement.

Our contention is that the lessons of experientially engaging brands will generalize across companies and product categories. These may require very different touch points, but the underlying logic is the same. Further, it is the logic of positioning the brand in terms of a specific kind of experiential engagement (e.g., Coca-Cola as being happy by making others happy) that itself guides the design of effective touch points that implement the branding. The kinds of touch points used may vary markedly, but the logic of experiential branding should remain the same.

WHAT ABOUT SOCIAL MEDIA BEHAVIOR?

Much of the growing interest in experientially engaging brands has revolved around the idea that engagement predisposes consumers to certain behaviors (Groeger et al. 2016); that is, that behavior is an integral part of being engaged, such as through interacting, participating in brand-related activities, etc. (Brodie et al. 2011; Hollebeek et al. 2017b; Maslowska et al. 2016). This is manifested in the view of engagement as an inherently "leaning forward" activity, with a participative nature. It follows from this idea that since social media is interactive and often entails user-generated content, it is ideal for creating experientially engaging brands (Brodie et al. 2013; Baumöl et al. 2016). Relatedly, Patterson et al. (2006) specifically identify *dedication* (a customer's sense of belonging to the brand), *vigor* (level of energy/effort in brand interactions), and *interaction* (two-way consumer/brand communications) as key engagement dimensions.

We must be careful, however, to separate the behavioral aspect of experiential engagement from its behavioral consequences. A consumer's level of brand-related engagement, such as with our newspaper brands, should translate into incremental consumer behavior. But reading the newspaper can still be an essentially passive experience, as could reading the news on Yahoo or Facebook. There is nothing to say that just because reading the newspaper, or using any other brand, is not a lean-forward activity, there cannot be an experientially engaging brand involved.

All the same, there is reason to think that experiential engagement can be increased in cases where consumers vigorously participate, advocate, or interact with the brand. A study of the Airmiles brand in Canada provides a case in point (Malthouse et al. 2016a, b). Airmiles is a loyalty program brand that rewards purchases of a large assortment of different products across many retail locations. The material/transactional brand benefit is the consumer's redemption of valued rewards with points. In an effort to evolve toward being an experientially engaging brand, Airmiles instituted a social media program in which consumers were invited to actively participate by sharing a goal that they had in mind. While they could merely name a product goal (e.g., saving for a toaster), Airmiles found that by allowing consumers to actively generate content about why they were collecting points, consumers were more likely to provide stories linking to life goals (e.g., I want to give a new toaster to my grandmother for her birthday).

The length of the social media content response, assumed to reflect whether the consumer had only a lower-order product goal or a higher-order life goal, correlated with the number of miles the customer accumulated during the period of the promotional period. In other words, actively generating a longer story about their goal (more elaboration), presumably expressing more relevance to a life goal, increased consumer's use of the brand. This is just the kind of result one would expect with the successful use of social media to build an experientially engaging brand that goes beyond satisfaction of a materialistic/transactional goal.

The implication is: "Engagement is not produced by simply being 'on' a certain kind of media, digital, social, mobile or otherwise. Marketers must design specific experiences using these media to make the brand-life goals(s) connection and elaborate on it (Malthouse et al. 2016b, p. 100)."

WHAT IS THE FUTURE SIGNIFICANCE OF EXPERIENTIALLY ENGAGING BRANDS?

Branding faces many challenges, from advertising clutter to the sheer proliferation of brands. Many worry about a general decline in the power of branding. Underlying these dynamics is the simple fact that it is becoming more difficult for marketers to distinguish products as materialistic/transactional brands. There is thus a pressing need for innovation in creating brands.

The foregoing analyses point to the importance of a relationship marketing perspective of branding (Palmatier et al. 2006, 2007, 2009) that is "directed toward establishing, developing, and maintaining successful relational exchanges" (Morgan and Hunt 1994, p. 34), in contrast to the classic transactional paradigm. Coviello et al. (2002) further divide this relational paradigm into two sub-types: (a) interactive marketing, which focuses on developing personal relationships to create co-operative interactions (e.g., between buyers and sellers) for mutual benefit, and (b) network marketing, which focuses on the development of relationships to allow for the coordination of activities among multiple parties for mutual benefit (Coviello et al. 2002, p. 34; Coviello and Brodie 2001).

Under this relational marketing paradigm, the importance of transacting is still pivotal. The framework should be viewed as a pyramid model where transactional marketing resides at the base of the pyramid (i.e., acts as the foundation for other marketing practices). Some marketing efforts will *extend* beyond the transactional foundation to include relational marketing practices, such as interactive marketing. The majority of contemporary marketing efforts will *extend* beyond the transactional foundation to include relational marketing practices. Transactional and relational marketing are best viewed as matters of relative degree on a continuum; that is, the two are likely to occur concurrently to various degrees (rather than being mutually exclusive).

The approach to experientially engaging brands discussed here can thus be seen as the adoption of a relational marketing paradigm, one not intended to supplant the materialistic/transactional paradigm of branding but to take a fundamentally different approach that offers the potential to make a greater contribution to consumer happiness or well-being as well as to enhance marketing effectiveness.

On a more concrete note, in the future we foresee brands, such as Oreo, embracing the relationship paradigm and experientially engaging branding. Presently the Oreo brand is becoming a way for consumers to connect more broadly over a range of brand-related contacts or touch points connecting to their life goal/value of a more carefree and fun life. This has led to marketing activities such as sending brand ambassadors out on the streets to ask consumers why they love Oreos and amplifying these contacts as social media content. This is not social media for the sake of having a social media budget but social media in the service of building an experientially engaging brand.

Acknowledgments The second author acknowledges Professor Amy Ostrom for a discussion on service, engagement, and well-being, and Dr Tom Chen for a discussion on engagement and experience.

REFERENCES

Aaker, J., Rudd, M., & Mogilner, C. (2011). If Money Does Not Make You Happy, Consider Time. *Journal of Consumer Psychology, 21*, 126–130.

American Marketing Association [AMA]. (2016). *Definition of 'Brand'*. Available at: https://www.ama.org/resources/Pages/Dictionary.aspx?dLetter=B. Accessed 11 Jan 2016.

Baumeister, R. F., & Tierny, J. (2011). *Willpower: Rediscovering the Greatest Human Strength*. New York: Penguin Press.

Baumöl, U., Hollebeek, L., & Jung, R. (2016). Dynamics of Customer Interaction on Social Media Platforms. *Electronic Markets, 26*(3), 199–202.

Brakus, J. J., Schmitt, B. H., & Zarantonello, L. (2009). Brand Experience: What Is It? How Is It Measured? Does It Affect Loyalty? *Journal of Marketing, 73*(3), 52–68.

Breidbach, C., Brodie, R., & Hollebeek, L. (2014). Beyond Virtuality: From Engagement Platforms to Engagement Ecosystems. *Managing Service Quality, 24*(6), 592–611.

Brodie, R. J., & Hollebeek, L. D. (2011). Advancing and Consolidating Knowledge About Customer Engagement. *Journal of Service Research, 14*(3), 283–284.

Brodie, R. J., Hollebeek, L. D., Jurić, B., & Ilić, A. (2011). Customer Engagement: Conceptual Domain, Fundamental Propositions, and Implications for Research. *Journal of Service Research, 14*(3), 252–271.

Brodie, R. J., Ilic, A., Juric, B., & Hollebeek, L. (2013). Consumer Engagement in a Virtual Brand Community: An Exploratory Analysis. *Journal of Business Research, 66*(1), 105–114.

Calder, B. J. (2010). Writing Positioning Statements and Brand Design. In A. Tybout (Ed.), *Kellogg on Marketing* (pp. 92–111). Hoboken: Wiley.

Calder, B. J., & Malthouse, E. C. (2004). Qualitative Media Measures: Newspaper Experiences. *International Journal on Media Management, 6*(1–2), 123–130.

Calder, B. J., & Malthouse, E. C. (2008). Media Engagement and Advertising Effectiveness. In B. Calder (Ed.), *Kellogg on Advertising and Media* (pp. 1–36). Hoboken: Wiley.

Calder, B. J., Malthouse, E. C., & Schaedel, U. (2009). Engagement with Online Media and Advertising Effectiveness. *Journal of Interactive Marketing, 23*(4), 321–331.

Calder, B. J., Isaac, M. S., & Malthouse, E. C. (2013). Taking the Customer's Point-of-View, *Marketing Science Institute Working Paper Series Report,* #13–102.

Calder, B. J., Isaac, M. S., & Malthouse, E. C. (2016a). How to Capture Consumer Experiences: A Context-Specific Approach to Measuring Engagement. *Journal of Advertising Research, 56*(1), 1–14.

Calder, B. J., Malthouse, E. C., & Maslowska, E. (2016b). Brand Marketing, Big Data, and Social Innovation as Future Research Directions for Engagement. *Journal of Marketing Management, 32*(5), 579–585.

Cooney, G., Gilbert, D. T., & Wilson, T. D. (2014). The Unforeseen Costs of Extraordinary Experience. *Psychological Science, 25*(12), 2259–2265.

Coviello, N. E., & Brodie, R. J. (2001). Contemporary Marketing Practices of Consumer and Business-to-Business Firms: How Different Are They? *v of Business & Industrial Marketing, 16*(5), 382–400.

Coviello, N. E., Brodie, R. J., Danaher, P. J., & Johnston, W. J. (2002). How Firms Relate to Their Markets: An Empirical Examination of Contemporary Marketing Practices. *Journal of Marketing, 66*(3), 33–46.

DeKeyser, A., Lemon, K. N., Klaus, P., & Keiningham, T. L. (2015). A Framework for Understanding and Managing the Customer Experience. *Marketing Science Institute Working Paper Series Report,* #15–21.

Dunn, E. W., & Norton, M. (2013). *Happy Money: The Science of Happier Spending.* New York: Simon & Schuster.

Dunn, E. W., & Weidman, A. C. (2015). Building a Science of Spending: Lessons from the Past and Directions for the Future. *Journal of Consumer Psychology, 25,* 172–178.

Dunn, E. W., Gilbert, D. T., & Wilson, T. D. (2011). If Money Doesn't Make You Happy, Then You Probably Aren't Spending It Right. *Journal of Consumer Psychology, 21,* 115–125.

Elliott, S. (2006, March 21). New Rules of Engagement. *New York Times.* Available at: http://www.nytimes.com/2006/03/21/business/media/new-rules-of-engagement.html

Gilovich, T., Kumar, A., & Jampol, L. (2015). The Beach, the Bikini, and the Best Guy: Replies to Dunn and Weidman, and to Schmitt, Brakus, and Zarantonello. *Journal of Consumer Psychology, 25,* 179–184.

Groeger, L., Moroko, L., & Hollebeek, L. D. (2016). Capturing Value from Non-Paying Consumers' Engagement Behaviours: Field Evidence and Development of a Theoretical Model. *Journal of Strategic Marketing, 24*(3–4), 190–209.

Harmeling, C. M., Moffett, J. W., Arnold, M. J., & Carlson, B. D. (2016). Toward a Theory of Customer Engagement Marketing. *Journal of the Academy of Marketing Science*. Forthcoming. doi:10.1007/s11747-016-0509-2.

Higgins, E. T., & Scholer, A. A. (2009). Engaging the Consumer: The Science and Art of the Value Creation Process. *Journal of Consumer Psychology, 19*(2), 100–114.

Holbrook, E. C., & Hirschman, E. C. (1982). The Experiential Aspects of Consumption: Consumer Fantasies, Feelings, and Fun. *Journal of Consumer Research, 9*(2), 132–140.

Hollebeek, L. D. (2013). The Customer Engagement/Value Interface: An Exploratory Investigation. *Australasian Marketing Journal, 21*(1), 17–24.

Hollebeek, L. D., & Brodie, R. J. (2016). Non-Monetary Social and Network Value: Understanding the Effects of Non-Paying Customers in New Media. *Journal of Strategic Marketing, 24*(3–4), 169–174.

Hollebeek, L. D., Glynn, M. S., & Brodie, R. J. (2014). Consumer Brand Engagement in Social Media: Conceptualization, Scale Development and Validation. *Journal of Interactive Marketing, 28*(2), 149–165.

Hollebeek, L. D., Malthouse, E. C., & Block, M. (2016). Sounds of Music: Exploring Consumers' Musical Engagement. *Journal of Consumer Marketing, 33*(6), 417–427.

Hollebeek, L. D., Juric, B., & Tang, W. (2017a). Virtual Brand Community Engagement Practices: A Refined Typology and Model. *Journal of Services Marketing, 31*(3), 204–217. Forthcoming.

Hollebeek, L. D., Srivastava, R. K., & Chen, T. (2017b). S-D Logic–Informed Customer Engagement: Integrative Framework, Revised Fundamental Propositions, and Application to CRM. *Journal of the Academy of Marketing Science*. Forthcoming. doi:10.1007/s11747-016-0494-5.

Homburg, C., Jozié, D., & Kuehnl, C. (2017). Customer Experience Management: Toward Implementing an Evolving Marketing Concept. *Journal of Academy of Marketing Science, 45*, 377–401.

Killingsworth, M. A., & Gilbert, D. T. (2010). A Wandering Mind Is an Unhappy Mind. *Science, 330*, 932.

Kotabe, H. P., & Hofmann, W. (2015). On Integrating the Components of Self-Control. *Psychological Science, 10*(5), 618–638.

Kumar, V., & Pansari, A. (2015). Measuring the Benefits of Employee Engagement. *MIT Sloan Management Review, 56*(4), 67.

Kumar, V., Aksoy, L., Donkers, B., Venkatesan, R., Wiesel, T., & Tillmanns, S. (2010). Undervalued or Overvalued Customers: Capturing Total Customer Engagement Value. *Journal of Service Research, 13*(3), 297–310.

Lemon, K. N., & Verhoef, P. C. (2016). Understanding Customer Experience Throughout the Customer Journey. *Journal of Marketing, 80*, 69–96.

Malthouse, E. C., Calder, B. J., Kim, S. J., & Vandenbosch, M. (2016a). Evidence That User-Generated Content That Produces Engagement Increases Purchase Behaviours. *Journal of Marketing Management, 32*(5), 427–444.

Malthouse, E. C., Calder, B. J., & Vandenbosch, M. (2016b). Creating Brand Engagement on Digital, Social, and Mobile Media. In R. Brodie, L. Hollebeek, & J. Conduit (Eds.), *Customer Engagement: Contemporary Issues and Challenges* (pp. 85–101). London: Routledge.

Maslowska, E., Malthouse, E. C., & Collinger, T. (2016). The Customer Engagement Ecosystem. *Journal of Marketing Management, 32*(5–6), 469–501.

Mersey, R. D., Malthouse, E. C., & Calder, B. J. (2012). Focusing on the Reader Engagement Trumps Satisfaction. *Journalism & Mass Communication Quarterly, 89*(4), 695–709.

Meyer, C., & Schwager, A. (2007). Understanding Customer Experience. *Harvard Business Review, 85*(2), 116–126.

Morgan, R. M., & Hunt, S. D. (1994). The Commitment-Trust Theory of Relationship Marketing. *Journal of Marketing, 58*(3), 20–38.

Nicolao, L., Irwin, J. R., & Goodman, J. K. (2009). Happiness for Sale: Do Experiential Purchases Make Consumers Happier than Material Purchases? *Journal of Consumer Research, 36*(2), 188–198.

Palmatier, R. W., Dant, R. P., Grweal, D., & Evans, K. R. (2006). Factors Influencing the Effectiveness of Relationship Marketing: A Meta-Analysis. *Journal of Marketing, 70*(4), 136–153.

Palmatier, R. W., Scheer, L. K., & Steenkamp, J.-B. E. M. (2007). Customer Loyalty to Whom? Managing the Benefits and Risks of Salesperson-Owned Loyalty. *Journal of Marketing, 44*(2), 185–199.

Palmatier, R. W., Jarvis, C. B., Bechkoff, J. R., & Kardes, F. R. (2009). The Role of Customer Gratitude in Relationship Marketing. *Journal of Marketing, 73*(5), 1–18.

Pansari, A., & Kumar, V. (2017). Customer Engagement: The Construct, Antecedents, and Consequences. *Journal of Academy of Marketing Science, 45*, 294–311.

Patterson, P., Yu, T., & de Ruyter, K. (2006). Understanding Customer Engagement in Services. In: *Proceedings of ANZMAC 2006 Conference*, Brisbane.

Pine, B. J., & Gilmore, J. H. (1998). Welcome to the Experience Economy. *Harvard Business Review, 76*(4), 97–105.

Pine, B. J., & Gilmore, J. H. (1999). *The Experience Economy.* Boston: Harvard Business School Press.

Rosenzweig, E., & Gilovich, T. (2012). Buyer's Remorse or Missed Opportunity? Differential Regrets for Material and Experiential Purchases. *Journal of Personality and Social Psychology, 102*(2), 215–223.

Schmitt, B., Brakus, J., & Zarantonell, L. (2015). From Experiential Psychology to Consumer Experience. *Journal of Consumer Psychology, 25,* 166–171.

Van Boven, L., & Gilovich, T. (2003). To Do or To Have? That Is the Question. *Journal of Personality and Social Psychology, 85*(6), 1193–1202.

Vargo, S. L., & Lusch, R. F. (2016). Institutions and Axioms: An Extension and Update of Service-Dominant Logic. *Journal of the Academy of Marketing Science, 44*(1), 5–23.

Venkatesan, R. (2017). Executing on a Customer Engagement Strategy. *Journal of the Academy of Marketing Science.* Forthcoming. doi:10.1007/s11747-016-0513-6.

Verhoef, P. C., Reinartz, W. J., & Krafft, M. (2010). Customer Engagement as a New Perspective in Customer Management. *Journal of Service Research, 13*(3), 247–252.

Viswanathan, V., Hollebeek, L. D., Malthouse, E. C., Maslowska, E., Kim, S. J., & Xie, W. (2017). The Dynamics of Consumer Engagement with Mobile Technologies. *Service Science.,* Forthcoming, *9,* 36–49.

Vohs, K. D., & Baumeister, R. F. (2011). What's the Use of Happiness? It Can't Buy You Money. *Journal of Consumer Psychology, 21,* 139–141.

CHAPTER 11

From Customer to Partner Engagement: A Conceptualization and Typology of Engagement in B2B

Werner J. Reinartz and Manuel Berkmann

INTRODUCTION

In the last decade, customer engagement has become a key topic for both practitioners and researchers. For Forbes Insights, "engagement is everything" (2015, p. 3). The increasing importance in marketing practice gets support from a recent study by McKinsey & Company that shows that 69% of CEOs consider customer engagement a top strategic priority for their business (McKinsey 2014). On the other hand, only 25% of CMOs state that they have a comprehensive understanding of the phenomenon customer engagement (CMO Council 2014).

Also in marketing research, engagement is regarded as a top priority as indicated by continued representation in the MSI Research Priorities (2010, 2014, 2016). In fact, there has been considerable progress in conceptualizing and measuring customer engagement (Brodie et al. 2011; van Doorn et al. 2010; Hollebeek et al. 2016; Kumar and Pansari 2016; Pansari and Kumar 2016). While some studies define customer engagement as behavioral manifestations beyond purchase (van Doorn et al. 2010),

W.J. Reinartz (✉) • M. Berkmann
University of Cologne, Department of Retailing and Customer Management, Cologne, Germany

© The Author(s) 2018
R.W. Palmatier et al. (eds.), *Customer Engagement Marketing*,
DOI 10.1007/978-3-319-61985-9_11

others argue that customer engagement is rather a psychological state of mind (Brodie et al. 2011). There is a general agreement, however, that customer engagement is a multidimensional concept (Beckers et al. 2014) which can be holistically defined as "the mechanics of a customer's value addition to the firm, either through direct or/and indirect contribution" (Pansari and Kumar 2016, p. 2). Yet, looking at the extant literature, it becomes apparent that the focus is almost exclusively on customer engagement in business-to-consumer (B2C) settings, while business-to-business (B2B) settings have largely been neglected (Vivek et al. 2016).

This is surprising given the tremendous importance of customer engagement in B2B settings. The lead user concept introduced by von Hippel (1986) was one of the first descriptions of customer engagement and originates in B2B innovation research. It states that firms can improve their innovation efforts by involving selected customers whose "needs will become general in a marketplace months or years in the future" (von Hippel 1986, p. 791). This approach is still valuable to B2B firms today. The software company SAP, for example, has implemented the lead user idea in the form of a Co-Innovation Lab intended to continuously gather insights from key clients and partners in order to leverage their innovation potential. As another instrument to foster collaboration with and among the many different partners (e.g. users, developers, implementation partners, etc.), SAP hosts a Community Network with 2 million unique visitors a month (Carboni 2014).

In addition, two trends are expected to increase the relevance of engagement in business markets and thus warrant a thorough understanding of the phenomenon. First, the digitization provides opportunities for increasing interconnectedness among the players. As firms and their products and services become parts of broader systems ("Industry 4.0"), the need for system interoperability and collaboration increases (Porter and Heppelmann 2015). Second, we witness an ongoing de-verticalization of value chains. For example, in the automobile industry the value added by Original Equipment Manufacturers (OEMs) like GM, Toyota or Volkswagen is projected to decrease from 44% in 1985 to 18% in 2015 (Statista 2016). The trend towards outsourcing and collaboration is also prevalent within the marketing function. Take, for example, the number and scope of players involved in digital marketing activities (internal marketing department, data provider, creative agency, publisher, ad networks, intermediaries for online shops, etc.), which has led to the creation of the role of lead agencies whose main responsibility is coordinating all players involved (Bauer et al. 2017).

Both trends exemplify that firms no longer operate in environments with a limited number of partners. Rather, they are part of complex networks comprising suppliers, competitors, partners and customers. Thus, it is of utmost importance to understand how B2B players engage with each other in order to create value.

Despite the high relevance of engagement for business marketing practice, marketing research on engagement in B2B is scarce. Except for the work of Vivek et al. (2016), the conceptual literature on engagement has largely focused on consumer markets (Brodie et al. 2011; van Doorn et al. 2010). Following the call for more B2B-specific research (Lilien 2015), we aim at addressing the void in the engagement literature and focus on a conceptualization of engagement in the domain of B2B relationships. Specifically, we seek to make the following contributions. First, we review specific properties of B2B markets and analyze their implications for engagement in business markets. Second, we suggest a broadening of perspective and an extended conceptualization of engagement in B2B. We propose to refer to this phenomenon as "partner engagement" instead of (just) "customer engagement". By taking a holistic view of the network a firm operates in, we seek to generalize recent initial work on B2B engagement by Vivek et al. (2016) and try to fully capture the complexity of B2B settings. Third, we develop a typology of partner engagement by adopting a framework from the organizational behavior literature. Fourth, based on the typology, we discuss different types of engagement with respect to the level of engagement (organizational vs. individual), underlying relational factors and special cases that help understand and manage partner engagement. Finally, we suggest several avenues for future research in the domain of partner engagement in B2B.

A B2B PERSPECTIVE ON ENGAGEMENT

Customer engagement is regarded as the new frontier in the domain of customer management and relationship marketing (Verhoef et al. 2010). Taking a historical perspective, Beckers et al. (2014) describe a three-stage development: Until the 1990s, marketing was focused on discrete transactions and one-way communication, from the firm to the customer, for example, by mass media advertising and direct mailings. The era of relationship marketing that followed (early 1990s to 2005) emphasized the importance of (two-way) firm–customer interaction and a joint value creation process. The current era of engagement is marked by a more holistic perspective, in which the classical firm–customer dyad has been opened up and considers interactions with other stakeholders (e.g. other customers) as well.

Against this background it is notable that although relationship marketing originated in B2B marketing (e.g. Dwyer et al. 1987), the literature on engagement today almost exclusively focuses on B2C settings. If we consider the almost similar economic weight of B2B and B2C trans-action volumes in the global economy, one should expect similar levels of academic attention for engagement in both markets (Lilien 2015). Yet, there is a clear mismatch between the importance in practice and the representation in research. Is this due to the fact that there is no difference between B2B and B2C with respect to engagement? Or, alternatively, is engagement simply less relevant in B2B? On the contrary, we argue that the specific properties of B2B markets make the concept of engagement highly relevant and yield distinct implications for its understanding. Therefore, the next section is intended to establish an overall theoretical framework for engagement in B2B. For that, we discuss specific properties of B2B markets and derive implications for engagement in these markets.

Specific Properties of B2B Markets and Their Implications for Engagement

The key difference between business-to-business and business-to-consumer markets is the fact that in B2B settings, organizations—and not the individual end consumer—act as decision-makers and buyers. While many specific properties of B2B markets have been described in extant literature (e.g. Grewal and Lilien 2012; Lilien 2015), we will focus on five properties that are most relevant for the concept of engagement since they deal with relational aspects (Homburg et al. 2013):

- The derived character of demand
- The multiperson nature of the buying process
- The high degree of interaction
- The formalization/rationality of exchange
- The small number of players in the market

First, the derived character of demand (Grewal et al. 2015) implies that compared to consumers, B2B buyers (only) purchase products and services to satisfy the needs of their respective customers. Thus, the demand of downstream partners in the value chain ultimately drives the behavior of firms in business markets. This requires a broader focus than just the focal firm–customer dyad and often entails approaches for marketing to the customers' customers (Dahlquist and Griffith 2014; Homburg et al. 2014). To add to the complexity, many firms collaborate with partners (e.g. consulting firms) or their own suppliers (e.g. special component manufacturers) in order to create value for their customers in a complex value chain system. This points to the importance of both a vertical and horizontal perspective and leads to the following implication for engagement in B2B.[1]

Implication 1: Engagement in business markets needs to be assessed within a broader context of a firm's network considering both horizontal and vertical relationships.

The second important property of B2B is the multiperson nature of the buying process (Lilien and Wong 1984). While in consumer markets, the most complex setup for decision-making is a household, in B2B markets, multiple functions and persons are involved in decision-making. The buying center concept, for example, describes five different roles (decision-maker, gatekeeper, influencer, user, buyer) that should be considered when analyzing organizational decision-making (Johnston and Bonoma 1981). Moreover, recent empirical research shows that relationship multiplexity is an important driver of firm performance. For example, multiple contacts at the individual level can help improve the value of supplier–customer relationships (Palmatier 2008). Thus, identifying those contacts within a partner's buying center that have a high likelihood for positive engagement is very important (Adamson et al. 2015). At an organizational level, multiple ties (e.g. standard product/service supply, R&D alliances, marketing alliances, joint ventures, mutual equity investments, board overlock) have been shown to positively influence overall sales while reducing sales volatility (Tuli et al. 2010). Hence, both forms of multiplexity create additional opportunities for engagement while making the analysis more complicated at the same time. This leads to the following implication.

Implication 2: Engagement in business markets should be analyzed taking a multi-level perspective and distinguish between individual and organizational level behavior.

Third, business market relationships often feature a high degree of interaction and integration of operating processes (Grewal and Lilien 2012). This goes along with an increased importance of personal selling and (long-term) relationships in general. The high degree of interaction is mainly due to the complexity and need for customization of many industrial products, which leads to the strong presence of direct sales models in business markets (Anderson et al. 2009). Moreover, process integration is often the result of strong mutual interdependence and the insight that integration serves the interest of both parties (Tuli et al. 2007).

Implication 3: In business markets, there are more "natural" opportunities to get engaged in order to improve the organization's own and/or the partner's situation.

Another important property of business markets is rationality and the high degree of formalization of exchange that comes with it. In contrast to consumer markets, impulse buying is rare, and purchase decisions are usually the result of clearly defined processes that are based on criteria and organizational requirements (Grewal et al. 2015). This implies less emotional, more rational benefit-oriented reasons for engagement (Vivek et al. 2016). Indeed, empirical research on community participation shows that—although personal motives such as experiential and symbolic benefits still play a role (Bruhn et al. 2014)—B2B community participants use the community for problem solving rather than socializing (Bone et al. 2014).

Implication 4: In business markets, there are different and additional types of engagement behaviors, which are more formally organized. The formalization can manifest itself in internal rules on how to interact with partners that are potentially hindering engagement on an individual level.

Finally, business-to-business markets usually comprise a smaller number of players for both supply and demand (Grewal and Lilien 2012). This can lead to competition among customers for a certain supplier or partner. For example, the concepts of preferred supplier (e.g. in automotive) or preferred partner (e.g. exclusivity agreements with retailers) both focus on getting exclusive access to an important market player instead of "sharing" with others (Kumar et al. 2007). This also applies to the "resource" engagement, which is limited for every market participant (van Doorn et al. 2010).

Implication 5: The small(er) number of players in business markets potentially fuels competition for engagement.

The discussion above shows that there are specific aspects to the concept of engagement in business markets. The insights derived here will serve as a theoretical basis for the subsequent steps of conceptualizing and developing a typology of engagement in B2B.

From Customer Engagement to Partner Engagement

The implication from the first property suggests that engagement needs to be assessed within a broader context of a firm's network. Figure 11.1 illustrates a simplified example of a business network. With the focal firm at the center of the network, the figure shows that there are numerous ties with partners both vertically and horizontally in the value chain. Downstream, firms often collaborate with their customers in order to better meet the needs of their customers' customers. The lead user approach (von Hippel 1986) that was introduced earlier is a good example for that. Similarly, the focal firm may turn upstream to collaborate with a supplier to improve its own offering. Finally, the lines from the focal firm to partners and competitors indicate that there are also relevant ties with other players on the same (horizontal) level of the value chain. In all situations, the behavior of the partner(s) is crucial for the success of the focal firm.

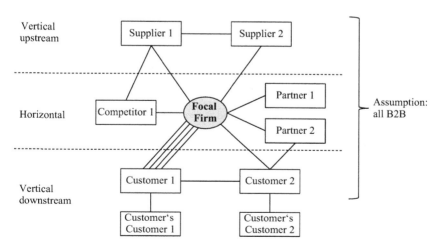

Fig. 11.1 Graphical illustration of a network in business markets (adapted based on Wuyts et al. 2004)

While the vertical (channel) perspective is well-understood, the horizontal collaboration with partners or competitors has received far less attention in the marketing literature (Rindfleisch and Moorman 2001). Yet, within the B2B network there is a host of specialized intermediaries that perform important functions for the value chain. These intermediaries may comprise financial partners (e.g. insurances, banks, brokers), advertising or promotion agencies, logistics specialists, sales and implementation support, IT vendors or market research firms (Palmatier et al. 2015). The relationship between the focal firm and these partners is often complex and typically based on informal arrangements (Plouffe et al. 2016) in which both parties collaborate based on aligned interests (Tuli et al. 2007). The B2B software and IT industry is a good example for that. Around major players like IBM, Oracle or SAP, an ecosystem of support firms has developed that assume different services like consulting, implementation or software customization. For example, SAP relies heavily on partners to market their software applications to small and medium enterprises (SMEs). In this setup, the partners fulfill important functions like generating leads, providing advice to clients and implementing the software. As many partners are not bound by exclusivity arrangements, their influencing behavior towards potential clients constitutes an important facet of engagement towards SAP.

Another aspect illustrated in Fig. 11.1 is the multiplexity of ties between the focal firm and potential engagement partners (as indicated by multiple lines between the focal firm and customer 1). In the case of a mechanical engineering company selling milling equipment, like Sandvik Coromant, we find ties between a sales account executive and several contacts in the customer firm (e.g. operations engineer, plant manager, purchaser), but also between employees of the service field force and users of the equipment. Depending on the respective importance, there may also be relationships between top management representatives. The partner engagement can occur at different levels of formalization. For example, innovation co-development initiatives are usually contract-based (i.e. formalized) and can thus be considered organizational engagement while we may also observe personal engagement at the individual level, for example, in the form of recommendations within the personal network that usually occur spontaneously and are unregulated.

The discussion of the structural framework shows that the context for engagement in business markets is complex. More stakeholders mean more opportunities for engagement. Thus, we posit that in business markets, the concept of customer engagement should be extended to partner engagement in order to reflect the importance of many stakeholders and their behavior for the success of the focal firm. This is in line with prior research in business markets. For example, scholars of the IMP group established a network perspective for studying business markets (Håkansson 1982). Moreover, "partnering" is regarded as a viable and focused market strategy (Anderson et al. 2009). With this conceptualization, we build on and extent recent work by Vivek et al. (2016) who focused on dyadic relationships between the focal firm and its business clients. We aim at generalizing the concept of engagement and apply it to both horizontal and vertical relationships as well as direct and indirect partners in the business network. The extended perspective for engagement is also reflected in relationship management tools in practice. Similar to the customer-focused approach in B2C, which has led to a widespread adoption of CRM tools, the importance of managing all partners effectively in B2B is mirrored in partner relationship management tools offered by leading software companies such as Oracle or Salesforce.com. These tools facilitate managing relationships with both partners and customers (e.g. in indirect multistage distribution channels), for example, with respect to certification and training, lead management or the coordination of marketing programs. These examples highlight the relevance of partner relationship management (PRM) as an extension of customer relationship management (CRM) in B2B.

Building on previous conceptualizations of (customer) engagement (van Doorn et al. 2010; Kumar et al. 2010; Pansari and Kumar 2016) and the discussion on business networks above, we consequently define partner engagement as a partner's volitional behavior towards any other stakeholder in the value chain affecting the focal firm's business, including both direct (purchase-related) but mainly indirect (referral, influence, knowledge) behaviors. Please note that this definition focuses on actual behavior as opposed to psychological or attitudinal aspects (van Doorn 2011). This is appropriate in the business market context for two reasons. First, a partner's action is what makes the difference and has a real impact on the focal firm's business (Bolton 2011). Second, given the multiperson nature of B2B relationships and the higher degree of formalization, individual psychological states are less relevant as well as more difficult to measure and aggregate. Thus, behavior can be interpreted as the outcome of individual- or group-based decision process.

A Typology of B2B Partner Engagement

Many types of engagement behavior are not new to marketing research and practice, yet, so far, they have been investigated separately. Only recently, scholars have started to consider these behaviors as part of the overarching phenomenon of customer engagement (Verhoef et al. 2010). Table 11.1 provides an overview of the many types of engagement classified into four different groups with regard to their value contribution to the firm, as suggested by Kumar et al. (2010). Engagement types more prevalent or specific to business market contexts are marked with an asterisk. The classification by Kumar et al. (2010) is a valuable first step for understanding different engagement types. Yet, the classification remains descriptive in nature and merely focuses on the value contribution to the firm. Therefore, we propose a typology that can help structure the various types of B2B partner engagement, analyze similarities and differences between them and, thus, gain important insights into the underlying mechanisms.

Overview of the Typology

Three criteria guided the development of our typology. First, the typology should build on previous engagement research and has to be able to accommodate all the different types of engagement. Second, it should reflect the specific properties of B2B markets. Third, it should help uncover similarities and differences between the different types of engagement, in particular, provide insights from a managerial point of view. Based on these criteria, we adopt a framework from the organizational behavior literature (Thomas 1976, 1992). Originally, it was applied to explain conflict resolution styles[2]. In this respect, Thomas' concept of conflict and the corresponding behavior can be interpreted as a form of (negative) engagement. However, the dimensions used in the framework are applicable to positive types of partner engagement as well.

Figure 11.2 shows the dimensions and resulting quadrants of the typology for partner engagement. The dimension *assertiveness* relates to a partner's focus on its *own* outcomes. For example, a partner may employ engagement behaviors to achieve its own goals such as increasing its own margins, securing channel access, or creating a distinct image (if necessary at the expense of other players in the network). *Cooperativeness* as the second dimension relates to the level to which the partner attempts to satisfy the *other party's* concerns (e.g. innovating the marketplace or

Table 11.1 Overview of types of engagement with exemplary articles for the B2B context

Indirect value contribution			Direct value contribution
Referral/Reference	Influence	Knowledge	Purchase
"Relates to the acquisition of new customers through a firm initiated and incentivized formal referral program" (Kumar et al. 2010, p. 299)	"Customers' influence on other acquired customers as well as on prospects" (Kumar et al. 2010, p. 299)	"Feedback provided to the firm for ideas for innovation and improvements, and contributing to knowledge development" (Kumar et al. 2010, p. 299)	"Repeat purchases or additional purchases through up-selling and cross-selling" (Kumar et al. 2010, p. 299)
Hada et al. (2014) Kumar et al. (2013) Godes (2012)	Word-of-mouth (WOM) Libai et al. (2010) von Wangenheim and Bayón (2007) C2C Support/ exchange Chakravarty et al. (2014) Gruen et al. (2007) Community participation Bone et al. (2014) Bruhn et al. (2014) Complaints Haverila and Naumann (2011) Homburg and Fürst (2005)	Co-development* Chang and Taylor (2016) Homburg and Kuehnl (2014) Joshi and Sharma (2004) Information sharing* Frazier et al. (2009) Fang (2008) Feedback/suggestions n/a Trainings* Ulaga and Reinartz (2011) Joint marketing/sales activities* Dahlquist and Griffith (2014) Homburg et al. (2014)	Grewal et al. (2015) Lacoste (2012) Kumar et al. (2008)

* = Engagement types more prevalent or specific to business markets

increasing overall channel volume). The dimensions used in the typology fit the criteria outline above well. They are consistent with previous conceptual work on customer engagement highlighting the importance of

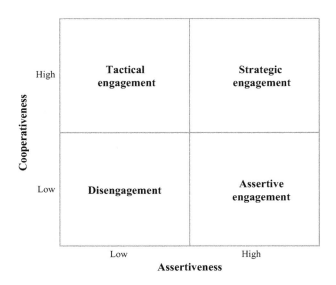

Fig. 11.2 Typology of partner engagement

customer goals (concern for oneself) and the purpose of engagement with respect to the focal firm (concern for the other) (van Doorn et al. 2010). Moreover, the dimensions are key parameters of B2B strategies (Anderson et al. 2009) and thus reflect the specific properties of B2B (e.g. the formalization of exchange). Compared to other potential dimensions that were initially considered (e.g. high vs. low, or positive vs. negative, or horizontal vs. vertical engagement), our typology also provides managerially relevant dimensions to uncover similarities and differences between the engagement types. It should be noted that in the context of partner engagement, this typology has to be analyzed from the perspective of the party that is exhibiting engagement behaviors. That is, we discuss a partner's engagement behavior and its underlying drivers in order to understand the implications for the success of the focal firm.

Crossing the two dimensions leads to four distinct types of partner engagement. If both assertiveness and cooperativeness are high, a partner is likely to show *strategic engagement* behavior. This could be, for example, the commitment of a supplier or customer to co-development activities with the focal firm. Similarly, a horizontal partner may be willing to offer trainings to the focal firm or have its employees participate in the focal firm's training program. Referring back to the SAP example above, this could mean that an implementation partner is willing to invest resources by having its employees attend trainings of SAP in order to learn more about the most recent product innovations and its value propositions.

If assertiveness is high but cooperativeness is low, a partner is likely to show behaviors that can have negative[3] effects on the focal firm. Examples for this group of *assertive engagement* are negative word-of-mouth (WOM), complaints or even lawsuits. This is in line with the previous research emphasizing that engagement can have positive or negative valence (van Doorn et al. 2010).

If, conversely, assertiveness is low and cooperativeness is high, we expect more *tactical engagement* behavior. Given the low own stakes, a partner may act in favor of the focal firm for different reasons. One motivation could be to give in to the demand of the focal firm in order to avoid open conflict (appeasement). On the other hand, tactical engagement behavior can be a means to make investments into a relationship at relatively low cost in order to generate goodwill at the focal firm.

Finally, we label the scenario when both dimensions are low *disengagement*. In this case, a partner is likely to show low intensity to no engagement behavior at all. This comprises, for example, deliberate disengagement, which is likely to occur if a partner has already entered into a preferred partnership with a competitor of the focal firm. The disengagement quadrant is an important part to complete the "engagement picture". As discussed above, resources for engagement are limited, so it is neither possible nor meaningful to have high engagement with every partner. In fact, anecdotal evidence suggests that only a minority of customers or partners is actually highly engaged, with 90% remaining rather passive (Libai 2011).

Insights from the Typology

In order to uncover similarities and differences among the types of partner engagement and generate deeper insights, we assigned the engagement types listed in Table 11.1 to the four quadrants of the typology. For each engagement type, the dimension assertiveness and cooperativeness were rated in terms of high vs. low. If available, we used information from the respective paper itself (e.g. Bone et al. 2014); for the remainder, the assignment was done based on the judgment of the researchers. We will discuss ambiguous cases subsequently. Figure 11.3 shows an overview of the final typology. For example, we assigned co-development to the strategic engagement quadrant, as the majority of co-development activities require both a high level of assertiveness and a high level of cooperativeness. Given the enormous size of resource investments necessary to make a co-development work, both partners will only engage if they expect value from the cooperation (Hoyer et al. 2010). Similarly, both high assertiveness and high cooperativeness are important prerequisites for open sharing of strategic information (Frazier et al. 2009). Conversely, a partner may show a high level of cooperativeness when referring other clients or contacts to the focal firm or spreading positive WOM while his or her own outcomes are of minor importance (i.e. low assertiveness).

Obviously, for some types of engagement, the position within the typology may vary depending on the specific business context. For example,

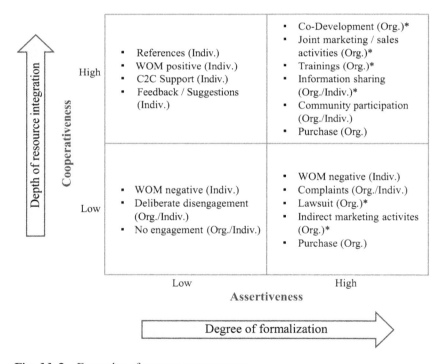

Fig. 11.3 Examples of partner engagement
(Indiv. = Engagement at individual level, Org. = Engagement at organizational level, * Engagement types more prevalent or specific to business markets)

the levels of concern for oneself and for the other party can differ for community participation (Bone et al. 2014). Similarly, a partner may generate positive WOM even if the concern for the impact on the focal firm is rather low (in this case, WOM may be triggered by the concern for a third party rather than by the concern for the party that is the object of WOM). From Fig. 11.3, some interesting patterns emerge. We discuss these insights next.

Level of Partner Engagement Behavior
The distribution of engagement behaviors in Fig. 11.3 that occur at the individual level vs. those behaviors that usually occur at the organizational level shows that individual engagement behaviors dominate if assertiveness is low, while organizational behaviors are important if assertiveness is high. Thus, the more important a certain behavior for the outcome of the partner, the higher the degree of formalization (Homburg et al. 2002; Pemer et al. 2014). If the engagement behavior takes place at the organizational level, it is reasonable to expect that internal rules and processes ensure that the behavior of several boundary-spanning actors is well aligned and consistent. This does not necessarily hold for individual-level engagement. Boundary-spanning employees may influence others by sharing their own experiences and evaluation with the focal firm outside of the own organization's influence (Wieseke et al. 2012). Thus, in a nutshell, high assertiveness usually translates into organizational-level engagement behavior and increased formalization, while other engagement behaviors with low assertiveness are mainly driven by personal motives.

Depth of Resource Integration
It is interesting to note that among the types of partner engagement shown in Fig. 11.3, some are mainly driven by one party, while others require action of both sides. WOM and deliberate disengagement are examples for one-sided actions of the partner; that is, the behavior is under full discretion of the partner with no or little involvement of other parties. Other types of engagement such as co-development or joint marketing activities require cooperation between the partner and the focal firm. Thus, a partner may strive for strategic engagement, but it will only become reality if the focal firm shows similar intentions and the willingness to cooperate (Ulaga and Eggert 2006). As indicated by the vertical

arrow in Fig. 11.3, higher levels of cooperativeness require higher levels of resource integration. This is in line with recent research that links customer engagement to the service-dominant logic and posits that resource integration is a foundational process for customer/partner engagement (Hollebeek et al. 2016). C2C support, for example, requires a stronger integration of (mainly operant) resources compared to disengagement, while information sharing or mutual participation in trainings also goes along with deeper resource integration as compared to complaints or lawsuits. It should be noted that the depth of resource integration is not to be equated with the overall level of resource investments, as the latter is rather conditional on the level of assertiveness (i.e. the determination of a party to influence the outcome in its own favor). As a takeaway, this implies that coordination is an important organizational capability (Teece et al. 2007) in order to extract value from a partner's tactical or strategic engagement.

Conditions for Different Partner Engagement Types
Several factors can help understand the conditions under which the different partner engagement behaviors are more or less likely to occur. These factors are all key concepts from the relationship marketing literature, in particular trust, commitment and dependence (Palmatier et al. 2007). They are considered important antecedents of engagement (van Doorn et al. 2010). Therefore, we briefly analyze the configurations of these factors for each of the four quadrants. In the case of *disengagement*, trust can be at any level (from low over medium to high), while commitment and dependence are at low levels. If we take the example of negative WOM: A partner may still have sufficient levels of trust into the integrity of the focal firm (Morgan and Hunt 1994), yet low commitment and low dependence create a situation in which nothing prevents the partner from spreading negative information about the focal firm. *Assertive engagement* is based on low levels of all three underlying factors. In particular, it requires either symmetric (i.e. mutual) dependence or even asymmetric dependence in favor of the partner (Scheer et al. 2014). *Tactical engagement*, in turn, is characterized by high levels of trust and low to medium levels of commitment which—in combination with the low concern for the own outcome—leads to a rather opportunistic utilization of this type of engagement. Moreover, it can occur at any level of dependence and can be characterized as "picking the low hanging fruit". *Strategic engagement*,

finally, requires high levels for trust, commitment and dependence. Most notably, symmetric dependence is a necessary requirement to make this type of engagement a success for both parties (Tuli et al. 2007; Vivek et al. 2016). Based on the reasoning above, we conclude that it is important for managers to consider the overall underlying relationship conditions in order to adequately judge a partner's engagement behavior.

Special Cases

Preferred or Exclusive Partnerships As already discussed above, in certain situations, B2B firms enter into preferred or exclusive arrangements with suppliers or partners (Ulaga and Eggert 2006). For the parties within the arrangement, this turns potential previous engagement into a formalized relationship. For players outside of the arrangement, this may result in deliberate disengagement of the respective supplier or partner. These kinds of constellations can occur both up- or downstream as well as horizontally. Due to the strategic importance of the arrangements, they are usually formalized on an organizational level and governed by detailed contracts (Sieweke et al. 2012). In some industries, for example in the consulting industry, exclusivity arrangements severely reduce the market potential. Therefore, in order to avoid exclusivity arrangements (and thus forego other business opportunities), consulting firms often employ "chinese walls" (i.e. organizational, personal and IT-system-related separation between teams working for competing clients) in combination with strict confidentiality rules for their employees.

Vertical Marketing Activities In B2B markets, it is common that firms collaborate with other players in the value chain for their marketing or sales activities (Dahlquist and Griffith 2014; Wuyts et al. 2004). This is particularly relevant when marketing to indirect downstream customers. In a recent study, Homburg et al. (2014) discuss three different marketing approaches to indirect customers: direct customer downstream support, cooperative indirect customer marketing and independent indirect customer marketing. As illustrated in Fig. 11.3, these vertical marketing activities can occur both under high as well as low cooperativeness. If we take, for example, a situation involving the focal firm, one of its suppliers and its customers (see Fig. 11.1): Direct customer downstream support and cooperative indirect customer marketing can be considered as strategic engagement behavior of the focal firm's supplier (high assertiveness and high cooperativeness). If the supplier, however, engages in independent, indirect marketing activities with the focal firm's customers, this can be classified as assertive engagement (high assertiveness but low cooperativeness towards the focal firm). The findings of Homburg et al. (2014) are in line with our reasoning for the underlying factor of dependence. In fact, they demonstrate that independent indirect marketing activities work best in the case of up- or downstream but not midstream locus of power, that is, an asymmetric dependence in favor of the supplier or the customer.

"Vertical Coopetition" Another interesting aspect illustrated in Fig. 11.3 is the dual classification of purchases as both strategic and assertive engagement. Depending on the underlying factors, customers exhibit different levels of cooperativeness when purchasing goods or services from its suppliers. This phenomenon can often be observed in the behavior of large multinational key accounts towards their suppliers when there is an asymmetric distribution of power in favor of the key accounts (e.g. Nestlé in the CPG market or OEMs in the automotive industry). By employing both cooperation and competitive market-based exchange (e.g. online auctions, tenders or competitive bidding) simultaneously, these key accounts exhibit an engagement behavior coined as "vertical coopetition" (Lacoste 2012, p. 649).

In summary, the discussion above shows that the typology is able to accommodate special cases of engagement as well. It further highlights the importance of considering the specific context in order to assign the behavior to the right quadrant and draw ensuing conclusions.

Importance of Strategic Engagement in B2B
Finally, it is interesting to examine the relative importance of each type of engagement. Overall, we find that strategic engagement is an extremely important type of engagement in B2B (Kumar and Pansari 2016). This is evident in the magnitude of different types assigned to the upper-right quadrant in Fig. 11.3. This finding is corroborated by a recent meta-analysis on innovation effectiveness that shows, for example, that integrating customers or partners in new product development activities is more promising in B2B compared to B2C contexts (Chang and Taylor 2016). Due to the specific properties of B2B (in particular formalization/rationality and high degree of interaction), we also posit

that both assertiveness and cooperativeness can reach higher levels in B2B settings. Overall, we conclude that strategic engagement is of great importance in B2B. This is driven by aligned interests and significant benefits for both parties, that is, a win-win situation if the business environment for engagement is designed properly.

Discussion

Summary

Customer engagement is a key topic for both practitioners and researchers. A review of the literature, however, suggests that there is a dominant focus on customer engagement in B2C settings, while the phenomenon has largely been neglected for B2B settings. Therefore, this chapter focuses on engagement in business-to-business contexts. First, we review specific properties of B2B markets and derive implications with respect to engagement. The insights show, for example, that engagement in business markets should be assessed within a broader context of a firm's network. Further, in business markets, engagement should be distinguished between individual and organizational behavior. Second, we offer an extended conceptualization of engagement in B2B. Specifically, we propose that the concept of customer engagement should be extended to partner engagement in order to reflect the complexity and network character of value chains in business markets. Third, we develop a typology of partner engagement behaviors in business markets based on the dimension of assertiveness and cooperativeness. The typology helps to better understand similarities and differences between types of partner engagement. Finally, we derive insights from the typology. For example, our analysis indicates that high assertiveness of a partner usually translates into organizational engagement behavior (e.g. co-development activities) and increased formalization, while other engagement behaviors (e.g. referrals) are mainly driven by personal motives. Moreover, the insights show that it is important for managers to consider the overall underlying relationship conditions (i.e. trust, commitment, dependence) in order to understand its partners' engagement behavior. We also show that special cases (in particular exclusive partnerships, vertical marketing activities, and vertical coopetition) fit into the typology.

Managerial Implications

The findings of our research bear important implications for managers. Most importantly, the extended conceptualization of engagement suggests that B2B managers are well-advised to broaden their focus and consider partner engagement in addition to customer engagement. This entails analyzing relevant stakeholders in the network with respect to positive and negative engagement behaviors and subsequently monitoring those systematically. The monitoring can be facilitated by using partner relationship management tools offered by many B2B software vendors (e.g Salesforce.com, Oracle, NetSuite, Relayware). From a managerial point of view, it is also important to acknowledge that certain types of engagement are often specific to certain departments (e.g. R&D, operations, marketing or sales). Thus, it requires centralized efforts to get an overview of the different engagement behaviors, but potentially a decentralized approach to deal with the different types of engagement.

Our typology of partner engagement provides managers with an actionable tool to understand and manage their partners' engagement. Based on the dimensions assertiveness and cooperativeness, each type of (potential) engagement behavior can be classified. The classification yields important implications, for example, with respect to the expected degree of formalization, the necessary depth of resource integration as well as the level (personal vs. organizational) of engagement. The typology, thus, can be used to devise partner engagement strategies.

In addition to that, the insights into the underlying factors of the typology provide proactive levers for managing partner engagement: First, gain power status in relationships to be able to counter assertive engagement strategies if necessary. Second, strengthen trust and commitment via relationship investments to build the foundation for strategic engagement of partners. Third, try to design business models and channel systems that align interests with partners to guard against opportunism and destructive engagement.

Avenues for Future Research

Our work follows the call of many scholars for more B2B-specific research of marketing phenomena (Grewal et al. 2015; Lilien 2015; Vivek et al. 2016). We offer an initial conceptualization of engagement in B2B and develop a typology of partner engagement behaviors. Yet, we believe further research is needed to fully understand the nature, drivers and consequences of engagement in business markets.

First, given the inherent heterogeneity of the B2B domain (Lilien 2015), we need to better understand the heterogeneity of engagement within B2B. What are differences in engagement with regard to different industries (e.g. financial services, commodities, automotive), different product types (goods vs. hybrid offerings vs. services), different stages of the value chain or different environmental factors (e.g. technological dynamism, level of competition)?

Second, we believe investigating the "level" of engagement could be an exciting area for future research. How does engagement on an organization level (formalized) differ from personal level (informal) engagement? Under which conditions are those behaviors complements, substitutes, or even countering each other? Which personal motives play a role for individual-level engagement behavior?

Third, it could be interesting to contrast the effectiveness of engagement from different partners for the same type of engagement. For example, whose inputs are most effective for co-development of innovation (suppliers, customers, partners, other)? What are differences in the impact of positive or negative WOM from different partners?

Finally, B2B managers would greatly benefit from insights on how to manage engagement successfully. On the "providing side", this comprises a better understanding of a "culture of engagement", management of organizational engagement, regulation of engagement behavior of individual employees and measurement of engagement effectiveness. On the "receiving side", it is about understanding how to create platforms or an environment for partners to show positive engagement behavior, how to develop organizational capabilities to extract full value from a partner's engagement behavior and how to protect the firm against assertive engagement of partners.

NOTES

1. One could argue that upstream and horizontal B2B relationships are also relevant for firms in B2C markets (e.g. banks, electronic equipment manufacturers, fashion). In that sense, firms marketing to the end consumer are a special case where there is only one stakeholder downstream. For the sake of consistency, however, we confine our analysis to the constellation when the direct customer of the focal firm is still an organization (see Fig. 11.1).
2. The idea of the original work by Thomas (1976) was to develop a generic theory of conflict and conflict management and the social processes involved. With respect to the framework, Thomas described five conflict-handling

modes (avoiding, accommodation, compromise, competition, collaboration) using a two-dimensional taxonomy based on assertiveness and cooperativeness.

3. It should be noted that under the condition of high assertiveness and low cooperativeness, a partner's engagement can also have positive effects, for example, by creating a pull effect in the value chain in the case of indirect marketing activities (Homburg et al. 2014). However, engagement types with negative effects prevail (see Fig. 11.3).

REFERENCES

Adamson, B., Dixon, M., Spenner, P., & Toman, N. (2015). *The Challenger Customer: Selling to the Hidden Influencer Who Can Multiply Your Results.* London: Portfolio.

Anderson, J. C., Narus, J. A., & Narayandas, D. (2009). *Business Market Management: Understanding, Creating, and Delivering Value.* Upper Saddle River/New Jersey: Prentice Hall.

Bauer, T., Heller, J., Jacobs, J., & Schaffner, R. (2017) *How To Get the Most From Your Agency Relationships in 2017 McKinsey Insights.* http://www.mckinsey. com/business-functions/marketing-and-sales/our-insights/how-to-get-the-most-from-your-agency-relationships-in-2017?cid=other-eml-alt-mip-mck-oth-1702. Date Accessed 15 Feb 2017.

Beckers, S. F. M., Risselada, H., & Verhoef, P. C. (2014). Customer Engagement: A New Frontier in Customer Value Management. In R. T. Rust & M.-H. Huang (Eds.), *Handbook of Service Marketing Research* (pp. 97–122). Northampton: Edward Elgar.

Bolton, R. N. (2011). Customer Engagement: Opportunities and Challenges for Organizations. *Journal of Service Research, 14*(3), 272–274.

Bone, S. A., Fombelle, P. W., Ray, K. R., & Lemon, K. N. (2014). How Customer Participation in B2B Peer-to-Peer Problem-Solving Communities Influences the Need for Traditional Customer Service. *Journal of Service Research, 18*(1), 23–38.

Brodie, R. J., Hollebeek, L. D., Juric, B., & Ilic, A. (2011). Customer Engagement: Conceptual Domain, Fundamental Propositions, and Implications for Research. *Journal of Service Research, 14*(3), 252–271.

Bruhn, M., Schnebelen, S., & Schäfer, D. (2014). Antecedents and Consequences of the Quality of E-Customer-to-Customer Interactions in B2B Brand Communities. *Industrial Marketing Management, 43*(1), 164–176.

Carboni, J. (2014). *The Importance of Online Communities with Cloud Computing-CIO Review.* http://sap.cioreview.com/cxoinsight/the-importance-of-online-communities-with-cloud-computing-nid-10088-cid-49.html. Date Accessed 15 Feb 2017.

Chakravarty, A., Kumar, A., & Grewal, R. (2014). Customer Orientation Structure for Internet-Based Business-to-Business Platform Firms. *Journal of Marketing, 78*(5), 1–23.

Chang, W., & Taylor, S. A. (2016). The Effectiveness of Customer Participation in New Product Development: A Meta-Analysis. *Journal of Marketing, 80*(1), 47–64.

CMO Council. (2014). *Maximize How You Individualize: Map the Operational Gap in Customer Insight and Experience.* http://www.cmocouncil.org/cat_details.php?fid. Date Accessed 15 Feb 2017.

Dahlquist, S. H., & Griffith, D. A. (2014). Multidyadic Industrial Channels: Understanding Component Supplier Profits and Original Equipment Manufacturer Behavior. *Journal of Marketing, 78*(4), 59–79.

van Doorn, J. (2011). Customer Engagement: Essence, Dimensionality, and Boundaries. *Journal of Service Research, 14*(3), 280–282.

van Doorn, J., Lemon, K. N., Mittal, V., Nass, S., Pick, D., Pirner, P., & Verhoef, P. C. (2010). Customer Engagement Behavior: Theoretical Foundations and Research Directions. *Journal of Service Research, 13*(3), 253–266.

Dwyer, R. F., Schurr, P. H., & Oh, S. (1987). Developing Buyer-Seller Relationships. *Journal of Marketing, 51*(2), 11–27.

Fang, E. (Er). (2008). Customer Participation and the Trade-Off Between New Product Innovativeness and Speed to Market. *Journal of Marketing, 72*(4), 90–104.

Forbes. (2015). *Customer Engagement: Best of the Best.* http://www.forbes.com/. Date Accessed 15 Feb 2017.

Frazier, G. L., Elliot, M., Antia, K. D., & Rindfleisch, A. (2009). Distributor Sharing of Strategic Information with Suppliers. *Journal of Marketing, 73*(4), 31–43.

Godes, D. (2012). The Strategic Impact of References in Business Markets. *Marketing Science, 31*(2), 257–276.

Grewal, R., & Lilien, G. L. (2012). Business-to-Business Marketing: Looking Back, Looking Forward. In G. L. Lilien & R. Grewal (Eds.), *Handbook of Business-to-Business Marketing* (pp. 1–14). Northampton: Edward Elgar.

Grewal, R., Lilien, G. L., Bharadwaj, S. G., Jindal, P., Kayande, U., Lusch, R. F., Mantrala, M., Palmatier, R. W., Rindfleisch, A., Scheer, L. K., Spekman, R., & Sridhar, S. (2015). Business-to-Business Buying: Challenges and Opportunities. *Customer Needs and Solutions, 2*(3), 193–208.

Gruen, T. W., Osmonbekov, T., & Czaplewski, A. J. (2007). Customer-to-Customer Exchange: Its MOA Antecedents and Its Impact on Value Creation and Loyalty. *Journal of the Academy of Marketing Science, 35*(4), 537–549.

Hada, M., Grewal, R., & Lilien, G. L. (2014). Supplier-Selected Referrals. *Journal of Marketing, 78*(2), 34–51.

Håkansson, H. (1982). *International Marketing and Purchasing of Industrial Goods: An Interaction Approach.* New York: Wiley.

Haverila, M., & Naumann, E. (2011). Customer Complaint Behavior and Satisfaction in a B2B Context: A Longitudinal Analysis. *Journal of Services Research, 10*(2), 45–62.

von Hippel, E. (1986). Lead Users: A Source of Novel Product Concepts. *Management Science, 32*(7), 791–805.

Hollebeek, L. D., Srivastava, R. K., & Chen, T. (2016). S-D Logic–Informed Customer Engagement: Integrative Framework, Revised Fundamental Propositions, and Application to CRM. *Journal of the Academy of Marketing Science*, in press, 1–25.

Homburg, C., & Fürst, A. (2005). How Organizational Complaint Handling Drives Customer Loyalty: An Analysis of the Mechanistic and the Organic Approach. *Journal of Marketing, 69*(4), 95–114.

Homburg, C., & Kuehnl, C. (2014). Is the More Always Better? A Comparative Study of Internal and External Integration Practices in New Product and New Service Development. *Journal of Business Research, 67*(7), 1360–1367.

Homburg, C., Kuester, S., & Krohmer, H. (2013). *Marketing Management: A Contemporary Perspective.* Maidenhead/Berkshire: McGraw-Hill Education.

Homburg, C., Wilczek, H., & Hahn, A. (2014). Looking Beyond the Horizon: How to Approach the Customers' Customers in Business-to-Business Markets. *Journal of Marketing, 78*(5), 58–77.

Homburg, C., Workman, J. P., & Jensen, O. (2002). A Configurational Perspective on Key Account Management. *Journal of Marketing, 66*(2), 38–60.

Hoyer, W. D., Chandy, R., Dorotic, M., Krafft, M., & Singh, S. S. (2010). Consumer Co-Creation in New Product Development. *Journal of Service Research, 13*(3), 283–296.

Johnston, W. J., & Bonoma, T. V. (1981). The Buying Center: Structure and Interaction Patterns. *Journal of Marketing, 45*(3), 143.

Joshi, A. W., & Sharma, S. (2004). Customer Knowledge Development: Antecedents and Impact on New Product Performance. *Journal of Marketing, 68*(4), 47–59.

Kumar, V., Aksoy, L., Donkers, B., Venkatesan, R., Wiesel, T., & Tillmanns, S. (2010). Undervalued or Overvalued Customers: Capturing Total Customer Engagement Value. *Journal of Service Research, 13*(3), 297–310.

Kumar, V., & Pansari, A. (2016). Competitive Advantage Through Engagement. *Journal of Marketing Research, 53*(4), 497–514.

Kumar, V., Petersen, J. A., & Leone, R. P. (2007) How Valuable Is Word of Mouth?, *Harvard Business Review*, October, 1–9.

Kumar, V., Petersen, J. A., & Leone, R. P. (2013). Defining, Measuring, and Managing Business Reference Value. *Journal of Marketing, 77*(1), 68–86.

Kumar, V., Venkatesan, R., Bohling, T., & Beckmann, D. (2008). The Power of CLV: Managing Customer Lifetime Value at IBM. *Marketing Science, 27*(4), 585–599.

Lacoste, S. (2012). Vertical Coopetition: The Key Account Perspective. *Industrial Marketing Management, 41*(4), 649–658.

Libai, B. (2011). The Perils of Focusing on Highly Engaged Customers. *Journal of Service Research*, 14(3), 275–276.

Libai, B., Bolton, R., Bugel, M. S., de Ruyter, K., Gotz, O., Risselada, H., & Stephen, A. T. (2010). Customer-to-Customer Interactions: Broadening the Scope of Word of Mouth Research. *Journal of Service Research*, 13(3), 267–282.

Lilien, G. L. (2015). The B2B Knowledge Gap. *International Journal of Research in Marketing*, 33(3), 543–556.

Lilien, G. L., & Wong, A. (1984). An Exploratory Investigation of the Structure of the Buying Center in the Metalworking Industry. *Journal of Marketing Research*, 21(1), 1–11.

McKinsey. (2014). *The Digital Tipping Point: McKinsey Global Survey Results.* http://www.mckinsey.com/business-functions/digital-mckinsey/our-insights/the-digital-tipping-point-mckinsey-global-survey-results. Date Accessed 15 Feb 2017.

Morgan, R. M., & Hunt, S. D. (1994). The Commitment-Trust Theory of Relationship Marketing. *Journal of Marketing*, 58(3), 20–38.

MSI. (2010). *2010–2012 Research Priorities.* Boston: Marketing Science Institute.

MSI. (2014). *2014–2016 Research Priorities.* Boston: Marketing Science Institute.

MSI. (2016). *2016–2018 Research Priorities.* Boston: Marketing Science Institute.

Palmatier, R. W. (2008). Interfirm Relational Drivers of Customer Value. *Journal of Marketing*, 72(4), 76–89.

Palmatier, R. W., Dant, R. P., & Grewal, D. (2007). A Comparative Longitudinal Analysis of Theoretical Perspectives of Interorganizational Relationship Performance. *Journal of Marketing*, 71(4), 172–194.

Palmatier, R. W., Stern, L. W., & El-Ansary, A. I. (2015). *Marketing Channel Strategy.* Upper Saddle River/New Jersey: Prentice Hall.

Pansari, A., & Kumar, V. (2016). Customer Engagement: The Construct, Antecedents, and Consequences. *Journal of the Academy of Marketing Science*, in press, 1–18.

Pemer, F., Werr, A., & Bianchi, M. (2014). Purchasing Professional Services: A Transaction Cost View of the Antecedents and Consequences of Purchasing Formalization. *Industrial Marketing Management*, 43(5), 840–849.

Plouffe, C. R., Bolander, W., Cote, J. A., & Hochstein, B. (2016). Does the Customer Matter Most? Exploring Strategic Frontline Employees' Influence of Customers, the Internal Business Team, and External Business Partners. *Journal of Marketing*, 80(1), 106–123.

Porter, M. E. & Heppelmann, J. E. (2015). How Smart, Connected Products Are Transforming Companies. *Harvard Business Review*, November, 97–114.

Rindfleisch, A., & Moorman, C. (2001). The Acquisition and Utilization of Information in New Product Aliances: A Strength-of-Ties Perspectives. *Journal of Marketing*, 65(2), 1–18.

Scheer, L. K., Miao, C. F., & Palmatier, R. W. (2014). Dependence and Interdependence in Marketing Relationships: Meta-Analytic Insights. *Journal of the Academy of Marketing Science*, 43(6), 694–712.

Sieweke, J., Birkner, S., & Mohe, M. (2012). Preferred Supplier Programs for Consulting Services: An Exploratory Study of German Client Companies. *Journal of Purchasing and Supply Management, 18*(3), 123–136.

Statista. (2016). *Automotive Suppliers' Proportion of Value Added to Worldwide Automobile Manufacture from 1985 to 2015*. https://www.statista.com/ statistics/269619/automotive-suppliers-share-of-worldwide-automobile-manufacture-since-1985/. Date Accessed 15 Feb 2017.

Teece, D. J., Pisano, G., & Shuen, A. (2007). Dynamic Capabilities and Strategic Management. *Strategic Management Journal, 18*(7), 509–533.

Thomas, K. W. (1976). Conflict and Conflict Management. In M. D. Dunnette (Ed.), *Handbook of Industrial and Organizational Psychology* (pp. 889–935). Chicago: Rand McNally.

Thomas, K. W. (1992). Conflict and Conflict Management: Reflections and Update. *Journal of Organizational Behavior, 13*(3), 265–274.

Tuli, K. R., Bharadwaj, S. G., & Kohli, A. K. (2010). Ties That Bind: The Impact of Multiple Types of Ties with a Customer on Sales Growth and Sales Volatility. *Journal of Marketing Research, 47*(1), 36–50.

Tuli, K. R., Kohli, A. K., & Bharadwaj, S. G. (2007). Rethinking Customer Solutions: From Product Bundles to Relational Processes. *Journal of Marketing, 71*(3), 1–17.

Ulaga, W., & Eggert, A. (2006). Value-Based Differentiation in Business Relationships: Gaining and Sustaining Key Supplier Status. *Journal of Marketing, 70*(1), 119–136.

Ulaga, W., & Reinartz, W. J. (2011). Hybrid Offerings: How Manufacturing Firms Combine Goods and Services Successfully. *Journal of Marketing, 75*(6), 5–23.

Verhoef, P. C., Reinartz, W. J., & Krafft, M. (2010). Customer Engagement as a New Perspective in Customer Management. *Journal of Service Research, 13*(3), 247–252.

Vivek, S. D., Dalela, V., & Beatty, S. E. (2016). Partner Engagement: A Perspective on B2B Engagement. In R. J. Brodie, L. D. Hollebeek, & J. Conduit (Eds.), *Customer Engagement – Contemporary Issues and Challenges* (pp. 53–66). New York: Routledge.

von Wangenheim, F., & Bayón, T. (2007). The Chain from Customer Satisfaction via Word-of-Mouth Referrals to New Customer Acquisition. *Journal of the Academy of Marketing Science, 35*(2), 233–249.

Wieseke, J., Kraus, F., Ahearne, M., & Mikolon, S. (2012). Multiple Identification Foci and Their Countervailing Effects on Salespeople's Negative Headquarters Stereotypes. *Journal of Marketing, 76*(3), 1–20.

Wuyts, S., Stremersch, S., Van Den Bulte, C., & Franses, P. H. (2004). Vertical Marketing Systems for Complex Products: A Triadic Perspective. *Journal of Marketing Research, 41*(4), 479–487.

CHAPTER 12

Engaging with Brands: The Influence of Dispositional and Situational Brand Engagement on Customer Advocacy

Richie L. Liu, David E. Sprott, Eric R. Spangenberg, and Sandor Czellar

INTRODUCTION

Firms have become increasingly interested in engaging customers with their products and services (Morgan and Hunt 1994). Driven by research on understanding such customer engagement and its impact on outcomes beyond purchasing, such as word-of-mouth (Van Doorn et al. 2010; Vargo and Lusch 2004), researchers have recently turned their attention to the processes by which consumers become engaged with brands (Brodie et al. 2011; Hollebeek 2011; Puligadda et al. 2012; Sprott et al. 2009). Furthermore, we are beginning to witness such brand engagement

R.L. Liu (✉)
Oklahoma State University, Stillwater, OK, USA

D.E. Sprott
Washington State University, Pullman, WA, USA

E.R. Spangenberg
University of California, Irvine, Irvine, CA, USA

S. Czellar
University of Lausanne, Lausanne, Switzerland

© The Author(s) 2018
R.W. Palmatier et al. (eds.), *Customer Engagement Marketing*,
DOI 10.1007/978-3-319-61985-9_12

processes playing out in practice. Recently, brands such as Coca-Cola, McDonald's, and Red Bull have allocated substantial marketing resources toward their Facebook pages to generate fanfare, leading to more "likes" and positive word-of-mouth (Thompson 2015).

Although the growing body of brand engagement literature has provided a number of theoretical and practical insights, researchers have devoted minimal attention to understanding how various forms of brand engagement influence one another and predict important marketing outcomes, especially outcomes that are non-transactional (i.e., advocating a brand via social media). In particular, prior work has neglected to consider simultaneously the impact of dispositional brand engagement (enduring, individual differences in how consumers engage with brands), along with situational engagement with a brand. In the current research, we address this situation by developing a theoretical framework that relates dispositional brand engagement to engagement with a specific brand.

In particular, we draw from research involving the self-concept and innate brand dispositions, wherein consumers have been shown to incorporate important brands in the self (i.e., brand engagement in the self-concept [BESC]; Sprott et al. 2009) and process product or service information in terms of the brand (vs. attributes; Puligadda et al. 2012). The influence of these dispositional forms of brand engagement is proposed to affect customer advocacy (i.e., word-of-mouth and posting in social media) via cognitive, affective, and behavioral dimensions of situational engagement with a brand (Hollebeek 2011). In addition to research on dispositional and situational brand engagement, the current research also relies upon insights from the co-creation of value with customers that has been shown to lead to post-purchase behaviors.

In terms of contributions, our work expands the field's theoretical understanding of dispositional and situational brand engagement and how each affects important market outcomes that do not necessarily occur at the point of purchase—a topic as yet to be addressed in the literature. Our research also provides insights regarding the differential degree to which cognitive, affective, and behavioral influences mediate the effect of brand engagement dispositions on customer advocacy, an important marketing outcome not yet empirically tested, but theorized in the brand engagement realm. In the remainder of our chapter, we review the relevant customer and brand engagement literatures in order to develop our conceptual model and associated hypotheses. We then present the method and results of a study providing empirical support for the model. Finally, we conclude with discussion of theoretical and managerial implications of our work.

Engagement from Customers to Brands

As with the evolution of brands extending from marketplace differentiators to symbols that can possess human traits (Fournier 1998; Levy 1959), the view of customers by marketers has similarly evolved. In particular, we have seen a major shift in marketing actions that were once product-centric to actions that are becoming increasingly customer-centric (Day and Montgomery 1999; Webster 1992). The idea that customers no longer act as passive recipients in relationships with organizations, but rather are co-creators of value in the exchange process is often referred to as customer engagement (Sashi 2012). As captured by the service-dominant logic paradigm (Vargo and Lusch 2004; Vivek et al. 2012), marketers no longer focus only on the transaction, but rather attend to the development of interactive (rather than unidirectional) experiences (Vargo 2009). It has been suggested that these co-created experiences between customers and firms result in behaviors from engaged customers that extend beyond a purchase, such as positive word-of-mouth or blogging (Van Doorn et al. 2010; Verhoef et al. 2010).

There are two main perspectives regarding customer engagement. One approach views engagement as behavioral in nature. From this perspective, behavior extends beyond the customer-firm transaction and serves as a motivational driver to a broad spectrum of interactions between the customer and the firm (e.g., Jaakkola and Alexander 2014; Van Doorn et al. 2010). A second view of engagement is psychologically based and focused on the interaction between the customer and firm, as reflected by cognitive, emotional, and behavioral states of the customer during the co-creative experience (e.g., Brodie et al. 2011; Calder et al. 2009; Hollebeek 2011).

Brand engagement is an extension of customer engagement. Rather than the interactive experience comprising value co-creation between a customer and a firm, the engagement now occurs between a customer and brand (Solem and Pedersen 2016). Brand engagement can occur with not only just one customer, but also between a brand and its community (Brodie et al. 2013). Two forms of brand engagement (the focus of our research) have been examined in the literature and include both dispositional and situational brand engagement. Dispositional brand engagement represents the enduring individual differences in how consumers engage with multiple (favorite) brands beyond a transaction in a particular consumption setting. We examine two forms of dispositional brand engagement, namely, brand engagement in the self-concept (BESC) and brand schematicity. BESC is the dispositional tendency to define the self-concept with important brands (Sprott et al. 2009), whereas brand schematicity is the disposition to process incoming product information in terms of the brand (vs. attributes; Puligadda et al. 2012). In contrast, situational brand engagement represents engaging with a specific brand beyond a purchasing context and is comprised of three dimensions: cognitive, affective, and behavioral.

Dispositional Brand Engagement

Research on dispositional brand engagement is grounded in work examining the role of brands within the self (e.g., Escalas and Bettman 2003, 2005; Johnson et al. 2011). Academics have long postulated that possessions can become integrated within a person's self-concept (e.g., James 1890)—an idea that forms the theoretical basis of Belk's (1988) influential treatment of the extended self. Brand research first explored the role of brands in the self-concept by theorizing and measuring self-brand connections (Escalas and Bettman 2003; Escalas 2004; Escalas and Bettman 2005). Building on this work, more recent research has conceptualized and developed measurement tools for enduring individual difference in brand engagement, namely, brand engagement in the self-concept and brand schematicity.

Brand Engagement in the Self-Concept Brand engagement in the self-concept (BESC) is conceptualized as a consumer's general propensity to incorporate important brands in the self-concept (Guèvremont and Grohmann 2016; Sprott et al. 2009). It is important to distinguish BESC and prior research on related branding constructs, such as self-brand connections; while the latter is often restricted to a relationship with a specific brand, BESC is viewed as a generalized tendency for consumers to include multiple brands as part of the self-concept.

The studies reported by Sprott et al. support the basic idea that consumers higher in BESC include their favorite brands as part of their self-concepts which in turn can lead to important reactions to brand-related marketing. In particular, these researchers demonstrated that consumers with a higher tendency to include brands in their self-concepts were able to access favorite (vs. least favorite) brands more easily from memory, recalled a greater quantity of branded products that they owned, and recalled a greater amount of brand names after incidental exposure. BESC was also shown to influence consumers' attention to favorite brands with overt logos, as well as to brand loyalty (operationalized by time insensitivity for waiting on new products to be offered by their favorite brands). More recently, research involving BESC has shown that consumers, with a stronger tendency to include important brands as part of the self, preferred national as opposed to private label brands (Liu et al. 2016).

Brand Schematicity Brand schematicity represents the degree to which consumers process information regarding a product or service based on the brand itself, rather than the features absent in the brand (Puligadda et al. 2012). Brand schematicity relies heavily on schemas within a consumer's self-concept (Halkias 2015). Schemas are cognitive structures (Higgins 1996) that enable a person to organize incoming information and help search for assimilating information when making sense of information on hand (Marshall 1995). Thus, brand schematicity is informed by Keller's (1993) customer-based brand equity framework and draws from the formation of brand knowledge and the storing of such information in associative memory.

Brand schematicity is regarded as a propensity to process brand information from the consumption environment generally, rather than for a specific brand. In such settings, brand schematic consumers will utilize incoming brand information to make sense of the product or service and then draw from prior information in self-schemas to form evaluations and make purchase decisions. Further, consumers with higher levels of brand schematicity have an innate intent to seek and integrate brand information in their memory. In contrast, brand aschematic consumers rely solely on the attributes of the product or service to make consumption decisions. The studies conducted by Puligadda et al. support the importance of brand information for brand schematic consumers in the context of brand extensions. Specifically, consumers higher in brand schematicity responded more favorably when a brand extension had a brand concept consistent with the parent brand. In contrast, brand aschematics did not show variability in evaluations regardless whether the brand extension was consistent or inconsistent with the parent brand. Recent work has also shown brand schematic consumers processing brand information that is aesthetic in nature (e.g., Apple brand logo that is an object vs. Samsung brand logo that is text). In particular, work by Jeon and Lee (2016) demonstrated a higher likelihood of brand schematic (vs. aschematic) consumers to purchase a moderate complementarity accessory (i.e., camera strap) from a highly aesthetic brand (i.e., Apple).

Situational Brand Engagement

When customers engage with a specific brand, the interaction has been described as a context-dependent, fluctuating, and iterative state (Hollebeek 2011). We refer to this state as situational brand engagement. Research on this form of engagement has explored the dimensions of interactive engagement between a customer and a particular brand. Similar to customer engagement, the majority of this research has concluded that interacting with a brand is multi-dimensional in nature. In particular, researchers have shown customers to invest cognitive, affective, and behavioral resources during the brand interaction (e.g., Higgins and Scholer 2009; Hollebeek 2011; Hollebeek et al. 2014). Cognitive activity during brand engagement is represented by brand-related elaboration, while affect is viewed as the degree of positive emotion. Situational engagement involving behavior reflects the effort invested while engaging with a brand (Hollebeek et al. 2014). Notably, some have associated the behavioral dimension of brand engagement with non-transactional activity such as positive word-of-mouth and liking on Facebook (Hollebeek 2011). The motivational state of situational brand engagement has been shown to positively influence brand usage intent (Hollebeek et al. 2014) and brand loyalty (Leckie et al. 2016) (Table 12.1).

Hypotheses Development

BESC and Situational Brand Engagement

Regarding the effect of BESC on situational engagement with a brand, we draw upon the foundational work by Sprott et al. (2009) where an individual difference measure of brand engagement (BESC) was developed and based on a cognitive view of the self-concept. Sprott et al. showed that consumers who are more likely to define themselves through important brands will incorporate such brands as part of their self-concepts. This work builds on the established view that the self can organize and maintain brands as part of the self-schema and associated memory structures (e.g., Keller 1993). Importantly, research finds that the inclusion of important brands within the self-concept can affect consumers' associated evaluations

Table 12.1 Overview of selected brand engagement research contributing to this chapter

Author(s) and year	Research type	Construct	Key content
Hollebeek (2011)	Empirical: Qualitative	Situational brand engagement	Conceptualizes and defines brand engagement with three dimensions (cognitive, affective, and behavioral) during an interaction between a brand and a customer.
Brodie et al. (2013)	Empirical: Qualitative	Situational brand engagement	Reveals the various sub-processes related to brand engagement in an online brand community.
Hollebeek et al. (2014)	Empirical: Quantitative	Situational brand engagement	Develops a brand engagement scale and validates the scale by testing its nomological net in a social media context.
Sprott et al. (2009)	Empirical: Quantitative	BESC	Conceptualizes the individual difference of brand engagement in the self-concept and develops scale. Predictive validity studies are presented.
Guèvremont and Grohmann (2016)	Empirical: Quantitative	BESC	Consumers with higher levels of BESC, when socially excluded, reported greater emotional brand attachment toward an authentic (vs. inauthentic) brand.
Puligadda et al. (2012)	Empirical: Quantitative	Brand Schematicity	Conceptualizes the individual difference of brand schematicity and develops scale. Predictive validity studies are presented.
Halkias (2015)	Conceptual	Brand Schematicity	Reviews brand schema, schema theory, and components of a brand schema.
Jeon and Lee (2016)	Empirical: Quantitative	Brand Schematicity	Brand schematic (vs. aschematic) consumers demonstrated a stronger likelihood to purchase an accessory with moderate complementarity from a high (vs. low) aesthetic brand.

and behaviors (Escalas and Bettman 2003; Markus 1983; Sprott et al. 2009). Thus, we expect that the cognitive nature of BESC will positively relate to cognitive engagement with a particular brand.

In terms of BESC's influence on affective situational engagement with a brand, we once again rely on Sprott et al.'s (2009) original research and their idea that Ball and Tasaki's (1992) work on attachment to possessions is a related, but distinct, construct from BESC. While BESC is focused on a dispositional tendency to include multiple important brands as part of the self, attachment to possession is focused on one specific object. Despite the cognitive basis of both BESC and possession attachment, attachment theory (which underlies both constructs) also includes an affective dimension, in terms of bonds that are formed with people (Bowlby 2012) and also brands (Thomson et al. 2005). Due to the relationships between possession attachment, BESC, and attachment theory, we believe that affect is an important consideration for BESC. Indeed, recent research has linked BESC and emotional brand attachment. In particular, work by Guèvermont and Grohmann (2016) showed high BESC consumers to report greater emotional brand attachment toward an authentic (vs. inauthentic) brand. Although the affective response from high BESC consumers only emerged when socially excluded, we propose that engagement of important brands in the self is unlikely to be void of affect. For this reason, we expect that BESC should have a positive relationship with consumers' affective engagement with a brand.

Lastly, we address the influence of BESC on behavioral engagement with a particular brand. Previous research has shown that higher BESC consumers have better recall of branded possessions, pay closer attention to incidental exposure to brand logos on others, and report longer willing-to-wait times for future products released by their favorite brands (Sprott et al. 2009). These results suggest that BESC leads to important behavioral marketing outcomes for consumers; as such, we predict that BESC will have a similar effect on consumers' behavioral engagement with a specific brand. Based on this reasoning, we hypothesize:

H₁ Brand engagement in the self-concept (BESC) is positively associated with the dimensions of situational brand engagement: **(a)** cognitive, **(b)** affective, and **(c)** behavioral.

Brand Schematicity and Situational Brand Engagement

Our second hypothesis considers the influence of brand schematicity on situational engagement with a brand. As previously discussed, brand schematicity primarily draws from research on cognitive schema (Puligadda et al. 2012). Brand schematic consumers have an inclination to process products/services at the brand (rather than attribute) level. While processing brand information from the marketplace, brand schematic consumers rely on self-schemas to assimilate brand knowledge (i.e., associations and awareness) from prior brand interactions and their current experiences. For example, when consumers engage with a brand in a co-created experience (e.g., participating in user-generated content), they heavily invest their cognitive resources in the relevant brand (i.e., think about the brand). Given the cognitive basis of brand schematicity, we expect this construct to have a positive relationship with the cognitive engagement with a brand.

Further, we also predict that consumers' tendencies to cognitively process brand information (e.g., for a brand that they are engaged with in a co-created experience) will have a positive relationship with behavioral brand engagement. While not necessarily drawn to every brand, a tendency for brand-schematic consumers is to process brand information for a particular brand, which should likely progress to an investment of behavioral resources when engaging with the brand. Finally, due to brand schematicity's heavy reliance upon cognitive self-schema, we do not expect brand schematicity to have an influence on a person's affective engagement with a brand.

Based on the preceding, we hypothesize:

H_2 Brand schematicity is positively associated with the (a) cognitive and (b) behavioral dimensions of situational brand engagement, but not with the (c) affective dimension.

Brand Engagement and Customer Advocacy

Our final hypotheses relate to the effect of dispositional brand engagement and the three dimensions of situational brand engagement on customer advocacy. We operationalize customer advocacy as non-transactional behavior benefiting a brand, such as positive word-of-mouth and "Liking" on Facebook (e.g., Van Doorn et al. 2010). Previous research has suggested, but not yet empirically tested, that engagement with a particular brand should positively influence customer advocacy (Hollebeek 2011; Verhoef et al. 2010). We agree with this view, as the context-dependent state of a consumer's encounter with a particular brand should activate cognitive, affective, and behavioral engagement with that brand, which will in turn lead to downstream non-transactional behaviors in favor of the brand. Each of the components motivates non-transactional behaviors that will ultimately and positively impact the firm, such as advocating on behalf of the brand to others.

Further, we also propose that dispositional brand engagement will have a positive influence on consumer advocacy given the importance brands play in defining the self-concepts of consumers who have stronger dispositional brand engagement (e.g., those higher in BESC and brand schematicity). Often, consumers are motivated to spread negative word-of-mouth when they are dissatisfied (Blodgett et al. 1993). In contrast, we expect that positive word-of-mouth will occur when consumers consider brands that help to define themselves. In any particular situation, we expect that situational engagement with a specific brand will serve as a mediator of these effects. Based on the preceding reasoning, we hypothesize the following:

H_3 Situational brand engagement along the **(a)** cognitive, **(b)** affective, and **(c)** behavioral dimensions is positively associated with customer advocacy.

H_4 Dispositional brand engagement is positively associated with customer advocacy, with the effect being mediated by situational brand engagement.

METHOD

The objective of the current work was to test the proposed framework in Fig. 12.1 comprised of dispositional brand engagement, situational brand engagement, and customer advocacy. We examined the effect of BESC $(H1_{a–c})$ and brand schematicity $(H2_{a–c})$ on the three dimensions of situational brand engagement (i.e., cognitive, affective, and behavioral). We also explored the relationship between engaging with a brand and customer advocacy $(H3_{a–c})$. In addition, we tested the mediating role of situational brand engagement for the relationship between dispositional brand engagement and customer advocacy (H_4).

Participants

U.S. respondents recruited from Amazon's Mechanical Turk (MTurk) service completed an online survey in exchange for $1.00 ($n$ = 481; 51.60% female; mean age = 35.18 years; 75.30% Caucasian).

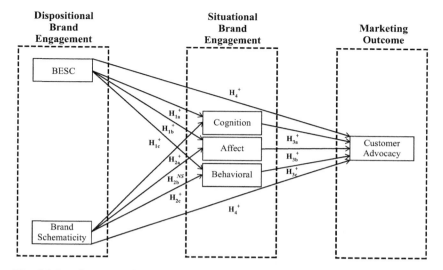

Fig. 12.1 Conceptual model
(Notes: *BESC* = brand engagement in the self-concept. H4 hypothesizes the positive relationship between the dispositional brand engagement constructs and customer advocacy and this effect being mediated by situational brand engagement with a specific brand)

Procedure

Participants first completed two individual difference measures assessing dispositional brand engagement: BESC (Sprott et al. 2009) and brand schematicity (Puligadda et al. 2012). Each of the brand engagement disposition scales were randomly presented. Next, participants were asked to recall an electronics brand that they often use and input the brand's name in the survey; participants proceeded to complete the situational brand engagement measure for that brand (Hollebeek et al. 2014). Each of the items of this measure referred to the electronic brand specified by the participant. Lastly, participants completed customer advocacy measures (i.e., positive word-of-mouth and "Like" on Facebook) and concluded the study by completing various demographic measures. All measures were assessed using seven-point scales (see Appendix for items).

RESULTS

Measurement Model and Common Method Variance

Prior to our main analyses, we evaluated the measurement model using confirmatory factor analysis (CFA) to ensure the items reflected their appropriate latent constructs (i.e., BESC; brand schematicity; cognitive, affective, and behavioral situational brand engagement; and customer advocacy). The CFA yielded a six-factor model that fit the data well (χ^2 (390) = 1243.95, $p < 0.001$; CFI = 0.92; SRMR = 0.04; RMSEA = 0.07), and all factor loadings were substantial (>0.58) and significant (*p-values* < 0.001).

Following recommendations of Fornell and Larcker (1981), we tested for convergent and discriminant validity. Analyses supported convergent and discriminant validity of our constructs: (a) average variance extracted (AVE) for all constructs exceeded the suggested value of 0.50; (b) AVEs exceeded the squared correlation between constructs; and (c) the composite reliabilities for all constructs were adequate (>0.75).

To rule out any significant influence of common method variance, we conducted two tests. First, we ran a Harman's one-factor test (Mossholder et al. 1998). All items from the latent variables were loaded on one-factor in a confirmatory factor analysis model. The one-factor model did not fit the data well (χ^2 (405) = 4237.53, $p < 0.001$; CFI = 0.68; SRMR = 0.11; RMSEA = 0.14). Second, we introduced a common-method factor to our six-factor measurement model (Podsakoff et al. 2003). Results of a confirmatory factor analysis revealed that the additional factor accounted for less than 4% of the variance in the indicator variables. Taken together, these ex-post analyses found no evidence for a significant influence of common method variance in our data.

Descriptive Statistics

Table 12.2 shows the means, standard deviations, AVEs, composite reliabilities, and correlations for the model variables. From the correlation matrix, the dispositional brand engagement constructs were positively related to all dimensions of engagement with a brand, which positively related to customer advocacy. As expected, dispositional brand engagement was positively correlated with customer advocacy.

Table 12.2 Correlation matrix and descriptive statistics for the model variables

	1	2	3	4	5	6
1. BESC	1.00					
2. Brand schematicity	0.73**	1.00				
3. SBE – Cognition	0.62**	0.51**	1.00			
4. SBE – Affect	0.59**	0.48**	0.64**	1.00		
5. SBE – Behavioral	0.40**	0.33**	0.49**	0.62**	1.00	
6. Customer advocacy	0.42**	0.30**	0.46**	0.54**	0.50**	1.00
Mean	3.61	3.21	3.76	4.94	5.05	5.16
SD	1.56	1.18	1.60	1.19	1.23	1.39
AVE	0.79	0.54	0.73	0.69	0.69	0.61
Composite reliability	0.97	0.92	0.89	0.90	0.87	0.75

BESC = brand engagement in self-concept, *SBE* = situational brand engagement, *SD* = standard deviation, *AVE* = average variance extracted

**$p < 0.01$ (two-tailed); n = 481 (listwise deletion)

Structural Equation Modeling (SEM) Analysis

Our primary analysis consisted of SEM using Stata 14. We also conducted logical follow-up indirect effect tests using Hayes' (2013) PROCESS macros (i.e., Model 4; multiple mediator test using bootstrapped samples). Building from the conceptual model depicted in Fig. 12.1, our estimation focused on customer advocacy regressed on situational brand engagement, which was, in turn, regressed on both dispositional brand engagement variables (i.e., BESC and brand schematicity). We also estimated the direct effects of the brand disposition variables on customer advocacy. Finally, dispositional and situational brand engagement variables were allowed to correlate among one another. The model and standardized path coefficients were estimated with a maximum likelihood estimation and resulted in good fit indices, $\chi^2 (392) = 1249.38$, $p < 0.001$, CFI = 0.93, SRMR = 0.04, RMSEA = 0.06 (Fig. 12.2).

We first predicted that BESC would be positively related to all three dimensions of situational brand engagement (i.e., cognitive, affective, and behavioral). Our model estimation supported these relationships; thus, $H1_{a-c}$ was supported. It is worth noting that BESC's influence on situational brand engagement was stronger for the cognitive and affective, compared to the behavioral, dimensions. BESC's varying effects on situational engagement suggest that consumers who include brands as part of their self-concepts are more likely to do so by thinking about the brand and how it makes them feel, rather than by using a particular brand. Given

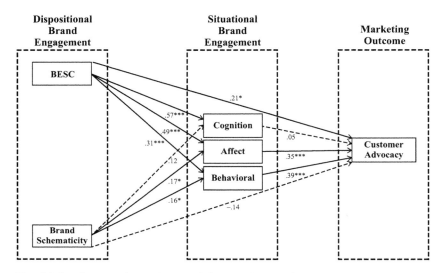

Fig. 12.2 Structural equation model estimation results
(Notes: $*p < 0.05$; $***p < 0.001$; $BESC$ = brand engagement in the self-concept. Model above was estimated using structural equation modeling and parameter estimates are standardized. For brevity, reflective items for constructs are not shown. Dispositional brand engagement constructs were correlated with one another as well as situational brand engagement constructs. Fit indices: χ^2 (392) = 1249.38 ($p < 0.001$); CFI = 0.93; $SRMR$ = 0.04; $RMSEA$ = 0.06)

the cognitive nature of BESC, its positive influence on cognitive engagement with a brand was not overly surprising. The same argument could be made for BESC's positive influence on behavioral engagement with a particular brand; however, this influence was less based on our data. While dispositional engagement in the form of BESC is primarily anchored in cognitive mechanisms, there is clearly a relationship to affective forms of engagement with a particular brand.

Our second set of hypotheses predicted that brand schematicity would be positively related to the cognitive and behavioral dimensions ($H2_{a-b}$) of situational brand engagement, but not to the affective dimension ($H2_c$). We found that brand schematicity had no influence on the cognitive dimension and a modest, positive influence on the behavioral dimension; these results support $H2_b$, but not $H2_a$. In addition, results revealed a positive influence on affectively engaging with a brand; thus, $H2_c$ was not supported. The magnitude of this effect was similar to brand schematicity's positive influence on behaviorally engaging with a brand. The entirety of brand schematicity's theoretical development is generally comprised of a consumer's cognitive processing of brand or product information. Due to the cognitive nature of brand schematicity, we found it surprising that brand schematicity did not have a positive influence on the cognitive component of engaging with a brand, but did have an influence on behavioral and affective engagement.

Overall, both BESC and brand schematicity influenced consumers' affective and behavioral engagement with a brand, with a stronger influence being witnessed regarding the emotional form of engagement. The fact that both BESC and brand schematicity had positive influences on affective engagement with a specific brand suggests that the branded schema (while cognitively based) is not void of emotion. Comparing the strength of effects between brand schematicity and BESC on situational brand engagement, we found BESC to have an overall stronger effect than brand schematicity. Interestingly, BESC also had a positive direct effect on spreading positive word-of-mouth and liking on Facebook, while brand schematicity did not.

The next set of hypotheses ($H3_{a-b}$) focused on the expected positive relationship between each dimension of situational brand engagement and customer advocacy. As discussed, previous research has suggested that engaging with a brand from cognitive, affective, and behavioral perspectives should have positive effects on outcomes such as positive word-of-mouth and liking on Facebook. However, no prior work has explored these assumptions in an empirical setting. Our results revealed that the affective and behavioral dimensions of engagement with a specific brand lead to customer advocacy, but contrary to expectations, there was no such effect regarding cognitive engagement with the brand. These findings suggest that thinking about a particular brand when engaging with it does not necessarily mean a consumer responds with valuable marketing outcomes (such as customer advocacy). This finding is somewhat unexpected given that engaging with a brand (at cognitive, affective, and behavioral levels) has been assumed to motivate consumers to act favorably toward the brand, not just during a transaction, but before and after as well. However, recent research aligns with our work by suggesting that cognitive brand engagement may not affect brand usage intent and may even negatively influence brand loyalty (Hollebeek et al. 2014; Leckie et al. 2016). These findings and our own research suggest that the influence of cognitive (compared to affective and behavioral) brand engagement on marketing outcomes may not be as important as originally presumed.

Our last hypothesis (H4) predicted the mediational effect of situational brand engagement regarding the positive influence of dispositional brand engagement on customer advocacy. To test this hypothesis, we conducted two follow-up indirect effect tests using bootstrapped samples. In each model (i.e., multiple mediators; Model 4; Hayes 2013), we tested for the direct effect of dispositional brand engagement on customer advocacy through the dimensions of situational brand engagement. Our first test focused on BESC's direct effect on customer advocacy through all three dimensions. Specifically, our analysis used 5000 bootstrapped samples and revealed 95% bias-corrected confidence intervals that were statistically different from zero (cognitive, 0.006–0.109; affective, 0.075–0.186; behavioral, 0.054–0.126) through three positive indirect effects (cognitive, 0.058; affective, 0.130; behavioral, 0.086). For our second test, we examined for brand schematicity's direct effect on customer advocacy through the affective and behavioral dimensions of engaging with a brand. Our analysis, using 5000 bootstrapped samples, revealed 95% bias-corrected confidence intervals that were statistically different from zero (affective, 0.138–0.279; behavioral, 0.061–0.161) through both tested dimensions for positive indirect effects (affective, 0.204; behavioral, 0.103). These findings support H_4.

GENERAL DISCUSSION

In the past two decades, branding research has focused on understanding how consumers engage with brands in various contexts (e.g., Aaker 1997; Aggarwal 2004; Johnson et al. 2011). Grounded in research on brand relationships (Fournier 1998) and self-brand connections (Escalas 2004), scholars have explored two different forms of brand engagement. At the dispositional level, brand engagement in the self-concept (BESC; Sprott et al. 2009) and brand schematicity (Puligadda et al. 2012) represent enduring individual differences in terms of how consumers engage with a variety of brands. Both forms of brand engagement rely on the cognitive nature of the self. At the brand level, in contrast, direct engagement with a specific brand has also been explored along cognitive, affective, and behavioral dimensions (e.g., Hollebeek 2011). Such a situational brand engagement represents a motivational state during the brand interaction that leads to both transactional and non-transactional outcomes positively impacting a brand (Brodie et al. 2011). While both views of brand engagement have received attention in the literature, there has been surprisingly little attention aimed at understanding how these approaches relate to one another and how they may influence consumers' responses to brands.

In the current work we propose that dispositional brand engagement (i.e., BESC and brand schematicity) positively influences cognitive, affective, and behavioral engagement with a particular brand, which in turn impacts consumer responses to the brand. Based on our empirical model, we find that BESC has a stronger influence on situational brand engagement than does brand schematicity, and that these effects differ depending upon the nature of engagement with a particular brand. Specifically, BESC has stronger effects on cognitive and affective engagement with a brand, but relatively less influence on behavioral engagement. In contrast, brand schematicity had no impact on cognitive engagement, but similar (yet modest) influences on behavioral engagement, and (unexpectedly) on affective engagement.

Our results also showed BESC, compared to brand schematicity, to have an overall stronger influence on situational brand engagement. In other words, the prevalence of defining one's self-concept with important brands had a stronger effect on how consumers engaged with a specific brand than the tendency to process brand information. In comparison to prior research, we found that affective and behavioral engagement with a specific brand had an equal and positive impact on consumers' advocacy for the brand, but cognitive engagement had no influence. We now turn to the theoretical and practical implications of our findings.

Theoretical Implications

Our research suggests that dispositional forms of brand engagement (BESC and brand schematicity) are influential antecedents of situational brand engagement. To our knowledge, this is the first research that has explored the interplay between these two different types of engagement with a brand. Our work also suggests that dispositional brand engagement influences market outcomes (namely, customer advocacy) in multiple ways—a finding that is consistent with prior research supporting brand engagement as a multi-dimensional construct (Brodie et al. 2011; Calder et al. 2009).

Dispositional Brand Engagement A central finding from the current work relates to dispositional engagement and BESC's positive influence on affective engagement with a specific brand. As previously discussed, BESC's theoretical development draws (at least partially) from attachment to possessions. Research examining possession attachment suggests owned possessions that reflect the owner originate in the self-concept, which by nature is a cognitive structure (Ball and Tasaki 1992). Yet one of attachment theory's main tenets is the emotional development in a relationship—an effect shown to occur in brand relationships (Bowlby 2012; Thomson et al. 2005). Despite our findings not resolving the potential conflicting views of affect in the branded self-concept, our findings at the very least suggest that affect is involved (at least partially) when defining the self-concept with brands. In other words, a consumer's engagement with a particular brand will not be solely based on cognitive processing but also in how the brand makes a person feel.

The impact of dispositional engagement on affective engagement with a specific brand was also supported by brand schematicity. These results also support our assertion that emotions do play a role to a certain degree in the cognitive branded self-concept. Although dispositions toward brand engagement are theoretically derived from the cognitive nature of the self-concept, our findings suggest that the role of affect is not void when the focus is on the brand schema.

Situational Brand Engagement Cognitive engagement was only influenced by BESC (not brand schematicity) and had no influence on customer advocacy for a particular brand. Much of the research on dispositional brand engagement has its theoretical roots in cognition, and thus similar to our finding that BESC influences cognitive brand engagement. For example, Sprott et al. (2009) found BESC to impact memory and attentional processes associated with brands. In contrast, brand schematicity was expected to positively influence cognitive brand engagement, as this disposition helps consumers make sense of incoming product/service information at the brand (not attribute) level.

Overall, our work suggests that the influence of consumers' dispositional brand engagement on marketing outcomes (such as customer advocacy) is more emotional (and behavioral) in nature, versus cognitive. Future research can usefully explore this issue with additional empirical research, perhaps featuring moderators that differentially influence the various forms of brand engagement. In addition, future work should investigate the role of affect when consumers define their self-concept with brands as well as when processing incoming brand information from the consumption environment.

Managerial Implications

Brand managers are increasingly concerned about how to engage consumers with their firms and brands (Van Doorn et al. 2010; Vivek et al. 2012). Indeed, our work suggests that two different dimensions of engagement should be considered when forming branding strategies at the cognitive, affective, and behavioral levels. To date, brand engagement research has not yet recommended that managers consider dispositional brand engagement while engaging customers with their brands.

Firms should consider the dispositional form and degree of brand engagement regarding their customers. As reviewed earlier, individual differences in brand engagement have been shown to impact a variety of marketing outcomes (Sprott et al. 2009; Puligadda et al. 2012). Yet, it is has been unclear how this type of engagement might impact the way consumers engage with a particular brand firm. Our work provides initial empirical evidence for brand managers that dispositional brand engagement is, at the very least, beneficial for understanding how target markets will respond to a brand in the marketplace. For example, if a brand's target market has higher levels of BESC or the proclivity to be brand schematic, then a manager can better position a brand to be differentially engaging from a cognitive, affective, or behavioral standpoint. In order for brand managers to gauge dispositional brand engagement among their customers, applicable items from BESC and brand schematicity scales could be embedded in customer satisfaction surveys. After determining the composition of dispositional brand engagement, managers could then develop brand positioning strategies that appropriately engage their customers from a cognitive, affective, or behavioral perspective.

Our findings indicate that dispositional engagement has differential impact on emotional, cognitive, and behavioral engagement with a brand. In particular, managers should place more priority on branding strategies that resonate on an emotional and behavioral level for consumers who are predisposed to all types of brands. The apparently unique influence of emotional engagement with a brand suggests that firms should carefully consider strategies that are affect-based. As previously discussed, brand engagement dispositions have primarily been associated with a cognitive framework due to the nature of the self-concept. Our findings suggest to brand managers that appealing to consumers' emotions is just as important as providing brand information, and, in some cases, may even trump communicating a brand's functional purpose.

Appendix: Scale Items

1) **Brand Engagement in the Self-Concept** (Sprott et al. 2009; 1 = strongly disagree, 7 = strongly agree)

   - I have a special bond with the brands that I like.
   - I consider my favorite brands to be a part of myself.
   - I often feel a personal connection between my brands and me.
   - Part of me is defined by important brands in my life.
   - I feel as if I have a close personal connection with the brands I most prefer.
   - I can identify with important brands in my life.
   - There are links between the brands that I prefer and how I view myself.
   - My favorite brands are an important indication of who I am.

2) **Brand Schematicity** (Puligadda et al. 2012; 1 = strongly disagree, 7 = strongly agree)

   - I couldn't care less what brands people around me are using. (R)
   - Product features are more important than brand names in my buying decisions. (R)
   - When I go shopping, I am always scanning the environment for brand names.
   - Brands are not at all important to me. (R)
   - Brand name considerably influences my buying decisions.
   - I like to surround myself with recognizable brand names at home.
   - When I am considering products, the brand name is more important to me than any other information.
   - Brands are important to me because they indicate social status.
   - The brand name is the least important information to me when I am considering a product. (R)
   - I keep abreast of the brands people around me are using.

3) **Situational Brand Engagement** (Hollebeek et al. 2014; 1 = strongly disagree, 7 = strongly agree)

Cognition

- Using "*the brand*" gets me to think about "*the brand.*"
- I think about "*the brand*" a lot when I'm using it.
- Using "*the brand*" stimulates my interest to learn more about "*the brand.*"

Affect

- I feel very positive when I use "*the brand.*"
- Using "*the brand*" makes me happy.
- I feel good when I use "*the brand.*"
- I'm proud to use "*the brand.*"

Behavioral

- I spend a lot of time using "*the brand*", compared to other electronic brands.
- Whenever I'm using electronic brands, I usually use "*the brand.*"
- "*The brand*" is one of the brands I usually use when I use electronic brands.

4) **Customer Advocacy** (1 = extremely unlikely, 7 = extremely likely)

- How likely would you be to "Like" "*the brand's*" Facebook page?
- Assuming your friend needs to purchase an electronics product, how likely is it that you would recommend that your friend buy from "*the brand*"?

REFERENCES

Aaker, J. L. (1997). Dimensions of Brand Personality. *Journal of Marketing Research, 34,* 347–356.

Aggarwal, P. (2004). The Effects of Brand Relationship Norms on Consumer Attitudes and Behavior. *Journal of Consumer Research, 31,* 87–101.

Ball, A. D., & Tasaki, L. H. (1992). The Role and Measurement of Attachment in Consumer Behavior. *Journal of Consumer Psychology, 1,* 155–172.

Belk, R. W. (1988). Possessions and the Extended Self. *Journal of Consumer Research, 15*, 139–168.

Blodgett, J. G., Granbois, D. H., & Walters, R. G. (1993). 'The Effects of Perceived Justice on Complainants' Negative Word-of-Mouth Behavior and Repatronage Intentions. *Journal of Retailing, 69*, 399–428.

Bowlby, J. (2012). *The Making and Breaking of Affectional Bonds* (2nd ed.). New York: Routledge.

Brodie, R. J., Hollebeek, L. D., Juric, B., & Ilic, A. (2011). Customer Engagement: Conceptual Domain, Fundamental Propositions, and Implications for Research. *Journal of Service Research, 14*, 1–20.

Brodie, R. J., Ilic, A., Juric, B., & Hollebeek, L. (2013). Consumer Engagement in a Virtual Brand Community: An Exploratory Analysis. *Journal of Business Research, 66*, 105–114.

Calder, B. J., Malthouse, E. C., & Schaedel, U. (2009). An Experimental Study of the Relationship Between Online Engagement and Advertising Effectiveness. *Journal of Interactive Marketing, 23*, 321–331.

Day, G. S., & Montgomery, D. B. (1999). Charting New Directions for Marketing. *Journal of Marketing, 63*, 3–13.

Escalas, J. E. (2004). Narrative Processing: Building Consumer Connections to Brands. *Journal of Consumer Psychology, 14*, 168–179.

Escalas, J. E., & Bettman, J. R. (2003). You Are What They Eat: The Influence of Reference Groups on Consumers' Connections to Brands. *Journal of Consumer Psychology, 13*, 339–348.

Escalas, J. E., & Bettman, J. R. (2005). Self-Construal, Reference Groups, and Brand Meaning. *Journal of Consumer Research, 32*, 378–389.

Fornell, C., & Larcker, D. F. (1981). Evaluating Structural Equation Models with Unobservable Variables and Measurement Error. *Journal of Marketing Research, 18*, 39–50.

Fournier, S. (1998). Consumers and Their Brands: Developing Relationship Theory in Consumer Research. *Journal of Consumer Research, 24*, 343–373.

Guèvremont, A., & Grohmann, B. (2016). The Brand Authenticity Effect: Situational and Individual-Level Moderators. *European Journal of Marketing, 50*, 602–620.

Halkias, G. (2015). 'Mental Representation of Brands: A Schema-Based Approach to Consumers' Organization of Market Knowledge. *Journal of Product and Brand Management, 24*, 438–448.

Hayes, A. F. (2013). *Introduction to Mediation, Moderation, and Conditional Process Analysis: A Regression-Based Approach*. New York: Guilford Press.

Higgins, E. T. (1996). The "Self Digest": Self-Knowledge Serving Self-Regulatory Functions. *Journal of Personality and Social Psychology, 71*, 1062–1083.

Higgins, E. T., & Scholer, A. A. (2009). Engaging the Consumer: The Science and Art of the Value Creation Process. *Journal of Consumer Psychology, 19*, 100–114.

Hollebeek, L. D. (2011). Exploring Customer Brand Engagement: Definition and Themes. *Journal of Strategic Marketing, 19*, 555–573.

Hollebeek, L. D., Glynn, M. S., & Brodie, R. J. (2014). Consumer Brand Engagement in Social Media: Conceptualization, Scale Development and Validation. *Journal of Interactive Marketing, 28*, 149–165.

Jaakkola, E., & Alexander, M. (2014). The Role of Customer Engagement Behavior in Value Co-Creation a Service System Perspective. *Journal of Service Research, 17*, 247–261.

James, W. (1890). *The Principles of Psychology.* New York: Henry Holt and Company.

Jeon, J. E., & Lee, J. (2016). Brand Schematicity Moderates the Effect of Aesthetic Brands on Brand Accessories Purchase Intentions. *Social Behavior and Personality: An International Journal, 44*, 1733–1746.

Johnson, A. R., Matear, M., & Thomson, M. (2011). A Coal in the Heart: Self-Relevance as a Post-Exit Predictor of Consumer Anti-Brand Actions. *Journal of Consumer Research, 38*, 108–125.

Keller, K. L. (1993). Conceptualizing, Measuring, and Managing Customer-Based Brand Equity. *Journal of Marketing, 57*, 1–22.

Leckie, C., Nyadzayo, M. W., & Johnson, L. W. (2016). Antecedents of Consumer Brand Engagement and Brand Loyalty. *Journal of Marketing Management, 32*, 558–578.

Levy, S. J. (1959). Symbols for Sale. *Harvard Business Review, 37*, 117–124.

Liu, R. L., Sprott, D., Spangenberg, E., & Czellar, S. (2016). *Consumer Preference for National vs. Private Brands: The Influence of Brand Engagement and Self-View*, Working Paper.

Markus, M. L. (1983). Power, Politics, and MIS Implementation. *Communications of the ACM, 26*, 430–444.

Marshall, S. P. (1995). *Schemas in Problem Solving.* New York: Cambridge University Press.

Morgan, R. M., & Hunt, S. D. (1994). The Commitment-Trust Theory of Relationship Marketing. *Journal of Marketing, 58*, 20–38.

Mossholder, K. W., Bennett, N., Kemery, E. R., & Wesolowski, M. A. (1998). Relationships Between Bases of Power and Work Reactions: The Mediational Role of Procedural Justice. *Journal of Management, 24*, 533–552.

Podsakoff, P. M., MacKenzie, S. B., Lee, J. Y., & Podsakoff, N. P. (2003). Common Method Biases in Behavioral Research: A Critical Review of the Literature and Recommended Remedies. *Journal of Applied Psychology, 88*, 879–903.

Puligadda, S., Ross, W. T., Jr., & Grewal, R. (2012). Individual Differences in Brand Schematicity. *Journal of Marketing Research, 49*, 115–130.

Sashi, C. M. (2012). Customer Engagement, Buyer-Seller Relationships, and Social Media. *Management Decision, 50*, 253–272.

Solem, B. A. A., & Pedersen, P. E. (2016). The Role of Customer Brand Engagement in Social Media: Conceptualization, Measurement, Antecedents and Outcomes. *International Journal of Internet Marketing and Advertising*, *10*, 223–254.

Sprott, D., Czellar, S., & Spangenberg, E. (2009). The Importance of a General Measure of Brand Engagement on Market Behavior: Development and Validation of a Scale. *Journal of Marketing Research*, *46*, 92–104.

Thompson, M. (2015). 8 Winning Habits of Social Media's Top Brands. http://www.socialmediatoday.com/marketing/2015-03-19/8-winning-habits-social-medias-top-brands. Date Accessed 12 Feb 2017.

Thomson, M., MacInnis, D. J., & Park, C. W. (2005). The Ties That Bind: Measuring the Strength of Consumers' Emotional Attachments to Brands. *Journal of Consumer Psychology*, *15*, 77–91.

Van Doorn, J., Lemon, K. N., Mittal, V., Nass, S., Pick, D., Pirner, P., & Verhoef, P. C. (2010). Customer Engagement Behavior: Theoretical Foundations and Research Directions. *Journal of Service Research*, *13*, 253–266.

Vargo, S. L. (2009). Toward a Transcending Conceptualization of Relationship: A Service-Dominant Perspective. *The Journal of Business and Industrial Marketing*, *24*, 373–379.

Vargo, S. L., & Lusch, R. F. (2004). Evolving to a New Dominant Logic for Marketing. *Journal of Marketing*, *68*, 1–17.

Verhoef, P. C., Reinartz, W. J., & Krafft, M. (2010). Customer Engagement as a New Perspective in Customer Management. *Journal of Service Research*, *13*, 247–252.

Vivek, S. D., Beatty, S. E., & Morgan, R. M. (2012). Customer Engagement: Exploring Customer Relationships Beyond Purchase. *Journal of Marketing Theory and Practice*, *20*, 122–146.

Webster, F. E., Jr. (1992). The Changing Role of Marketing in the Corporation. *Journal of Marketing*, *56*, 1–17.

CHAPTER 13

The Emotional Engagement Paradox

Lerzan Aksoy, Timothy L. Keiningham,
Alexander Buoye, and Joan Ball

Customer engagement (CE) is widely viewed as an important component of a firm's long-term success. The purpose of this exploratory investigation is to examine how customers' WOM behaviors differ based upon emotional engagement (EE) levels towards the brands that they use in different industry categories. This research contributes to the engagement literature by providing new insight into the relationship between EE and WOM behaviors. Specifically, we examine how customers' WOM behaviors relate to different levels of positive and negative EE. We find that high self-brand connection among consumers that are high in both positive and negative EE generates the most positive and negative online WOM. We refer to this surprising relationship as the *Emotional Engagement Paradox*.

Kumar et al. (2010) propose four core dimensions by which CE creates value for the firm: (1) customer purchasing behavior, (2) customer referral behavior (CRV), (3) customer influencer behavior (CIV), and (4) customer knowledge behavior (CKV). The researchers argue that CE value provides an "umbrella metric" (p. 299) for consumer behavior in and outside of the realm of transactions. Interestingly, outside of customer purchasing behavior (i.e. CRV, CIV, and CKV), the components of CE

L. Aksoy (✉) • A. Buoye
Fordham University, Bronx, NY, USA

T.L. Keiningham • J. Ball
St. John's University, Jamaica, NY, USA

© The Author(s) 2018   293
R.W. Palmatier et al. (eds.), *Customer Engagement Marketing*,
DOI 10.1007/978-3-319-61985-9_13

value are directly related to word of mouth (WOM connections and interactions.

Despite this recognition, however, there is no consensus among academics and practitioners regarding the definition of CE. CE has been conceptualized as a psychological state (Brodie et al. 2011; Jaakkola and Alexander 2014), a behavioral manifestation (van Doorn et al. 2010), or a combination of psychological, behavioral, cognitive, social, and other dimensions (Vivek et al. 2012; Patterson et al. 2006). For a review, we direct the reader to Maslowska et al. (2016). See Table 13.1 for a review of relevant literature. While all of these definitions differ, there are also general points of commonality. Simplistically, customer engagement reflects a level of involvement or absorption with a brand/firm that generates attractive or repulsive emotional or behavioral responses (Higgins and Scholer 2009).

As noted earlier, one of the most important behavioral responses from a managerial point of view is the generation of WOM. While research exists on WOM and CE, much of this research actually infers engagement from the presence of positive WOM behavior (e.g. Dwyer 2007). This research takes a different approach in the hope of gaining new insights into the relationship between CE and WOM behaviors. Specifically, we

Table 13.1   Review of relevant literature

Key concepts		References
Customer Engagement	Customer engagement as a psychological state	Brodie et al. 2011; Jaakkola and Alexander 2014
	Customer engagement as a behavioral state	Van Doorn et al. 2010
	Customer engagement as an emotional/affective state	Mano and Oliver 1993; Higgins and Scholer 2009
	Customer engagement as a combination of psychological, behavioral, cognitive, social, and other dimensions	Berger 2014; Vivek et al. 2012; Patterson et al. 2006)
	Customer engagement ecosystems	Maslowska et al. 2016
	Customer engagement and value creation	Kumar et al. 2010; Higgins and Scholer 2009
Routes to Word of Mouth	Customer engagement as a route to WOM	Kumar et al. 2010; Dwyer 2007
	Self-brand connection as a route to WOM	Kwon and Mattila 2015; Park et al. 2008
	Consumption emotions as route to WOM	Ladhari 2007

refer back to the early research in marketing on engagement, specifically the work of Mano and Oliver (1993) on engagement, and examine its relationship to WOM behaviors in order to better understand how WOM behaviors differ based upon EE levels towards brands they use in different industry channels. To do so, we examine data from 3022 US consumers who provided EE information and linked this to their WOM behavior across different channels.

In some ways, our findings support prior research. In particular, EE driven by positive affect tends to generate positive WOM, EE driven by negative affect tends to generate negative WOM, and a lack of EE (either positive or negative) results in lower positive and negative WOM behaviors. Interestingly, however, consumers high in both positive and negative EE generate the most positive and negative online WOM and provide the most recommendations to family and friends. We argue that this happens because these customers also have the highest self-brand connection; we refer to this as the *Emotional Engagement Paradox* (i.e. customers with high positive and negative EE engage in greater positive and negative WOM than would occur if either positive or negative affect was absent).

EMOTIONAL ENGAGEMENT

As noted earlier, there is no consensus regarding the definition of consumer engagement. Rather than seek to define CE, however, our goal is to gain a better understanding of the relationship between WOM and engagement. To that end, we examine engagement using the framework of Mano and Oliver (1993; Oliver 2010, p. 318) who use the affect circumplex of emotions to equate engagement with a high level of arousal associated with either positive or negative affect. We recognize that researchers in CE likely believe that this notion of engagement is incomplete, particularly given the numerous investigations into the nature of CE. We argue, however, that because CE value—and in some cases the proposed definition of CE itself (e.g. Dwyer 2007)—involves WOM behaviors, important information regarding the relationship between engagement and WOM may be convoluted.

To make explicit that our examination of engagement focuses on high arousal emotion levels, we refer to this as *Emotional Engagement (EE)*. By disentangling EE from WOM behavior, our investigation can better examine how these constructs relate to one another.

Numerous studies have investigated WOM behavior. For a review, we direct the reader to Berger (2014) and King et al. (2014).

The growth of social media has dramatically changed the opportunities for consumers to engage in WOM. Moreover, it has expanded the breadth of a consumer's WOM reach (e.g. online, blogs, forums, etc.) in addition to the traditional voice communication (largely to family and friends). Keiningham et al. (2016) find that WOM channel impacts the type and level of WOM activity.

Specifically relevant to this investigation, researchers have found that both pleasure and arousal are positively associated with WOM behaviors (Ladhari 2007). Because to date, however, all studies (of which we are aware) have examined the relationship between consumers' pleasure, arousal, and WOM behaviors regarding a single brand or industry category, it is unclear if the relationships in these constructs reflect a general customer characteristic (e.g. consumer positivity or negativity predisposition) or experience-dependent arousal. Specifically, do consumers' WOM behaviors differ significantly when their levels of arousal and pleasure for different brands diverge?

DATA AND METHODOLOGY

We collected cross-sectional survey data that gathered information about positive and negative WOM, giving volume across a variety of channels including friends and family, online, forums, and blogs. We also collected information on common drivers of WOM reported in the literature (e.g. overall satisfaction, repurchase intention, positive and negative emotions, self-brand connection, and consumer demographics). Data were collected from 3022 unique respondents in the United States. The sample was 51% male and 49% females representing a broad distribution of age ranges: 5% age 18–24, 18% age 25–34, 25% age 35–44, 28% age 45–54, and 24% age 55+.

Respondents were asked about their product/services usage of different industry categories and then given the opportunity to fill out the survey for up to two different product/services categories depending on whether or not they made purchases in the category. Out of all respondents, 1656 (55%) evaluated only one brand, whereas 1366 respondents (45%) evaluated two brands that represent different product/services categories. In total, 4388 brand ratings were provided by 3022 respondents. Thus, the unit of analysis in the final file is best described as "respondent-rating level" (sometimes referred to as a "stacked" data file) containing 4388 records and where each record represents the rating of one brand by one respondent and where the number of records in the file corresponding to each respondent is equal to the number of brands he or she rated. Brands rated were distributed across nine industries in the USA: Automotive (11%), Gaming Consoles (10%), Handheld Devices/PDA (9%), Hotels (9%), Mobile (10%), Pharmacy (10%), Software OS (10%), Software Websearch (10%), and Retail (11%).

Measures

WOM Behavior WOM giving behavior was measured via the following question. "How many times in the last year, have you [given WOM in a particular way]?" The one-year time frame is adopted from Yang et al. (2012). WOM behavior was further divided by whether or not recommendations/complaints were made to family and friends or online. We also distinguish between "when asked" and "spontaneously" to disentangle whether someone gave the WOM information with or without active solicitation (Wien and Olsen 2014).

Emotions Respondents were asked to indicate on a 10-point scale, where 1 = strongly disagree and 10 = strongly agree, the extent to which they agreed that the brand/firm made them feel an emotion. The list of 24 included both positive and negative emotions: angry, irritated, regret, afraid, nervous, worried, sad, helpless, miserable, embarrassed, humiliated, self-conscious, secure, fulfilled, peaceful, delighted, thrilled, happy, loved, desired, warm-hearted, pride, important, and self-respect (Oliver 1993, 2010).

Self-Brand Connection Because we expect engagement and self-brand connection to be related (Sprott et al. 2009), we asked a battery of eight questions designed to gauge the extent to which respondents felt a personal connection to the brand (per Escalas and Bettman 2005). Principal components analysis strongly suggests a single-factor solution, with only a single eigenvalue over 1 (6.86) accounting for 86% of the variance across variables.

Analysis

The 24 emotions variables were included in a principal components analysis (using varimax rotation) to determine the dimensionality of emotions and to create factors for use in our analysis. The principal components analysis suggests a two-factor solution that accounts for 80% of the variance across variables. The first principal component is comprised of the positive emotions (pride, warm-hearted, important, etc.), such that higher values characterize positive emotional engagement with the brand, while lower values characterize the absence of positive EE. The second principal component conversely is comprised of the negative emotions (afraid, sad, humiliated, etc.), such that higher values characterize negative emotional engagement with the brand, while lower values characterize an absence of negative EE. Our findings support those of Watson and Tellegen (1985), who argue for a circumplex characterized by positive and negative affect. As a result, we are able to cross the two factors on at their medians to create EE quadrants: a brand characterized by both high (i.e. above average) positive and negative EE would fall into the upper-right quadrant. A brand characterized by positive EE would fall into the upper-left quadrant. A brand with no EE would be in the lower-left quadrant, while a brand high on negative EE would fall in lower-right quadrant.

We then conducted a simple exploratory means analysis of WOM behavior by quadrant accompanied by one-way ANOVA tests (see Table 13.2).[1] Some generalities become immediately apparent. As would be generally expected, the absence of both positive and negative EE corresponds to the lowest levels of all forms of giving WOM. Paradoxically, however, with the exception of giving negative WOM to family/friends, the highest levels of WOM behavior occur when customers' experience demonstrates both positive and negative EE. By contrast, the highest satisfaction, recommend intention, and repurchase intention levels are associated with the presence of positive EE only. The highest levels of self-brand connection, however, are associated with having both positive and negative EE. Figure 13.1 summarizes the key information contained in Table 13.2.

Since our goal is to differentiate WOM behaviors between brands with different levels of emotional engagement, we conducted additional examination limiting our sample to only those respondents who provided feedback on two brands and who also demonstrated different levels of emotional engagement between the two brands rated with respect to placement in the EE grid. Of the 1366 respondents who provided information

Table 13.2 Word-of-mouth behavior means by emotional engagement quadrant

	Positive and negative EE	Positive-only EE	Negative-only EE	No EE	One-way ANOVA Sig
N	1252	1004	813	1319	
Brand Identification	0.75	0.33	-0.67	-0.55	***
Recommended [company/brand] to family and friends (Spontaneously)	2.32	1.72	0.62	0.75	***
Given negative feedback about [company/brand] to family and friends (Spontaneously)	0.24	0.06	1.18	0.14	***
Posted positive comment about [company/brand] on forums/blogs (Spontaneously)	0.89	0.20	0.07	0.12	***
Posted negative comment about [company/brand] on forums/blogs (Spontaneously)	0.20	0.01	0.11	0.06	***
Given a positive review about [company/brand] online (Spontaneously)	0.80	0.18	0.07	0.11	***
Given a negative review about [company/brand] online (Spontaneously)	0.13	0.01	0.13	0.05	***
Recommended [company/brand] to family and friends (When asked)	2.57	2.12	0.86	1.12	***
Given negative feedback about [company/brand] to family and friends (When asked)	0.26	0.09	0.86	0.18	***
Posted positive comment about [company/brand] on forums/ blogs (When asked)	0.84	0.22	0.08	0.16	***
Posted negative comment about [company/brand] on forums/ blogs (When asked)	0.15	0.03	0.10	0.08	
Given a positive review about [company/brand] online (When asked)	0.86	0.26	0.09	0.16	***
Given a negative review about [company/brand] online (When asked)	0.18	0.02	0.12	0.08	**
Recommend Intention	8.41	8.85	5.68	7.59	***
Repurchase Intention	4.40	4.46	3.66	4.20	***
Overall Satisfaction	8.39	8.76	6.24	7.90	***

***p < .001, **p < .01, *p<.05

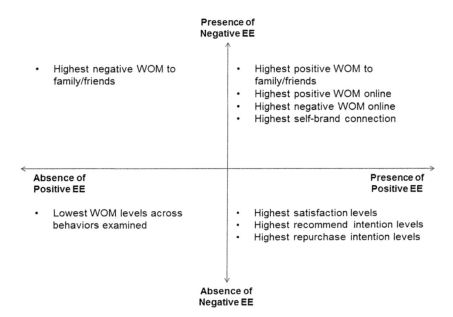

Fig. 13.1 Average word-of-mouth behavior by emotional engagement quadrant

on two brands, 696 (51%) demonstrated different levels of emotional engagement for those two brands. The final analysis file consists of two records for each respondent, producing a final stacked data file of 1392 records. The main results of the EE quadrant analysis were unchanged.[2]

CONCLUSION

This exploratory investigation provides new insight into what we know about the relationship between emotional engagement (EE) and word-of-mouth (WOM) by examining how customers' WOM behaviors relate to different levels of positive and negative EE. In keeping with prior research, our findings indicate that positive/negative EE are associated with positive/negative WOM behaviors. Our findings, however, also identified an *Emotional Engagement Paradox*—specifically, the highest levels of positive and negative online WOM, as well as the most recommendations to family and friends, occur for customers having both positive and negative EE.

We argue that this paradox is related to Hirschman's observations regarding the voicing of complaints in his seminal work, *Exit, Voice and Loyalty* (Hirschman 1970). Hirschman argues that more loyal individuals are also more likely to voice their concerns than less loyal individuals. Specifically, the combination of the positive and negative EE is also associated with the highest levels of self-brand connection.

Self-brand connection has already been shown to be associated with higher WOM levels (Kwon and Mattila 2015). The literature to date, however, tends to associate this connection with favorable WOM behavior (e.g. Park et al. 2008). By contrast, we argue that customers holding a higher self-brand connection are also more likely to be loyal to the brand. As a result, they are more likely to be actively engaged with the brand, and therefore are more likely to voice their concerns as well as their praise. Anecdotally, we can think of fans that are intensely loyal to particular sports teams; it is common to hear their laments at coaching decisions, player errors, and so on, in addition to praise for their beloved teams.

These findings have important implications for researchers and managers. First, our findings indicate that emotionally engaged consumers are more likely to spread positive and negative WOM than are customers who hold only positive or negative EE. Therefore, the simple notion that customers high on EE recommend a brand and those low on EE complain about a brand is incomplete. Given that the general goal of many firms is to have more intensely engaged customers, the end result of these efforts is likely to be an increase in both positive and negative online WOM. Therefore, managers need to develop systems to monitor and manage online WOM (e.g. Gatorade's Mission Control (Ostrow 2010)). Moreover, where possible, managers need to identify customers who are providing both positive and negative online WOM, as these customers are more likely to be personally connected to the brand. These engaged customers need to have their concerns recognized and addressed to maintain the strength of their relationships.

What's Next? Relative Metrics and Share of Engagement

Researchers and managers have come to accept the importance of customer engagement, particularly as it relates to increasing firm performance through WOM behaviors (Kumar et al. 2010). We believe, however, that research into engagement still has many things yet to be understood. In particular, research into customer engagement is almost always examined for a single firm/brand (as opposed to firms/brands used by a customer in a category). This unit of analysis is easy to understand since it is the level most strongly under management control, and it is the level that is easiest to link to firm/brand-specific outcomes.

The primary problem with this level of analysis, however, is the strong possibility that heavy users in a particular category may be "category" engaged, and therefore demonstrate engagement behaviors towards multiple brands in the category. Research has demonstrated that heavy users in a category are much more likely to divide their spending among multiple brands in the category (Stern and Hammond 2004). Moreover, there is empirical evidence that a brand's best customers (in terms of spending with the brand) are also its competitors' best customers (Cameron 2014; Cushion 2016). Given this, we argue that heavy users in a category are more likely to demonstrate engagement behaviors across competing brands.

Additionally, research shows that consumers allocate their category spending across brands by assigning a relative rank to each of the brands used in terms of their ability to satisfy them (Keiningham et al. 2015). Given this, it is logical to believe that multi-brand customers use a similar ranking system when engaging in WOM related to the industry category. This notion argues that there is indeed a "share of engagement" that is distinct from the more commonly used "share of category spending" (aka share of wallet).

Of course, it is also indeed possible that multi-brand customers with high category engagement use different criteria to drive WOM behavior. For example, it is easy to imagine a scenario where lower ranked brands receive greater negative WOM precisely because of their inability to raise performance to the level of the perceived first place brand.

Therefore, there is a clear need for future research that identifies whether share of engagement reflects a managerially relevant outcome. If that is the case, research needs to identify how customers decide to which firms they are both positively and negatively engaged, and how what level of engagement is assigned to each brand.

Notes

1. Respondents were allowed to provide answers regarding up to two brands. As such, the cases are not entirely independent. So in addition to the one-way ANOVA tests (the assumptions of which are not entirely satisfied), we also ran mixed regression models, including respondent ID as a random effect and

controlling for sector of the brand(s) rated. The results of the mixed models are substantively similar to the ANOVA tests with regard to the statistical significance of quadrant assignment. We present the significance test results of the ANOVA in Table 13.1 for simplicity sake. Averages in the table are calculated directly from the respondent-rating level data without any intermediate aggregation to the brand level (i.e. a brand rated by multiple respondents is included in the calculation of the quadrant average multiple times).

2. The highest mean repurchase intention was associated with high positive and negative EE instead of positive EE only. It should be noted that in both analyses, the mean repurchase intention levels were very close for the positive/negative EE quadrant and the positive-only EE quadrant. Additionally, "Posted negative comment about [company/brand] on forums/blogs (When asked)" and "Given a negative review about [company/brand] online (When asked)" appear in the no EE quadrant.

References

Berger, J. (2014). Word of Mouth and Interpersonal Communication: A Review and Directions for Future Research. *Journal of Consumer Psychology, 24*(4), 586–607.

Brodie, R. J., Hollebeek, L. D., Juric, B., & Ilic, A. (2011). Customer Engagement: Conceptual Domain, Fundamental Propositions, and Implications for Research. *Journal of Service Research, 14*(3), 252–271.

Cameron, S. (2014). Loyalty Lost? Your Best Customers Are Cheating On You. *Forbes.* http://www.forbes.com/sites/mckinsey/2014/09/04/loyalty-lost-your-best-customers-are-cheating-on-you/#2760d4492e4b. Accessed 16 Nov 2016.

Cushion, D. (2016). Loyalty through Two Lenses: Part I: Are Your Loyal Customers Really Loyal? *Cardlytics.* http://www.cardlytics.com/blog/loyalty-two-lenses-part-loyal-customers-really-loyal/. Accessed 16 Nov 2016.

Dwyer, P. (2007). Measuring the Value of Electronic Word of Mouth and its Impact in Consumer Communities. *Journal of Interactive Marketing, 21*(2), 63–79.

Escalas, J. E., & Bettman, J. R. (2005). Self-Construal, Reference Groups and Brand Meaning. *Journal of Consumer Research, 32*(3), 378–389.

Higgins, E. T., & Scholer, A. A. (2009). Engaging the Consumer: The Science and Art of the Value Creation Process. *Journal of Consumer Psychology, 19*(2), 100–114.

Hirschman, A. O. (1970). *Exit, Voice, and Loyalty.* Cambridge, MA: Harvard University Press.

Jaakkola, E., & Alexander, M. (2014). The Role of Customer Engagement Behavior in Value Co-Creation a Service System Perspective. *Journal of Service Research, 17*(3), 247–261.

Keiningham, T. L., Cooil, B., Malthouse, E. C., Lariviére, B., Buoye, A., Aksoy, L., & De Keyser, A. (2015). Perceptions are Relative: An Examination of the Relationship Between Relative Satisfaction Metrics and Share of Wallet. *Journal of Service Management, 26*(1), 2–43.

Keiningham, T. L., Rust, R. T., Lariviere, B., Aksoy, L. & Williams, L. (2016). *A Comprehensive Roadmap for Driving Word of Mouth*. Working Paper, St. Johns University, Queens, NY.

King, R. A., Racherla, P., & Bush, V. D. (2014). What We Know and Don't Know About Online Word-of-Mouth: A Review and Synthesis of the Literature. *Journal of Interactive Marketing, 28*(3), 167–183.

Kumar, V., Aksoy, L., Donkers, B., Venkatesan, R., Wiesel, T., & Tillmanns, S. (2010). Undervalued or Overvalued Customers: Capturing Total Customer Engagement Value. *Journal of Service Research, 13*(3), 297–310.

Kwon, E., & Mattila, A. S. (2015). The Effect of Self–Brand Connection and Self-Construal on Brand Lovers' Word of Mouth (WOM). *Cornell Hospitality Quarterly, 56*(4), 427–435.

Ladhari, R. (2007). The Effect of Consumption Emotions on Satisfaction and Word-of-Mouth Communications. *Psychology & Marketing, 24*(12), 1085–1108.

Mano, H., & Oliver, R. L. (1993). Assessing the Dimensionality and Structure of the Consumption Experience: Evaluation, Feeling, and Satisfaction. *Journal of Consumer Research, 20*(3), 451–466.

Maslowska, E., Malthouse, E. C., & Collinger, T. (2016). The Customer Engagement Ecosystem. *Journal of Marketing Management, 32*(5–6), 469–501.

Oliver, R. L. (1993). Cognitive, Affective, and Attribute Bases of the Satisfaction Response. *Journal of Consumer Research, 20*(3), 418–430.

Oliver, R. L. (2010). *Satisfaction: A Behavioral Perspective on the Consumer* (2nd ed.). Armonk: M.E. Sharpe.

Ostrow, A. (2010). Inside Gatorade's Social Media Command Center. *Mashable.* http://mashable.com/2010/06/15/gatorade-social-media-mission-control/#oApMCw3pEkqs. Accessed 13 Nov 2016.

Park, C. W., MacInnis, D. J. & Priester, J. (2008). Brand Attachment: Constructs, Consequences and Causes. *Foundations and Trends in Marketing Series, 1*(3), Hanover, MA: Now Publishers Inc.

Patterson, P., Yu, T., & De Ruyter, K. (2006). Understanding Customer Engagement in Services. *Advancing Theory, Maintaining Relevance: Proceedings of ANZMAC 2006 Conference*, Brisbane: Queensland University of Technology, School of Advertising, Marketing and Public Relations, pp. 4–6.

Sprott, D., Czellar, S., & Spangenberg, E. (2009). The Importance of a General Measure of Brand Engagement on Market Behavior: Development and Validation of a Scale. *Journal of Marketing Research, 46*(1), 92–104.

Stern, P., & Hammond, K. (2004). The Relationship Between Customer Loyalty and Purchase Incidence. *Marketing Letters, 15*(1), 5–19.

Van Doorn, J., Lemon, K. N., Mittal, V., Nass, S., Pick, D., Pirner, P., & Verhoef, P. C. (2010). Customer Engagement Behavior: Theoretical Foundations and Research Directions. *Journal of Service Research, 13*(3), 253–266.

Vivek, S. D., Beatty, S. E., & Morgan, R. M. (2012). Customer Engagement: Exploring Customer Relationships Beyond Purchase. *Journal of Marketing Theory and Practice, 20*(2), 122–146.

Watson, D., & Tellegen, A. (1985). Toward a Consensual Structure of Mood. *Psychological Bulletin, 98*(2), 219–235.

Wien, A. H., & Olsen, S. O. (2014). Understanding the Relationship between Individualism and Word of Mouth: A Self-Enhancement Explanation. *Psychology & Marketing, 31*(6), 416–425.

Yang, S., Hu, M., Winer, R., Assael, H., & Chen, X. (2012). An Empirical Study of Word-of-Mouth Generation and Consumption. *Marketing Science, 31*(6), 952–963.

CHAPTER 14

Conclusion: Informing Customer Engagement Marketing and Future Research

Colleen M. Harmeling, Jordan W. Moffett, and Robert W. Palmatier

Over the past ten years, there has been a transformation in marketing theory and practice that we cannot begin to understand without acknowledging the changing role of the customer. Often at lower costs and greater effectiveness, customers are increasingly serving as pseudo-marketers, actively and voluntarily contributing to marketing functions, such as customer acquisition, expansion, and retention; product innovation; and marketing communication. The chapters collected in this book present various perspectives on customer engagement and represent a compilation of current thought leadership in this domain. Importantly, each perspective contributes to our understanding of how to effectively execute customer engagement marketing initiatives in which the firm deliberately motivates, empowers, and measures customer contribution to marketing functions beyond their financial patronage (Harmeling et al. 2017a). In this final chapter, we summarize these perspectives to provide a practical

C.M. Harmeling (✉)
Florida State University, Tallahassee, FL, USA

J.W. Moffett
Louisiana State University, Baton Rouge, LA, USA

R.W. Palmatier
University of Washington, Seattle, WA, USA

© The Author(s) 2018   307
R.W. Palmatier et al. (eds.), *Customer Engagement Marketing*,
DOI 10.1007/978-3-319-61985-9_14

guide for implementing customer engagement marketing as well as offer potentially fruitful areas of future research.

Customer engagement marketing actively enlists customers as pseudo-marketers for the firm. It is distinct from marketing strategies such as promotion marketing, which uses a special offer to raise a customer's interest in and influence over focal product purchases versus competitor product purchases, and relationship marketing, which captures "marketing activities directed towards establishing, developing, and maintaining successful relational exchange" (Morgan and Hunt 1994, p. 22). The objective of engagement marketing is to encourage active customer contribution to the firm's marketing functions, which differs from promotion marketing's focus on inducing a single transaction with the focal firm and relationship marketing's focus on motivating future repeat transactions with the customer. In addition, in promotion marketing the customer is merely a receiver of value through marketing actions and in relationship marketing the customer negotiates value received in that particular customer—firm relationship directly with the firm. However, with engagement marketing, the customer can exercise a high level of control over value creation and can affect outcomes that move beyond their particular customer-firm relationship to the broader customer population.

Probably the most essential point of differentiation from other marketing strategies, however, is the engagement marketing view of the customer. Both promotion and relationship marketing take more of an economic perspective, focusing on the customer's current and future financial contributions. Engagement marketing, however, views the customer as possessing resources beyond their financial contribution that are desirable and otherwise unattainable to the firm. Accordingly, Harmeling et al. (2017a) identify four key customer-owned resources. First, customer network assets represent the number and diversity of a customer's interpersonal ties within his or her social network, which benefit the firm by increasing the reach of marketing initiatives and providing access to otherwise inaccessible or particularly influential customer groups. Second, customer persuasion capital represents the "trust, goodwill, and influence a customer has with other existing or potential customers" (Harmeling et al. 2017a, p. 316–17) and can improve the authenticity and diagnosticity of customer engagement (e.g. word of mouth) over other firm driven marketing actions. Third, customer knowledge stores capture a "customer's accumulation of knowledge about the product, brand, firm, or other customers" (Harmeling et al. 2017a, p. 317) and can improve the quality and relevance of marketing initiatives, enhance product developments, and improve customer-to-customer interactions. Fourth, customer creativity captures the customer's "production, conceptualization, or development of novel, useful ideas, processes, or solutions to problems" (Kozinets et al. 2008, p. 341) and provides unique insights beyond those available within the firm. Therefore, customer engagement marketing differs from other marketing strategies in its objective, creation of value, and, importantly, view of the customer.

Designing Customer Engagement Marketing Initiatives

The aspects of customer engagement marketing that make it distinct from promotion and relationship marketing suggest tactics that are effective in these other domains may not be effective for engaging customers, thereby requiring a new perspective. Several of the chapters in this book focused on antecedents of customer engagement and can inform the design of customer engagement marketing strategies. In Table 14.1, we summarize the implications to marketing practice as well as research directions emerging from this new perspective.

Facilitating Customer Engagement

Engagement marketing requires designing customer interactions outside of the core economic transaction in which customers will be both motivated and empowered to contribute to the firm beyond their financial patronage. Many engagement initiatives take the form of shared interactive experiences that are meant to stimulate voluntary customer contributions to marketing functions (Harmeling et al. 2017a). Vivek, Beatty, and Hazod (Chap. 2) suggest that providing an optimal balance between the customer's ability and the challenge of the experience can improve the effectiveness of these initiatives. Yet, calibrating the engagement event may require dynamically adapting based on customer learning, which suggests personalization is also relevant in delivering the engagement initiative (Bleier, De Keyser, and Verleye, Chap. 4). Calder, Hollebeek, and Malthouse (Chap. 10) suggest that experiential initiatives may provide a means for brands to connect with customers in their attainment of higher life goals. Therefore, personalizing the initiative to the target customer's current abilities as well as their broader life goals could potentially enhance the effectiveness of experiential engagement initiatives.

Table 14.1 Summary of future research directions in customer engagement marketing

Research Direction	Key Topics	Informative Research
Designing Customer Engagement Marketing Initiatives		
Facilitating customer engagement	• Calibrating the availability window of an experiential engagement initiative such that it is brief enough to create a sense of novelty but extended enough to provide accessibility	Arnould and Price 1993; Vivek et al. 2012
	• Empowering customer contributions with engagement tools (e.g. amplification, connective, feedback, creative tools)	Harmeling et al. 2017b; Kozinets et al. 2008; Fuchs et al. 2010
	• Creating effective engagement platforms and engagement environments (i.e. brand communities)	Kozinets et al. 2008; Nambisan 2002; Schau et al. 2009
Incentivizing customer engagement	• Optimizing customer engagement incentive structures to motivate each unique form of customer engagement	Ryu and Feick 2007; Verlegh et al. 2013
	• Calibrating effective rewards and incentives for engagement marketing initiatives	Ryu and Feick 2007; Trusov et al. 2009; Verlegh et al. 2013
	• Understanding how each of the benefits of different incentive structures affects perceptions of the resulting customer engagement	Trusov et al. 2009; Verlegh et al. 2013
	• Investigating the group aspects of certain engagement marketing initiatives	Harmeling et al. 2017b; Schau et al. 2009

Capturing value from customer engagement	• Understanding the differences in future customer engagement between "earned group membership" and "given group membership"	Henderson et al. 2011; Steinhoff and Palmatier 2014
	• Identifying effective strategies for collecting, filtering, and analyzing engagement data	Smith 2014
	• Designing learning algorithms and systems that interactively audition and incorporate new data to adapt marketing mix elements in real time	Bleier and Eisenbeiss 2015a; Chung et al. 2016
	• Assessing consumers responses to the engagement data collection processes (e.g. privacy issues)	Aguirre et al. 2016; Bleier and Eisenbeiss 2015b; Martin et al. 2017

Deploying Customer Engagement Marketing Initiatives

Targeting customers for engagement initiatives	• Determining which assessments of customer value are effective for different engagement objectives	Kozinets et al. 2010; Schmitt et al. 2011; Kumar et al. 2010a
	• Identifying potential customers through a combination of value to the firm and likelihood to engage	Harmeling et al. 2017b; Kumar et al. 2010a
	• Targeting customers with promotions to stimulate engagement (e.g. word of mouth) versus purchase behaviors	Kumar et al. 2008; Kumar et al. 2010b
	• Investigating how engagement marketing targeting may differ when focusing on customer groups (e.g. sports teams, clubs) rather than individuals	Dholakia et al. 2004; Harmeling et al. 2017b

(continued)

Table 14.1 (continued)

Research Direction	Key Topics	Informative Research
	• Investigating areas of differentiation between engagement with consumers (B2C) versus business customers (B2B)	Kumar et al. 2010a; Kumar and Pansari 2016; Pansari and Kumar 2017
	• Investigating the unique influence of trust, commitment, and dependence in the B2B domain, to assess how consumer-based strategies might need to be adapted	Kumar et al. 2010a; Kumar and Pansari 2016; Pansari and Kumar 2017
	• Understanding motivation, norms, and engagement processes in the B2B domain	Kumar et al. 2010a; Kumar and Pansari 2016; Menguc et al. (2017)
Determining timing of engagement initiatives and exposure to customer engagement		
	• Investigating the influence of dynamic relational expectations on the effectiveness of customer engagement initiatives, including insights into the strategic deployment of engagement initiatives	Harmeling et al. 2015; Kumar et al. 2010a; Kumar and Pansari 2016
	• Adapting and taking a dynamic perspective (e.g. stages of value chain) for customer engagement strategies for B2B exchanges	Harmeling et al. 2015; Kumar et al. 2010a; Kumar and Pansari 2016
Potential Dangers of Customer Engagement Marketing		
	• Investigating proactive and reactive means of managing firm vulnerabilities specific to customer engagement initiatives (e.g. turning a firm supported channel into an avenue for brand terrorism and negative word of mouth)	Henderson et al. 2014; Roehm and Brady 2007; Van Doorn et al. 2010
	• Exploring how engagement data is captured, stored, used, and protected, including the implications this has from a data privacy standpoint	Martin et al. 2017; Martin and Murphy 2017

Notes: B2B = Business to Business, B2C = Business to Consumer

Part of the appeal of experiential engagement initiatives is that they offer unique, often one-time, experiences. However, because of this high perishability, Calder, Hollebeek, and Malthouse (Chap. 10) suggest poorly delivered initiatives can induce not only dissatisfaction and disappointment, but also a sense of lost opportunities and regret. Thus, calibrating the availability window such that it is brief enough to create a sense of novelty but extended enough to provide accessibility is key (Arnould and Price 1993; Vivek, Beatty, and Morgan 2012). Future research is needed in this domain.

Although the design of the engagement initiative is critical for motivating customers, just as critical is the firm's ability to empower contribution in ways that make it impactful. Therefore, effective customer engagement requires investment in engagement tools that facilitate both customer-to-customer and customer-to-firm interactions. Harmeling et al. (2017a) identify four types of tools. First, amplification tools diffuse engagement behaviors among the participating customers' existing network structures (e.g. share buttons). Second, connective tools link the participating customer to other customers, the firm, or the engagement initiative (e.g. tagging, following buttons). Third, feedback tools enable the customer to react to a particular action by the firm or other customers (e.g. comment boxes, likes). Fourth, creative tools facilitate the creation, development, and contribution of unique ideas (e.g. filtering and editing tools). Determining when and how to use these tools warrants future research.

Engagement tools are rarely used in isolation but rather contribute to the design of an overall platform (e.g. My Starbucks Ideas) or environment (e.g. brand communities) that enables customer-to-customer and customer-to-firm interactions (Schau et al. 2009). In taking this more holistic view, culture and norms become relevant to facilitating the self-disclosures that are inherent in customer engagement. Vivek, Beatty, and Hazod (Chap. 2) suggest that the customer's perception of the authenticity of interactions and feelings of psychological safety are key to designing an effective environment for customer engagement. They further suggest that authenticity can be achieved through the acceptance of conflicting viewpoints (e.g. positive and negative reviews), whereas psychological safety develops when people believe others will not think less of them if they make a mistake, ask silly questions, or ask for help, information, or feedback. Future research should investigate the role of engagement tools in both enhancing customer engagement independently and holistically, to create effective engagement platforms (Kozinets et al. 2008; Nambisan 2002).

Incentivizing Customer Engagement

If engagement marketing shifts the role of the customer to that of a pseudo-marketer (i.e. pseudo-employee), then the firm must assume the role of pseudo-employer. From this perspective, motivating, recognizing, and rewarding customer work and productivity are essential for effective engagement marketing initiatives. In Chap. 6, Bijmolt and colleagues examine the possibility of augmenting traditional programmatic incentive structures (e.g. multi-tier loyalty programs) to motivate engagement behaviors. They suggest that effective incentivizing requires a balance between instrumental benefits, or those that enhance economic utility (e.g. money, prizes), symbolic benefits (e.g. status), and emotional benefits (e.g. customer company identification). In addition, Vivek, Beatty, and Hazod (Chap. 2) suggest "people find an activity worthwhile when they feel they can make a difference and are not being taken for granted". Thus, nontraditional incentives such as amplified voice, or the "amplification of a customer's engagement efforts through the firm's paid, earned, or owned channels", may also be effective (Harmeling et al. 2017a, p. 331). Providing feedback on how customer contributions are used could be an additional incentive for customer engagement. It is possible, however, that the effectiveness of an incentive may depend on the nature of the requested engagement behavior. If the requested behavior requires a high degree of self-disclosure (e.g. product ideas, product uses), incentives that increase its visibility (e.g. amplified voice) may appear intrusive and potentially erode effectiveness. Future research is needed to examine optimal incentive structures to motivate each unique form of customer engagement (Ryu and Feick 2007). In addition, research on incentivized word of mouth suggests that knowledge of an instrumental reward can erode the perceived authenticity of the resulting recommendation (Verlegh et al. 2013). Research into how each of the benefits of the incentive affects other customers' perceptions of the resulting customer engagement could be investigated.

Beyond the direct incentives, a person's membership in a multi-tier incentive program (e.g. Starbuck's Gold Member) can create feelings of being part of an exclusive group (Bijmolt et al. Chap. 6). Because group members often share similar experiences (e.g. earning and experiencing rewards), this membership can enhance in-group feelings in which the customer may take actions to support and protect that group, therefore, perpetuating further customer engagement (Harmeling et al. 2017b). Future research should investigate the group aspects of certain engagement incentives (Schau et al. 2009). Building on this, a potentially fruitful area of research is to investigate the differences in future customer engagement between "earned group membership" and "given group membership".

As a final note on incentivizing customer engagement, Bijmolt and colleagues (Chap. 6) present an interesting dynamic in which encouraging customer engagement (e.g. word of mouth) about the incentive itself (especial symbolic rewards) can enhance the incentive's effects. However, caution must be employed when deploying this strategy in that symbolic rewards require a small, exclusive, elite group to be effective, which can trigger negative bystander effects among customers that are not part of that group if not carefully managed. Thus, visibility of the reward is a double-edged sword that could produce status effects for one customer but could also produce perceptions of unfairness or jealousy for others (Steinhoff and Palmatier 2014). Therefore, a key area of research is in calibrating effective rewards and incentives and how engagement (e.g. word of mouth) about the reward or incentive can (positively or negatively) affect its effectiveness.

Capturing Value from Customer Engagement

Customer engagement behaviors (e.g. word of mouth, customer feedback) can directly benefit the firm by contributing to customer acquisition, product innovation, marketing communication, and other marketing functions. Yet several of the chapters in this book touch on indirect sources of value through data benefits that can enhance the product offering and improve strategic decision-making. Customer engagement inherently involves a degree of customization where the customer voluntarily discloses self-relevant information to actively adapt the marketing initiative to fit his or her preferences. Bleier, De Keyser, and Verleye (Chap. 4) suggest that customization and self-disclosure not only provide visibility to customer behaviors outside the core economic transaction but also create a more complete description of the customer's preferences. The resulting "mass engagement data" then increases the breadth and speed of data collection, which facilitates learning (e.g. Nest Thermostat and Apple autocorrect) and aggregation of feedback to the customer that can improve the firm's offering, both of which were previously not possible (e.g. "25 people liked you since you last checked Tinder"). Thus, engagement data provides the necessary resources for the firm to monitor, adapt, and personalize product offerings and general interactions with customers over the entire customer journey.

One of the major benefits of a customer engagement marketing strategy is the increased visibility of customer behaviors outside the core economic transaction, which can be particularly informative in assessing customer value (Kumar et al. 2010). Venkatesan, Petersen, and Gussoni (Chap. 3) suggest that assessing customers based on this additional engagement data can often provide a more accurate view of the value of a particular customer to the firm such that customers with low purchase frequencies or amounts may possess valuable resources such as extraordinary reach and influence to particularly valuable potential customers previously unaccounted for in traditional measures of customer value. This more holistic view can influence strategic decisions such as who to target or how to structure key account teams. With a traditional customer lifetime value perspective, teams are typically dedicated to the most profitable customers, but it may be more effective to allocate teams to the most vocal customer or most informative customers (Chap. 3). These structural and indirect benefits warrant future research.

Extracting the value from engagement data requires three major processes (data collection, data analysis, and strategic adaptation). As a first step, customer data must be collected and matched to customer profiles. This requirement reinforces the value of investments in engagement tools that capture behaviors outside the core economic transaction and loyalty programs that provide a means of linking those behaviors to the customers, which together creates the conditions necessary to extract value from these data. Once collected, however, the magnitude of potential data can create challenges in which data filtering becomes necessary before engagement data can be analyzed and incorporated into strategic decision-making (Smith 2014). Learning algorithms and systems that interactively audition and incorporate new data to adapt marketing mix elements in real time may be potentially useful (Chung et al. 2016), yet requires future research. Bleier, De Keyser, and Verleye (Chap. 4), however, caution that learning "too quickly" could be seen as invasive and potentially trigger defensive responses. Finally, the firm should provide transparency and control to customers on their data management policies to reap benefits from customer engagement data and not cause future feelings of violation (Martin et al. 2017). Future research should investigate effective strategies for collecting, filtering, and analyzing engagement data as well as consumer responses to such processes and potential privacy issues (Aguirre et al. 2016).

Deploying Customer Engagement Marketing Initiatives

Beyond designing the engagement initiative, marketers must determine who to target for engagement initiatives and when it is best to target them. When considering these two strategic decisions from a traditional perspective (e.g. promotion or relationship marketing), decision-making criteria is typically narrowly focused on economic factors (e.g. share of wallet or customer lifetime value). The more holistic view of the customer embraced in engagement marketing suggests enhancements to these criteria.

Targeting Customers for Engagement Initiatives

The first key decision in deploying engagement initiatives involves targeting customers. The chapters in this book identify two perspectives on determining which customers are the most effective targets of customer engagement initiatives, customer value, and success likelihood. In engagement marketing, valuations go beyond the traditional economic-focused assessments to acknowledge and capture valuable customer-owned resources. Venkatesan, Petersen, and Gussoni (Chap. 3) present and evaluate three enhanced measures of customer value; customer influence value, customer referral value, and customer knowledge value. For example, customer influencer value measures the size of the customer's social network and therefore captures the customer's network assets. Although these valuation criteria provide new insights, the authors suggest that, because of the rules of sameness, the traditional measure of customer lifetime value may still be a useful proxy for assessing the economic value of a customer's network assets as an indicator of "rich friends". Thus, a combination of or triangulation across measures may be more effective. Reinartz and Berkmann (Chap. 11) suggest using lead users as a proxy for identifying customers with high knowledge stores, whose needs will become general in the marketplace sometime in the future. Although a significant amount of work has been done in this area, determining which assessments of customer value are effective for different engagement objectives is a fruitful area of future research. For example, valuations based on customer knowledge stores may be more effective for enhancing product innovations, whereas valuations of customer network assets more beneficial for marketing communication.

As an alternative perspective, several chapters provide insights into a success rate perspective in which customers are chosen on their likelihood to engage rather than their potential resource value. Liu et al.'s (Chap. 12) work suggests that customers who are predisposed to incorporate brands into their self or process information from a brand perspective may be effective targets for an engagement initiative. Vivek, Beatty, Hazod (Chap. 2) suggest customers high in experience-, cognition-, sensation-, and novelty-seeking are likely candidates for customer engagement. In addition, a customer's perceived psychological availability, or his or her level of physical, emotional, and cognitive resources available for the engagement marketing initiative, will influence his or her level of engagement. Finally, they suggest role readiness, or the customer's willingness and ability to contribute, is a key predictor of engagement and can potentially be enhanced through encouragement, support, socialization, and training (e.g. how to engage videos). Venkatesan, Petersen, and Gussoni (Chap. 3) suggest a customer's response rate to other marketing campaigns or their previous engagement behaviors (e.g. referral performance, number of previous suggestions, or comments) may also be significant predictors of future engagement behavior. Ultimately, a combination of value to firm and likelihood to engage may be the best means of identifying potential customers, which warrants future research.

Beyond targeting customers with engagement initiatives, Venkatesen, Petersen, and Gussoni (Chap. 3) suggest future research should assess the effectiveness of targeting customers with high persuasion capital and network assets (e.g. influencers) with cross-sell promotions on products that are not necessarily effective at stimulating purchases but rather more effective at generating customers engagement behaviors (e.g. word of mouth) about the products. Similarly, different customer resources may be more or less appealing based on the product type. For example, complex products may benefit more from customer knowledge stores than other customer resources. In addition, the authors suggest that future research should investigate how targeting may differ when focusing on customer groups (e.g. sports teams, clubs) rather than individuals.

While the majority of research focuses on engaging consumers, Reinartz and Berkmann (Chap. 11) suggest more research is needed on how to effectively engage business customers. The multi-person buying process, need for customization, and narrowly rather than generally focused customer knowledge may make engagement among business customers challenging and potentially less valuable. In addition, high degrees of dependence and resource integration between firms will likely alter the effectiveness of engagement. The authors also acknowledge the distinction between individual (referrals) and organizational level engagement (co-development), which can have implications for the design and management of engagement initiatives. Future research should investigate these areas of differentiation as well as the unique influence of trust, commitment, and dependence in the B2B domain to assess how consumer-based engagement strategies might need to be adapted.

Beckers et al. (Chap. 7) offer an additional concern for engaging business customers such that there is a fundamental disconnect between the users of engagement platforms and decision-makers that has implications on both the participation and value of engagement efforts. For example, employee contribution to the engagement initiative (e.g. posts, responses to other participant posts, etc.) may not be valued by the employer and may actually simulate punishment if viewed as distracting to the employees core purpose to the employer. Thus, motivation, norms, and engagement processes in the B2B domain warrant future research.

Determining Timing of Engagement Initiatives and Exposure to Customer Engagement

The second key decision in deploying engagement initiatives is determining the timing of deployment. The contributing chapters examine this from both a functional perspective, in which engagement helps to inform other customers throughout the purchase decision process, and a relational perspective, in which engagement contributes to and is affected by the relational aspects of exchange (e.g. trust and commitment). Minnema et al. (Chap. 5) examine this question by investigating the role of engagement across the purchase cycle and how it impacts product returns. They suggest that exposure to customer engagement from other customers (i.e. product reviews) in the prepurchase stage can influence the effects of imperfect information on product returns and that this is especially true of online purchases. If there is not enough customer engagement, it could spark returns because of poor fit, but too much (or too positive of reviews) could increase expectations and also spark returns. Thus, this requires careful consideration of stimulating the appropriate amount of customer engagement among postpurchase customers. As Hochstein and Bolander (Chap. 9) recognize, exposure to customer engagement early in the buying process can alter the effectiveness of traditional elements of the selling process, suggesting that there has been a shift that requires salespeople to take on more of a knowledge broker role. Thus, research on properly calibrating when to expose customers to other customers' engagement behaviors, when to stimulate customer engagement through direct requests, and how to respond to increased customer engagement throughout the purchase cycle is needed.

Participation in an engagement initiative requires a degree of self-disclosure that, if managed improperly, can spark negative responses among consumers. Consequently, Bleier, De Keyser, and Verleye (Chap. 4) suggest adapting engagement requests over the customer lifetime with more restrictive and less invasive requests early on, but, more general, autonomous requests later on as familiarity, knowledge, trust, and emotional attachment build. Research that investigates the influence of dynamic relational expectations on the effectiveness of customer engagement initiatives could provide insights into the strategic deployment of engagement initiatives (Harmeling et al. 2015). On the other hand, for B2B customers, Beckers et al. (Chap. 7) suggest customer engagement should be managed over the stages of value chain rather than the customer life cycle. The adaptations necessary in B2B exchanges and taking dynamic perspective are interesting avenues for future research.

POTENTIAL DANGERS OF CUSTOMER ENGAGEMENT MARKETING

Engagement marketing is intended to improve firm performance by either providing access to customer resources that were previously unattainable to the firm or shifting value generation from internal to external entities. Works by both Vivek, Beatty, Hazod (Chap. 2) and Bleier, De Keyser, and Verleye (Chap. 4) suggest, however, that engagement initiatives often require complex customization. Because of this, they need high levels of technical support and large investments of human capital. Firms should carefully assess the potential management and implementation costs of customer engagement initiatives versus the potential benefits. For instance, Minnema et al. (Chap. 5) suggest that high levels of engagement can increase customer's overall expectations, often leading to increased dissatisfaction and potentially to product returns.

For engagement marketing to be successful, firms must empower customers; however, this relinquishing of control can create potential risks (Van Doorn et al. 2010). Engagement marketing initiatives are designed to extract value from customers and require investment in tools and platforms that amplify the consumer voice and impact on other current and potential consumers. This creates conditions where the value producer can become a value destroyer (Roehm and Brady 2007). For example, customers have turned engagement initiatives such as the McDonald's hashtag

#McDstories into "bashtags", thus turning a firm supported channel into an avenue for brand terrorism and negative word of mouth. Future research should investigate both proactive and reactive means of managing these potential vulnerabilities.

The data collection aspect of customer engagement can create improved visibility of customer behaviors outside the core economic transaction. This increased visibility comes with increased responsibility for the firm. Customers are now more cognizant than ever before of data privacy issues. Thus, future research could explore how engagement data is captured, stored, used, and protected as well as what implications this has from a data privacy standpoint (Martin et al. 2017).

In summary, the radically transformed marketing environment in which customers can exert greater influence over marketing functions than ever before has offered a new avenue for strategic advantage over competitors (Kumar and Pansari 2016). There is now a need for engagement marketing research to understand the most effective ways for firms to motivate, empower, and measure customer contributions to marketing functions. The work presented in this edited book provides a foundation for examining this new perspective, yet much work remains to be done. Research areas include investigating the elements of the engagement initiative as well as engagement platforms that most effectively stimulate customer engagement, incentivizing customer engagement, targeting customers for participation in engagement initiatives, deploying customer engagement initiatives across the entire customer journey, and assessing the potential dark side of customer engagement marketing. This book and the collection of chapters within it should serve as a guide for academics advancing research in this domain and practitioners designing and implementing engagement marketing strategies.

References

Aguirre, E., Roggeveen, A. L., Grewal, D., & Wetzels, M. (2016). The Personalization–Privacy Paradox: Implications for New Media. *Journal of Consumer Marketing, 33*(2), 98–110.

Arnould, E. J., & Price, L. L. (1993). River Magic: Extraordinary Experience and the Extended Service Encounter. *Journal of Consumer Research, 20*(1), 24–45.

Bleier, A., & Eisenbeiss, M. (2015a). Personalized Online Advertising Effectiveness: The Interplay of What, When, and Where. *Marketing Science, 34*(5), 669–688.

Bleier, A., & Eisenbeiss, M. (2015b). The Importance of Trust for Personalized Online Advertising. *Journal of Retailing, 91*(3), 390–409.

Chung, T. S., Wedel, M., & Rust, R. T. (2016). Adaptive Personalization Using Social Networks. *Journal of the Academy of Marketing Science, 44*(1), 66–87.

Dholakia, U. M., Bagozzi, R. P., & Pearo, L. K. (2004). A Social Influence Model of Consumer Participation in Network-and Small-Group-Based Virtual Communities. *International Journal of Research in Marketing, 21*(3), 241–263.

Fuchs, C., Prandelli, E., & Schreier, M. (2010). The Psychological Effects of Empowerment Strategies on Consumers' Product Demand. *Journal of Marketing, 74*(1), 65–79.

Harmeling, C. M., Palmatier, R. W., Houston, M. B., Arnold, M. J., & Samaha, S. A. (2015). Transformational Relationship Events. *Journal of Marketing, 79*(September), 39–62.

Harmeling, C. M., Moffett, J. W., Arnold, M. J., & Carlson, B. D. (2017a). Toward a Theory of Customer Engagement Marketing. *Journal of the Academy of Marketing Science, 45*(3), 312–335.

Harmeling, C. M., Palmatier, R. W., Fang, E., & Wang, D. (2017b). Group Marketing: Theory, Mechanisms, and Dynamics. *Journal of Marketing, 81*(July), 1–24.

Henderson, C. M., Beck, J. T., & Palmatier, R. W. (2011). Review of the Theoretical Underpinnings of Loyalty Programs. *Journal of Consumer Psychology, 21*(3), 256–276.

Henderson, C. M., Steinhoff, L., & Palmatier, R. W. (2014). *Consequences of Customer Engagement: How Customer Engagement Alters the Effects of Habit-, Dependence-, and Relationship-Based Intrinsic Loyalty* (Marketing Science Institute Working Papers Series).

Kozinets, R. V., Hemetsberger, A., & Schau, H. J. (2008). The Wisdom of Consumer Crowds: Collective Innovation in the Age of Networked Marketing. *Journal of Macromarketing, 28*(4), 339–354.

Kozinets, R. V., De Valck, K., Wojnicki, A. C., & Wilner, S. J. S. (2010). Networked Narratives: Understanding Word-of-Mouth Marketing in Online Communities. *Journal of Marketing, 74*(2), 71–89.

Kumar, V., & Pansari, A. (2016). Competitive Advantage Through Engagement. *Journal of Marketing Research, 53*(4), 497–514.

Kumar, V., George, M., & Pancras, J. (2008). Cross-Buying in Retailing: Drivers and Consequences. *Journal of Retailing, 84*(1), 15–27.

Kumar, V., Aksoy, L., Donkers, B., Venkatesan, R., Wiesel, T., & Tillmanns, S. (2010a). Undervalued or Overvalued Customers: Capturing Total Customer Engagement Value. *Journal of Service Research, 13*(3), 297–310.

Kumar, V., Petersen, J. A., & Leone, R. P. (2010b). Driving Profitability by Encouraging Customer Referrals: Who, When, and How. *Journal of Marketing, 74*(5), 1–17.

Martin, K. D., & Murphy, P. E. (2017). The Role of Data Privacy in Marketing. *Journal of the Academy of Marketing Science, 45*(2), 135–155.

Martin, K. D., Borah, A., & Palmatier, R. W. (2017). Data Privacy: Effects on Customer and Firm Performance. *Journal of Marketing, 81*(1), 36–58.

Menguc, B., Auh, S., Yeniaras, V., & Katsikeas, C. S. (2017). The Role of Climate: Implications for Service Employee Engagement and Customer Service Performance. *Journal of the Academy of Marketing Science, 45*(3), 428–451.

Morgan, R. M., & Hunt, S. D. (1994). The Commitment-Trust Theory of Relationship Marketing. *Journal of Marketing, 58*(3), 20–38.

Nambisan, S. (2002). Designing Virtual Customer Environments for New Product Development: Toward a Theory. *Academy of Management Review, 27*(3), 392–413.

Pansari, A., & Kumar, V. (2017). Customer Engagement: The Construct, Antecedents, and Consequences. *Journal of the Academy of Marketing Science, 45*(3), 294–311.

Roehm, M. L., & Brady, M. K. (2007). Consumer Responses to Performance Failures by High-Equity Brands. *Journal of Consumer Research, 34*(4), 537–545.

Ryu, G., & Feick, L. (2007). A Penny for Your Thoughts: Referral Reward Programs and Referral Likelihood. *Journal of Marketing, 71*(1), 84–94.

Schau, H. J., Muñiz, A. M., Jr., & Arnould, E. J. (2009). How Brand Community Practices Create Value. *Journal of Marketing, 73*(5), 30–51.

Schmitt, P., Skiera, B., & Van den Bulte, C. (2011). Referral Programs and Customer Value. *Journal of Marketing, 75*(1), 46–59.

Smith, D. (2014). Tuning In and Turning On: Leveraging Customer Engagment Data for Maximum Return. *Loyalty Management.*

Steinhoff, L., & Palmatier, R. W. (2014). Understanding Loyalty Program Effectiveness: Managing Target and Bystander Effects. *Journal of the Academy of Marketing Science, 44*(1), 1–20.

Trusov, M., Bucklin, R. E., & Pauwels, K. (2009). Effects of Word-of-Mouth Versus Traditional Marketing: Findings from an Internet Social Networking Site. *Journal of Marketing, 73*(5), 90–102.

Van Doorn, J., Lemon, K. N., Mittal, V., Nass, S., Pick, D., Pirner, P., & Verhoef, P. C. (2010). Customer Engagement Behavior: Theoretical Foundations and Research Directions. *Journal of Service Research, 13*(3), 253–266.

Verlegh, P. W. J., Ryu, G., Tuk, M. A., & Feick, L. (2013). Receiver Responses to Rewarded Referrals: The Motive Inferences Framework. *Journal of the Academy of Marketing Science, 41*(6), 669–682.

Vivek, S., Beatty, S., & Morgan, R. (2012). Customer Engagement: Exploring Customer Relationships Beyond Purchase. *Journal of Marketing Theory and Practice, 20*(2), 122–146.

Index[1]

A
acquisition, 6, 17, 55–7, 60, 63,
64, 68–70, 76, 87–9, 307,
315
assertiveness, 252, 254–62, 264n2,
264n3
attribute-specific information,
215, 216
authenticity, 32, 40, 41, 43, 44, 47–9,
308, 313, 314

B
brand engagement in the self-
concept(BESC), 270–6, 278–88
brand relationships, 284, 286
brands, 4, 31, 55, 75, 96, 119, 141,
174, 216, 221–38, 269–89
brand schematicity, 23, 271–88
business networks, 249, 251
business-to-business (B2B), 10–12,
14, 19–22, 57, 78, 123, 124,
127, 133, 141–64, 178, 181,

182, 186, 189, 190, 243, 261,
312, 319, 320
business value chain, 36, 244, 246,
251, 261
by-alternative customization, 79
by-attribute customization, 79

C
consumer engagement, 295
consumer experience (CX), 21, 221–38
consumer learning, 19, 124, 129, 130
cooperativeness, 252, 254–6, 258–62,
264n2, 264n3
customer advocacy, 22, 23, 269, 270,
277–81, 283–6, 289
customer behaviors, 18, 95, 96, 110,
120, 124, 127, 129, 191, 315,
316, 321
customer engagement, 1–25, 31–49,
53–71, 75–90, 95, 119–35, 141,
173–95, 203–16, 243, 269, 293,
307–21

[1] Note: Page numbers followed by "n" refer to notes.

R.W. Palmatier et al. (eds.), *Customer Engagement Marketing*,
DOI 10.1007/978-3-319-61985-9

Printed by Printforce, the Netherlands